Library of
Davidson College

SOCIAL SCIENTISTS AND
INTERNATIONAL AFFAIRS

Social Scientists and International Affairs

A CASE FOR A SOCIOLOGY OF SOCIAL SCIENCE

Edited by
ELISABETH T. CRAWFORD
ALBERT D. BIDERMAN

*Bureau of Social Science Research, Inc.
Washington, D.C.*

John Wiley & Sons, Inc.
New York • London • Sydney • Toronto

300.72
C899s

75-172

Copyright © 1969 by John Wiley & Sons, Inc.

All rights reserved. No part of this book may
be reproduced by any means, nor transmitted,
nor translated into a machine language without
the written permission of the publisher.

Library of Congress Catalog Card Number: 68-55333
SBN 471 18530 2
Printed in the United States of America

Preface

This book examines the relationship between social scientists and the activities of the United States Government in the international field since the beginning of World War II. The plan for this volume of reprinted articles, commented on by the editors and supplemented by an extensive bibliography, was developed in the course of a research project supported by the Behavioral Sciences Division of the Air Force Office of Scientific Research on the use of social science knowledge in international and military affairs. This research and its sponsorship is of some pertinence to our subject matter.

Our manner of selecting, organizing, and commenting on the articles suggests some conceptual and methodological guidelines for the sociological study of the activities of social scientists in relation to an important area of practical political concern. In the past these activities have all too frequently been treated in the hortatory and passionate manner that characterizes a high degree of subjective involvement of writers with their subject matter. The subtitle of this book, "a case for a sociology of social science," can be taken both as a plea for a dispassionate, scientific study of the social science institution in its interactions with other institutions and as an indication of the particularly prominent role of international affairs as a case for such study.

Just as science constitutes only a part of all the organized processes by which society perceives and comprehends its environment, the social sciences are but one of many social activities that attend to the meanings of social phenomena. Most broadly considered, sociological attention to the social sciences would select from all individuals who have felt impelled to take aspects of the social world into account those for whom this has become a differentiated and organized activity. Further, within the broad array of activities oriented to social knowledge such studies would focus on that small portion which has become the domain of the social sciences. There is particular interest in differentiating those areas into which the social sciences have extended because of a felt need on the part of clienteles, those in which they have established legitimacy in the absence of any recognition of dependence on the part of others and those into which their extension has been contested.

In conducting inquiries in the sociology of social science, social scientists will undoubtedly be stimulated by the same urge to "debunk" and to shatter existing myths that has moved them to examine other areas of social concern. This important function of many intellectual endeavors in the social sciences has been described by Glazer (VI, 1967), who writes with special reference to sociology:

"The chief illusion, then, that is fostered among sociologists—the chief ideological function of sociology, I suspect—is that there are more illusions around than there actually are. Thus people *do* know that there are classes, do know that patriotism is abetted by profit, do know that factory owners have different interests from workers, and so on. The social groups from which sociologists are recruited are new groups, aspiring groups—or if we may indulge in that harsh illusion-stripping language sociologists like to use, parvenu and *nouveau riche* groups—and it is understandable that sociologists want to see where things are not what they claim to be. Thus, when we say the sociology of religion, we mean the part that is *not* religion. When we say the sociology of industry, we mean the part that shows how people gum up productivity in the factory. When we say the sociology of health, we mean the part that shows that doctors and nurses are moved by prestige and status rather than simply the needs of patients. The sociology of politics deals with the nonpolitical reasons why people act the way they do in political life. And the sociology of social science will emphasize all the less pleasant reasons why people become social scientists. Since, as a matter of fact, people are moved by status, prestige, face, wealth, power, sociologists have something to say and are often enlightening to the practitioners in all these fields . . . (pp. 75–76)."

The hesitancy of social scientists to apply to themselves even a fraction of the energies that they have used in scrutinizing the behaviors of others may account for the slow development of the sociology of social science as a field of empirical research. That there should be a built-in aversion to shattering the illusions of one's own world is easily understood. A more important and less easily remedied condition hindering development in this area of inquiry is the inability of many social scientists to discern the commonalities that exist between their own behavior or organizations and those of other social and professional groups. For it is only on the basis of the discovery of these nonunique or, to use Glazer's term, "nonsocial-scientific" aspects of the social sciences that we will be able to generalize concerning characteristics that indeed make them distinct social activities or institutions.

The limitations of our book are numerous. Some of them inhere in the anthology format; others are the result of our arbitrary decision to restrict our subject matter in time or in scope. Although the book is an anthology, it is one, however, with a synthetic purpose in that we have tried to fit writings from different time periods and with different orientations into the broad framework of the sociology of social science. The authors of these selections, obviously, had not necessarily oriented their discussions to the particular issues and formulations that we would have them illuminate in the framework of this volume. Although many editors of anthologies face this problem, in our case the task of compilation was rendered more difficult by our wish to develop a new way of approaching the subject matter that the literature as a whole now lacks.

In selecting and editing the articles included here, we have given first consideration to the importance of the contribution the author has to make to the overall purpose of the book. Given the disparity that exists between our aim to describe the relationship between social scientists and government bodies in a dispassionate and scientific manner on the one hand and the hortatory tone of much of the literature on the other, the contributions of our selected authors do not necessarily lie in the stated objective of the article.

In some instances the entire article can be regarded as "data" or as a sort of specimen for analysis. As such, it may illustrate the reaction of a particular segment of the social science community to a specific event, or a perspective on a role of social science in government characteristic of a particular time, such as World War II or the Cold War. In cases in which the author may show little detachment in treating his subject matter the article still contains useful data or information, often in anecdotal form, on some aspect of the relationship between government and social science. In still others, however, the article may be based on interesting empirical work that is more tangential to the problems with which we are concerned. In selections taken from such fields of study as, for example, decision making or military sociology, questions of the influence of social science research on policy end an inquiry that started with the more general problem of the many different influences that shape the perspectives and doctrines of foreign and military policy makers.

This book deals with the relationships of the Federal Government and the social sciences as they have evolved in the United States. Although it includes occasional excursions into what many social scientists would regard as a distant past, the time period covered is for the most part that from the beginning of World War II to mid-1967. This focus on the wartime and postwar periods directs attention to research oriented toward international and military policy, for, as we show later, during this period government support of social science research received much of its original impetus from defense needs and was most easily justified by reference to the symbols of national and international security. Many of the selections and introductory material deal with the interaction of government and social science in the international and military field; they also include more general propositions and observations that would be applicable to other areas as well.

We have attempted to keep the topic of social scientists and international affairs at the forefront while, at the same time, systematically exploring its ramifications for the organization and conduct of social science research activities in support of other practical concerns. This has led us to treat as tangential a number of important aspects of the main topic. Thus we have neglected international or multinational collaborative research and scholarly relations except when they have influenced, or have been influenced by, the relation of American social scientists to government agencies and departments. The "Camelot affair" is perhaps the most prominent example of such reciprocal influences. Nor have we treated in depth the complex organizational and other relationships between government-supported research in the social sciences on the one hand and the physical and natural sciences on the other.

The selections were made and the book organized to touch on major conceptual and methodological problems for study of the sociology of social science. At the same time the essays provide numerous concrete illustrations and insights concerning interactions between social scientists and government agencies active in international affairs.

The papers by Znaniecki and Shils in Chapter I suggest *theoretical and methodological* bases for the sociological study of the social sciences. These selections, together with the Editors' Introduction review the contribution of the sociology of knowledge as well as that of intellectual history and the sociology of science to an emergent sociology of social science. Although the essay by Znaniecki is easily classified as being in the tradition of sociology of knowledge, that by Shils defies conventional categorization. It merits a prominent place, however, in that it discusses, often in original and propositional form, most of the problems that have occupied those writing on government and social science in the postwar period.

In Chapters II and III we move from methodological considerations to the *concrete issues and problems* raised by the activities of social scientists in relation to military and foreign policy bodies. Here questions are put regarding the organization of policy-oriented research activities within government or outside it; about those differences in the backgrounds and professional experiences of social scientists and administrators that are seen as limiting the influence of social science knowledge; of the relevance of the social sciences at their present stage of development to problems on the international scene; and of the divergence of the values and goals of academic social scientists from those of governmental officials. Although the selections in Chapter II treat these matters in a descriptive-analytic fashion and those in Chapter III in what is often a polemical and hortatory manner, the differences that exist between them are more a question of format and style than of actual substance. The uniformity of viewpoint among the writers in regard to the problematic features of policy-oriented social science reflects the shaping of their perspectives by the normative culture of science.

In Chapter IV we present and extend *some general synthesizing treatments* of the roles of the social sciences. Characterized by an analytic orientation frequently absent in the problem-oriented part of the literature, these writings generally represent examples of functional analysis. Not that we regard functional models as necessarily the only or best mode of synthesis. Indeed many of those presented here have limited independence from the restricted viewpoints and prejudgments of writers highly involved with their objects of study.

For the benefit of those interested in gaining a wider perspective on the subjects treated in the text, we have included a bibliographic appendix. This consists of five parts containing annotated references and one part listing references to cited works that have not been annotated, since they fall outside the scope of the main bibliography. References to the bibliography are made in the text by indicating the part and section (e.g., IV.2 meaning Part IV, section 2) in which the material is found. The authors' index provides an overall guide to the bibliography.

In order to accommodate the selections, our own materials, and the bibliography, most of the articles have had to undergo some cutting. Although the editing in some cases has amounted to major surgery, we have tried to limit it to sections containing illustrations, elaborations, or other materials unessential to the main theses or arguments that the authors have wished to propound. To alert the reader to what has been lost we have used ellipses (. . .) or, in the case of a whole paragraph or more, asterisks (*****).

The preparation of this volume was carried out as a project of the Bureau of Social Science Research, Inc. Nadine Pitts assisted in adapting the selections for inclusion in the volume, and Carol Busch contributed a variety of research tasks in connection with the compilation of the articles and the bibliography. Paul de Forest helped in the preparation of some of the introductory materials, and Rhoda Holtzman did most of the work of annotating the references in the bibliography. Albert E. Gollin and Gerald C. Bailey commented on parts of the manuscript. In the early work of preparing this volume we profited from several discussions with Morris Janowitz. We are grateful for the valuable assistance provided by all these individuals in this undertaking. We also want to thank the authors and publishers of the selections who gave us permission to use the writings for a purpose not originally intended.

ELISABETH T. CRAWFORD
ALBERT D. BIDERMAN

Washington, D.C.
January 8, 1968

Contributors

WARREN G. BENNIS

Mr. Bennis is Provost of the Social Sciences and Administration at the State University of New York at Buffalo. From 1959 to 1967 he was Professor of Organizational Psychology and Management at M.I.T. He has served as a consultant to the Department of State, the American Management Association, and private industry. Among his publications are *The Planning of Change* (1961), *Interpersonal Dynamics* (1963) and *Changing Organizations* (1966).

LEONARD S. COTTRELL, JR.

Mr. Cottrell spent most of his academic career as Professor of Sociology at Cornell University. In 1951 he joined the Russell Sage Foundation in the position of social psychologist and secretary, which he held until his retirement in 1967. He has served on numerous Department of Defense and Department of Health, Education and Welfare advisory groups and occasionally held research positions in those departments. Among his publications are *Predicting Success or Failure in Marriage* (1939) with E. W. Burgess, *The American Soldier* (1949) with S. A. Stouffer et al., and *Identity and Interpersonal Competence* (1955) with N. N. Foote.

ELISABETH T. CRAWFORD

A political scientist and sociologist, Mrs. Crawford has been a member of the staff of the Hudson Institute, Harmon-on-Hudson, N.Y., and of the Bureau of Social Science Research, Washington, D.C. Among her publications are several articles on the organization and use of social science research on international and military affairs.

GEORGE W. CROKER

Mr. Croker has spent most of his career conducting or administering social science research programs in the Armed Forces. He was Associate Director and Director of the Human Resources Research Institute of the United States Air Force, 1949-1954, Chief of the Research Division, Industrial College of the Armed Forces, 1955-1958, and has been Director for Contracts and Grants at the University of Alabama since 1963. He has been an advisor to several state and federal agencies.

ROBERT H. DAVIS

Mr. Davis directs the Learning Service of Michigan State University. His doctoral work at M.S.U. was in experimental psychology and the philosophy of science. After teaching at Allegheny College, he was engaged in systems work from 1955 to 1967 at the RAND Corporation, the Denver Systems Laboratories, and the System Development Corporation. His publications display his special interest in systems applications to arms control as well as his experimental work on learning.

CONTRIBUTORS

PAUL DE FOREST

At the Bureau of Social Science Research, 1965-1967, Mr. De Forest collaborated with the editors of this book in studies of relations between the social sciences and other institutions. His chapter is based on research also reported in the dissertation for his Ph.D. in Georgetown University's political behavior program. He was instructor in government at Georgetown and is currently on active duty with the United States Army.

LEONARD W. DOOB

Mr. Doob has spent most of his academic life at Yale University, where he is now Professor of Psychology and Chairman of the Council on African Studies. During World War II he was associated with the Office of the Coordinator of Inter-American Affairs, the Military Intelligence Division of the Army, and the Office of War Information. His book *Public Opinion and Propaganda* (1948) derives primarily from the war period; other more recent works include *Communication in Africa* (1961) and *Patriotism and Nationalism* (1964).

MAURICE L. FARBER

Mr. Farber is Professor of Psychology at the University of Connecticut. He has also been associated with the Bureau of Applied Social Research at Columbia University, where he worked on voting behavior. During World War II he directed public opinion studies for the United States Army in Europe. He has published extensively on national character, the psychology of politics, and the theory of suicide.

LLOYD A. FREE

Mr. Free is Director of the Institute for International Social Research at Princeton, which specializes in public opinion surveys in foreign countries. He headed the worldwide information program of the Department of State that later became the United States Information Agency. He has served as a consultant to President Eisenhower and for many years to the USIA. Among his publications are *Six Allies and a Neutral* (1959) and numerous reports dealing with the political opinions of foreign populations.

HAROLD GUETZKOW

Mr. Guetzkow has had long involvement in establishing links between advanced developments in the social sciences and industrial, governmental, and international applications. His appointment in 1957 as Professor of Sociology, Psychology and Political Science at Northwestern University suggests the breadth of his interest. His special work in recent years is reflected in his *Simulation in the Social Sciences* (1962) and, more particularly, *Simulation in International Relations* (1963).

PAUL Y. HAMMOND

Mr. Hammond has been a Senior Staff member of The RAND Corporation since 1964. Before that he was a member of a number of university staffs—the longest time at Yale University and most recently at the Washington Center of Foreign Policy Research of the Johns Hopkins University. He has served as a consultant to the Institute for Defense Analyses, the System Development Corporation, and the Department of Defense. He is author of *Organizing for Defense* (1961) and coauthor of *Strategy, Politics, and Defense Budgets* (1962) and *American Civil-Military Decisions* (1963).

PHILIP M. HAUSER

Mr. Hauser's career has included academic, United States government, and United Nations posts. He is currently Professor of Sociology and Director of the Population Research and Training Center at the University of Chicago. He was Deputy Director and Acting Director of the United States Bureau of the Census, 1938-1950, and has served in a number of capacities for the United Nations and UNESCO. Among his publications are *Population and World Politics* (1958), *Population Dilemma* (1963) and *The Handbook for Social Research in Urban Areas* (1965).

IRVING LOUIS HOROWITZ

Mr. Horowitz is Professor of Sociology at Washington University (St. Louis) and Director of Studies in Comparative International Development at its Social Science Institute. He has often written and spoken on problems concerning the relationship between government and social science. Among his publications in the area of social science and policy are *The Idea of War and Peace* (1957), *The War Game: Studies in the New Civilian Militarists* (1963), and *The Rise and Fall of Project Camelot: Studies in the Relationship Between Social Science and Practical Politics* (1967).

MORRIS JANOWITZ

Mr. Janowitz is Chairman of the Department of Sociology of the University of Chicago. One of his major interests since his association with Lasswell's War Communications Research Project in 1941 has been the sociological study of violence institutions and their roles in domestic and international affairs. He has contributed to this end by fostering the work of other American and foreign scholars as well as in such books as *The Military in the Political Development of New Nations* (1964), *The Professional Soldier* (1960), and *Sociology and the Military Establishment* (1959).

HAROLD D. LASSWELL

Mr. Lasswell has been at Yale University since 1946 as Professor of Law and Political Science. He served as Director of the War Communications Research Project in the Library of Congress during World War II and has been a consultant to the Departments of State and Justice and other government agencies. Past and present conceptions of policy-oriented social science owe much to such works by Mr. Lasswell as *The Policy Sciences* (1951), which he edited with Daniel Lerner. His numerous publications include *Propaganda Technique in the World War* (1927), *World Politics and Personal Insecurity* (1935), and *Language of Politics* (1949) with Nathan Leites.

MAX F. MILLIKAN

For the last 15 years Mr. Millikan has been Director of the Center for International Studies (CENIS) at the Massachusetts Institute of Technology. His government service includes positions with the War Shipping Administration, the Department of State, and the Central Intelligence Agency. His major publications are *A Proposal. Key to an Effective Foreign Policy* (1957) with W. W. Rostow, *The Emerging Nations: Their Growth and United States Policy* (1961) with D. L. M. Blackmer, and *No Easy Harvest* (1967) with David Hapgood.

MARTIN OPPENHEIMER

After obtaining his Ph.D. at the University of Pennsylvania in 1963 Mr. Oppenheimer joined the staff of the American Friends Service Committee. His contribution to this book was an outgrowth of his work for the AFSC. He is presently Assistant Professor of Sociology at Vassar College. His is co-author of *A Manual for Direct Action* (1965) and is completing a book on Negro protest movements.

CHARLES E. OSGOOD

Mr. Osgood is a Research Professor in the Department of Psychology and the Institute of Communications at the University of Illinois, Urbana. He has served as consultant to the Air Force, the Navy, and the Arms Control and Disarmament Agency. His major publications include *The Measurement of Meaning* (1957), *An Alternative to War or Surrender* (1962), and *Perspective in Foreign Policy* (1966).

ROBERT A. PACKENHAM

Mr. Packenham has been Assistant Professor of Political Science and Faculty Associate, Institute of Political Studies, Stanford University since 1965. He has done research in the areas of Latin American studies, political development, and the use of research in foreign aid programs. He has written articles on all of these subjects.

DON K. PRICE

Mr. Price is Dean of the Kennedy School of Government at Harvard, at which in 1958 he established the Inter-disciplinary Science and Public Policy Seminar. His previous career, which had been with the Federal Government and the Ford Foundation, included a period as Deputy Chairman of the Research and Development Board of the Defense Department. Among his publications are *Government and Science* (1954) and *The Scientific Estate* (1967).

PETER H. ROSSI

The versatile applicability of sociological research to a broad range of public concerns has been exemplified by Mr. Rossi's work, particularly as director (1960-1967) of the National Opinion Research Center of the University of Chicago. He is editor of the 12-volume *N.O.R.C. Monographs in Social Research* and author of a number of books, including *The Politics of Urban Renewal* (1961) with Robert A. Dentler and *The Education of the Catholic American* (1966) with A. M. Greeley. Mr. Rossi is currently professor in the Department of Social Relations of Johns Hopkins University.

EDWARD A. SHILS

Since translating Mannheim's *Ideology and Utopia* (1936) with Louis Wirth and *Man and Society* (1940), Mr. Shils has lent emphasis to the importance of a social theory of knowledge for a politically relevant social science. His long tenure at the University of Chicago is regularly interspersed with work at British universities. His appraisal of *The Current State of American Sociology* (1948) was originally prepared for a British audience. With Talcott Parsons he edited *Toward a General Theory of Social Action* (1951) and is author of *The Torment of Secrecy* (1956).

FLORIAN ZNANIECKI

Politically barred from Polish university posts, Mr. Znaniecki found work in the emigration service. This led to his association with W. I. Thomas in the study of *The Polish Peasant in Europe and America* (1918-1920). His subsequent influence on basic conceptions of the appropriate substance and methods for sociology, from which his ideas on the sociology of knowledge reprinted here are derivative, are set forth in such works as *The Method of Sociology* (1934), *Social Actions* (1936), *Cultural Sciences . . .* (1952), and *Modern Nationalities* (1952). He was Professor of Sociology at the University of Illinois from 1940 until his death in 1958.

Contents

EDITORS' INTRODUCTION   1

I. Perspectives on the Social Roles of the Social Sciences   27

Sociology and Theory of Knowledge   29
Florian Znaniecki

Social Science and Social Policy   35
Edward A. Shils

II. The Social Organization of Policy-Oriented Social Science   51

The Organization of Policy and Research—An Overview

The Structure of Policy   61
Don K. Price

The Informal Organization of Policy-Oriented Social Science   69
Elisabeth T. Crawford

Organizations Producing Research

Researchers, Scholars and Policy Makers: The Politics of Large-Scale Research   85
Peter H. Rossi

Values and Organization in a University Social Research Group   92
Warren G. Bennis

The Utilization of Social Scientists in the Overseas Branch of the Office of War Information   100
Leonard W. Doob

Government Organizations Using Research

Political-Development Doctrines in the American Foreign Aid Program   111
Robert A. Packenham

The Soldier and International Relations   128
Morris Janowitz

The Social Sciences in the Foreign Policy Subsystem of Congress   135
Paul De Forest

III. The Affairs of Social Scientists with the Affairs of State   151

Political and Professional Issues

The Psychologist in International Affairs   163
Charles Osgood

The Peace Research Game   170
Martin Oppenheimer

The Life and Death of Project Camelot   174
Irving Louis Horowitz

Organizational Issues

Some Principles Regarding the Utilization of Social Science Research Within the Military   185
George W. Croker

Social Research and Psychological Warfare   195
Leonard S. Cottrell, Jr.

xiv CONTENTS

Methodological Issues

The Problem of National Character: A Methodological Analysis 207
Maurice L. Farber

The Role of Public Opinion in International Relations 214
Lloyd A. Free

International Influence Process: How Relevant is the Contribution of Psychologists? 223
Robert H. Davis

IV. **The Functions of Policy-Oriented Social Science** 233

Engineering and Intelligence Models

Social Science and Social Engineering 247
Philip M. Hauser

Conversion Barriers in Using the Social Sciences 253
Harold Guetzkow

The Relation of Ideological Intelligence to Public Policy 259
Harold D. Lasswell

Enlightenment Models

Foreign Policy Making and Administrative Politics 269
Paul Y. Hammond

Inquiry and Policy: The Relation of Knowledge to Action 277
Max F. Millikan

BIBLIOGRAPHIC APPENDIX 285

I. **Social Roles of the Social Sciences: General and Introductory Writings** 287

II. **Approaches to the Study of the Role of Social Science in Public Policy: Theory and Method** 291

  1. Sociology of Knowledge, Sociology of Science, and Sociology of Social Science 291

  2. The Value-Contexts of Policy-Oriented Social Science 294

  3. Theories of Decision-Making and Bureaucracy 296

III. **The Organization of Policy-Oriented Social Science** 298

  1. An Overview of Organizational Developments in Applied and Policy-Oriented Social Sciences 299

  2. The Involvement of the Federal Government in Social Science Research (General) 301

  3. The Involvement of the Federal Government in Social Science Research on International and Military Affairs, 1940-1966 302

  4. Problematic Aspects of the Relationship of the Government and the Social Science Professions 304

IV. **Decision-Making Structures and the Use of Social Science Research** 307

  1. The Use of Research in the Federal Government (General) 307

  2. Characteristics of International and Military Decision-Makers and Decision-Making Structures Affecting the Use of Research 308

  3. Uses of Social Science Knowledge and Expertise in Departments and Agencies Concerned with International and Military Affairs 309

V.	**The Substance of Social Science Knowledge and Policy Concerns in International and Military Affairs**	312	3. Applying Social Science Knowledge in the Area of Peace and International Cooperation 316
	1. Translating Basic into Applied Social Science 312		VI. **Other Works Cited** 318
	2. The Applicability of Social Science Methods and Materials to International and Military Policy Problems 313		**AUTHOR INDEX** 325
			SUBJECT INDEX 329

SOCIAL SCIENTISTS AND
INTERNATIONAL AFFAIRS

Editors' Introduction

The concern of social scientists with their proper relationship to the body politic is as old as social science itself. In this century there is hardly a prominent social scientist who has not spoken or written on this subject at one point or another in his career. To a considerable extent this concern is integral to a social science perspective. For, as Myrdal (I, 1958: 9)[1] points out, "the social sciences have all received their impetus much more from the urge to improve society than from simple curiosity about its working." The attempts of some contemporary social scientists to draw a sharp dividing line between science and politics have not alleviated the concern. Rather they have intensified it and created an aura of forays into forbidden territory when social scientists enter into the political sphere.

Yet of all the writings on the relationship between social science and public policy, little is based on empirical or even objective research. Few studies of the actual roles and functions of social scientists have been made. In dealing with these matters social scientists have almost invariably acted as missionaries, apologists, social philosophers, or official representatives of their disciplines.

[1] In citations, roman and arabic numbers preceding the date indicate respectively the Parts and Sections of the Bibliographic Appendix in which the cited work is found. This appendix is topically organized into six parts, and some of the parts, in turn, into sections.

In general their writings along these lines are frankly speculative or impressionistic. Case studies by social scientists who have themselves been involved in policy-oriented research activities have constituted the most adequate evidential basis for assertions. Only rarely have these activities been subjected to systematic, detached analysis by social scientists practicing science.

The purposes of this book are to demonstrate that the subject of social science research in government can be approached in an analytic and empirical fashion rather than a prescriptive one; to suggest some conceptualizations that will permit statements on this topic to be cast in propositional form; to suggest some propositions even though this usually involves hazardous stretching of the thin evidence that now exists; and to suggest some ways in which more substantial evidence for such propositions may be developed by further research.

Through the selection of articles and our own comments we wish to describe policy-oriented research as a social activity and to give some data on its actors, norms, scope, and institutions. On the whole, this book raises many more questions than it answers, which is to be expected, for we are building on selections that in many instances are as diverse and inconclusive as the literature from which they are drawn.

I. POLICY-ORIENTED SOCIAL SCIENCE IN HISTORICAL PERSPECTIVE

The kind of dispassionate self-examination for which we are making a somewhat impassioned plea becomes especially important at times like the present when a language of crisis characterizes discussions of the relationships of government and the social science community.[1] In the present instance, however, we want to look beyond current controversies and relate our inquiry to the radical alterations in these relationships that have occurred since the emergence of modern, university-based social science in the latter part of the nineteenth century.

It has not been common to apply a perspective of some 100 years to the study of the policy roles of the social sciences. Instead, the majority of writers in the field have limited their inquiries to the period from the beginning of World War II to the present time. Earlier developments are usually disposed of by passing references to "early greats" such as Plato, Aristotle, and Machiavelli as the precursors of the modern policy-oriented social scientist.

The predominance of a short-range time-perspective is not surprising in view of the youth of the "newer" social sciences and the ahistoricity of most social scientists. When, as in the case of American sociology, the entire history of a discipline spans at most four generations, there is a great temptation to make this history seem longer by considering everything that happened before one's own time as the dark past. Working in the same direction is a tendency on the part of many social scientists to base their descriptions of disciplinary developments on what they, themselves, have observed or experienced.

Yet the scientific study of the policy roles of the social sciences requires inquiries based on other than the self-experienced, the anecdotal, and the tidbits of information exchanged in the government research cocktail-circuit or the bars of convention hotels.[2] By applying a longer time perspective we might hope to speed up the process whereby the roles of social scientists become objects of disciplined study rather than merely subjects of privatized concern and moralistic discussion. Similarly, we would probably acquire a more detached perspective if, instead of discussing these roles in shallow abstractions and self-serving prescriptions, we were able to relate them to developments within the institutional spheres in which they have occurred.

Three principal spheres are involved: the university, the federal government, and the "twilight zone" of overlapping public and private functions created by a growing volume of governmental intervention and "planning." The sheer growth in size of each of these spheres and in the volume of their activity has had much to do with the alteration of the policy roles of the social sciences. From the 1890's to the present time the number of government employees in the competitive civil service has grown from some 50,000 to well over two million. This large corps of civil servants and the professional status toward which they have aspired have provided policy-oriented social scientists with a large potential market for scientific knowledge and esoterica. The annual rate of earned doctorates is one measure of the increase in the number of individuals with a formally recognized

---

[1] We find it indicative that in 1966 and 1967 the journals of the socal science professions devoted several issues in whole or in part to the relationship of government and social science. See, for example, "'Camelot and Psychological Tests" (III.4, 1966); "Congress and Social Science" (III.2, 1967); "Editor's Column" (III.4, 1966 and 1967).

[2] Since the literature abounds with writings based on self-experience and since quite a few of these offer insights which might form a basis for more analytically oriented discussions, obviously, this kind of information cannot be disregarded. Some of these writings figure in the selections in subsequent chapters, others are included in the bibliography.

competence to produce such knowledge. In the period from the 1890's to the present this rate has risen from around 300 annually to close to 12,000. In 1962 approximately one-tenth of this number was earned in social science disciplines. The growth of governmental intervention into the social life of the nation, finally, has not only created "social engineering" tasks for the social sciences but has also given rise to the varied institutional arrangements which now link the government and the university spheres.

In this introductory chapter we examine some of the specific ways in which developments in these three spheres have affected the policy roles of the social sciences. Although the several social science disciplines —social psychology, sociology, anthropology, political science and economics—vary greatly in subject matter, techniques, and internal organization, they show enough commonality in their relationships to policy making bodies to be treated as a single entity. The representatives of these disciplines who have oriented their work toward governmental policy and planning share many of the same general goals and values: to infuse governmental structures and actions with rationality, to use scientific knowledge in systematic attempts to shape the future, and to achieve reliable social planning.[1] They also share the problems of finding the institutional means for bringing research findings to bear on policy, and of reconciling their role of scientist with that of participant in the policy process. Still, there are important differences between the disciplines; some authors, for instance, have felt that the earlier and much more thorough "institutionalization" of economics in government would warrant its treatment as a special case. If sociology stands out as *our* special case, this is a reflection not so much of the importance of its policy roles, but rather of our own professional biases and the relative dearth of materials pertaining to other disciplines.

Policy Concerns of Early Social Scientists

In explaining the ways in which social scientists have performed their policy roles at various points in time it would be erroneous to place too heavy a burden on the simple fact of the growth of governmental activities and the proliferation of governmental functions involving social scientists. Scholarship influenced policy and social scientists played roles in policy formation long before the growth of governmental activities had created the institutional and organizational mechanisms that now link the university and government spheres. Published scholarship, by means of book or article, still dominates conceptions of how the scholar can exert influence. Despite the development of mechanisms for placing scholarship in highly specific service to policy, the largest part of the scholar's influence may still derive from this medium. Myrdal (I, 1958), in discussing historical developments in the relationship of the social sciences and public policy, states:

"My thesis is that, while there was little participation on the part of social scientists in the actual technical preparation of legislation and still less in administering induced social changes [before World War I], their influence was nevertheless very considerable, and that this influence was due in the main to their exposition and propagation of certain general thoughts and theories.

"Malthus's theory of population pressure was in its time one such powerful influence and molded a whole generation's general attitude towards social policy; in our time very different general thoughts on the population

---

[1] We are in general agreement with Lasswell's characterization of the policy orientation as being "in part directed toward the policy process, in part, toward the intelligence needs of policy" (Lerner and Lasswell, I, 1951: 3). Lasswell's observation that the "policy sciences" should not be taken as identical with the "applied social sciences" is also worth noting. We view applied research as being directed more toward narrowly formulated operational and adminstrative problems than toward broad matters of domestic and international policy.

issue have in a radical way determined social policy in Scandinavia and Britain. Ricardo's thoughts about prices and distribution and about currency, taxation and tariffs, Marx's thoughts about surplus value and the economic determination of history, Darwin's and Spencer's about social evolution and the survival of the fittest and, in our time, Keynes's about how the state by increasing total demand can prevent or mitigate depressions and mass-unemployment, are other such general theories which have strongly influenced the direction of social policy (pp. 16–17)."

The currently dominant role of the university institution in knowledge production, and its key place in the relationship of knowledge to policy may lead one to overestimate its historical importance in both respects. Shils points out the following in his article in Chapter I:

"The great schemes of interpretation and judgment formulated by the masters of social science grew up outside the universities and in a fairly close connection with politics and practical affairs. Except for Adam Smith no major figure of social science outside Germany, until the latter part of the nineteenth century, was a university teacher."[1]

When a university-based social science, recognizably modern in approach, started to develop in this country in the late nineteenth century, close contact with social problems and practical affairs remained an important feature, at least among many of its first-generation practitioners. Practical and policy orientations were perhaps the most pronounced in economics, or, more pertinently, "political economy," which, according to Riesman (VI, 1958: 71), "in a society of great extremes of wealth, of booms and busts, of trusts and tycoons, . . . offered the promise of the greatest intellectual leverage on what was going on and hence the promise of political and more broadly human relevance." But such early sociologists as Ward and Giddings, who had spent their formative years outside the universities, also maintained throughout their lifetimes a passionate interest in social reform(Bramson, II.1 1961: 75; Hinkle and Hinkle, II.1, 1954: 12–14). Political scientists, although only slowly separating themselves from moral philosophy and law, were nevertheless active in the municipal reform movement, and participated in the founding of many of the bureaus for research in public administration that were an important part of this movement (Waldo, III.1, 1960: 1–5).

In many cases, however, this concern with socioeconomic problems entailed neither political participation nor an insistence that governmental intervention was the best means for their solution. Shils points out that even the sociologists, for all their concern with "social problems," seldom expected these to be solved by governmental actions. In the case of the political scientists their involvement in governmental affairs was largely concentrated in the municipal reform movement whose major goal was to separate administration from politics.[1]

Isolation of University Social Science

From the first World War to the second, the history of the social sciences was, with some notable exceptions, that of the development of university disciplines. Teaching was the primary work activity of most of its practitioners. The drive to gain academic respectability, the emphasis on methodological and theoretical development, and the quest for scientific rigor were all factors that tended to confine social scientists to the university sphere. It was also during this period that the influence of German social science, with its strongly rooted university and "pure" science traditions, was the strongest. The period between the wars, finally, was one of tremendous growth in graduate education, with the number of doctorates granted annually rising from around 600 in 1920 to close to 3000 in

---

[1] P. 36.

[1] Pp. 36–37.

1938. With the proportionate number of doctorates in the social sciences rising at an equal rate—from 111 to 533—the emphasis on teaching and discipline-building is not surprising.

The developments that we have sketched here had important consequences for the research carried out in the universities. The emphasis on the training of future social scientists, for instance, tended to lessen the concern over the relevance of the research for the solution of social and practical problems. So long as the research gave the desired training in methods and techniques, it had served its most important purpose.

The quest for respectability and academic legitimacy caused a similar isolation from the broad social problems of the time. Wirth (II.1, n.d.) has described how in sociology, as a result of these pressures,

". . . there followed a period of fact-gathering and intensive, but more or less aimless, study of small and often disconnected 'problems' and the immersion into the development of super-refined techniques for ordering and summarizing the crude data thus gathered. . . . [T]his accumulation of mountains of authentic but meaningless facts yielded a minimum of either practically useful or scientifically generalizable conclusions (p. 274)."

Nor were these impulses tempered by a need to orient the research toward the problems of government and business for the purpose of obtaining financial support from these bodies. Several writers have commented on the relative prosperity that hit the university social sciences in the decade following World War I in the wake of both university and foundation support. In the period 1921–1930, for instance, private foundations made grants of 27 million dollars to the social sciences (U.S. National Resources Committee, III.2, 1938: 180). Given the average annual income of college professors in the 1930's, this was the equivalent of the compensation for 900 man years of social science time per year—a considerable investment at a time when the combined membership of all the professional associations in the social sciences was roughly 7000.

Early Social Science Programs in Government

The most notable exceptions to the relative separation of the government and university spheres during the period from early in this century to the time shortly before World War II were the areas of social statistics, economics, and rural sociology. Further exceptions occurred during the brief interlude represented by World War I when academic psychologists were active in the United States Army. In all of these areas the government maintained social science programs of considerable size in which academic social scientists actively participated.

To a considerable extent the work of the Federal government in collecting and analyzing socioeconomic data antedates similar endeavors by academic social scientists. In a monograph that formed a part of the U.S. National Resources Committee report (III.2, 1938), *Research—A National Resource,* Samuel Stouffer describes how the decennial census, originally instituted for the purpose of allocating seats in the House of Representatives, in the course of the nineteenth century was extended to include statistics on agriculture, commerce, and schools. Although the decennial census was still almost entirely under political patronage and before the establishment of a permanent statistical agency in 1902, these kinds of data were collected on a fairly extensive basis. In discussing this period Stouffer says:

"The social science research in Francis A. Walker's census of 1880, and in publications of the 1890 census completed under Carroll D. Wright, probably was more significant, both in quantity and quality, than all the university research of that period put together (p. 205)."

Analytical research as an adjunct to the

census continued to be important in the 1910's and 1920's when these kinds of studies were transformed into separate monographs. By the 1930's, however, rapid expansion of data-gathering facilities and proliferation of federal statistical agencies had caused something of a decline in the position of the Bureau of the Census as a leader in the development of statistical and survey methodology. More important than this, perhaps, was the explicit recognition in the National Resources Committee report of "the collection of data national in scope . . . as a function of the Federal Government (pp. 49–50)."

With their emphasis on data-production and "fact finding," governmental research programs were not in conflict with the academic social sciences which also stressed empirical work. While the profession as a whole, as discussed earlier, was not oriented toward public policy, there were still individual social scientists who did concern themselves with the relationships of their disciplines to governmental bodies. Among these social scientists the collection and analysis of data concerning socioeconomic conditions and popular attitudes were seen as the primary contributions of social science to public policy. Presented within the superstructure of ideology with which social scientists like to adorn their relationships with governmental bodies, these contributions became the "intelligence function" which was regarded as vital to the proper workings of a democratic society. In a discussion of this function in 1922 Walter Lippmann (V.2, 1946) presents the vision of a permanent intelligence section in each governmental department, staffed by social scientists who would be involved neither in decision nor in action. He sees this as a means of overcoming the central difficulty of self-government, "the difficulty of dealing with an unseen reality (p. 299)."[1]

[1] See also the article by Harold D. Lasswell, "The Relation of Ideological Intelligence to Public Policy," in Chapter IV and the introduction to that chapter.

Yet in spite of the mutual dependence of government statistical agencies and university social scientists during this period, there were few institutional mechanisms for linking the two spheres. In the majority of cases the only way in which an academic social scientist could do research for governmental agencies was to leave the university and become an employee of the Federal government. The absence of the many arrangements—contracts, grants, etc.—through which the government currently supports social science research is shown in the U.S. National Resources Committee report which states: "Cooperative financing . . . that is the use of Federal funds by a non-federal agency such as a private university, a State government, or a research foundation for carrying on cooperative research, now exists only in a few specially authorized instances . . . (p. 84)."

The chief exceptions to this general pattern were the agricultural experiment stations, which, early in this century, started to make grants to universities for research in agricultural economics and rural sociology. Presidential committees, such as the President's Committee on Social Trends which was active from 1929 to 1933, also sponsored a considerable amount of university-based research. The fact that much of this research, although conducted for a governmental body, was paid by private foundations is another indication of how the government had yet to assume the sponsorship of academic research.

The major effects of this institutional separation are shown in the quantity and quality of professional social scientists in government in the period between the wars. Although changes in definitions and inadequate reporting preclude meaningful numerical comparisons, it should be possible to measure the quality of interwar and present-day government social scientists, for instance, by the prestige of their academic affiliations. If we use the academic and professional visibility of the individuals involved as a first approximation to such a measure, it is apparent that the "in-house" research offices of the interwar period, contrary to what has often been assumed in discussions of intellectuals in the public bureaucracy, were able to attract and hold prestigious social scientists.

Growing Interdependence in National Crises

For most writers the beginning of World War II stands out as Year One in the history of government and social science. The dependence of the social sciences on government funds, the institutional mechanisms for linking the university and government spheres, and social scientists' present conceptions of their roles in policy making are all seen as originating during this period. We would contend, however, that although many of these changes may not have come to fruition until World War II or its aftermath, they were largely foretold by developments in the 1930's.

The depression and the New Deal were primary conditions in bringing about these changes. The repudiation of laissez-faire brought a tremendous expansion of the government's welfare and regulatory functions. The increased volume of public interventions into the private sphere that occurred at this time placed new demands on the social sciences. The need for data on which the government could base its planning and regulatory activities increased greatly. Antidepression and social-welfare programs created opportunities for the application of scientific propositions to practical problems and for "social engineering." The influence of social scientists extended into policy making spheres. One measure of the effect of New Deal programs is the number of social scientists active in governmental agencies in a professional capacity: from 1931 to 1937 this increased from 680 to 2150 (*ibid.,* 49). More key positions of power were occupied by men drawn from the social sciences during the Roosevelt administration than at any time before. Another measure is the extensive use of emergency funds: in 1938, for instance, such funds accounted for 73 percent of a total of 41 million dollars expended for social science research and data-collection (U.S. National Resources Committee, III.2, 1938: 49, 69).

Also in the New Deal period we find emerging among university social scientists a new awareness of social and practical problems and an expanded conception of the role of social science knowledge in policy. Waldo, in a contribution to the Brookings Institution dedication lectures in 1960 (Herring, I, 1961), was to characterize these new roles in the following manner:

". . . In the past generation or so social science research has become 'institutionalized,' increasing in amount and acceptability to a degree that we can say is historically unique. It is implied—and again—I agree—that it would be impossible without disaster to return to a situation in which public decisions are made without a substantial amount of research produced by a large number of researchers. . . . Social science has and will have to the extent that it explains or justifies our policy choices not just a clinical and rejective function, but a symbolic, a *legitimatizing* and an *ideological* function. I argue, in other words that in the sociological-anthropological perspective, social scientists will have *religious* and *political* functions (p. 28)."

In the Depression this new orientation was most pronounced in economics. Myrdal (I, 1958: 27), in speaking of this period, observed that "a new generation of economists, who, on the whole, were better equipped ideologically and intellectually, for the task of planning and controlling became available. . . ." But several writers have also commented on the shift within sociology which occurred at about the same time toward an emphasis on making it useful to society. In one form or another all of the presidential addresses at the annual meetings of the American Sociological Society during the years 1933–1938 dealt with the role of sociology in planning and social action. Perhaps the most forceful statement urging social scientists to assume roles which would include not only data-gathering but also the application of scientific principles to the solution of societal problems is contained in Robert Lynd's (I, 1948) *Knowledge for What?* originally delivered as a series of lectures in 1938.

The breaking-down of the isolation of the university social scientists and their recognizing government and business as "clients" for social science research have to be seen in the context of the economic changes brought about by the depression. As a result of the decline in available university and private foundation funds, the Federal government came to play a more important role in supporting research. This trend not only affected social science research in support of governmental functions and programs; it also encompassed basic research conducted in the universities. The U.S. National Resources Committee (III.2, 1938) report, for instance, observes that "the two significant agencies to which research in the universities must turn for large financial help are the Foundations and the Government . . ." and predicts that "the Federal government will be asked to give more largely to research. . . (p. 189)." Its very title—*Research—A National Resource*—signalled a change in the relationship of the government and the universities.

Affinities in political and ideological beliefs were another major factor making for more frequent interactions between academic social scientists and governmental bodies. Many of the former saw the Roosevelt administration as at least a partial embodiment of the reformist or Marxist orientations that formed an important part of prevailing social science ideologies. At that time, as well as later, however, there were many others who were skeptical of any kind of political involvement and who preferred to remain on the outside. For those who did take up governmental positions such a move was facilitated by the fact that they often came to work for new agencies whose climates and operating styles were very different from those that characterized "old-line" departments.[1]

In many respects World War II represented a continuation, if not an accentuation, of patterns established in the New Deal. The total mobilization made the governmental sphere close to all-embracing. The extensive use made of university expertise in government can be explained not only by Leonard Doob's observation that "it was somewhat vaguely felt that all kinds of brains, even academic ones, were necessary to win a total war . . . ,"[2] but also by a very real concern over the effect that the war might have on the intellectual resources of the nation. With large numbers of both students and teaching personnel engaged in the war effort, the government came to assume a large share of the responsibility for keeping university instruction and research going. It did so by increasing its support for research, tailoring it to the needs of the war agencies, and by sending military personnel to the campuses for training or continuing education.

The harmony of the ideological stances of the government with that dominant among the intellectual community continued throughout the war. Among the social scientists the war brought into focus the antifascist sentiments that had been an important part of social science ideologies in the 1930's. Basic feelings on this issue had also been strengthened by the entrance into the social science community of a large number of European refugees. Feeling that this was a "just war," many social scientists put aside their pacifist orientations, at least for the time being.

The intensity of the consensus around a completely superordinate end facilitated intellectual activity in an interesting way. The ultimate value—winning the war, liberation,

---

[1] These distinctions have rarely been recognized in writings on intellectuals in the public bureaucracy. Instead the government is most commonly treated as a monolith (Merton, II.3, 1945).

[2] P. 100.

and defeat of Nazism—allowed the transforming of what ordinarily would be fundamental value questions into purely instrumental ones. Hence what had previously been value questions became questions accessible to science—open to scientific judgment. The effects of bombing upon the morale of populations; the degree of democratization appropriate to the armed forces; the functions of true and false atrocity accounts and propaganda, domestic and foreign; all could be treated as purely instrumental issues. When this consensus started to erode in the postwar years, there were renewed concerns with questions of values in research and in regard to the duty of the social scientists to examine not only the means but also the ends of governmental policies.

In two important respects the war represented a departure from prewar patterns. In sheer numbers social science involvement in government research at this time was more extensive than ever before. It was the first occasion when there was the degree of organization and financial support that permitted the pursuit of research activities on anything like the scale approaching what has now become common. Habits of thought, action, and work of many of the most prominent contemporary social scientists were set during the war period. Many of the conflicts that we are witnessing at present between government-supported social scientists and those who prefer to remain on the outside could probably be traced to the succession of a new generation of social scientists who did not share in the wartime experience.

The war also opened up whole new areas of governmental activity as fields of inquiry for social scientists. Psychological warfare research, morale studies, and propaganda analysis became firmly established as specialized fields. More of a continuation of prewar patterns, but not less dramatic in its impact, was the tremendous expansion of the government's intelligence function. As a result of the war, information and data-gathering activities were extended to include most foreign countries. As before in the area of domestic statistics, "intelligence research" became an "umbrella" for analytical research.

Paralleling these developments were important changes in the recruitment of social scientists into government research programs. Most significant was undoubtedly the large-scale entrance of behaviorally oriented social scientists—psychologists, social psychologists, sociologists, and anthropologists—into the governmental, and more specifically, the military sphere. Important results of the wartime involvement of these groups were the claims that they came to stake out in areas formerly dominated by professional military men, or, in the foreign policy sphere, by experts on diplomatic history and international law.

Although during the war the social and psychological sciences were almost always tied directly to operational organizations, independent organizational structures were being developed for military research and development by the "hard" sciences. In the immediate postwar period the social sciences began to find niches in this military-scientific research and development structure. From tenuous beginnings the acceptance of social science in the programs that were directed to the development of new weapons, defense operations, and the management of the military establishment grew to where the broad involvement of social science in military R&D came to have major consequences for the orientation of social science research as a whole.

These R&D programs helped enhance the scientific ambitions of social scientists desiring to shift their activities away from information gathering and descriptive analysis of data. Even where the work to be done had very poor fit to conventional scientific models, it had to be rationalized in experimental, nomological, or engineering terms. These programs were also consequential in another sense in that they enabled the social sciences to share in the tremendous growth in the volume of federal allocations to scientific research. In the war and its aftermath the symbols of "defense" and "national security" became major bases for such allocations. After having reported no expense for social science research and a modest 14 million dollars for research in natural and physical science in 1938, in the early 1950's the national military establishment was spending over a billion dollars for scientific R&D and 20 million dollars for research in the social sciences alone (U.S. National Resources Committee, III.2, 1938: 69; *Federal Funds* . . . , III.2, 1953: 29).

Conflict and Tension in the Postwar Years

As we move closer to the present it becomes more difficult to generalize concerning long-term trends in the relationship of government and social science.[1] It is easier to be dispassionate about events of a fairly distant past than about contemporary ones. This is evident in the literature dating from the postwar years, much of which is topical, parochial, and typically lacking in empirical data. On the whole it has little to offer as a basis for firm generalizations.

Primarily in a speculative vein, then, we suggest that many of the problems which have troubled the relationships between successive postwar administrations and the social science community can be traced to two developments. One is the extent to which the government has come to rely on extragovernmental organizations—the universities and nonprofit research organizations—to produce knowledge and expertise for use in decision-making. The other is the Cold War and the drastically changed conditions —intellectual, ideological, and organizational—of government-sponsored research on foreign areas and peoples.

As a consequence of the first of these developments research designed to meet the needs of governmental agencies for information and knowledge has more frequently than before come to be performed by individuals in institutions whose norms, values, and objectives differ from those of sponsoring institutions. The greater responsiveness of the academic social scientist to the needs of his discipline can be illustrated by the frequency with which the solution to practical problems calls for the creation of new knowledge rather than the application of existing theory or data. While conflict between individuals working within different systems of institutional requirements and responsibility can be seen as endemic to policy-oriented social science, in the postwar period these conflicts have been exacerbated by divergences of political opinion. Disparities of outlook of representatives of the two institutions concerning the substance of governmental policy and action in international and military affairs have become more common and more intense.

The expansion of the university domain brought about by the infusion of federal funds in the postwar period is apparent when we consider that in 1936 only an estimated 10 percent of the federal government's research expenditure of 70 million dollars went to the universities (U.S. National Resources Committee, III.2, 1938: 189). In fiscal year 1967, educational institutions proper and educational institution research centers received 30 percent of a total federal research budget of 5.5 billion dollars (*Federal Funds* . . . , III.2, 1966: 77).[2] In addi-

---

[1] For descriptive overviews of the interactions of social scientists with foreign policy and military departments and agencies, see Archibald (I, 1968); Bowers (IV.3, 1967); Crawford and Lyons (III.3, 1967); and Davison (IV.3, 1967).

[2] No tabulations exist which show the amount of federal funds going to different types of recipients in specific research areas such as the social or life sciences. The Subcommittee on Research and Technical Programs has estimated that in fiscal year 1965 the universities and colleges received 65 percent of the funds for all government-sponsored projects reported to the Science Information Exchange (*Research and Technical Programs* . . . ,

tion the universities have benefited from the creation of new types of organizations to perform research and development activities for the federal government. In fiscal year 1966 close to half of the 1.2 billion dollars allocated to federal contract research centers, for instance, was spent in centers managed by educational institutions (*Federal Funds* . . . , III.2, 1966: 25).

The expansion of the university domain has resulted not only from tremendous increases in government spending for scientific research but also from the entirely new economic and administrative system for support of science instituted after the war. The major features of this system and the conditions that brought it into being have been described by Price (III.2, 1954):

"When it became necessary to bring the country's leading scientists into the war program, it was far easier, and less disturbing to all of the career relationships involved, to make arrangements with the existing companies and institutions than to bring the individual scientists in as government employees. After V J Day, when the incentive of wartime patriotism was gone, it was all the more necessary to make the same choice. As soon as this choice was made its dynamic features became evident by contrast with the previous systems of government support of science.

"First of all, as the scientists eagerly left special military work to go back to their industrial laboratories or universities, the necessity of using private careers for public purposes became all the more evident. It was easy enough to say that certain defense research had to be continued. But the scientist, like the common soldier, wanted to get back to his home institution. The contractual system made it possible to have government work done under private salary scales, with none of the civil service red tape, without the restrictions of personnel ceilings, and with a greater appearance of long-term security.

"The system was comparable in some ways to that of the agricultural grants-in-aid program. But there had been endless Congressional haggling over the question whether any given state should be permitted to have more than one experiment station in the federal program and over rigid statutory formulas for the distribution of research grants among states. By contrast, here was a system in which the federal agencies could do business not only with state government agencies, but with private universities and industrial corporations as well.

"In addition, it gave the federal agency, . . . the advantages of flexibility and initiative. The Department of Agriculture could not create a new state, but the Air Force could bring about the creation of a new corporation. The new system was an absolute necessity for the Air Force as it sought to build up the various supporting services that had formerly been provided for it by the Army (pp. 77–78)."

The widespread use of the contract and granting mechanisms in the postwar period has affected the institution of social science in a number of ways. It has permitted the university-based social sciences, for instance, to take on a considerable portion of the government's data-gathering activities. The creation of new types of organizations—federal contract research centers and nonprofit independent research organizations—has involved social scientists in new career patterns, research specialties, and styles of work.[1] The emergence of research as the

III.2, 1967: 41). The reporting of projects to this organization, however, is far from complete. The absence of National Science Foundation tabulations according to field of science and performers of research is one of several examples of inadequacies in the data on which most discussions concerning the role of the federal government in sponsoring scientific activities currently have to be based. The production and uses of official statistics describing scientific activities could well be subjected to the kind of scrutiny that crime statistics have undergone recently (Biderman, II.1, 1966: 111 ff).

[1] A National Science Foundation report states that independent nonprofit institutions employed more than three times as many scientists and engineers in 1965 than in 1954 and that during the same period expenditure for their intramural research and development activities increased fivefold (*Scientific Activities* . . . , III.2, 1967:

primary work activity of a substantial number of social scientists derives in considerable measure from new work opportunities in these organizations.[1]

In the social sciences the new system for government support of scientific activities has created a division of labor through which governmental needs for narrowly applied or mission-oriented research are fulfilled by the organizations most responsive to these needs, most frequently the federal contract research centers. This has left to the universities not only their traditional basic research functions but has added the whole area of policy-oriented research as well. Whether exploring political conditions favoring arms control agreements, ways of building sociopolitical institutions in developing areas, or broad aspects of the war on poverty, such studies are for the most part performed, under government contract or grants, by researchers at universities or university-affiliated institutions.

It is partly against a background of growing affluence and power that one must view recent protests by many academic social scientists over the threats to academic freedom and the dangers of corruption posed by the infusion of government research funds into the university sphere. Particularly in the 1960's, activities seen as needing the attention of social scientists have increased more rapidly in scale and scope than has the supply of social scientists available to perform the work. This "seller's market" during much of the decade has allowed picking, choosing, and bargaining for the individual social scientist as well as for the profession collectively. Recent protests against government support of social science research, especially support by the military, are regarded by some commentators as an effort to stave off subservience of university social science to government influence. But since most of the protestors call for more, rather than less, public support of research, these protests may also be seen as part of a bargaining process by which social scientists attempt to retain the benefits of governmental support while at the same time setting their own conditions for such support.

Much of the recent conflict surrounding government sponsorship of academic social science has centered on the presence in the university sphere of funds which do not meet current academic standards of ideological cleanliness. That the change lies more in the greater assertiveness of academic social scientists than in the number or character of governmental strings attached is demonstrated by a comparison of wartime or early postwar foreign area and military research programs with present ones. The early postwar programs, which rarely caused objections, did, in fact, have much more stringent security and loyalty requirements than most present ones. Orlans (III.4, 1967), in writing about the aversion of some scholars to Defense Department sponsorship, observes:

"Shortly after World War II, the issue of conducting classified research on campus was of greater practical importance than it is today, when both government and university officials concede that it is preferable, in peacetime, not to do this work in a setting designed for unfettered inquiry and instruction. In any event, the volume of classified work at universities has declined and alternative sites for its prosecution have increased, so that the problem has dwindled (p. 9)."

Social scientists have recently protested provisions for governmental review and oversight of research and for censorship of research products that for long encountered little objection. Rice (III.2, 1967) points out that organized social scientists in the

---

5–7). The data in this document relating specifically to economists and sociologists, however, suffer from obviously egregious underenumeration.

[1] Of the sociologists and economists in the National Register of Scientific and Technical Personnel in 1964, 22 percent and 19 percent, respectively, reported research and development as their primary work activity (Hopper, III.1, 1966: 151; "The Structure of . . . ," III.1, 1965: 22).

1940's were sponsors of the legislation requiring Budget Bureau review of federally sponsored interview and questionnaire studies. He discusses the change in the nature of the relationships between the federal government and social research that now leads social scientists to see these procedures as an alarming threat to essential research freedom.

In Chapter II we discuss in greater detail divergences of opinion between academic social scientists and government officials with respect to the substance of policy during the Cold War and its aftermath. The multiple effects—broadly organizational as well as intellectual—of the Cold War on foreign area research are best illustrated by the area of intelligence research. This is a particularly pertinent case not only because intelligence research involved the most extensive use of the Cold War innovation of covert sponsorship of research, but also because the intelligence function had appeared to hold the promise of an important social science contribution to the formulation and execution of foreign policy.[1]

As we commented earlier, World War II saw the extension of the domestic intelligence function, long performed by social scientists, to include a wide range of sociopolitical and economic information concerning foreign countries. In the war that part of intelligence work which relied on open sources—newspapers, radio broadcasts, and interviews with refugees—was carried out more openly than was later to be the case. Much of it was unclassified work. Even when it was not, the community of scholars with access to the relatively permissively employed "Restricted" and "Confidential" classifications was so broad in wartime that these classifications imposed relatively few impediments to scholarly interchange. The work of the Research and Analysis Branch of the Office of Strategic Services (OSS), for instance, resulted in more than 300 published reports and monographs[2] dealing with every conceivable aspect of foreign areas and cultures.

With the cloak of secrecy in which intelligence work came to be shrouded as a result of the Cold War and the particular ways in which the Central Intelligence Agency interpreted its mission, there was less room for open participation by social scientists. The concept and the word "intelligence," whether used in reference to research or action, became a creature of the shadows—the property of a nether world of agents, codes, plots, and paid-for putsches. The cool professionalism with which these tasks were to be executed is illustrated by a statement of Allen Dulles before the Committee on Armed Services (VI, 1947). While observing that more than 80 percent of the information collected by the proposed central intelligence organization would come from open sources, Dulles also stated that "the agency should be directed by an elite corps of men with a passion for anonymity. . . . Whatever may have been their previous professions, . . . once they take position in the central intelligence organization they should 'take the cloth' of the intelligence service" (p. 525).

As a result of the secrecy surrounding intelligence work, academic social scientists presumably have had less opportunity to influence information concerning foreign areas brought to the attention of the makers of foreign policy. Most of them were cut off from many sources of data concerning foreign countries, such as those gained by the monitoring of foreign broadcasts. One

---

[1] Hilsman (IV.2, 1956: 7) has stated that ". . . it is in the strategic intelligence agencies that research—and even the social sciences—will find their real home within the formal structure of government." It is significant that Hilsman's entire analysis of the production and use of strategic intelligence is carried out without his citing a single academic social scientist.

[2] Figure obtained from a count of cards in the Library of Congress catalogue. By contrast the Central Intelligence Agency is represented in the catalogue by only a handful of cards.

might speculate, for example, that there would have been markedly different developments in the methodology and substance of international studies had extensive foreign broadcast monitoring and translation services been a resource available to all scholars during the last 20 years.

The refinement of techniques for studying "cultures at a distance" in the postwar years were the result not only of the Iron Curtain but also of this embargo on information. The CIA's near-monopoly on intelligence research also prevented other governmental agencies from undertaking much of this kind of research. The low ranking of empirical research in the Department of State, which is the subject of much adverse comment by social scientists, is doubtless due in large measure to the fact that substantive foreign political and social intelligence was primarily a CIA mission during the period of the most rapid growth and institutionalization of social science. In the Department of State in the postwar years there was only a small intelligence research office (Bureau of Intelligence Research or INR) which maintained open, although limited, contacts with the academic community. The department's ability to draw on the products of academic research has, however, been greatly impaired by organizational arrangements which linked intelligence and research.

Currently we are experiencing a collapse of the fragile innovations and relationships that developed during two decades of partially covert sponsorship. Doubtless, covert financing allowed intelligence agencies to promote and supply some scholarly activities which more politically responsive agencies would have had to shun. The special kinds of relationships that were formed between covertly sponsored research scholars, their sponsors in the intelligence agencies, and the remainder of the academic world are yet to be fully understood. Only on the basis of such knowledge of the past can we determine what may be the future involvement of the social sciences in the foreign intelligence function.

II. THE SOCIOLOGY OF SOCIAL SCIENCE: ISSUES OF THEORY AND METHOD

For many social scientists, including the editors of this book, the thought of a sociology of the social sciences is slightly discomforting. For one thing, such inquiries suggest an endless process. We have immediate sympathy for reviewers of this book who will be thrust into the meta-meta level if they seek sociological explanations for the generation of a book such as the present one. Some may see us urging our colleagues to adopt the behavior of the notorious bird that flies in ever narrower circles until it disappears into its own innards. Those who may fear the development of a sociology of the sociology of the social sciences, however, can seek solace in the fact that the first meta-level has barely been explored.

Many social scientists have doubts concerning the legitimacy of inquiring into their own activities. If polled, they would probably feel that such inquiries divert scarce intellectual resources from other, more important problems. Although rarely vocalized, questions of propriety are also involved. Realistic inquiries into the financial aspects of research, for instance, would be considered gauche in many social science circles. These feelings may be explained partly by an interest in protecting the "secrets of the trade" and partly by scientific norms, which insist on the minimization of such extrascientific concerns as money.

These doubts are evident in the elaborate justifications which preface studies of social science activities. For the most part the argument is that "if we study what we are doing, we will be able to do it better." In other cases the relative lack of attention given social scientists, compared with the extensive study of other social groupings, is used as an argument. Merton's (II.1, 1957: 458) observation about the wealth of studies of hobos and salesladies, professional thieves and professional beggars, and the dearth of those concerning social scientists, has been quoted so often that it is beginning to sound almost true.

In contrast to the sociology of science which has established itself as a specialized field of empirical inquiry, work done along the lines of a sociology of social science has almost always been subsidiary to other intellectual endeavors and activities. Most frequently examinations of social science as an institution or a social activity are linked to the interests of the profession and carried out to meet needs for professional self-understanding, internal control, or external relations. In the less frequent instances in which social science has been studied independently of its perceived self-interests, it has been from perspectives of intellectual history or the traditional sociology of knowledge.

Only on very few occasions has the theoretical framework of the sociology of science been applied to social science. The social scientific adequacy of this treatment of the institution of science, as well as its adaptability to social science, should be examined before settling for a simple transfer of the same perspectives and products to social science. We examine here in some detail the propositional and conceptual bases of the sociology of science. Before doing so, we review briefly the contributions of the "professional affairs" literature, the sociology of knowledge, and intellectual history to a sociology of social science.

Self-Scrutiny in the Profession

Social scientists are no different from other professionals in being interested in the state of their profession, both internally and in relation to the outside world. In fact, peculiar features of the profession such as its marginal position in relation to other social groupings, its concern with autonomy, and the nonspecific nature of its calling may have made its members unusually prone to introspection and self-scrutiny. These matters are habitually discussed at the meetings of professional associations. The professional journals frequently feature articles examining employment and other characteristics of practicing social scientists, problems of recruitment and training, and questions of professional standards. Some of the major associations—the American Psychological Association, the American Statistical Association, the American Sociological Association—now have journals exclusively devoted to matters of professional interest.

An example of this type of self-scrutiny is the "whence and whither social science?" themes often chosen as topics for presidential addresses at the annual meetings of the professional associations. Discussion of what should be the relationship of social scientists to their "clients" in business and government, and of research ethics, are others. In this literature we also see the effect of a series of specific incidents that have given a particular issue high and temporary visibility: the 1948 election forecast debacle, for instance, prompted a debate on "overselling" of the social sciences (Social Science Research Council, VI, 1949); the 1955 Chicago jury case caused widespread soul-searching over the ethicality of the methods through which social scientists sometimes obtain their data (Shils, VI, 1959: 114–157); in 1965 the "Camelot affair" brought to the surface, among other things, the question of "covert" sponsorship of research ("'Camelot' and Psychological Tests," III.4, 1966; Horowitz, III.4, 1967; Silvert, III.4, 1965).

Although conducted on a higher level of intellectuality, many of these writings and discussions are not very different in kind from similar exercises among lawyers, doctors or morticians. In intensity, for instance, the reaction of the social science community to the "Camelot affair" might well be compared to that of organized morticians when confronted with Jessica Mitford's *The American Way of Death.*

Although the professional self-scrutiny of social scientists in public has generally been carried out on a low analytical level, it is our experience that in private, nonbusiness settings—such as those associated with annual meetings and conferences—they bring to bear on the question of social science as a profession much of the conceptual and theoretical apparatus with which they are most at home. The informality of the setting also permits going beyond what, in the terms used by Goffman (VI, 1964: 22–30), would be called the "front" of public presentation. For indeed, as is true of any human activity, social science has both its "fronts" and its "backs." Much of the effectiveness of social science in going beyond the commonplace in the knowledge it provides of institutions, or human behavior, generally, derives from its willingness and ability to explore "backs."

Thus it is only in these settings that one hears analyses[1] of such "back" topics as the effects of ethnic succession in the profession on the directions of its intellectual activity; of specifics of the workings of competition and cooperation in the "grants economy"; of politics and personality as they have affected the granting policies of a great foundation; of the "cognitive dissonance" inherent in research roles.

A somewhat different kind of professional self-scrutiny relates more directly to the work methods, practices, and experiences of social scientists engaging in scientific research. Writings in this genre may merely form the introduction to a larger work which presents the results of a study, or they may be independent articles or books describing the origins of a particularly well-known research project, the steps involved in its execution, the contacts with sponsoring bodies and with the individuals and organizations being studied, and the hardships and frustrations of the investigators. Although frequently presented as studies in social science methodology, in this context methodology means more than simply the mechanics of research. Vidich and Bensman (VI, 1964: vii), for instance, in their introduction to *Reflections on Community Studies,* describe this other dimension as ". . . the personal quality of community studies, that is the intimate connection between the investigator, his methods of investigation, his results, and his own future intellectual development."

The individualistic character of many of these writings renders difficult their use as a basis for generalized descriptions of research behavior. Although they frequently, and often candidly, describe the "backs" as well as the "fronts" of research activities and are lively and insightful, these writings rarely achieve the degree of detachment from the object of study that is usually characteristic of social science work. Instead, here as well as in the literature oriented to other professional concerns, the information is ordered and presented from the standpoint of what it means to social scientists, personally, as members of a professional group. The results seldom yield comprehensions of the social sciences as institutions or behavioral systems in terms of general sociological concepts and propositions. Broader knowledge of the operation of society is poorly applied to comprehending the social sciences and the information gathered about the social sciences does not contribute to a broader understanding of the society.

Sociology of Knowledge and Intellectual History

To the extent that the study of the social sciences has been infused with perspectives broader than professional self-interest, these orientations have come primarily from the sociology of knowledge and from intellectual history. The basic hypothesis of the sociol-

---

[1] See also the article by Horowitz in Chapter IV.

ogy of knowledge is undoubtedly so well-known by now that it hardly needs to be restated. Knowledge whether in the form of subjective beliefs or objective "truths" is seen as socially conditioned. The perception, cognition, and conation of reality are viewed as socially determined in the sense of their being a function of the social position of individuals.[1] This notion is frequently merged with one of the recurring themes of intellectual history, that is, that historical events not only shape ideas directly, but they also shape the social and cultural institutions which in turn generate new knowledge and ideas.

Environmental influences on ideas and the influence of the thoughts of one man on the thoughts of another are the two themes forming the explanatory bases of most histories of the social sciences. This is the case with the historical sketch in the earlier part of this introductory chapter. A more specific example of how these perspectives are used to gain understanding of developments in the social sciences is found in a history of sociology such as that by Hinkle and Hinkle (II.1, 1954). In presenting evidence supporting the view ". . . that sociology emerged largely as a response to the industrialization and urbanization of the post-Civil War era," they use explanations such as the following:

1. *The social backgrounds of early sociologists:* "The vast majority of eminent sociologists prior to 1920 came from rural and religious environments."
2. *The academic setting of sociology in its formative period:* This "was of such a nature and so located (in the Midwest) as to be acutely sensitive to effects of urbanization."
3. *The professional organization of sociologists:* Sociology was "a lineal descendant of a general intellectual movement committed to the betterment of urban social conditions (pp. 2-4)."

Apart from infusing writings on the social sciences with a certain degree of "perspectivism," a more important contribution of the sociology of knowledge perhaps is the precedent it sets and, hence, the legitimation it offers for inquiring into the production and use of social science knowledge. But it also sets the tone for the genre that this field of inquiry represents. Regardless of time, method, or subject matter, writings in this area have certain common characteristics. These have been outlined by Merton (II.1, 1957: 458):

". . . whatever the intention of the analysts, their analyses tend to have an acrid quality: they tend to indict, secularize, ironicize, satirize, alienate, devalue the intrinsic content of the avowed belief or point of view. . . . Statements ordinarily viewed in terms of their manifest content are "debunked," . . . by relating this content to attributes of the speaker or the society in which he lives."

In tone as well as in choice of problems and methodology inquiries bearing the sociology of knowledge label have themselves been strongly influenced by the social and cultural contexts in which they have been launched. It is entirely fitting then that Mannheim (II.1, 1948; II.1, 1951; II.1, 1952), writing in the 1930's, should choose the rise of authoritarian ideologies as the focus for a generalized treatment of the existential bases of belief systems.

In its methodology, too, the sociology of knowledge has been influenced by the particular milieus in which it has been cultivated. Given the strong empirical orientation of American sociology before World War II, it is not surprising that the major American contribution to the sociology of knowledge came to be a methodological one. This was the proposition advanced, among

---

[1] Znaniecki in Chapter I, pp. 31-32. For a paradigmatic overview of the sociology of knowledge as of its development at the time of World War II, see Merton (II.1, 1945). Other writings in the sociology of knowledge deemed important to this volume are included in the Bibliography, II.1.

others, by Znaniecki, that we view systems of knowledge "simply as empirical realities, trying to reach by their comparative analysis theoretic generalizations about them."[1] Although far from being achieved in actuality, this has remained the ambition of most contemporary sociologists of knowledge. In this respect, however, the study of social science knowledge has lagged far behind that of such other "mental productions" as physical science, the humanities, or religious beliefs.

In the substance of its concerns the sociology of knowledge has undergone changes which set the general theoretic framework for a sociology of social science. In earlier periods it dealt primarily with the thought and knowledge of an entire society or culture. It examined the shaping of "mental productions" by the social position of their producers. Only incidentally, however, did these positions involve knowledge-producing roles. In this aspect it reflected prevailing conceptions of "men of knowledge" in eighteenth and nineteenth century Europe.

In its later developments, especially after its transfer to this country, the sociology of knowledge has come more and more to concern itself with individuals and groups who specialize in the production and application of knowledge. These are often seen as orienting their activities not toward the total society but toward specialized audiences, or, to use Znaniecki's term, "social circles." As a result, the field has come to be split up into a number of subareas labeled after the particular cultural product being studied. Here the sociology of social science can be placed alongside such other specialized fields of inquiry as the sociology of science, of art and literature, and of religion.

In these fields the concern has come to be not, as before, with mental productions per se, but with the social behavior, roles, and institutions that are specific to their creation and use. In certain fiields this reversal of foci has advanced to the point where the product itself is seen as incidental to the social activities surrounding it. This development has been most pronounced in the study of disciplines where the application of existing knowledge or techniques is more important than the production of new knowledge. It is not accidental, therefore, that the frame of reference for a sociology of psychiatry, for instance, should be that of the sociology of work and professions (Schatzman and Strauss, II.1, 1966: 4).

A similar development has occurred in the study of such a predominantly knowledge-*producing* activity as science. In a brief history of the sociology of science, Storer (II.1, 1966: 5-6) points out how in earlier times science was seen primarily "as the part of society that produces new information about the empirical universe. . . ." Since about 1940, however, he believes we have rapidly moved ". . . toward the investigation of science as a particular sort of social behavior, one which can be studied as an independent part of society. . . ."

The Sociology of Science

The sociology of science represents the most elaborate attempt thus far to apply to the institution of science "the kind of sociological analysis that has proved fruitful when directed to many other kinds of social activities" (Barber, II.1, 1952: 5). Despite this programmatic pronouncement, we find that in basic theoretic statements regarding the sociology of science its concepts and propositions are for the most part derived teleologically from methodology and epistemology.[2] Abstract conceptions of "the scientific method" rather than the concepts and

---

[1] P. 30.

[2] It should be noted that the writings on which we focus here are theoretic statements of the sociology of science such as those of Barber, Merton and Storer (all in II.1). Historical descriptions and empirical studies of scientific organization are often marked by a more objective and detached appreciation of social determinants of scientific institutions and activities than the attempts at contemporary or timeless social system analysis discussed here.

theories that social scientists have used to explain other social phenomena are at the center of these theories and their analytic applications. This is so despite the contention that the study of science presents merely a "special case" of generally applicable institutional and behavioral analysis. In giving primacy to methodology, especially the truth-seeking goals of science, sociologists of science may be disposed to label certain features of science as central problems which are more peculiar to their own discipline.

More specifically, in such discussions sociologists of science commonly mix conceptions of science as an *abstract philosophical system* (or systems) for gaining valid knowledge, with that of science as an *ideal cultural system* embodying certain values, norms, and techniques. In turn the principles of both of these systems are confused with those of the *phenomenal systems of action* when the latter are the purported referents of the discussions. Abstract conceptions of the scientific method are ideas central to each of these systems. But each system also involves other prescriptive elements. Most functional descriptions of science confound the purely epistemic elements of each of these systems with other elements that are at most only partially derivative from their epistemological basis.

Merton (II.1, 1957), for example, makes a somewhat similar distinction between the philosophical and cultural systems. He distinguishes between the "technical methods" by means of which knowledge is certified and the "ethos of science." His models, however, appear unsatisfactory to us for pursuing his particular interest in the paper in question, which, he says, is concerned with:

". . . one limited aspect of science as an institution. Thus, we shall consider, not the methods of science, but the mores with which they are hedged about. To be sure, methodological canons are often both technical expedients and moral compulsives, but it is solely the latter which is our concern (p. 551)."

The shortcoming of his models derives from a functional formulation that begs some of the central questions toward which his analysis is directed. A goal is postulated that is common to these systems, as follows:

"The institutional goal of science is the extension of certified knowledge. The technical methods employed toward this end provide the relevant definition of knowledge: empirically confirmed and logically consistent predictions. The institutional imperatives (mores) derive from the goals and the methods. The entire structure of technical and moral norms implements the final objective. The technical norms of empirical evidence, adequate, valid and reliable, is a prerequisite for systematic and valid prediction; the technical norm of logical consistency, a prerequisite for systematic and valid prediction. The mores of science possess a methodological rationale but they are binding, not only because they are procedurally efficient, but because they are believed right and good. They are moral as well as technical prescriptions.

Four sets of institutional imperatives—universalism, communism, disinterestedness, organized scepticism—comprise the ethos of modern science (pp. 552–553)."

The goal stated by Merton can be posited, as it and similar formulations have been, for abstract epistemological formulations, or as a goal for devising concrete methods of study, or as a basis for axiological examinations of the workings of the "ethos of science." We would find it preferable, however, to treat as empirical questions whether the moral imperatives are derivative, historically, from the goal, or, if the functionalist perspective is taken, whether a particular imperative "implements the final objective" or serves some other system demand.[1]

An additional difficulty of Merton's model

---

[1] Kaplan (II.1, 1964: 855–858) raises the additional question of whether these moral imperatives, which Merton derived from studying writings and documents of the seventeenth century, have indeed remained as unchanged as sociologists of science usually assume.

is that it tends to confuse those particular technical expedients which form the contemporary, methodologically prescriptive culture of science, as well as those technical expedients adopted in any concrete setting, with the theoretically open universe of all possible methods that would be axiologically consistent with a given epistemic formulation of science. An alternative culture-system model would be one whose form is not as directly inferable from the philosophical system.

Merton does not assue, however, that the ends from which institutional imperatives are derived and which they serve are necessary or primary motivational determinants of the behavior of all (or any) scientists. He makes this statement, however, in defending himself against arguments that a concern with "social contexts of science" is a corrupting intrusion of matters alien to science proper or that it impugns the disinterested motives of the scientist:

". . . scientists may be most variously motivated—by a disinterested desire to learn, by hope of economic gain, by active (or, as Veblen calls it, by idle) curiosity, by aggression or competition, by egotism or altruism. But the same motives in different institutional settings take different social expressions, just as different motivations in a given institutional setting may take approximately the same social expression. In one institutional context, egotism may lead a scientist to advance a branch of science useful for the military arts; in another institutional context, egoism may lead him to work on research with apparently no military use. To consider how and how far social structures canalize the direction of scientific research is not to arraign the scientist for his motives (p. 532)."

Merton escapes from his concern with whether or not his sociology of science impugns scientists' motives by climbing on a higher pedestal from which he pronounces a resounding endorsement of science as a cultural and social system. He is doubly safe in that his teleological analysis not only concludes that science (as a cultural system) is functionally necessary to science (as an expanding body of valid knowledge), but also that science (both meanings) thrives as a direct function of the degree of democracy in the social order and of a handful of other virtues. Our point may be illustrated by remarking that this concern with whether science or scientists' motives are impugned is "unscientific" from the standpoint of some norms of the ethos (those supporting objectivity) but consistent with other norms powerfully binding on the profession (those supporting in-group solidarity).

The models implicit in Merton's writing might be depicted as follows. Science has the goal of valid knowledge at its center. Flowing from this goal and encircling it, is the body of basic epistemic principles which constitutes the scientific method. Around this, in turn, is an epiphenomenal normative culture which serves to constrain the activities of scientists into the forms required by the method and goal. The ethos controls and patterns divergent inner and outer forces so that the scientist is not led into temptation but rather pursues the virtues consistent with expanding the area of scientific truth.

The Action Systems of Science

Storer (II.1, 1966), writing 20 years after Merton, recognizes a tendency to confuse the real and the ideal inherent in Merton's formulation and he turns his attention from

". . . the 'ideal' organization of science, the social *system* of science to a consideration of certain general patterns of behavior in which scientists actually engage. Such patterns constitute the social *structure* of science. The principal distinction between system and structure as I use the terms here, lies in the fact that *structures* represents the working out of *system* in the 'real world' (p. 99)."

In contrast to Merton, then, Storer adds a construction—the social structure of science—which sounds equivalent to the third type of system to which we referred, that is, the systems of action. This construction is more open to influences from the social environment of the scientific social system than those considered by Merton.

Adding this third system, however, does little to free Storer from ideal functional presuppositions equivalent to those of Merton's earlier discussion. The organization of Storer's analysis rests on the same kind of teleological postulate. He, too, posits a normative cultural system that constrains activities in keeping with the ideal goal of the advancement of knowledge. His discussion of the social structure of science consists of instances of inconsistencies among these norms confronted in actual practice and of conflicts between these norms and extra-system impingements on scientific activities.

All of the relationships of scientists and extrascientific institutions he treats as sources of conflict—as embodying disintegrative tendencies for science as a goal, as a social system, and as a social structure. The conception of contacts between science and the rest of society is much like that of the concerns of the pious of the ghetto regarding their contacts with the gentile.

This discussion of "social structure" thus is exclusively a discussion of "problems of science." For each norm of science he presents illustrative "problems." Thus he talks about problems of disinterestedness, that is, factors that detract from the scientist's concern with preserving both the integrity and value of science's "native commodity" and that encourage his interests in other commodities. Or he looks at examples of the "problem of organized scepticism," such as the reliance on personal authority as a certification of the value of a work. The integrative principle keeping scientific activity in line with the teleological principle in Storer's analysis is, in effect, peer-group pressure. The scientist's major motivation is not assumed to be directly that of expanding valid knowledge, but rather that of receiving "competent response from his colleagues." This response, however, is received only when work is performed in a manner that serves the abstract goal of science. Scientists are not assumed to apply the controls to themselves, but only to each other. Storer's social structure proves no system at all, but rather selective interferences with his ideal social system—a system equivalent to Merton's ethos of science.

Thus Storer's analysis of the "working out of the ideal system in the real world" differs from his analysis of the ideal system of science only in being somewhat more concerned with more concretely illustrated extrasystem influences than with internal dynamics. For example in discussing the "ideal system," he analyzes controls that keep scientists from working on problems that are primarily of importance to nonscientists. In the later discussion of the "social structure" the problems the scientist is constrained from working on, for example, become those of the government. No new principle is involved and the assumptions foreclose possibilities of disconfirmation (pp. 88–90 and 113–114).

This may be illustrated by the "explanations" of aspects of scientific systems that serve to protect and extend the autonomy of the individual scientist and of science as a whole in terms of the need to protect scientific activity from contaminating external influences. Both Merton and Storer describe much of the ethos of science as serving this central need. They see as the rationale for these controls the protection of the manifest function of science, that is, the extension of scientifically certified knowledge. But can this function suggest when, where, and with what intensity mechanisms to protect autonomy will come into play?

Storer emphasizes that science differs fundamentally from service professions, such as medicine and law, in support of his general theory that an internal dynamic—the drive for esteem of colleagues—is the primary driving force of its culture and social system. Scientists, as contrasted with service professionals, he asserts, are driven to far greater dependence on their colleagues' esteem because ". . . the service professional is typically supported by nonprofessionals, his colleagues do not have the collective power to regulate the 'rewards' he receives" (p. 18).

The elaboration of an ethos to extend and protect the autonomy of the profession, however, is fully as great, if not greater, in these service professions as it is in science; and, indeed, is a dynamic found in all self-conscious, occupational groups. Direct lay dependence may, in fact, intensify the need for devices to foster autonomy and self-sufficiency. The intensity of the perceived need for the professional service on the part of lay publics, further, is a basis for economic and political power that often makes possible the extensions of autonomy in these service professions. Other social forces than the willingness of clients to pay for services, determine the ability of a highly organized system to control the rewards, economic or otherwise, a professional receives. (Lynn et al., I, 1967: 3, *passim.*)

Kuhn (II.1, 1962: 167-168) argues identically, as does Storer, placing particular stress on the highly esoteric character of science. The insulation of science from demands of the laity, which Kuhn believes exceeds that of any other profession, allows scientists to work exclusively on such problems that they are likely to be able to solve. But these properties, too, are characteristic of all esoteric professions. There is a tendency in these theses about science to ignore the degree to which relationships between professions and laity may involve asymmetries of power and, further, to confuse the situation of elite members of the profession with those of its rank and file.

It should be apparent that we regard such treatments of science as Merton's and Storer's as more likely to lead to simple affirmations of the faith, or at most scholastic elaborations of inherited doctrine, than to increased understanding of science, if they are taken as the models for what we have called the social action systems of science. When explicitly addressed to the cultural system, they may usefully delineate important, but only semiexplicit, norms of the culture; they may provide measures of the degree to which scientists' behavior conforms to one or another of these norms in a given context; and they may investigate why these norms are taken to be "right and good." It is more on the basis of assumption than verification, however, that these normative elements of the scientific culture can be accepted as the driving forces determining how much scientific knowledge is produced, how many people are engaged in it, with what kind of resources, toward what particular ends, and with what particular success in ordering reality, either predictively or for adaptation and manipulation.

Kaplan (II.1, 1964) also complains that writers on the sociology of science have been prone to accept the behavior-determining character of the posited values and norms of science without sufficient theoretical clarification of them and without empirical study of their operation. He draws extensively on illustrations of scientific communication and various inconsistencies between the assumed communal imperative and various systemic characteristics of contemporary science (e.g., the privately circulated "preprint"). He also illustrates how following the imperative against secrecy may interfere with scientific progress (e.g., by the "publication explosion" overloading the system with trivia and ephemera). He gives other illustrations relating to communication patterns in science, which suggest that the customary formulations are also too general to suggest which of various alternative forms consistent with such a general imperative as communality will be followed in actual practice (pp. 856–860).

The approach to the study of science as a system of action would be improved by models (a) that do not posit norms derived exclusively from the philosophical systems; (b) that incorporate the many normative and technical alternatives of the culture of science which are not necessarily either logically consistent with one another nor consistent in the specific action they suggest in any concrete situation; (c) that pay greater attention to the requirements of the viability of a system which is not so self-sufficient economically, politically, socially, culturally, and demographically as it aspires (and pretends) to be; and (d) that do not obscure the applicability of general principles of behavior and organization to science by unnecessarily postulating its uniqueness.

The Sociology of Social Science—A Product of "Big Social Science"

The sociology of social science as it is now developing is the product of what some observers have called "big social science" ("New Intelligence Requirements," III.3, 1965: 173). The production of social science knowledge, especially that involving mass collection of data, has become a large-scale enterprise requiring a combination of skills, a fairly elaborate division of labor and considerable mechanical and administrative resources. The costliness of this enterprise has created an intricate structure for support of research which ties the social sciences to such other social institutions as business, government, and the world of foundations. Although the total amount of economic resources required to maintain the current level of social science research activities is difficult to calculate, one estimate, made in 1961, sets this figure at 652 million dollars. Of this the Federal government provided an estimated 32 percent. We get a better feeling for the size of the current social science research budget of the Federal government—an estimated 222 million dollars for fiscal year 1967—if we consider that it involves outlays of more money than what it costs annually to operate the entire legislative branch (Ellis, III.2, 1964; *Federal Funds for Research,* III.2, 1966: 78).

In the last few years the affairs of the social science professions have become public and political concerns. This is true not only of those matters that relate to the larger society and to government, but of many internal matters as well. A large portion of the unprecedented attention currently given social science in Congress[1] has been directed to questions of how economic allocations to social science are to be justified, how research should be organized in and out of government, and of how the activity may be regulated to keep it consistent with the sensitivities and sensibilities of other social groupings. Much of this debate has been characterized by an ambivalence toward the social sciences. On the one hand, there is the fear that a powerful social science may create an omniscient and omnipotent Big Brotherish state; on the other hand, there is concern over turning over to what is deemed to be a feeble, impotent, and camouflaged pseudoscience, a role in engineering social lives which it cannot perform, at least not yet.

The parallel trends of the emergence of "big social science" and the increased attention given it by political bodies have forced attention to the institutions which produce, use, and support social science research. In the growing volume of writing and thinking about the relationship of social science and government, systematic examinations have

---

[1] In 1967 a handful of congressional committees were considering aspects of the role of social science in government and the larger society. Among these committees were: the Subcommittee on Government Research of the Senate Committee on Government Operations (the Harris Committee); the Subcommittee on International Organizations and Movements of the House Foreign Affairs Committee (the Fascell Committee); the Research and Technical Programs Subcommittee of the House Committee on Government Operations (the Reuss Committee); and the Subcommittee on Science, Research, and Development of the House Committee on Science and Astronautics (the Daddario Committee).

so far primarily taken the form of studies[1] bearing on such questions in the debate as the utility of social science for public policy, what might be a national policy for developing the social sciences, and what should be the level of government support of social science research activities. Some of these studies are conducted under official auspices[2] (with participating social scientists acting as representatives of their respective disciplines or professional associations). They have the explicit purpose of providing guidance to decision-makers concerned with national science and social science policies. The Behavioral and Social Science Survey (BASS), for instance, was launched in 1966 by a committee of the National Academy of Sciences. It is described as being undertaken "in response to the widespread and increased interest in the behavioral and social sciences on the part of government agencies, the Congress, a number of influential natural scientists, and others concerned with national policy for science" (*Behavioral and Social Science Survey . . . ,* VI, 1967). Since the conduct of research or formulations of questions for such research are not primary functions of these study groups, their contribution to a sociology of social science is likely to be mostly indirect. Their work, for example, may well stimulate the development of better data concerning government support of social science research.

In the future the institution of social science is certain to be a more frequent object of research as an important social phenomenon in its own right. The emergency of "big social science" is the most effective stimulus to such research. This development is likely to affect not only the subject matter but also the methodology of a sociology of social science. Overall, we can expect this field of inquiry to spawn increasingly specialized empirical investigations of the role of the social sciences in society. This trend will derive from the oft-noted tendency of social science to split up into multiple subject fields. While the label "sociology of social science" will probably continue to be used, in the future it will comprise specialized inquiries into the economics and politics of social science as well as its history.

We have spoken earlier of the hesitancy of social scientists to inspect, publicly, the "back" of social science activities. Yet the sociology of social science, in order to provide understanding of the dynamics of social science as an institution, must consider the "back" as well as the publicly presented "front." A growth in the size, the strength, and security of this institution makes it possible to accomplish with propriety the invasions of privacy involved in such studies.

By dealing with larger numbers of individuals or units of analysis, we can insure the anonymity of the subjects. As the furor over the ethics of Vidich and Bensman's (VI, 1960) study, *Small Town in Mass Society,* demonstrated, if the community is small enough, research invades the privacy both of the individual and the collectivity when social scientists display the "backs" of their activities. The anonymity of numbers also facilitates the development of an appropriately clinical style of rhetoric. As demonstrated in the study of political and economic as well as sexual activity, "backs" can be hygienically arranged for public scholarly presentation.

A larger scale of social science activities increases both the feasibility and utility of generalizations concerning different aspects of the social science institution. With more units of observation at our disposal, propositions can be validated against findings that have statistical significance. A research project seeking to develop generalizations con-

---

[1] A distinction between "research" and "study" in policy-oriented social science is suggested in the Introduction to Chapter II, p. 56.

[2] In 1967 within the National Academy of Sciences—National Research Council, there were two committees examining the social sciences. These were the Advisory Committee on Government Programs in the Behavioral Sciences and the BASS Committee mentioned later in text.

cerning the effectiveness of different ways of organizing social science research, for instance, would relate a significant number of "team" and "individual" research projects to such factors as productivity, work satisfaction, and career advancement. In a situation where large sums of money go into social science research, such generalizations will also be of pragmatic value.

The growth of social science and the many links it has established with other social institutions make concepts and theories developed in other fields of sociological inquiry more pertinent to the study of the institution of social science. As organizations for social science research grow larger and come to involve an elaborate differentiation of roles, they can profitably be studied within the conceptual frameworks of professional organizations. The institutionalization of social science research in government makes theories of bureaucracy, administrative behavior, and decision-making appropriate means of comprehending the interactive behaviors of social scientists and government officials. The growth in the economic requirements of the institution of social science and the complex ways in which allocations of funds are made to this activity renders economic theory useful, especially that pertaining to public value goods and services. By setting up models that do not rest exclusively on elements that are intrinsic to the institution of social science, it also becomes feasible to separate those characteristics of the institution and its behavioral components that are indeed unique to science and social science from those that are merely adaptations of principles and forms found in other social institutions.

CHAPTER I

Perspectives on the Social Roles of the Social Sciences

Sociology and Theory of Knowledge

FLORIAN ZNANIECKI

Sociology is still young and inclined to be imperialistic. Her forefathers claimed for her the entire domain of culture, and many of her faithful courtiers are trying to make those claims good by extending her sway over the fields of law, economics, technology, language, literature, art, religion, knowledge.... It is all very well to cultivate the borderlands between the special sciences, but each science should first cultivate properly its own field by its own methods.

We are concerned here with that particular set of borderland problems that has recently been termed the "sociology of knowledge"—a term parallel to "sociology of religion," "sociology of art," "sociology of language." Interest in these problems goes back to the very beginnings of modern sociological thought. The central idea of Comte's famous "law of three states" was that between certain types of philosophy or—more generally—of knowledge (theological, metaphysical, positive) and certain forms of social structure there exists a relationship of mutual dependence. Half a century later, the French sociological group centered around Durkheim tried in a series of highly significant studies to show the social origin of the fundamental forms of human experience and thinking. More recently, German sociologists, especially Max Scheler and Karl Mannheim, have made systematic efforts to trace the dependence of knowledge on social conditions.

The term "sociology of knowledge" seems to us rather unfortunate, for it suggests that knowledge as such is an object matter of sociological investigation. Now, every science deals with a specific class of systems and of processes. Sociology is primarily concerned with that class of systems which is called "social" (for example, a "social group," a "social relation") and with processes which occur within or between such systems. The distinctive characteristic of social systems is that their chief components are interacting men, whereas systems of knowledge, or theories (using this term in the most general sense), are obviously not social systems. Nor are linguistic, aesthetic, religious, or technical systems "social": there is little similarity between a compound sentence, a poem, a painting, a sacrifice, an automobile, on the one hand, and a political party, a club, a conjugal or parental relation, on the other hand, beyond the fact that each of them has an inner order holding its constituent parts together.

Of course, between social systems on the one hand and other kinds of cultural systems on the other hand there are many dynamic relationships of one-sided or mutual dependence, some of which we are going to investigate presently. But there are likewise relationships of dependence between other kinds of systems. If the existence of such relationships entitles us to use the terms "sociology of knowledge" and "sociology of art," by the same token we should be

• Florian Znaniecki, *The Social Role of the Man of Knowledge,* New York: Columbia University Press, 1940, pp. 1–22. Reprinted by permission of the publisher.

justified in speaking of "linguistics of religion," "religionistics of art," "economics of knowledge," and so on.

However, there is no need of wrangling about words. Since the expression "sociology of knowledge" has by now gained a wide recognition in sociological literature, we may as well adopt it with the emphatic reservation that it does not mean a "sociological theory of knowledge." Otherwise, sociology would find itself in a curious position. As a theory of knowledge, a "science of the sciences," it would have to determine its own character as sociology; whereas as sociology it would determine its own character as a "science of the sciences." (von Schelting, II.1, 1936.)

Many misunderstandings might be avoided if we had a fully constituted "science of knowledge," a comparative, inductive study of the various systems of knowledge which empirical research would disclose in the past and the present . . . . [A] science of knowledge parallel to modern sociology or linguistics would not attempt to standardize normatively the systems it studies but would view them simply as empirical realities, trying to reach by their comparative analysis theoretic generalizations about them. Such a science has only begun to emerge out of historical and ethnological studies. Its development is apparently a slow and difficult task, and the sociologist is hardly competent to participate in it.

For an objective investigation of systems of knowledge in their composition, structure, and relationships must take fully into consideration that which is an essential characteristic of every system of knowledge: its claim to be *true,* that is, objectively valid. The sociologist, however, is not entitled to make any judgments concerning the validity of any systems of knowledge except sociological systems. He meets systems of knowledge in the course of his investigation only when he finds that certain persons or groups that he studies are actively interested in them, that they construct, improve, supplement, reproduce, defend, or popularize systems which they regard as true or else reject, oppose, criticize, or interfere with the propagation of systems which they consider untrue. In every such case the sociologist is bound to abide by whatever standards of validity those individuals or groups apply to the knowledge in which they take an active share. For, as an observer of cultural life, he can understand the data he observes only if he takes them with the "humanistic coefficient," only if he does not limit his observation to his own direct experience of the data but reconstructs the experience of the men who are dealing with them actively. (Znaniecki, VI, 1934.) Just as a conjugal relation which he observes is to him really and objectively what it is to the conjugal partners themselves, or an association what it means to its members, a given system of knowledge must be to him also what it is to the people who participate in its construction, reproduction, application, and development . . . . He must resign his own criteria of theoretic validity when dealing with systems of knowledge which they accept and apply . . . . [I]t is their judgment, not the sociologist's, which conditions whatever influence their knowledge has on their social life, and vice versa.

But how ought the sociologist behave when he finds that some people deny the validity of a system which other people regard as true? Does not this conflict of authorities compel him to make a decision? We do not think so. If we apply consistently the humanistic coefficient, we shall conclude that when a man takes a negative attitude toward a system of knowledge which others recognize, this is only a more or less interesting fact of his personal life, not affecting at all the objective composition, structure, or validity of the system which he rejects. In the same way, the fact that a person does not like the English language, impressionism in painting, or Calvinism in religion is entirely irrelevant to the intrinsic pattern and significance of those cultural systems as experienced by their adherents. Such a negative valuation may, however, be instructive in other respects. If a man rejects, for example, voluntaristic psychology because he applies to it the standards of behavioristic psychology which he recognizes as true, this fact (though it has no bearing upon voluntarism) throws light on the composition, structure, and claims to validity of behaviorism . . . .

. . . . In observing, however, the actual functioning of these multiform "truths" in the sphere of active experience of the people who regard them as valid—in observing the influence which the recognition of certain truths has upon the conscious lives of people as experiencing and active subjects —we can say generally that whatever is regarded as a truth functions as a *norm of thinking,* imposes upon the conscious agent who recognizes it a distinctive selection and organization of some data of his experience. The data acquire thereby the character of object matter of knowledge. The "truth" itself—and even more so the whole system of which it is an element—possesses in the active experience of all those who recognize it an "objective" significance which makes its validity seem to them independent of their "subjective" emotions, wishes, representations. They *participate* in a system of knowledge, ...

Now, sociological investigation discovers that there are two kinds of connection between knowledge and social life. On the one hand, upon men's participation in a certain system of knowledge often depends their participation in some social system and their conduct within the limits of the latter. A person who is "instructed" or "learned" in certain theories is admitted to the performance of certain roles and to the membership of certain groups in which the "ignorant" are not allowed to share. . . . The development and popularization of modern physical and biological sciences have markedly affected the composition and structure of many social groups, either directly by changing traditional beliefs or indirectly by the technological applications of those sciences.

On the other hand, the participation of men in certain social systems often determines (though perhaps not entirely or exclusively) in what systems of knowledge they will participate, and how. Many social groups require that all their members know certain sacred doctrines or the rudiments of some lay sciences, while some groups forbid their members to meddle with certain theories. Men who are destined for professional occupations must acquire the knowledge regarded as necessary for those occupations according to social rules and regulations. And there are various socially prescribed ways of participating in systems of knowledge. Sometimes men are expected and taught merely to memorize formulas in which knowledge is expressed, whereas at other times understanding of all the implications of a system is required. Exclusive emphasis may be put upon the practical application of the "truths" included in a system or, on the contrary, upon their purely theoretic significance. In many cases no modification of the system is allowed; in other cases it is regarded as not only permissible but meritorious to improve, develop, modify, supplement a system and in rare cases even to construct a new system.

Individual conformity with the various social demands relative to knowledge is obtained by specific methods of education, encouragement, and control. The success or failure of these methods in particular cases is conditioned, of course, by the psychological capacities and dispositions of the individuals to whom they are applied. But why individuals manifest such psychological capacities and dispositions as they possess by participating the way they do in certain systems of knowledge and not in others is a question which can be answered only by a study of the society in which those individuals live.

Thus, while admittedly systems of knowledge—viewed in their objective composition, structure, and validity—cannot be reduced to social facts, yet their historical existence within the empirical world of culture, in so far as it depends upon the men who construct them, maintain them by transmission and application, develop them, or neglect them, must in a large measure be explained sociologically. And this is what "sociology of knowledge" has actually been doing, whenever it was not vainly trying to become epistemology. Even thus limited, the task is sufficiently vast and difficult to occupy many sociologists for generations to come, especially as the conceptual framework hitherto used in dealing with these problems seems rather inadequate.

In our present outline we attempt to survey a certain portion of the field which "sociology of knowledge" tends to cover. We assume from experience and observation, direct and indirect, that knowledge as it has historically grown is the agglomerated product of specific cultural activities of numberless human individuals. Further, we are familiar with the fact that some individuals for longer or shorter periods of their lives specialize in cultivating knowledge, in distinction from other individuals who specialize in performing various other kinds of cultural activities—technical, economic, artistic, and so on. We call them "scientists," using the word in its etymological sense as derived from *scire*, "to know," and equivalent to "men of knowledge" (like the French term "savants"). This is obviously a different and much more extensive meaning than that in which this word is used by epistemologists and logicians, who define a "scientist" in terms of objective achievements in the field of knowledge . . . . [T]o us as sociologists, applying the humanistic coefficient to our data, all knowledge is valid which is regarded as such by the people who participate in it, and a "scientist" is any individual who is regarded by his social milieu and who regards himself as specializing in the cultivation of knowledge . . . .

Now, individual specialization in any kind of cultural activity is generally recognized as a phenomenon which is socially conditioned. Sociologists have given considerable attention to it. Spencer was the first to treat it systematically in his *Principles of Sociology,* though we find some of his views anticipated in earlier works in social philosophy. For the most part, however, the attention of sociologists has centered upon the collective aspect of this phenomenon; viewing society as a whole, they regard individual specialization as a question of social structure, a differentiation of the total set of activities by which society is maintained. This is, for instance, what Durkheim emphasizes in his famous work *De la division du travail social,* in which progressive differentiation of functions is treated as the most significant collective process in the history of human societies.

But specialization has also an individual aspect: the persons who specialize in any kind of activity can be comparatively studied, irrespective of the part this activity plays in the total structure of a group or of society at large. Such studies may be psychological or sociological. In the former, attention centers upon the individual himself as a psychobiological being viewed apart from his social environment, and the problem is whether any typical psychological characteristics are associated with specialization in the given kind of activity and, if so, how this association is to be explained . . . . In sociological studies of specialized persons, it is the connection between the individual and his social milieu which is the main object of interest; and his specialized activities are viewed with reference to the cultural setting in which they are performed . . . .

. . . . In recent years the term "social role" has been used by many sociologists to denote the phenomena in question . . . .

Every social role presupposes that between the individual performing the role, who may thus be called a "social person," and a smaller or larger set of people who participate in his performance and may be termed his "social circle" there is a common bond constituted by a complex of values which all of them appreciate positively. These are economic values in the case of a merchant or a banker and the circle formed by his clients; hygienic values for the physician and his patients; . . . . On the other hand, the person obviously cannot perform his role without the coöperation of his circle —though not necessarily the coöperation of any particular individual within the circle . . . .

The person is conceived by his circle as an organic and psychological entity who is a "self," conscious of his own existence as a body and a soul and aware of how others regard him. If he is to be the kind of person his social circle needs, his "self" must possess in the opinion of the circle certain qualities, physical and mental, and not possess certain other qualities . . . .

The psychological qualities ascribed to persons performing social roles are enormously diversified: in every Western language there are hundreds of words denoting supposed traits of "intelligence" and "character"; and almost every such trait has, or had in the past, an axiological significance, that is, is positively or negatively valued, either in all persons or in persons performing certain kinds of role . . . .

A person who is needed by a social circle and whose self possesses the qualities required for the role for which he is needed has a definite social *status,* that is, his circle grants him certain rights and enforces those rights, when necessary, against individual participants of the circle or outsiders . . . .

He, in turn, has a social *function* to fulfill; he is regarded as obliged to achieve certain tasks by which the supposed needs of his circle will be satisfied and to behave toward other individuals in his circle in a way that shows his positive valuation of them.

. . . . But our knowledge of a social role is not complete if we know only its composition, for a role is a dynamic system and its components may be variously interconnected in the course of its performance. There are many different ways of performing a role, according to the dominant active tendencies of the performer. He may, for instance, be mainly interested in one of the components of his role—the social circle, his own self, the status, or the function —and tend to subordinate other components to it. And, whatever his main interest, he may tend to conform with the demands of his circle or else try to innovate, to become independent of those demands. And, again, in either case he may be optimistically confident in the opportunities offered by his role and tend to expand it or else he may mistrust its possibilities and tend to restrict it to a perfectly secure minimum.

The possibility of reaching such general conclusions about all social roles and more specific, though still widely applicable, generalizations about social roles of a certain kind—such as the role of peasant, priest, merchant, factory worker, or artist—points obviously to the existence of essential uniformities and also of important variations among these social phenomena. Social roles constitute one general class of social system, and this class may be subdivided into less general classes, these into subclasses, and so on; . . . .

Systematic sociology stands before a task similar to that of systematic biology . . . . But, manifestly, the source of uniformities in the social field is different from that in the field of biology. Although in both fields differentiation is due to variations of individual systems, biological uniformities are due in the main to heredity; whereas uniformities of social systems, like those of all cultural systems, are chiefly the result of a reflective use of the same *cultural patterns* in many particular cases.

* * * * *

Sometimes a pattern is explicitly formulated as a system of legal or ethical norms prescribing what all the roles of a given class within a particular political or religious society ought to be: such a pattern is then imposed by a dominant group upon all the candidates to those roles. For example, this is how the patterns of the several military, administrative, legislative, and judiciary roles are maintained and transmitted by state legislation . . . . In other cases, patterns of social roles are not explicitly rationalized but are included in the mores of a community and transmitted from old to young through a process of educational guidance and imitation . . . .

As to the diffusion of the patterns of social roles, or their spread from community to community and from society to society, there are various well-known ways by which this process goes on: borrowing from neighboring cultures, travel, trade, migration, colonization, conquest, dissemination of book lore. But not all the similarities of roles found in different communities or societies can be thus accounted for; in many cases we must admit independent evolution along similar lines . . . .

The conception of social roles here outlined furnishes the background for our present problems in the "sociology of knowledge." First of all, we presume hypothetically that individuals who specialize in cultivating knowledge and are therefore called "scientists" perform social roles of a definite class. This means that there must be social circles to whom knowledge in general or systematic knowledge in particular appears to be positively valuable. Participants in these circles must be convinced that they need the coöperation of "scientists" to realize certain tendencies connected with this valuable knowledge. In order to be qualified as a scientist whom his circle needs, a person must be regarded as a "self" endowed with certain desirable characteristics and lacking certain undesirable characteristics. Social status must be granted to a person who is thus needed and qualified as a scientist. And this person must perform social functions which will satisfy the needs of his circle . . . .

Are there indeed such social roles? If so, what is their essential composition and structure? Are there any specific varieties among them? How are they as a class related logically to other classes of social role? . . . . What is the origin of scientists' roles in general, and how did specific variations of those roles evolve? (Znaniecki, VI, 1934.)

This gives us our first set of problems. They are of the same kind as all problems of systematic description and classification of social phenomena. But because this is a study in the "sociology of knowledge," there are other borderland problems which we have to face. Are there any relationships of functional dependence between the social roles which scientists perform and the kind of knowledge which they cultivate? More specifically: Are the systems of knowledge which scientists build and their methods of building them influenced by the social patterns with which scientists are expected to conform as participants in a certain social order and by the ways in which they actually realize those patterns?

Social Science and Social Policy

E. A. SHILS

The line of thought from which contemporary Social Science has come forth was occupied with problems of public policy in a way which has since become very much less prominent in the work of social scientists. The classic figures of social thought—Aristotle, Plato, Adam Smith, Montesquieu, Jeremy Bentham, James and John Stuart Mill, Ricardo, Hobbes and Locke, Burke, Machiavelli and Hegel—were all involved in the consideration of the fundamental problems of policy from the point of view of the man who had to exercise power and to make practical decisions. . . . The politician's problems, reduced to fundamentals, were their problems. The problem of maintaining order through the prince's exercise of power was the point of departure of classical philosophy; it was extended by modern liberalism to the maintenance of liberty in a framework of order. Political philosophy was regarded by those who professed it, as a means of enlightening rulers —and citizens—as to the right ends and the approximate means. . . . Early economic theory accepted the same task. Even after mercantalism gave way to liberalism, economic theory was still intended to be a guide to policy.

A rather fundamental change occurred in the course of the nineteenth century. The social sciences became de-politicised; even the study of politics adulterated its preoccupation with policy by concrete recipes of administration and the aproblematic description of governmental processes. The other social sciences—economics and the slowly-growing sociology and anthropology—were explicitly and implicitly apolitical. The problems were not selected in accordance with an explicit standard of relevance to the making or execution of a policy-maker's decision; the policy-making process did not become the object of realistic investigation and finally the practitioners of these subjects even disavowed any interest in policy-making.

This general tendency towards de-politicisation might in part have resulted from the "separation" of the various spheres of

---

• *Philosophy of Science,* Vol. 16, July 1949, pp. 219–242. Reprinted by permission of The Williams & Wilkins Company, Baltimore, Md., 21202, and the author. E. A. Shils was the first to discuss many of the questions of the postwar relationships between social science and government with which the present work is concerned. The editors have abridged Shils' paper extensively to eliminate redundancy with later writings in this anthology which provide either more extensive or more current treatments of some of his topics. The desire of the editors to eliminate material which is now commonplace causes this version of Shils' article to reflect less fully than it might Shils' ability to foresee matters that would come to preoccupy future attention to the role of the social sciences in policy. Shils also was among the voices which cautioned against tendencies at the time toward what might be termed a predominantly cameralistic social scence. That he felt it necessary to make this plea for the preservation of theory-oriented social science in the universities may be evidence of how strong the trend at the time was toward research with a governmental orientation rather than an academic one. That the editors have felt it appropriate to abridge this part of his discussion reflects their estimation of how drastically this trend has been reversed.

life in the liberal society of the nineteenth century. The relative autonomy of the spheres fostered a belief in the possibilities of separate fields of study, with the resultant expulsion of political elements from sociological and economic discipline. . . . Moreover, the nature of the ideal economy, "prescribed" by the liberal economic theory, which was the most striking product of this intellectual division of labor, minimized the importance of large decisions. It dispersed decisions into a great multitude of organs and interpreted them as automatic. The intellectual preponderance of economic theory among the social sciences in the English-speaking world thus reinforced this tendency of each social science to rid itself of any political traces in content and especially in its conception of its calling.

The development of the universities of the nineteenth century and their relations with the world of affairs also appears to be an important factor in the de-politicisation of the social sciences. The great schemes of interpretation and judgment formulated by the masters of social science grew up outside the Universities and in a fairly close connection with politics and practical affairs. Except for Adam Smith no major figure of social science outside Germany, until the latter part of the nineteenth century, was a university teacher. The University teaching of social science, as distinct from political and moral philosophy, developed on a considerable scale only in the second half of the Nineteenth century.

The great efflorescence of philological studies and the natural sciences and the much greater specialization of research in history and the social sciences tended to increase the distance between the universities and the making of the large and small decisions which affect the commonwealth, at the very time when the social sciences were becoming university subjects. The humanistic tradition in the universities in Great Britain, Germany and the United States was, except in the two older universities in Great Britain, put on the defensive early in the twentieth century by departmental specialization in all fields and further specialization within the departments.

* * * * *

At the same time for a variety of reasons, this same period witnessed a pronounced alienation of intellectuals—university and free-lance—from the existing holders of power.

These conditions then facilitated a condition in which the majority of eminent social scientists were cut off from the two main courses of concern with the major problems of policy, namely, the great tradition of Western political philosophy and practical business and governmental affairs.

The multiplication of post-graduate students with no inspiration of their own and usually unsustained by their teachers' own dim visions of policy, bore dry fruits in the numerous monographs on local, state, federal, and comparative administration. A pecularily apolitical political science grew up. . . .

Sociology which set out, or at least claimed, to cure the deficiencies of political science did nothing to compensate for the apolitical character of political science. In the first place, in order to prove their rights to existence, sociologists sought to find a sphere of events left untouched by the older social sciences. The distinction between the state and civil society was ready to hand in a liberal society and sociologists seized upon it. Even though they found a justification for their independent existence in the numerous "*social* problems" which had arisen in connection with urbanization and immigration, they seldom expected them to be solved by governmental action and even where they did, they did not incorporate this relationship with reality into their theory. Their theory was indeed often accented towards the view that political decisions were impotent to affect "social processes." The persistence of evolutionary biologistic and instinctual theories in French, British and American sociology (even in Sumner and Park) obstructed the formulation of a theory of action in which knowledge and decision are important categories and even hampered the correct interpretation of those sociologists who were more adequate in this regard (e.g., Durkheim). Neither in substance nor in general theoretical categories did sociology concern itself with politics, with political decisions or with decision-making in other spheres. . . .

The fifty years which end the last and open the present century saw all over the Western world the growing prestige of the natural sciences with their apparent divorce from all questions of metaphysics, morals and politics. This model aroused the admiration and the emulation of the insecure social scientists who, as newcomers in the university environment and as the browbeaten objects of the contempt of the humanists on the one side and the natural scientists on the other, sought to legitimate their status as scientists and as searchers for truth in the same way as the already established branches of university life. The humanistic tradition did not seem to offer sufficiently immediate sustenance, and a misunderstood pattern of natural science procedure and outlook came to dominate the minds of social scientists. Even where methodologically they struggled to discern differences between the subject matters and, consequently, the procedures of the two fields of scientific work, it was believed almost universally that academic disciplines could become scientific to the extent that they ceased to seek concrete evaluations. The expulsion of value judgments as the result of scientific work sometimes even went so far as to refuse to accept the empirical analyses of value judgments as a task of social study.

There is no doubt that logically the proposition which distinguishes judgments of fact from judgments of value is the correct one; what is incorrect is the deduction that because scientific knowledge can offer no direct guidance in the determination of the ultimate ends of individual conduct or social policy, scientists are not only unqualified to discuss value-questions but that their very profession as scientists forbids a serious involvement in evaluative problems in any way—and particularly in the selection of problems.

It is, of course, true that social scientists did serve on Governmental commissions, testified before governmental committees and participated in various political reform movements, but on the whole they were relatively exceptional. Woodrow Wilson as Professor of Political Science and President of the United States was a great exception to the prevalent attitude among American university social scientists which rejected politics as unclean. This attitude was common even among those who participated in reform politics since for them, the improvement of politics consisted in the elimination of politics, the city-manager movements. (The ordinary economic activity of the entrepreneural class was also regarded as unworthy of positive moral identification.) This contemptuous and fearful alienation from the holders of power and the makers of important decisions helped psychologically to disqualify social scientists from the realistic study of the exercise of power and the responsible choice of problems of investigation in the light of their relevance to the making of decisions. Moreover, the social sciences at that time had much less to offer to policy-makers and administrators than they have at present. It was the First World War which showed particularly in the United States, that academic social scientists could be used by governments and by all organizations interested in controlling and modifying human behavior. The important work of psychologists in the United States Army during the First World War gave rise to a new conception of the relevance of the scientific study of man for political practice, and it also indirectly affected the line of development of psychology, and, therewith of social sciences. Immediate uses were also found for political scientists, historians and geographers in political warfare and in the organization of the peace. After the war, psychologists immediately found many practical applications for their skills in testing, and many powers, private and public, sought to employ them. The great extension of advertising and propaganda after the first world war and the increased prestige of psychologists in associated activities, provided many opportunities in the world of affairs for academically trained social scientists. The turning by enterprisers toward industrial psychology—which was also accentuated by the war and particularly by the disturbances in industrial relations following the war—was another stimulus to the increasingly mature science of psychology and an additional opportunity for the social sciences to aid in the manipulation of reality.

Today governments and private, civic and economic organizations are beginning to surpass universities and endowed research institutes as employers of social scientists. It is a trend which probably cannot be reversed. Truth is always useful to those who exercise power, regardless of whether they wish to share that truth with those over whom their power is exercised, or whether they wish to bring about particular patterns of behaviour in consequence of their monopoly. As governments incline more and more towards interventionism and comprehensive planning a more specific knowledge of the data to be manipulated becomes pressingly necessary.

* * * * *

Social scientists . . . work in consultative and advisory roles and they perform intelligence functions. The latter engages the vast majority of the social scientists in power-exercising bodies. This means that social scientists are not drawn upon for their wisdom as counsellors in the delineation of fundamental alternatives nor as guides in the choice from among these alternatives once discovered. Neither in the main are they looked to for basic truths about human behaviour derived either from rigorous scientific research or from the slow accretion of wisdom. Social scientists are rather viewed as instruments for the reporting of descriptive data about particular and concrete situations. . . . This type of knowledge is not of interest to policymakers simply out of idle curiosity. In their very role as policymakers they are concerned with the future and with the consequences of particular changes in their own behaviour on the behaviour of others. . . . The point of departure of these predictions is an approximate description of the present and recently past situation. This means that the inventories of estimates of magnitude with which social scientists furnish policy-makers are used by policy-makers as data for *their own* predictions or "interpretations." The social scientist may indeed accompany his inventory with *his* own interpretations of the way in which these magnitudes will affect the various intended policies, but in the majority of cases at present, it is not the "interpretation" which the policy-maker or administrator seeks from the social scientist. This does not, of course, completely exhaust the type of intelligence functions carried out by social scientists for policy-makers. Social scientists also execute what might be called "dynamic applied research."[1] Here the social scientist

[1] It is neither in the logical structure of the propositions with which an investigation concludes, in their subject matter nor even in the aims of the investigator that the significant differences between applied social research and other types of social research can be found. The term "applied research" in the social sciences may be understood to refer to investigations performed for policy-makers who use or intend to use the resulting propositions as elements in their decisions. It is simply research, the results of which are to be applied in some way in practice by those who have in their charge the care of practical affairs. It is not applied research in the sense of the application of scientifically tested general principles obtained in "basic" or "pure" research, to the explanation of concrete and

determines not merely isolated magnitudes such as the gross national output for the preceding year or even for the ensuing year or years, but rather analyses the structure of the situation in its causal relations with those magnitudes. In this latter type of applied research the concrete inventory or description of the situation remains central to the research, while the causal explanation is added as a separate and indeed separable part.[1] . . .

. . . [T]he important feature of "dynamic" research is that the social scientist adduces explanatory hypotheses which create a certain coherence among the events under investigation. These explanatory hypotheses are in almost all cases *not* derived from systematic scientific research. They represent either a somewhat jargonic translation of the wisdom of the race, or the prevailing wisdom or drift of opinion, reinforced by clinical insight, of that particular segment of the social science profession with which the investigator in question identifies himself.

* * * * *

From this intermediate function we pass now to *roles* occupied by social scientists much closer to the actual making and execution of decisions. There are first of all social scientists as formally defined policymakers, e.g., Woodrow Wilson as President of the United States, Gunnar Myrdal as Swedish Secretary of Commerce, Hugh Dalton as Chancellor of the Exchequer, Harold Wilson as President of the Board of Trade, Luigi Einaude as Minister of Finance and many more. In such roles social scientists, if they believe what they write and teach, will, to the extent that considerations of political tactics render it feasible, act in accordance with the general principles of their discipline. It should be noted that with the exception of Woodrow Wilson, who was a political scientist of a sort which could certainly not be called scientific, all the other instances cited are economists, the one social discipline which has elaborate and explicit general principles—which have not, however, been subjected to the rigorous testing which the status of scientific propositions demands.[2] Presumably, empirical research will be used by the type of politician-social scientist primarily as a means of obtaining data, i.e., assessments of particular magnitudes, since he will not require additional interpretative propositions to those he already possesses from his own professional experience. . . .

The relationship with policy and decision is more complex at the level of the "Chief Advisor" whether it be psychiatric or economic advice which is solicited or offered. At this level frequently the end in the mind of the politician is so vague or general that it allows for a variety of constructions. In this situation the "advisor" recommends a policy in which are contained his own preferences as to right ends to be pursued and a series of specific legislative and administrative measures. These flow from his own ethical standards, his general views about human nature and society (themselves most frequently only to a *very* limited extent products of scientific research) and an assessment of the concrete constellation in which the politician will have to act—only a fraction of which has usually been described by the techniques of social science research.

particular situations or to the management or construction of concrete and particular constellations of actions. . . .

To summarize the difference from applied research in the better established sciences consists (a) in the absence of rigorously tested general propositions and (b) in the absence of rigorous intellectual controls over the results of the manipulations introduced in accordance with those hypotheses.

[1] It is not a matter here of a sharp line which separates these two types of investigation; it is only a question of proportion.

[2] It would be relevant for our present purposes to know just how much of the elegant and precise propositions of economic theory find application in the recommendations for policy and in the actual policies made by professional economists.

Thus where the social scientist as counsellor devises a policy, there are notable limits to the role played by scientific knowledge in the construction of policy; these limits are in some part variable with the improvement in scientific techniques and in the extension of the area of scientific knowledge; in other respects, they are fixed by the irreducibility of ethical judgments. Between these two there is an area of indeterminateness where general scientific laws (assuming our possession of them) must be applied to concrete cases and where concrete ethical goals must be subsumed under general ethical standards. In any case, the results of social research, whether they be simply propositions about concrete magnitudes, concrete explanatory propositions or universal propositions about human behaviour—though they could play a greater part than they do at present—do and can play only a restricted part on the higher levels of policy.

The *third* of the roles in which social scientists are closely involved in policy-making and execution occurs in action, or "therapeutically-oriented" research as it is called in the United States and Britain. Here the social scientist simultaneously discovers and modifies the situation. As the doctrine has been elaborated by the members of the Tavistock Institute, it proposes a unification of the functions of intelligence, interpretation in the light of general principles and decision-making and execution.[1] This procedure allows, more than any other, an approach to the application of social science knowledge by a democratic sharing of insight and the joint modification of behaviour through the shared possession of that insight. It does not, however, in its present form concern itself with the opportunity for the establishment of new general propositions. It does rather assume that such general propositions already exist in verified form and are ready for application. In consequence the chief scientific product of this type of research—where it is not coupled with the more conventional type of non-manipulative scientific procedure—is an increase in clinical sensitivity. In the terminology used above, it is "dynamic applied research" with a very novel method of application.[2]

We should now consider some of the consequences for the development of social science of these functions of social scientists in the exercise of power. There can be no doubt about the great advantages for social science of involvement in practical affairs. The rich development of research techniques which has been the most heartening development in the empirical social science in the past quarter of a century, has, to a very large extent, been stimulated by the interest of power-exercising bodies.

[*Editors' Summary*. Among research techniques that have depended heavily on contacts with practical problems for their origin and refinement are: sampling, polling, attitude-scaling, content analysis, and the sociometric technique.]

This is not to say, of course, that all research techniques in contemporary social science have developed in connection with the execution of researches in the service of practical ends. It is doubtful, for instance, whether the Thurstonian extension of the

[1] The Tavistock doctrine also requires the close association of the persons under study, the persons with formal policy-making executive powers and the "therapeutic" investigators.

[2] Operational research merits mention in passing, not because it represents a genuine innovation in scientific procedure, in the choice of problems or indeed in any other respect, but rather because some of its proponents claim that it is all of these and more. As a matter of fact, it seems to be nothing else than the ordinary method of research applied to the problem of determining the relative efficiency of different techniques for achieving a given end. To this is added a certain political dictum regarding the superiority of applied, as over against pure science, the superior skill of natural scientists in the study of social processes and similar propositions which have little to do with the methodology or technique of scientific research.

principle of equal-appearing intervals and its application in attitude scales arose from a practical interest, nor—for that matter—can it be said that factor analysis—although obviously finding important applications in practice—arose in connection with research projects which were performed at the behest of the exercisers of power.

This, of course, does not exhaust the possible gains for social science from close association with practical demands. Social research in the present century has been characterized by an extraordinary scattering of attention over a great variety of unco-ordinated problems which were investigated on a very concrete level. Although our knowledge of contemporary society has been greatly increased in consequence of these numerous investigations carried out by university teachers and post-graduate students, our systematic knowledge of human behaviour has not increased correspondingly.

* * * * *

It is, of course, by no means certain that these deficiencies will be cured by a greater orientation of social research towards practical problems. Indeed, there are numerous arguments as to why it should not be so, but it is at least conceivable that a greater concentration of attention resulting from a practical orientation might occur about a small number of definite problems. The likelihood of continuity in the growth of general knowledge is perhaps somewhat greater if a larger number of the better minds in the field apply their attention to a given problem, even though the problem has a quite concrete point of departure. The gradual formation in this way of a pool of general hypotheses has more chance of giving rise to the demand for resources to test them than if they are produced by a few isolated and scattered investigators.

It is scarcely necessary to emphasize that social research is expensive. Both basic and applied research, if carried out in accordance with the requirements of technical rigour, entail numerous interviewers, complex systems of codifying and tabulating the data gathered by interviewers, and highly-skilled analysts and statisticians.

The funds traditionally assigned to social research are probably inadequate for permitting the kind of scientific work which could take its place with the achievements of the better-established sciences. It is only by large grants—such as only governments or large private corporations or wealthy civic bodies can endow—that scientifically adequate research can be carried out.

Under present conditions it appears to be quite certain that governments will provide an increasingly large share of the funds to be expended on social sciences and the total sum is also likely to increase by a large multiple. Hence, insofar as the importance of basic scientific research is recognized by governmental authorities, the wealth of governments allows some hope that the scientific knowledge of man will really begin to grow in earnest. It must, however, be recognized that the necessary condition for the growth of social science, namely sufficient financial support, might not be forthcoming from governments simply because government officials who do not understand the nature of social science, will conceive of it as consisting exclusively of factual inventories or manipulative recipes and will accordingly fail to see that the utility and reliability of both of these are dependent on the advance of general theoretical or fundamental knowledge. Hence, the extent to which governmentally financed social research will have beneficial results for the growth of science depends on whether the universities which must remain the main centres of training will so clarify the minds of their students concerning the relations between general theoretical propositions and empirical research, between basic scientific knowledge and its concrete application, that government officials who will be drawn from these circles will come to understand the issue.

There is perhaps another, in the long run more important, consequence of the practical orientation of research. Those at whose command "applied" social research is carried out are not university teachers or administrators. They are less likely to share the generally prevailing academic prejudices about the self-sufficiency of the different academic departments in the social sciences. Their interests lie in obtaining the data which they believe they need for making a decision and when they summon the aid of social scientists—unless they themselves are bound by an academically inculcated prejudice or by the counsel of a departmental prejudiced academic observer—they are more likely to bring together on the research staff social scientists from the different social science departments of universities. Thus, to take a single instance, they are more likely —if they are governmental economists and not purely academic economists—to employ psychologists to work with them in certain types of investigations. . . .

In addition to these scientific benefits which might flow from the marriage of social research and practical policy, there is an extra-scientific consequence which should be mentioned. For those social scientists whose moral standards require that each action which they perform should directly serve the public welfare, this intimate connection is double-edged, since the truths, concrete or abstract which they discover, might, of course, be used by the holders of power in ways which are contrary to the individual social scientist's own conception of the public good. For those who are concerned solely with the application of social science to social practice and do not inquire too closely into the direction of the particular policy which is in part based on the data provided by the social scientist, the moral danger of the misuse of knowledge is obviously no problem. For the social scientist of the latter outlook nothing but good can come from the governmentalization of social science or to similar development by private business enterprise. For the social scientist who holds firm moral convictions about the ultimate ends of social policy, conflicts can and undoubtedly will arise—regardless of the scientific level of the investigation. These conflicts will be more specific, more frequent and often more acute because of the greater proximity of the decision but in a very fundamental respect, the moral position of the applied social scientist working in government is not so very different from that of the social scientist in the universities—assuming that they are both working on problems of equal scientific importance.

The likelihood of action on the basis of systematically acquired knowledge is certainly greater where the social scientist is directly related to the policy-maker than where he seeks to work on him through his scientific and popular writings, through occasional interviews and the like.

Where the policy-maker orders an investigation he is probably much more likely to take its results into account than if it is pressed to his attention by someone who has performed it independently. He is, moreover, likely to be more cooperative in the execution of the research, not merely from the point of view of the provision of funds, but of making himself, and those over whom he exercises his power, accessible as objects of investigation.[1]

---

[1] This is not by any means always the case. Policy-makers with strong convictions about the correctness of their own perception power are not infrequently disposed to reject as wrong or irrelevant factual representations which contradict their own impressions or which bring to their attention facts which are unpleasant, i.e., which are incompatible with certain measures which they are using to attain a given end. This especially is likely to be the case with those investigations which consist more of the clinical insights of the investigator than of quantitatively handled data. The more amorphous the structure of the data, the less persuasive it is likely to be with a policy-maker with strong personal convictions. There is, also, of course, the policy-maker who orders an investigation to be conducted by social scientists not because he is interested in the results in order to instrument a policy but because it is expedient as a political tactic.

We should now consider some of the disadvantages of this practical orientation of social science. It is often characteristic of policy-makers that they should wish to retain the reins of policy in their own hands, and to renounce as little as possible of their authority and initiative to those who advise them. Insofar as they behave in this way they will regard social scientists only as providers of facts of a specific and concrete sort, which they can take into account in making their decisions by themselves. . . .

There is no reason, of course, why results of investigation into concrete variables should not contribute to scientific knowledge, if there are other social scientists in the world sufficiently free in the movement of their attention and in the disposition of their resources to follow the problems which they think are important. But in that case, the concrete material provided by the practically oriented social scientists will be used as a stimulus and not as a link in the chain by those more freely-ranging social scientists for their own speculations and for the construction of their own hypotheses. The work of the practically oriented investigator will be simply a source of hypotheses, in the same way that novels, phantasies or dreams may be the source of hypotheses. Science will grow only if the attempt to test hypotheses results in at least the partial confirmation of previously held hypotheses and the creation of more differentiated hypotheses. If the research begins without any hypotheses other than purely descriptive ones, or even with none at all, as is the case in most social science research undertaken for practical purposes, then it is most unlikely that the usual practically oriented type of investigation will contribute anything directly to the growth of scientific knowledge.

Under these conditions of investigation, it is only too likely that when the policy-maker does come under the influence of social science in a deeper and more comprehensive way than he does when he merely uses its concrete description results, he will become the victim of a general proposition which has never been adequately tested. It might indeed—under such "scientific" conditions the probability is particularly great —be some adage of common sense, or an ingenious insight rubbed down and worn into a cliche which the results of concrete investigations, if not too rigorously scrutinized, seem to exemplify and which seems to "explain" the concrete results.[1] Nothing can be worse for the long-run material and intellectual prosperity of social science than to live on such winds of fashion.

But although there are strong grounds for not expecting those who exercise power to order investigations other than those which appear to be directly useful to them, it is not inevitable that they should do so. It depends in part on the attitude toward science of those policy-makers who themselves are responsible for the expenditure of funds for social science. If they recognize either that basic scientific knowledge is good in itself, or that the material and social benefits which basic scientific knowledge can confer are unpredictable but genuine (so that no particular scientific research should be excluded simply because it does not promise immediate practical benefits) then research subsidized by public bodies can indeed contribute much to science. (But it is no longer practically-oriented research in the sense in which we have been discussing it above.)

This awareness of the function of general theoretical propositions in concrete analyses and hence in policy-making might come about in a number of ways. Well-qualified social scientists who themselves appreciate the problem, or who see the right solution and who are also sympathetic with the needs of policy-makers for concrete data, might be able to persuade those with whom they work of the importance of testing by the

---

[1] The general propositions about "human relations" in formal structures, especially in industry, are illustrative here. These practically oriented researches have never rigorously formulated or tested any hypothesis, yet they have to an increasing extent conveyed a general proposition into the minds of policy-makers.

same kind of rigorous techniques which are used for description, the general explanatory propositions which are always being used.

In this event some of the resources available for research will then be used to test the validity of the general explanatory propositions and science will certainly benefit considerably. Likewise, if those who ascend to high administrative and policy-making positions have been properly educated in the universities on the appropriate relations between theory and concrete research, they will themselves devote part of their resources to basic research—either on their own initiative or through an easier recognition of the correctness of the arguments of social scientists, etc. If this occurs, we shall be able to perceive the possible convergence of the practical orientation and the right and imminent development of fundamental social science.

As long as research is practically oriented and particularly if it is exclusively dominated by the therapeutic approach, certain kinds of problems will be excluded, while other problems will be prescribed, with some damage to the development of science. Thus, the study of small groups, of "human relations" face-to-face might come into a great inheritance of research funds, while certain important problems such as identification with the symbols of a larger community, will be left unstudied. These choices will be made because some problems appear to be subject to easy manipulation within the time which administrators or policy-makers feel is available to them, while other problems of great importance will be neglected because they do not appear to be at all manipulatable with the currently available, or morally permissible, resources.

The concentration of research on current practical problems whether in universities or in governmental and private organizations, will also perhaps tend to limit the freedom of idle curiosity and phantasy from which science derives much nurture. Imaginative powers will be concentrated largely on the development of the most accurate method of observing the events, the manipulation of which is necessary for the achievement of practical ends. No satisfactory scientific work is possible without the continuous improvement of technique, but technique can develop too disproportionately and without relationship to the problems set by the general hypotheses of systematic theory. If so, special prizes will be awarded technical virtuosity, and the recruitment of social scientists will become unbalanced. For a long time social science suffered from a preponderance of philosophically trained persons whose fear of scientific procedure held back scientific development.

The opposite tendency has already begun to appear in certain fields and anything which will accentuate it to an extreme is to be watched with care. Moreover, an unbalanced relationship between technique and general theory will determine in a way which is frequently sterile and wasteful the selection of research problems. Thus the early development of attitude scales before psychologists had worked out hypotheses about the genesis of attitude studies, led to an overconcentration of research efforts on attitude studies, the vast majority of which have been utterly inconsequential for the growth of theoretical knowledge and the techniques of investigation. This misdirection of effort has still not been halted. . . .

* * * * *

. . . [I]t is clear that there is no unresolvable conflict between the practical orientation of scientific work and the development of a general scientific theory. The real incompatibility is between the *level of concreteness* of most practically orientated investigations and the development of science.

Another point of conflict might emerge when the policy-maker sees the invasion of his own sphere of judgment and interpretation by the results of basic social science research. The fundamental maxims for the estimation of the conduct of others, the theory of human nature by which policy-makers—and everyone else—guide their decisions and conduct, are very close to the centre of personality. Resistance to the acceptance of these kinds of propositions is therefore much more likely and so, therefore, is the resistance to the support of the type of research which will produce such propositions. The best method of dealing with resistances by policy-makers to the acceptance and application of the results of research have been associated with the "therapeutic" approach. The successes of this approach have not, however, been in the field of obtaining support for basic research from policy-makers—they have rather been achieved mainly in obtaining the acceptance of recommendations for practice derived in part from general clinically-founded maxims about human behaviour. Nonetheless, there is no logical reason —although there are some empirical grounds—to believe that it would not be possible to use the same procedure to extend the understanding of policy-makers to the recognition of the importance of basic research.

The extensive call for help from practical bodies at present carries with it the danger of the "over-selling" of social science before it is in a position to deliver more than a fairly accurate descriptive inventory. On the one hand this might culminate in disillusionment with social science—a recognition that it is not yet science and consists largely of a set of fairly gross techniques, which—although probably better than impressionistic observations—provide no incontestably valid answers; and that it has promised more than it has delivered. This might then result in governmental unwillingness to support social science research on a scale necessary for its continued improvement and a greater resistance against the acceptance of the counsel of social scientists—which though seldom scientific, still is occasionally wise and hence worthy of serious consideration. It can also in this period of immaturity in which no consensus has yet been achieved, regarding standards of quality, accentuate the role of irrelevant criteria in the competition for eminence, office and income among social scientists. The policy-maker is left, in this pre-scientific situation, to choose arbitrarily on the basis of his own impressions, and his accidental personal relations with one block of social scientists or another, or he is forced to depend upon some formal system of certification, such as membership in a given Society, as a qualification for entry into his service. Since no valid consensus exists as yet among social scientists, any system of licensing would be damaging. The bureaucratization of science is to be feared at all times but especially is it to be feared in a science which is still in a formative state.

The intellectual situation in social science today—particularly in anthropology, sociology and psychology—is undergoing rapid changes in techniques and hypotheses and the rate of obsolescence of intellectual capital is rather high. Any institutional arrangement which would slow down the process of writing off obsolete intellectual capital would be pernicious. Yet that might well be a consequence of the promotion of an institutional monopoly, in which the older hands, who profiting by age and "political" experience have the advantage in the distribution of strategic positions from which research funds would be controlled. The centrally unified control of research funds is not desirable even in the well-established sciences where standards are fairly clear and where the ethics of the profession, organized around the pursuit of truth, is well incorporated. In the social sciences which have as yet few wholesome traditions of devotion to truth and few models of rigorous achievement, free competition is even more necessary. An over-development of practically oriented research with its dependence for finances on the decisions of laymen or on the hierarchy of a single professional body advising the laymen, would choke off this free competition and retard the formation of the necessary standards.

There is one other negative consequence of the practical orientation which should be mentioned here. As we have already indicated, the practical orientation provides greater sums of money for social research. The greater sums require a more complex organization for their proper administration. The greater the task of administration, the greater the likelihood that talented and promising scientists will be drawn from scientific research into the administration of scientific research. Another prominent and perhaps too probable alternative is for those who have little talent and understanding for research to become the administrators of science so that crucial decisions affecting the future development of science pass into the hands of those who are not intellectually qualified to decide. . . . The solution probably is to be found in the rotation of the personnel of the top administration post of scientific organizations, with some sacrifice of administration efficiency for the sake of more satisfactory relations between the heads of scientific organizations and those actually doing scientific work.

* * * * *

We have thus far concerned ourselves mainly with what might happen to social science if its energies are given over mainly to the service of practical affairs. We have considered only indirectly what social science can contribute to practice. A few more direct remarks are appropriate.

There is no doubt and there are no grounds for doubting or rejecting the claims of contemporary social science to be useful to the making of policy. Since every human decision assumes knowledge of conditions, resources, and the alternatives into which they can be formed, social science today even on its present primitive state can go far beyond the capacity of a single policy-maker and a handful of advisers in the creation of a moderately accurate picture of the various magnitudes with which the policy-maker will have to cope. This is a role in which social scientists are now almost universally accepted by governments, businessmen, and by themselves. It is probable that this acceptance—of this role at any rate—will become more intense and more widespread in the future.

It belongs within the logically proper limits of scientific work—in its relation to the practical pursuits of ends—to contribute not only information about conditions and resources but also predictions about consequences of the pursuit of one end for the realization of other ends. Even the most concrete predictions presuppose general propositions. Hence all assertions about the "cost" of one policy in terms of the amount of effort which would have to be introduced in order to overcome resistance, or in terms of the consequences set into motion in other spheres of life by the particular policy, involve a type of knowledge in which the social sciences today are not especially rich. There are many hypotheses afloat on this general abstract level and some which even have a reasonable measure of plausibility. Their plausibility is a function of a perhaps higher order of plausibility which rests on clinical observation in "microscopically similar" situations and an extrapolation to macrocosmic conditions.

Here the plausibility becomes attenuated in proportion to the span of extrapolation and it is reinforced by impressionistic assessments of congruance between the hypothesis and at least some elements in concrete situations. This is, however, very far from genuinely scientific validity. At present, therefore, propositions of this sort offered to policy-makers are more in the nature of "wisdom." Even more than scientific truth it rests on the personal genius, "tact," sensibility, and responsiveness of the social scientists and the criteria for assessing its validity are much more obscure than those by which the validity of scientific propositions are assessed.

* * * * *

The simple distinction between judgments of value does not, however, either exhaust the categories of decision-making or draw an adequate boundary to the ultimate powers of social science and social scientists. Even in the sphere of empirical knowledge —of judgments of fact—there are limits to what the social scientist as such can do for the policy-maker. "Tact" or the "sense of the situation" which is one of the great virtues of the policy-maker can never be replaced by scientific knowledge, even when our techniques of research and our general knowledge have both been greatly improved. Time will always elapse between the moment at which a research is made and the moment of decision, and during this interval changes will have occurred in the situation. The policy-maker will have to improvise for himself some estimate of the situation derived from his knowledge of the recent past as described by the research and a co-efficient describing the rate of change which he himself will have to make. A perhaps more important zone in the assessment of facts which the policy-maker will necessarily have to reserve to himself unless he renounces policy-making altogether, lies in the application of general propositions to concrete situations. (We assume at this point that social science has reached the stage at which it can provide such propositions in a scientifically valid form). General propositions are, by definition, abstractions, and the rules for their application to the concrete situations which they are to explain necessarily involve a fairly high degree of discretion. Their application is an art which is no more peculiar to science than to any other field of human activity and the special logical qualities of scientific work constitute no better qualification than administrative or other experience. The same problem arises, only in a rather accentuated form, with respect to the subsumption of concrete ends under general ends. Here, too, we find a gap between the abstract and the concrete which can be filled in only by the exercise of discretion and although it is not a value judgment per se which is involved here, it is not an area in which the social scientist, unless he is also a wise man, can do very much.

We have not raised the question of the ethical desirability of the application of social science knowledge to the execution of policy. Inasmuch as the use of scientific knowledge to facilitate the achievement of an end usually represents an increased skill in manipulation of other human things, its ethical status is perhaps dubious. (This applies more to "scientific" research than it does to those types of descriptive inventories of "wants" which are produced by public opinion polls). Yet there is no reason why social science knowledge should not become self-knowledge, the self-knowledge of individuals and the self-knowledge of the community. If it does become self-knowledge and modification of behaviour becomes self-modification then its ethical status is unquestionable. . . .

It might also be said that even if an adaptation of the "therapeutic" approach in research is not invented, the more conventional type of application of social science knowledge by an administrator is not contrary to the principles of representative democracy as long as the *ends* and *procedure* of representative democracy are respected. The reasons for many laws and administrative measures are not understood by the citizens of a democracy who obey them and who obey them simply because of the democratic legitimation of the legislators and the rational-legal legitimation of the administrators. The situation would be no different in the case of the conventional application of social science knowledge to the tasks of making and executing policy.

Finally, the increase and improvement of social science knowledge is certainly invaluable for the criticism of policy—of both ends and procedures. Hence it is a valuable instrument of political democracy.

These foregoing reflections show that the objections may be raised against the close involvement of the social sciences with social policy are nearly all to be found on the side of the consequences of such a relationship for the development of science. We have already dealt at some length with the possible dangers to the development of social science which might arise from too close an attachment to the sphere of policy. Nonetheless it does not seem possible that the social sciences can develop from their present menage to the level of science if they cut themselves off entirely from the sphere of practical valuation. We have stressed above that the chief deficiency of contemporary empirical social research is the absence of general theory and the virtually random scatter of concrete attention—in other words the absence of a common problem on the general level which could serve as a criterion for the selection of research problems. This criterion must in its ultimate derivation, rest on the value-relevance of some social phenomenon. Our problems are then formed by our interest in the conditions of the coming to be, persistence and passing away of the phenomenon in question and indeed in the whole class of which this phenomenon is one instance.

This method of choosing a problem is completely compatible with the utmost rigor in research procedures, the freedom from political partisanship in the execution of the investigation and the maximum degree of scientific systematization. . . .

Let us set forth the criterion by which problems are to be selected. We postulate the value of order in human relations. By order, we mean the integration of ends in which the actions of diverse individuals are concerted in such a way that the ends of these diverse individuals are fulfilled to a significant extent. The one particular form of order which we value highly is one which allows within the framework of order an optimal amount of individual freedom in the setting of ends and in the choice of procedures, and which regulates access to resources in accordance with generally acknowledged moral rules. If we accept this object of evaluation as our point of departure, our scientific knowledge will accumulate in a way which will give us more insight into the conditions under which this valued combination of liberty in order can exist and of the conditions which threaten its existence.

* * * * *

In the course of time a coherent theory of the working of institutions, of the conditions which reproduce them or change them would accumulate and with it both truth about the nature of human behaviour as well as guidance in the implementation and criticism of policy.

There are undoubtedly other evaluation points of departure, e.g., equality, from which reality might be observed. But it seems less fruitful from a scientific point of view in the sense that it subsumes fewer problems and is of less practical and ethical value as well. Equality as an end of policy is less "permeative" than order which is entailed in every policy both as a partial end (in association with other values) and as a pre-condition. Propositions about the condition of order would moreover subsume propositions about the consequences of equality; the interest in order raises more ramified scientific problems and offers the basis for a more comprehensive general theory.

There is thus no incompatibility between the orientation of social research towards value-related problems and the growth of social science—as long as the values which are involved in the problems are not too concretely and immediately defined. In other words, as long as the values and consequently the variables to be investigated are conceived in certain general categories and as long as the hypotheses to be tested are not simply descriptive or concrete, social science can develop fruitfully alongside or even in employment by governmental and other power exercising organs.

[*Editors' Summary*. The development of a scientific policy, however, depends on recognition of the necessity to invest substantial resources —intellectual as well as financial—in basic research and in the construction of general theory. The universities will have to bear chief responsibility for these tasks. It is important that in sponsoring basic research, governments and foundations do not disregard the university in favor of in-house government research offices and independent research institutes. In the universities, training in empirical social research is combined with the cultivation of a philosophical sense of relevance so as to bring forth the renewal of social science which would simultaneously serve science and policy.]

CHAPTER II

The Social Organization of Policy-Oriented Social Science

THE ORGANIZATIONAL SETTINGS OF KNOWLEDGE TRANSACTIONS

In contrast to medicine or law, in which knowledge and advice is transmitted in private, face-to-face interaction with clients, social science knowledge by its very nature is almost always solicited and applied in more elaborately organized settings. This is particularly true in government.

To the extent that governmental agencies experience a need for social science knowledge this is almost always linked to certain identifiable organizational requirements. Organizational and administrative rules determine the ways in which these needs are expressed in action. When these rules, as is often the case, are routinized and formalized so that they prescribe a certain dollar-amount of social science research to be sponsored annually, we can speak of the institutionalization of research in a given department or agency.

Organizational requisites play an important role in the application of social science knowledge to problems of policy and planning. Although personal relationships between social scientists and government officials help in the promotion of research and although attitudes toward social science knowledge vary radically among officials, in the final analysis the wedding of knowledge and action depends on the official in question being in a position, organizationally, that enables and impels him to act

The production and formulation of social science knowledge are themselves organized activities that, for the most part, have been carried out in organizations—university departments and research institutes—especially established for this purpose. To the extent that the last 25 years have added new organizational forms these activities have involved separations of social science *research* from teaching. Social research activities have developed organizational bases of their own, apart from traditional university structures (Lazarsfeld, III.1, 1961: 3–4 and 7). Included is a variety of organizations with no university affiliation and the many centers and institutes that have established themselves as satellites in the orbit of the modern "multiversity." Some of these new forms are examined in this chapter.

Of the many ways in which organizational

settings and requisites affect social science research activities, those most pertinent to the present work are the consequences for (a) the occupational roles and work activities of social scientists; (b) the selection of social phenomena as objects of social investigation; and (c) the generation and application of modes of investigation to these phenomena. These factors, too, exert a reciprocal influence; organizational forms are changed and modified by new conceptions of the professional social scientist. Such changes may develop through interactions with outside groups and institutions, and from the application of new techniques such as computerology or systems analysis.

In this chapter we are concerned with the implication of these factors for the interrelationship of government and social science. We have selected for inclusion articles describing (a) some research organizations whose work was, or is, largely oriented toward governmental policy or planning (Rossi, Bennis, and Doob); (b) characteristics of governmental bodies which relate to their role as actual or potential users of social science research (Packenham and Janowitz).

In addition we have included articles that, at least by implication, suggest some conceptual models for studying the different kinds of relationships which link government and social science. Since there are few studies of this latter kind, we have prepared original materials (Crawford and de Forest) or, as in the case of the article by Price, drawn on studies examining the institutional interrelationship of government and science.

GOVERNMENT AND SCIENCE AS SEPARATE SOCIAL INSTITUTIONS

This organization of the articles reflects the commonly held conception of government and science as social institutions, each with its own set of norms, goals, and values. In the literature this notion is represented by two different strands of inquiry. One concerns itself with the internal organization of science. Here the sociological study of the organization of *social* science has not yielded anything as impressive as is found among the list of publications on the organization of physical and biological scientific activities.[1] Still beginnings have been made in the survey by Lazarsfeld (III.1, 1961 and 1964) and others of university social research organizations; in the case-study by Bennis (III.1, 1955) of individual social research organizations; in comparative studies of structural variations in institutional settings on researchers' roles and the conduct of social research, primarily in health or medicine (Rosengren, III.1, 1961; Gordon and Marquis, III.1, 1966); in several studies of the training, recruitment, and social characteristics of social scientists (Sibley, III.1, 1963); and in "profiles" of individual social science disciplines (Somit and Tanenhaus, III.1, 1964).[2]

Several of the articles in this chapter contain descriptions and evaluations of the effect of government sponsorship of research on the organization of social science. Thus the government is described by Rossi as providing some of the impetus behind the establishment of large-scale university-affiliated research organizations, especially those engaging in sample surveys. The institutionalization of social science in government has also brought important changes in the work orientations of social scientists. Bennis, for example, describes this as an overall trend toward a more purposive orientation, manifesting itself in the numerous extrascientific concerns—administration, public relations,

---

[1] Kaplan (II.1, 1964: 864–869) contains an overview of research in this area.

[2] For additional studies of social science research organizations, see Bibliography III.1.

and fund-raising—which now crowd and sometimes dominate the work days of social scientists.

As was suggested in the Editors' Introduction, larger systematic inquiries into the organization of social science research activities may well become important by-products of "big social science." A systematic study of the elaborate social system in which research is embedded will probably show that the emergence of new organizational forms, and the strains and stresses that affect many of the existing ones, result from the interplay of such factors as (a) the cultural norms of the system of science which dispose social scientists to favor highly personalized and highly autonomous work units; (b) the economic and technical requirements of large-scale social science—the need for funds, facilities, equipment, and differentiated skills; (c) the degree to which social scientists can successfully lay claim to economic resources and the terms on which these are secured; (d) patterns of recruitment into the social sciences and career choices among social scientists, exemplified by the type of data presented by Bennis. The operation of some of these factors is exhibited in isolated form in studies of individual research organizations or in surveys of a particular organizational type, such as university-affiliated research institutes.

The other strand of inquiry which is pertinent to an examination of policy-oriented social science is the study of governmental organization, administrative behavior, and decision-making.[1] Although many of these studies touch upon the policy roles of the social sciences, few writers have made this topic the primary focus of inquiry. Those who have done so base their observations on narrow personal experience or speak as representatives of a "fraternity of scholars" or of a "policy making elite." Commentary in the latter vein typically arises when administrators confront social scientists on panel discussions at professional meetings, or when each in the confines of his own circle, gives vent to low opinions of the other for being ignorant of his world. (Barber, 1964; Polk, 1965; Rostow, 1957; Yarmolinsky, 1963; all in IV.2.)

Strategic Intelligence and National Decisions, by Hilsman (IV.2, 1956) which draws on interviews with intelligence specialists and "operators" in the Department of State and on White House staffs, is perhaps the only empirically-based study dealing with the involvement of "social science" (in the broadest sense of the term) in international policy making. More general studies of policy elites are also important sources of data and propositions concerning factors affecting the role of social science and scientists in government. This is illustrated by two articles in this chapter. For example several of the generalizations concerning the changing roles and functions of the professional military suggested by Janowitz have implications for the role of social science knowledge in the military establishment. As examples of changes that may foreshadow a growing social science influence, we might mention: "the concern of professional officers with the political and social aspects of military operation," the prediction that officers are likely to spend "an increased amount of time in extraorganizational activities . . ." which provide "an area of initiative outside of specific hierarchical control . . . ," and "the emergence of the civic action concept in which the military seek to be agents of social change . . . ." A factor which may or may not work in the reverse direction is the "increasing number

---

[1] Obviously we have not been able to review here the entire literature. Included in the bibliography are examples of writings that we feel are more than tangentially relevant. These are of two types; theoretical materials included in II.3, empirical or discursive studies with particular reference to international and military decision-making found in IV.2.

of senior officers now following scientific and technical careers . . . ."[1] The impact of officer specialists will determine, and in turn, depend on the degree to which social science will continue as a part of the military-scientific research and development structure, rather than become merged into policy, planning, and intelligence activities.

The article by Packenham throws light on the effect of the educational backgrounds and operating doctrines of foreign aid officials, and on their exposure to and use of social science knowledge. That these officials appear little influenced by scholarly studies dealing with long-range, broad-scale social and political development can be explained by such factors as the predominantly economic orientation of the officials studied, their negative evaluation of political as opposed to technological aid, and their short-term time perspectives.

More importantly, perhaps, this article illustrates one of several ways of viewing the role of knowledge in decision making. In the frame of reference in which Packenham places his analysis, the policy goals of political development are seen as flowing from the particular interpretation given the "national interest" by foreign policy elites. Once the overall policy objective is set, knowledge becomes an aid in finding the practical means to implement already established goals. The kinds of scholarly knowledge sought then are tested propositions suggesting the lines of action to be pursued in order to bring about the goal of political development.

We could also examine the roles that other students of policy making have assigned to knowledge. It would be important to attend to the more traditional literature as well as behaviorally oriented studies. We can expect that there would be significant variations, for instance, between models based on power theories from those models oriented to process or bargaining theories or to those with legal-institutional or social-systems approaches. We know that writers differ in their assumptions about such matters as the degree of organizational or individual rationality present when making decisions, and the extent to which policy makers are seen as acting on ideological beliefs, interest or power calculations, or universalistic or particularistic orientations.

In most of these models the role of knowledge is subsidiary to the author's primary concern. His concern may be, for instance, to seek explanations for the actions or preferences of nations, to understand the considerations behind the formation of alliances, or to find the sources of international conflict. Although not directly focused on the making of public policy, writings on information and intelligence as it relates to communication and control in political or other systems appear to be the most fruitful source of propositions regarding the role of knowledge. (Deutsch, II.3, 1963; Wilensky, II.3, 1967.) These writings, however, rarely relate the role of information and intelligence in the receiving system to characteristics of the individuals or institutions from which it emanates. A theory of the role of social science knowledge in policy making would not only have to include propositions regarding these relationships with respect to the social science institution, but also consider the claims made on the attention of policy makers by competing knowledge-producing institutions.

[1] Pp. 128–130.

SOME REQUISITES OF EMPIRICAL STUDIES

Ideally a theory of the role of social science knowledge in decision making would flow from empirical studies of how decision makers perceive the utility and validity of such knowledge and of its many different practical uses. At present we know of no attempt, at least not in the field of international affairs, to trace through concrete instances the precise ways in which such perceptions affect the selective use of knowledge. This is understandable since such an enterprise would not only be time-consuming and costly, but also presents formidable problems of access and research design. It has also been widely assumed that the influence of social science knowledge on policy is too limited, infrequent, and unpredictable to make such a systematic treatment feasible. As social science research oriented toward problems of policy and planning continues to grow in volume, however, social scientists, whether motivated by simple curiosity or an urge to improve the usefulness of their products, may become more interested in developing this area of inquiry.

Such step-by-step studies would have to deal with a reality that is much more complex than that commonly depicted in discussions of the uses of social science knowledge in policy making. The primary concern of these studies has been the problem of nonuse or misuse of research. An expression of the latter is the frequently heard complaint that social science knowledge is not used to further scientific goals but rather as ammunition for groups or parties holding contending views or as a basis for righteous self-assertions. If viewed in relation to the scientific study of the use of knowledge, however, a number of other ways of viewing nonuse and abuse will assume greater prominence.

Price states that "[a] science itself cannot tell how its own data are to be used."[1] If we interpret him correctly, he implies that in any field of science one can neither prescribe nor predict how findings are to be used. While scientific findings often strongly suggest implications for use, these can never be binding. As a consequence, how a science is applied will depend on the needs and interests of whoever may be the user—an engineer, a social worker, a government official, or a politician. While it is true that the individual sciences of which Price is speaking cannot describe or predict the uses to which their findings have been or will be put, this is not valid for science as a whole. Information science is perhaps the most telling example of a specialty that not only attempts to describe and predict, but also, through its applied arm, to control and direct such uses. This latter is accomplished through information systems design, library organization, and programming. Studies of social science knowledge in decision making, although limited to selected parts of a few social science disciplines, constitute a similar field of meta-study.

The range of considerations that have to be accounted for in such studies is easily imagined. By taking even the simplest case —an individual decision maker faced with a product that carries with it recommendations for scientific uses—the broad range of considerations can be appreciated. In the simple case it is assumed that the findings are used in accordance with the rules set by the producer, that is, as a means to scientific understanding and control. A number of aspects of the operative context, however, work to limit the feasibility of scientific uses of knowledge. Many of these limitations are similar to those catalogued by Simon (II.3, 1947: 61–78) in a discussion of departures of actual decision making behavior from the model of objective rationality.

In addition, and partly as a result of the difficulties that inhere in scientific uses of knowledge, there are nonscientific functions which may be equally legitimate once the knowledge has passed from the scientific system. These functions include knowledge and research used as ammunition in controversies, as a rallying-point or in support of the *credenda* and *miranda* of social and political life (Biderman, II.1, 1966: 102–103). While nonscientific uses may seem wholly nonrational to the social scientist who produces the research, they are rational within the operative context if they "work," that is, if the particular use to which the

---

[1] P. 66.

research is put constitutes an efficient means to a given end. To the "operator," the uses prescribed by the social scientist may appear equally nonrational.

Perceptions of the utility of the product is only one of many factors entering into decision makers' judgments of the worth of research. Such judgments, too, are often based on criteria other than the products' scientific merit. Among these are the scholarly reputation of the author, the prestige of his organizational affiliation, or that of the sponsor of research, and even personal likes and dislikes. A lack of scientific training makes it perhaps even more likely that decision makers' evaluations will be based on whatever prestige or authority symbol may be attached to the study—a stamp of officialdom, a recommendation from a superior, an organizational label, or the authoritativeness suggested by appropriate typographical treatment. The sheer volume of research brought into the governmental sphere obviously increases the significance of these kinds of evaluative criteria.

When we move from individual to systemic aspects of the use of social science knowledge, we must confront an even more complex and varied reality. If we look at the total social science research input to the foreign and military policy-making sphere, we would probably also find that decision makers' opinions of what constitutes useful research play a relatively limited role in determining which products enter into the system. With the specialization of functions that characterizes large-scale government, decisions concerning sponsorship or support of research have come to rest with specialized offices, which often maintain only limited contacts with those in charge of policy and operations. In many instances several layers or independent pillars of administrative structure separate the former from the latter; the research offices of the Army, Navy, and Air Force, for instance, are located in separate research and development commands.

Although government research officials must act on the basis of anticipated problems of policy, these officials may be more intimately enmeshed in the social and symbolic world of science and research.[1] In this respect "research"—being the routinized and delegated commissioning of scientific products—is different from the "studies" which often come under the direct control of potential users. In speaking of the latter Price points out how "the very decision to undertake a study on a given subject may be a major political decision."[2] Such a decision may, in fact, have a much larger impact than anything that will ever result from the study. While this may be less true for studies with a scholarly orientation than for official commissions of inquiry whose composition must meet certain principles of interest representation, even there the point has some validity. One illustration is the decision in 1958 of the Senate Foreign Relations Committee to conduct a series of Studies on various aspects of United States foreign policy as well as its selection of personnel for these studies (Halperin, III.3, 1960).

Taking a broad, systemic view, rather than a case perspective, complicates analysis by broadening the span of attention with regard to such matters as the number and categories of scholarly products, potential utilities of research, and interactions between scholars and policy makers. But it also simplifies the design of inquiries into

---

[1] Uyeki (VI, 1966: 516–517), in a questionnaire study of scientist-administrators in the federal government, found that 50 percent of those interviewed deemed the esteem of colleagues in the academic world "very important." The academic world as an organizational context was second only in importance to government (64.5 percent). The symbolic significance of the former is shown in that only 24.8 percent of the respondents reported university colleagues as one of the groups with which they "talked the most." It should be pointed out that the sample of scientist-administrators did not include social scientists.

[2] P. 65.

the uses of knowledge. By looking at the system as a whole, we can formulate generalized hypotheses concerning the behavior of government officials in using research, and their interactions with different categories of social scientists. We would also be in a better position to study the extent to which such behavior is influenced by organizational and institutional requirements, as opposed to the individual's own predilections. The article by Crawford, for instance, contains a number of impressions concerning the formation and functioning of "networks of actors" in these fields of research that are translatable into propositions. The same holds true for the observations, now often stated as accusations, concerning the difficulties behavioral scientists have in gaining access to policy-making and planning offices in the Department of State as contrasted with the more frequent acceptance of their products by the military.

Finally generalized descriptions of the use of knowledge in decision making raise the possibility of predicting and controlling the types and amount of information entering into the military and foreign policy-making system. Crude mechanisms exist for directing the attention of government officials to the types of knowledge that are considered important to their specialized concerns, in the form of information storage and retrieval systems, such as the Defense Documentation Center or the bibliographic services of the State Department's External Research Staff. At present these systems are organized around semantically derived categories or based on crude measures of use. Sociological studies of the nonrational elements of such patterns might help information science from being a captive of these early forms of organization. Basing the design of these systems on such studies would undoubtedly also make them more efficient and economical.

THE ORGANIZATION OF POLICY AND RESEARCH
—AN OVERVIEW

The Structure of Policy

DON K. PRICE

A couple of centuries ago a government of laws and not of men was the ideal of those who distrusted arbitrary power. They hoped to make human affairs conform more closely to natural law, which was the will of God as manifest in nature . . . .

Since 1776 scientists have come down from the lofty philosophical interests of a Thomas Jefferson to deal with a great many specific problems of government. The efforts to apply science to social problems, for example, have been at the heart of our national programs for the improvement of agriculture and the development of our resources. They have stimulated the development of city planning and the hope that business management and public administration may create something like a science of organization. And most recently the techniques of operations research, by bringing the mathematical and physical sciences into closer co-operation with economic and sociological studies, have gone far beyond those of management engineering in their depth and precision.

It is no wonder that many a social scientist, looking at the spectacular accomplishments of the natural scientist, begins to dream of a society in which scientific method will replace the accidents of politics or the arbitrary decisions of administrators in determining the policies of society . . . .

• Don K. Price *Government and Science,* New York: New York University Press, 1954, pp. 160-189. Reprinted by permission of the publisher and the author.

Are there, indeed, any limitations on the use of science to guide the decisions of government? Why should not every major policy decision be based on scientific findings? Why should not every major executive be guided by an authoritative scientific adviser? Ultimately, why should not a scientist be chosen, by scientific techniques, to occupy every position of power?

* * * * *

The scientist likes to think in quantitative and pragmatic terms. Is there any way to approach this question in such terms? Let me try.

I have to start with a couple of assumptions. The first is the idea that there is a government, and that it has an executive head. The second is that the executive must give some measure of direction to the whole organization through some kind of organized structure, in which he deals mainly with the heads of major departments, and each of them in turn deals with his subordinates through a hierarchical and subdivided structure. An organization chart is a very crude (usually a deceptively crude) model of such a hierarchy. Each of the millions of persons at the bottom level of this pyramid is different from every other; his work and his abilities are unique. The process of administration is to identify or imagine some uniform patterns; to set up general standards and general goals; and to select for consideration at the top the individual issues of the most general significance, so that decision on them will give the greatest amount of effective direction to the organization as a whole. . . .

If the organization chart is the model of a government, a university curriculum is the crude model of science. Here the process works in the direction, not of artificial integration, but of natural division and subdivision. The scientist is an analyst. He breaks each scientific discipline down into subdisciplines and multiplies their subordinate specialties. . . . If you start a scientist on a simple concrete problem, he can build on top of it an inverted pyramid of abstract specialized sciences and refined research projects.

When you try to match up the pyramid of the government organization with the inverted pyramid of science, you are bound to run into trouble.

It is true, no doubt, that in the higher reaches of abstract science new unities are discovered—simpler patterns that account for the great diversity of the things that appear on the surface. . . . But unhappily it is not possible to relate these grand abstractions to the immediate problems of public affairs in any very practical system of organization. The most important truths can be dealt with only by the individual mind and the individual conscience. We are still faced, then, with this problem: At the lowest levels of the government hierarchy the worker must deal with problems each of which could be solved perfectly, as an individual problem, only by a considerable number of scientists; and in the process of solution each of those scientists would open up enough new questions, all needing to be answered before a final solution could be obtained, to keep their research going indefinitely.

I have already spoiled my effort to put this discussion in quantitative terms by letting my answer reach infinity. In practice, of course, nothing of this sort happens, because very few scientists are interested in pure science. Most of them are partly engineers at heart; they want to use the scientific method, or rather some particular scientific method, to solve the key part or a new part of some problem, while they rely on arbitrary policy, general experience, tradition, or guesswork to fill in the gaps.

As they do so they are likely to notice that the higher in government an issue goes for decision, the less likely it is that it can be answered by scientific research. Some will argue that this is not so. A very eminent diplomat, in a moment of exasperation, once remarked to me that if the hierarchical pyramid of the State Department were turned upside down, the only result anyone would notice would be that the typing would not be done very well. In a similar mood a scientist might argue that the reason why scientific issues are not taken to the top of an organization is that the executives are not competent to handle them.

This is doubtless a true reason, but it is not the only reason, or the effective one. A better reason is that only in the lower reaches of the government pyramid do problems become specialized enough to correspond to the structure of specialization of the sciences and to the specialized training of the scientist.

In the lower levels of the pyramid of policy the problem may be mainly scientific —that is to say, it may be a problem that can be solved by the precise research methods of one of the sciences. How can an explosive be made more powerful? What kind of testing process will identify the man with the fastest reaction time? What can be done to make an airplane fly faster? These are questions that science can take hold of. To get an airplane that will fly faster you put to work an aeronautical engineer, or rather a propulsion engineer and an aerodynamic engineer, supported by a number of more specialized colleagues. Their purposes and their skills correspond to the purposes of certain very specialized subdivisions of several government agencies.

Just a little higher on the pyramid of

government policy the sciences begin to give less precise answers, and usually in terms of statistical probability rather than absolutes, because the questions themselves are of a different nature: What combination of bomb load and fuel load should a bomber of a certain type have in order to get the maximum speed, with acceptable armor protection, at which pilots may be expected to fly with reasonable safety? At this level a number of different types of scientists need to work together on operations research, which in turn must be guided by a number of policy assumptions supplied by operating officials.

Finally, when you go still farther toward the top of the organization, the problems begin to frustrate science completely: What proportion of our resources shall be put into bombing planes, by comparison with land forces or naval vessels or air defense? How much shall we rely on building up supplies of weapons, and how much on encouraging a stable economy? How do we appraise the intentions of any potential enemy?

Much more often than not, the controlling elements in the vast web of government decisions . . . . are least likely to be the questions that can readily be answered precisely by scientific research. Aerodynamics has been one of the more dynamic of the sciences in its social consequences. Yet the way in which it will make its contribution is often prescribed by the answer to the questions being considered at the next higher level of the pyramid. Whether applied research in that field will receive support and what problems it will be asked to consider will depend (in the hypothetical example we have been using) on decisions about the bombing system as a whole and about the relative demands of speed and range and armament and maneuverability. And as we look at still higher levels on the pyramid of government it is clear that whether we develop more long-range bombers or more battleships or interceptor planes will depend mainly on the military strategists, and that whether we develop any of them (and how many) will depend on the still less scientific judgments of the diplomats and the politicians about our views of other nations and on our decision concerning how much national armament is required for national security.

Scientific methods are the most useful in determining *how* a specific thing is to be done; the more specific the thing, the more precise the determination. They are less often and less immediately useful in determining *whether* or *when* such things are to be done and *how much* effort or money is to be spent on them. But these are the controlling decisions, the decisions that must be made in the upper levels of the hierarchy if a government is to have any unity of purpose and action. This necessity, too, leads the higher officials to deal with the less scientific aspects of their major problems.

A final reason is one that has to do with the way in which responsibilities are delegated in any organization. Any issue that can be reduced to precise and objective terms is one that a superior can delegate with confidence to a subordinate. No matter how intricate and difficult the operation, no matter how much skill and training may be required for its performance, the executive will be willing to delegate it to a subordinate if there are precise standards to use in judging its performance . . . .

But then we come to questions that, step by step, become less objective in their nature. How many bacteria can the water system tolerate? How much should the city spend on reducing infant mortality by public health measures? How much salary should it pay the public health officer? These questions become progressively . . . . more dependent on factors on which research does not give a conclusive and verifiable answer and on which the scientist's opinion may be as prejudiced as any layman's.

For the sake of simplicity I have been talking as if each problem in government were either precise and scientific or the opposite. This alternative, of course, is not so. Most problems of any importance are made up of a mixture of factors, some of which can be stated in quite precise terms and tested by objective research, while others are much more vague and general and more dependent on interests, values, and ideals. Any system of staff work for an executive then becomes a sort of sieve, screening out those aspects of the problems that can more nearly be solved by science (as well as the quite different category of problems that are not important enough) and bringing to the executive for decision only those aspects of the problem that he is not willing to delegate.

This relationship means, of course, that a much lower level of purely intellectual ability may be required for the decisions that come to the top of the government pyramid than for those that are made nearer the bottom. I suppose that it took much more detailed knowledge of the latest specialized discoveries in nuclear physics, and greater concentration on the purely scientific aspects of the program, to do the work of many a junior scientist at Los Alamos than to do the work of Dr. Bush or General Groves, who had top-level responsibilities for atomic devolopment. And they, in turn, needed to know a great deal more about the scientific aspects of the atomic bomb than did the President of the United States. When the President made at Potsdam the fateful decision to use the bomb he may have been right or wrong, but whether he was right or wrong was surely not the result of a lack of scientific advice or understanding. For the scientists themselves divided immediately and bitterly on just that type of issue, and are still divided, apparently according to the same kind of idealistic or temperamental differences that characterize the rest of us.

[*Editors' Summary.* Some social scientists believe that such confusion and division will disappear as soon as there is a much more advanced science of society and human behavior; that the distinction between science and values is not a real one. In my skeptical view, the greater the advances of all the sciences, the greater and more difficult the burdens of responsibility and of judgment placed on the government's principal executives. Every day in our technological society the modern executive and legislator must make decisions that would have signified a major crisis in the last century.]

In short, scientific discoveries . . . enlarge the opportunities and broaden the possibilities for discretionary judgment in governmental affairs, just as they do for the acquisition of further knowledge.

. . . . At the same time every new change in our national system of economy or technology brings a few more policy issues to the harried government official. As new technology creates new social problems the governmental executive may solve a few by asking scientists to provide him with the answers. But there will always be at least three reasons why he cannot submit all questions to research to get the answers.

(1) The first is that some types of question call for an immediate answer—the kinds of question on which inaction or delay is itself an answer, and the worst kind. As long as there is conflict in human affairs this type of question will remain important. President Truman at Potsdam could not have referred to a study commission the issue whether to drop the bomb. On the other hand, many an executive has discovered an easy way to avoid doing something that he has decided not to do. The way is simply to appoint a research committee to study the matter until the issue has cooled off, and then to advise him why he should not do it.

(2) The second reason is that each question, if it is to be answered by formal research, leads to another. It is a matter of infinite regression. You cannot get anywhere if you first make a complete study of what

you ought to study; and then a complete study of the methods that you ought to use in making the study; and then a complete study of the way in which the results of your study should be applied. By that time, of course, you would need to study the extent to which changes in the situation had made the original question obsolete. Studies of all these types are, within limits, useful and necessary, but only by the application of arbitrary judgment can the process be shortened to such a point that it can be applied to the problems of the real world.

(3) Third, there is the question how to take into account the political implications of a research project. It is a sign of political maturity—from the point of view of one who has faith in both democracy and the freedom of science—when the public is willing to accept and support the findings of science in its proper fields. But it is important to remember that some societies have not been willing to do so at all and that no society has been willing to do so all the time. Even in our own country today there are a great many forces that are willing to attack science in order to prevent it from even considering certain subjects.

As long as people like power, and some have more than others, the very decision to undertake a study on a given subject may be a major political decision. Certainly the terms of reference of the study and the selection of the personnel to make the study are political decisions. That is to say, they are decisions that must be based on discretionary if not arbitrary judgment. This is not to say that the appointment of personnel for a study is always made with intent to determine the answers; even in a public study of a highly political subject, it may be greatly in the interest of the appointing authority to select men whose objectivity and balanced judgment will give wisdom and weight to their recommendations. But major official commissions of inquiry on public affairs are not likely to be selected in the near future on the basis of competitive objective examinations.

*   *   *   *   *

. . . [F]or the reasons that we have just been discussing, no decision is so controlling as the selection of top personnel. This is the most important way in which a chief executive can control his departments. It is also the most important way in which the electorate can control the chief executive and the legislature. At the apex of the pyramid the issues are reduced, in effect, to a choice between candidates, and the democracies in which popular control has been the most real and the most effective have been those in which the people are limited, in their formal power, to a choice between two major parties. It has always seemed to me that some of the most able atomic scientists have overstated their case in arguing that the public ought to demand to know more about the details of our atomic energy program— . . . . I am inclined to think that, on the contrary, we should consider that most of these matters—like all the most delicate diplomatic negotiations and all the most important war plans—have to be left to the proper legislative and executive authorities, and that we should concentrate our attention on getting better ones. I personally do not want to know how many atomic bombs we have, and the figure would not mean much to me if I knew it. I do want to know that the bomb and the processes of planning for its custody and its possible use are fully under the control of properly constituted authorities who are effectively responsible to the people. Responsibility to the people, I must add, means that the key decisions of the executive authorities should be subject to the criticism of an adequate number of well-informed and independent experts and to the criticism and control of the legislators who may draw their technical advice from those experts.

But even if we are not on our way toward

a system in which science takes the place of political responsibility and executive leadership, we are clearly well along in an era in which political leaders and administrators can further public policies far more effectively by making adequate use of science. And we have certainly developed a system of government in which more and more of our administrators, and perhaps some of our political leaders, will begin their careers as scientists or at least will have some training in science.

* * * * *

The policy staff work around the President would doubtless benefit from a great deal more use of scientific insight and scientific advice. But it would be a mistake, it seems to me, to try to attain this end by providing by law for new members, or for specialized staff advisers, attached to the National Security Council. This is the process of specialism that makes our top policy staff work so weak. On the contrary, we need instead to strengthen the executive generally and to provide him with the discretionary authority and the career staff that he needs in order to bring together all pertinent points of view—certainly including the scientific point of view—before making his decision.

A science itself cannot tell how its own data are to be used. Its findings cannot be taken undiluted by top political authorities, any more than a scientist's invention can ever be produced by industry just as the scientist invented it. In private industry an invention has first to be developed into a workable product by the engineers; next the production engineers have to make it suitable for mass output by designing it to fit, so far as possible, the machine tool and production facilities already available; and simultaneously it has to be designed so as to fit in with the company's sales program. This is only a pale counterpart of the problem in government, which must decide on the use of any major scientific development in the light of an immense range of policy considerations—social, economic, political, and perhaps military and diplomatic.

* * * * *

In application to practical affairs the sciences as such have no common denominator. In a physical sense the engineer provides the common denominator; in a policy sense, the administrator. One of the administrator's tools is the budget, which ought to provide a stable basis for sustained scientific effort and ought to be the means for distributing resources in the most effective way among the various branches of science. It is a poor enough tool in practice, but no one has ever invented a substitute . . . .

The budget, of course, is only one of a number of methods by which the administrator creates a program out of an infinite variety of ill-assorted facts and random possibilities. This is not a feat of individual brilliance, but of group competence; for a group to develop competence, it has to have some continuity and some stability. The reason why civilian scientists are often frustrated in their relation with the military is that the military, with all its faults, does have such continuity and group competence and is not adequately counterbalanced by any corresponding organization or career service on the civilian side of government.

The personnel system of the United States government does not even recognize the need for such an administrative service. Under its rules of civil service classification there is no arrangement for a corps of generalists to deal with the major issues of policy; the administrative officer, indeed, has to justify his existence by making his work into something like a technical specialty or pseudo-science. In this respect, of course, government in America simply follows the example of society as a whole, which in business and in education has glorified the specialties and neglected the over-all problem of developing the generalist. When I speak of the administrator and his function

I am not thinking of him as he is defined for civil service purposes by the classification experts. That kind of administrator and his function are only an inferior kind of specialty. I am thinking instead of the function described by Brooks Adams (VI, 1913):

"Administration is the capacity of co-ordinating many, and often conflicting, social energies in a single organism, so adroitly that they shall operate as a unity. . . . Probably no very highly specialized class can be strong in this intellectual quality because of the intellectual isolation incident to specialization; and yet administration or generalization is not only the faculty upon which social stability rests, but is, possibly, the highest faculty of the human mind (pp. 207-208)."

Many scientists, especially those from universities, never feel the need for such a function. The purpose of organization and administration in a university is mainly to care for the material needs of a collection of independent disciplines. There have been some ambitious efforts to bring them together in the name of general education, but the going has been rough. On the other hand, in public affairs (including the great foundations as well as government) the administrator is not motivated by a merely philosophical purpose: he sees the need for stamping out hookworm or the boll weevil; he sees the need for an improved system of communications; he sees the need for an effective system of air defense. And it is his job to marshal the forces of science into an effective program and to keep them from going off into the entirely different directions of their several disciplines and specialties. Unless this essential job of the administrator is done, the whole program of government will not become coherent enough to be controlled by the political authorities who in turn are responsible to the people.

* * * * *

On the aspects of administration that are managerial in the narrow sense of the word, the scientist whose only experience has been the laboratory is often poorly prepared. Moreover, he is likely to dismiss as unimportant those aspects of an administrative job that have to do with keeping the organization and procedures in good repair and keeping the majority of the staff satisfied with their work. The reason may be that he is tempted by force of mental habit to concentrate on those aspects of his job that are most interesting to the individual student as intellectual problems—a temptation which the administrator usually cannot afford to yield to.

These considerations argue, it seems to me, for having a few men with quite general administrative background in the top ranks of even those agencies with heavily scientific programs. On the other hand, I would argue with equal emphasis that the administrative personnel of almost all agencies ought to have a fair proportion of men with some training and experience in science and engineering. If administration is to serve as a useful layer in the pyramid of policy between the peak of political power and the base of science and technology, it needs in its composition an appropriate mixture of general competence and special knowledge.

Many policy problems that cannot be solved precisely by scientific research can in practice be solved satisfactorily only by men with scientific knowledge as well as administrative ability. In military affairs, for example, there are many issues on which it is not practical to look to operations research for the answers, but which cannot be handled properly without the kind of judgment that comes from scientific background. The Canadian government recognized this principle when it made its leading civilian scientist a member of its equivalent of the Joint Chiefs of Staff. The scientist should take part as a responsible administrator, right up to the highest levels, in making decisions that cannot be based entirely on objective research, and on which no irresponsible adviser can ever expect to be consulted.

In the administrative corps some mixture of general and special qualifications is desirable. In the long run, however, a mere mixture of unrelated skills is not what is needed. What is needed is a corps of men whose liberal education includes an appreciation of the role of science and technology in society and whose scientific education has not been a narrowly technical or vocational one, but has treated science as one of the highest intellectual endeavors of men who also have responsibility as free citizens. The humanities and the social sciences are too often taught in America as narrowly technical subjects. We can hardly found a new generation of administrative generalists on them as they are commonly taught today.

It will not do to adopt as our ultimate ideal the pattern of a completely separate administrative class, set up in an administrative career that is a lifetime business and virtually closed to men whose experience in their twenties and thirties has been in science or technology. This is the pattern of the Administrative Class of the British civil service, which . . . richly deserves the praise that it has long received as a keystone of integrity and efficiency for the government of the United Kingdom.

The British Administrative Class is a great deal more efficient than its chaotic counterpart in the United States government . . . . But I do not think that our main possibility of improvement lies in an effort to imitate it.

Any such closed service is a profoundly conservative force— . . . in the sense of looking on the government and its program as a single coherent machine in which inconsistencies cannot be permitted. Any novel idea is an inconsistency that could cause temporary waste and disorder and inefficiency and would probably detract from the current program.

As much as I should like to see a more satisfactory administrative service in the United States government, offering a much more attractive permanent career to a larger proportion of its officials, it seems to me that there is a great deal of merit in continuing to have many of its members drawn from earlier experience in the professional and scientific specialties, in private as well as public life. With all the disadvantages of the American public service as it now exists, we can see even now some advantages in basing our system of administrative careers on such a mixed foundation. The professional ties that the government administrators retain with their professional colleagues outside the government keep them from considering current issues solely from the point of view either of the party in power or of the convenience of the governmental organization. Those same ties help to keep them alert to new ideas and willing to support a certain number of varying and independent programs. Their variety of experience gives them more sympathy with the functions and the point of view of the private and local institution, and it helps to keep the federal system and the system of contractual relationships truly decentralized, varied, and more likely to retain the vigor and initiative that characterize a free society.

The Informal Organization of Policy-Oriented Social Science

ELISABETH T. CRAWFORD

INTRODUCTION

The field of policy-oriented social science presents an unusual challenge to the social scientist who is concerned with defining its boundaries and scope. The problems that would normally be present in trying to map a field of social activity in which the acting persons and organizations assume a variety of roles and identities are in this instance made more complex by the social scientist bearing the burden of being both observer and observed. The resulting lack of agreement concerning what constitutes policy-oriented social science has often left the individual writer free to tailor his definitions to a particular purpose or viewpoint.

In this paper we will introduce some conceptual models which might help in building a common language to deal with a variety of phenomena in the field of policy-oriented research. Our aim has been to choose models which will enable us to gain an overview of the field by suggesting propositions regarding the interrelationships of its structural parts. Although our immediate concern is research dealing with international and military policy, many propositions and observations pertinent to this case may be equally applicable to other areas of government-related social science.

In searching for applicable models, it becomes immediately apparent that the peculiar features of policy-oriented research require that we think in terms of complex social organizations. This means that we will be stressing informal rather than formal organizational properties. We will also suggest that alternate modes of structuring the field are applicable, depending on which particular variable we choose to bring into focus.

Specifically, we will suggest three ways of structuring the field. Firstly, we will discuss a model—suggested by Barton (II.1, 1961)—in which applied research is viewed as a social system based on certain influence patterns. Secondly, we will examine the extent to which the informal organization of the field corresponds to "communities of profession" as these have been described by Goode (VI, 1957). Thirdly, we will outline a model of our own which orders the field in terms of "networks" formed around the patterns of communication which link social scientists working in similar areas of research to each other and to their sponsors in government.

PROBLEMS IN SURVEYING THE FIELD OF POLICY-ORIENTED RESEARCH

The complexity and fluidity of policy-oriented social science makes it unusually difficult to define its boundaries and scope.[1]

• This is a modified version of an article which appeared in *Background*, Vol. 10, No. 2, 1966, pp. 131–149, under the title, "Organization and Values in Social Science Research on International and Military Policy." Reprinted by permission of the International Studies Associaton.

[1] For a discussion of the organization of knowledge within the framework of an analysis of com-

These problems have been keenly sensed by social scientists who have tried to survey the field using such traditional measures of a given social activity as the number of participating actors, funds expended for the activity in question, or the institutional and organizational units involved. These surveys are a good starting point in that each affords an overview of the field, while at the same time making us aware of various difficulties involved in finding concepts and labels that adequately describe its functioning.

A simple way of describing the scope of any organized social activity is to count *the number of individuals* engaged in this activity at a given point in time. Without detailed information concerning the work activities of social scientists, however, such a count would provide scant enlightenment of the area of our concern. Some information of this type is collected by the professional associations and entered into the National Science Foundation's *Register of Scientific and Technical Personnel*. At present, this register includes economists, psychologists, and sociologists. On the basis of this data and that drawn from other sources, the overall population of social scientists in colleges and universities has been estimated at 43,000–45,000 individuals. Of the ones listed in the register, 24 per cent of the psychologists (16,800 in all), 22 per cent of the sociologists (2,700) and 16 per cent of the economists (12,100) give research as their primary work orientation.[1] We do not know, however, whether these are engaged primarily in "basic" or "applied" research or the number and categories that derive most of their support from governmental sources. Nor is any information of this kind collected for the majority of social scientists—those who combine teaching and research. The exclusion of political scientists as well as of social scientists active in such interdisciplinary fields as international relations or area studies from the register places further limitations on its usefulness.

Apart from these limitations of data, a more useful way of getting a measure of the number of individuals involved in policy-oriented research may lie in the use of "sociometric" techniques. Collectivities of policy-oriented scholars could be revealed by analyzing existing data concerning scholarly interaction, e.g. citations in books, articles and papers or the names of individuals attending conferences on a given topic. Original data would be collected through a questionnaire study where the respondents would be asked to make choices as to the colleagues with which they would like to engage in different scholarly activities. Adding up the populations of the groupings that such an operation would yield in the field of international and military affairs, for instance, would provide us with an approximation of the total population. It would also have the advantage of showing features such as permanence of groupings and visibility of individuals within a certain group, that otherwise could not emerge.

A commonly used indicator of the scope of research activities is *the funds expended* for research; in this case, expenditures by governmental agencies. Federal expenditures for research and other scientific activities, including work in the social sciences, are reported annually by the National Science Foundation in *Federal Funds for Research, Development and Other Scientific Activities*. A privately sponsored survey of the government's involvement in social science research which relied heavily on funding figures was conducted in 1963 with Ellis as the study director. To this should be added a host of surveys of government agencies and private organizations of re-

---

plex organization, see Etzioni (VI, 1964: 75-93). For a general work see Etzioni (VI, 1961).

[1] For recent analyses of economists, psychologists, and sociologists in the register, see "The Structure of Economists' Employment and Salaries, 1964" (III.1, 1965); Compton (III.1, 1966); Hopper (III.1, 1966 and 1967). The 1966 article by Hopper contains a discussion of weaknesses in the specialties categorization used for sociologists in the National Register (pp. 73–75).

search activities in such specialized fields as arms control and disarmament studies, "counterinsurgency" research and area research.[1]

In this context we are not directly concerned with the accuracy of the funding figures used. This does not mean that we accept them. On the contrary, in most instances they require a great deal of interpretation. Taking as an example the overall annual federal expenditure for social science research as reported in various sources, we find that in 1964, Ellis (III.2, 1964: 5) sets this at 210 million dollars, whereas the *Federal Funds* estimate for 1966 is 188 million dollars (III.2, 1966: 78).[2]

Here we shall only mention a few factors militating against the use of funding figures as a valid measure of scope. These are (a) funding figures are tailored to administrative and budgetary needs and hence do not reflect the organizational and social functioning of the field; (b) the special nature of research in the social sciences means that funds are in no way a uniform measure of activity in terms of personnel resources used, output, etc.; (c) the fact that social science research is often a component of scientific research or development programs, e.g. in the fields of medicine, weapons development, or technical innovations such as Supersonic Transport; (d) the use of indirect sponsorship and "in-house" research facilities.

Lastly we will concern ourselves with some attempts to delineate the field of policy-oriented research in terms of the *institutions and organizations* involved. Here it has been common to differentiate between types of sponsoring and producing organizations. A simple typology of the latter would include universities, university-affiliated research centers, independent nonprofit research corporations, operating foundations, and research divisions of manufacturing corporations. A complication is that a given organization may figure both as a producer and a sponsor of research.

For our purposes organizations are not very good units of analysis. One drawback is that the boundaries of policy-oriented research in the social sciences rarely coincide with formal organizational boundaries. It has been common, for instance, to identify certain types of policy-oriented research with a few, highly visible organizations such as RAND, etc. A closer look at these organizations will reveal the often very marginal position of social scientists or others working on the nonhardware or noneconomic aspects of military and foreign policy. At RAND, for instance, in 1964 the social scientists (excluding economists but including historians) numbered 41 out of a total of 577 professionals (B. L. R. Smith, VI, 1964: 499).[3]

Surveys of government offices and agencies sponsoring social science also bear out our thesis that the study of policy-oriented research is not easily accommodated within a formal organizational framework.[4] There is general agreement that research represents behavior which is socially regulated and carried out within identifiable social and organizational units. What is not always

---

[1] See *Federal Funds for Research, Development, and Other Scientific Activities* (III.2, 1953–1966) and subsequent volumes. For surveys of specialized fields see e.g. *Research in Arms Control and Disarmament 1960–1963* (VI, 1963); Orlansky and Blumstein (VI, 1965).

[2] The Ellis survey (p. 4) included "in-house" research as well as some federal statistics-gathering activities. *Federal Funds* . . . (III.2, 1966: 60, 162) excludes the psychological sciences from social science and applies a more stringent definition of "research." Similar variations in definitions make it practically impossible to achieve reliable comparisons of figures reported by individual government agencies.

[3] To some it may also be surprising that the behavioral parts of the social sciences were not better represented at RAND; of 41 social scientists, 20 were political scientists, 9 historians, 7 psychologists, 4 sociologists, and one an anthropologist.

[4] See, e.g., U.S. Department of State (III.3, 1967).

recognized, however, is that the units that are important for the structuring and functioning of the field do not have characteristics which make them "organizations" as commonly conceived or as formally defined in most of the literature on organization and bureaucracy (Caplow, VI, 1964: 1-3; Etzioni, VI, 1961: xi). Instead they are built around interactive patterns which cut across the boundaries of formal organization. These units are therefore best described by concepts stressing informal rather than formal organizational elements.

APPLIED SCIENCE AS A SOCIAL SYSTEM

A model which suggests a number of propositions regarding the informal structuring of the field is put forth by Barton (II.1, 1961) in a study of the "Sociology of Reading Research." He proposes that reading research should be viewed as a social system made up of the various status-groups (reading researchers, schoolbook writers, school teachers, etc.) that operate in the field and the lines of influence that tie these together. The status-groups are seen as roughly corresponding to universities, publishing companies, and local school systems, but Barton also points out that statuses are not always defined by position in the formal institutions. The overall system is depicted with lines of influence flowing from the allocators of research funds through researchers, writers, and teachers, down to the "users"—school children (pp. 95-97).

In the same way as reading research, policy-oriented research in international and military affairs can be seen as a social system made up of interrelated status-groups (researchers, allocators of research funds, "operators," etc.). But there is also enough dissimilarity in the organization of the two fields to make us doubt the total applicability of Barton's model to policy-oriented research. The main value of the model for us, therefore, is its ability to point up some distinct characteristics of this type of research.

Although we can speak of status-groups in the policy field, these are not as clear-cut as the ones making up the system of reading research. This applies particularly to the "users" of research (policy-makers) who cannot be assumed to have the same kind of uniform identities as do Barton's school children and teachers or, to take an example from the related field of medical sociology, doctors and nurses. This has important implications in that it makes the lines of influence structuring the field less easy to unravel.

More important, however, in order to make the system of policy-oriented research fit Barton's model, the model would have to be turned upside down; that is, the direction of influence flow reversed to be from "low status" to "high." This may sound strange, but is perfectly reasonable if we consider the hierarchical arrangement of status-groups in reading research. Here, as in many other systems of applied research, the predominant lines of influence, and also the channels by which research findings will have to travel in order to influence practices in the field, run from institutions operating on a high level in the social or governmental hierarchy (federal government, State boards of education, large school systems, etc.) down to status-groups on much lower levels (local school systems, individual schools, local teachers' associations).

In research on military and international policy, the picture is almost the reverse. Here the presumptive "users" of research commonly operate on a higher level of social organization (executive or congressional leadership, policy-making bodies in governmental agencies and departments) than the "producers" or "sponsors" of research. Put in simple terms, this means that products of research will have to travel "upwards" more often than they can travel "downwards" in the system. While treatment of the upward flow of information and advice is common enough in the treatment of complex organization (Simon, Smithburg & Thompson, II.3, 1950: 235-237), or indeed, the small group, intraorganizational flow through the kind of networks we posit here has received less consideration.

Since we are dealing with the field in terms of a model, the picture that we have drawn here is, of course, oversimplified. In reality, the lines of influence are much more complex; perhaps so much so that they defy being fitted into the kind of schematic representation that Barton suggests.

Two other conditions add to the complexity of the influence structure in policy-oriented research. One is that many of the groups engaged in policy-oriented research operate outside an influence structure such as the one suggested in Barton's model. They do not have a legal relationship with other statuses, nor do they have an economic one. This is the case, for instance, with the groups engaging in "peace research" whose relationship with "user" groups is more of a political or lobbying type. Even where we find economic-legal relationships, as with government research contracts, these are of very little consequence for the utilization of research findings when compared to political, ideological or organizational factors. Here the situation differs from that of reading research where groups with a primarily economic motivation, such as publishers or textbook writers, have a considerable influence over the dissemination of research findings.

A second important way in which research findings influence international and military policy is through their becoming part of the general culture and incorporated into a system of generally accepted concepts, beliefs and values. This is fairly common to research on public affairs but is rarely the case in more specialized fields of knowledge, such as reading research or medical sociology.

COMMUNITIES OF POLICY-ORIENTED SOCIAL SCIENTISTS

Some writers have used the term "community" to describe groupings that have some but not all of the attributes of organizations (Caplow, VI, 1964: 24-25). This term has become as familiar in its application to professional groupings as to geographical ones, for our present topic notably in the usages "the intelligence community" or "the social science community." Goode (VI, 1957) has specified some of the characteristics of the "community of profession": (a) its members are bound by a sense of identity; (b) once in it, few leave, so that it is a terminal or continuing status for the most part; (c) its members share values in common; (d) its role definitions vis-à-vis both members and nonmembers are agreed on and are the same for all members; (e) within the areas of communal action there is a common language, which is understood only partially by outsiders; (f) the community has power over its members; (g) its limits are reasonably clear, though they are not physical and geographical but social; (h) though it does not produce the next generation biologically, it does so socially through its control over training and socialization (p. 194).

As shown here, Goode's criteria stress not only the structural elements of the field, but also its normative and motivational aspects. As a result they bring to attention a whole new set of questions and propositions regarding the functioning of a given social grouping.

Although the people who do research on international and military policy show many indications of constituting a community (e.g., in the sense that they are bound by a sense of identity and that the social limits are reasonably clear), they only partially meet several other of Goode's criteria. The weakest relationships are those involving the characteristics most closely associated with professionalism. When applied to our occupation, Goode's criteria appear to be statements of goals rather than existing realities.

There is, for instance, very little overall control over recruitment and training in the field of research on international and military affairs in the sense of the members of the occupation having a say over who carries out research and how it is done. It has not been uncommon, in fact, to define policy-oriented social science on the basis of its subject-matter, e.g., the study and analysis of human and social factors pertaining to international and military affairs and to consider any individual, whether he be a nuclear physicist, a journalist, or a former diplomat, writing on these subjects as practicing some form of "social science" (Gilpin and Wright, I, 1964: 7n).

This lack of professional control through monopoly over skills—those of social scientists or others—exists not only in the field as a whole but also within its specialized subfields. Psychological warfare is one example of a field which social scientists have tended to regard as intrinsically "social scientific" in character and as requiring *their* specialized skills. To their surprise and dismay, social scientists who have gone into government research in this area have often found themselves competing with a number of other "experts" such as journalists, public relations men, and intelligence specialists.[1]

There is, of course, some variation in the field. Subfields which require technical or analytic skills, e.g., international opinion research or political development studies, seem subject to a larger measure of control from the social science profession than do fields dominated by factual knowledge or "experience" (e.g., area studies). In many instances, however, where social scientists have established "exclusive rights" over a field, this has been due more to the fact that it has not been a very rewarding one—for other groups—in terms of money or prestige than to its intrinsically "social scientific" character. Had political development programs been more popular with policy-makers, social scientists would undoubtedly have had much more competition from other groups. In other instances, exclusivity may be a question of labeling, hence somewhat artificial. Nobody but a sociologist is likely to venture into the field of "sociology of war and peace," although it does not take a great amount of specialized skills to duplicate most studies that have been carried out under this label.

On the whole it seems that the element of community or communities of profession that we find among scholars in the field of international and military affairs stems not so much from the special characteristics of the field as it does from the actors being members of other professional communities (such as a social science community, an academic community, or a community of anthropologists). These other communities are also the source of whatever professional control there is in the field. An exception to this general pattern are the civilian-military strategists who seem to meet many of Goode's criteria and consequently comprise a field of policy-oriented research that has developed into a "community of profession" in its own right.

If we were to examine the values of policy-oriented social scientists, we would undoubtedly find more evidence of the importance of membership in other large communities. Thus, we might classify a sample of actors according to their position in relation to values that may be regarded as important for the functioning of the field. This could be done by having them place themselves on value scales such as "pacifism—acceptance of violence," "internationalism—Fortress America," "rigorous scien-

---

[1] See, e.g., Doob, in this chapter, p. 103; Cottrell in Chapter III, p. 197.

tific method—intuition," "pure science—applied science."

We would undoubtedly find large variations in the value positions of different respondents but also some element of consistency in the values of each individual respondent in the sense that his position on any particular scale would be a function of his pattern on the other, and thus would form a predictable "profile." The position of individuals on these value scales probably are correlated with their positions in broader communities such as disciplinary ones. We could hypothesize, for instance, that social scientists tending toward the left-hand side of each of the value scales used illustratively above are (a) likely to belong in the academic community; (b) likely to have strong disciplinary ties; (c) likely to belong to social science disciplines with a behavioral orientation (sociology, anthropology, or psychology).

NETWORKS OF COMMUNICATION IN POLICY-ORIENTED SOCIAL SCIENCE

Although the normative questions raised here are important, they do not significantly affect the workings of the field of policy-oriented social science. Instead, they come into focus at special occasions such as when the profession discusses its relationship to other social groupings or at times of disruptive events such as the "Camelot Affair." In the ordinary course of their professional lives, however, the actions of social scientists are shaped less by lofty ideals than by the demands of the "trade" in which they are involved. Foremost among these demands is the necessity to communicate with colleagues working in similar or related fields and with sponsors or clients in governmental departments and agencies. Consequently, the field has become structured along the lines of communication patterns or "networks" the function of which is to permit the easiest and most satisfying flow of ideas, information and decisions.

These networks can be regarded as adaptive mechanisms in the sense that they bridge the gaps created by artificial boundaries of organizations and institutions. They provide means of communication without which research tasks could hardly be accomplished. In many instances, they also serve the function of mitigating the cleavages created by conflicting ideological positions. If we were to examine the interactional patterns of two groups such as the "sociologists of war and peace" and the "civilian-strategists" who stand far apart in their value or policy positions, we would probably find that they interact more frequently with each other than with outside groups. Such interactions were aptly characterized by Kenneth Boulding at one of a string of conferences that took place in 1962-1963 on arms control and disarmament. He remarked, "This is like a meeting of the WCTU and the drunks."[1] To push his figure further, even those meetings during the period sponsored by WCTU'ish interests could not have been nearly as well attended nor would as much elaborately researched material have been presented at them were not so many of the participants financed by the "distillers."

Rather than thinking of the field as a single network, it is more realistic to look at it in terms of a number of different networks. These can be identified using such points of reference as are suggested in the following:

1. The *forums* where social scientists meet and exchange views (journals, professional meetings, etc.).

2. The *audiences* at which the different networks aim the products of their research (State Department, Department of Defense, the individual Armed Services, or, more

[1] Recorded in unpublished notes by Albert D. Biderman on a Conference on Arms Control and Disarmament, University of Michigan, 1962.

typically, policy-making organs within departments, or configurations cutting across departmental boundaries).

3. The *"levels of social organization"* at which are found the policy problems with which they are concerned (a simple classification of problems on this basis would range from issues having global significance to those involving relations with one country or segments thereof or, along another dimension, from relations involving "high matters of state" to those of a more peripheral character such as scientific exchanges).

4. The *"distance"* of the actors from the making of policy (this would range from actors concerned with clarifying policy alternatives or expressing their views on policy choices to those who provide knowledge on the contexts in which a given policy will operate or on the problems encountered in the implementation of policy-decisions).

5. *The methods, modes of analysis and interpretations* which have become the "trademarks" of various groupings (behavioralistic, historical, simulation or gaming as devices for policy analysis, etc.).

We are suggesting that one or several of these points of reference be used to identify and draw profiles of the various networks operating in the field. At the same time it is important to recognize the unusual degree of fluctuation and change both in the spawning of new networks and in the high and often temporary visibility of some particular network when heed is paid to it by policy-makers and "operators."

What are some of the networks that can be found operating in the field? Firstly, there are the civilian strategists. Most so identified are associated with the nonprofit research corporations (RAND Corporation, Institute for Defense Analyses, etc.) set up by defense agencies to produce knowledge for use in high-level decision-making. They form a convenient starting-point because of their concern with the "great issues" of international politics.

Whether at the focus of attention, or as the central underlying assumption, nuclear weapons have set the problem concerns of the civilian strategists. These have been the problems of the use of such weapons (deterrence), ways of controlling their use (arms control), or the various alternatives that can be found to using them (e.g., conventional or limited warfare). Some boundaries can be noted that distinguish the "systems analysis" or "cost-effectiveness" part of this community from its more politically-oriented groupings. This distinction becomes more clear if one looks at the forums which seem most congenial to these subgroupings of the community. For example, the "political" civilian strategists have in recent years been attending the annual meetings of the American Political Science Association and International Studies Association. The "systems analysis" and "cost-effectiveness" groups, however, have their own meeting grounds.[1]

A second network consists of psychologists, sociologists, and some others, usually with a university rather than a research corporation affiliation, who are active in a field

---

[1] In a personal communication to the author in 1965, Albert Wohlstetter, who in recent years has emerged as one of the "political" civilian strategists, makes some points which illustrate this discussion. Wohlstetter says: "As someone whose basic training was in mathematical logic, who, after completing graduate work in logic, studied economics, and who now is professor of political science, I might venture saying (1) that, in World War II and immediately after, mathematicians, physicists and biologists made perhaps the largest contribution to operational research on policy decision in the small, including many decisions which involved social science components, (2) that in the 1950's while these mathematicians and natural scientists continued to be important, by far the largest contributions were made by economists or men with some economic training (they produced the most influential systems analyses affecting larger decisions than had hitherto been subject to major analytic influence), and (3) that in the 1960's the role of sociologists and political scientists may hopefully increase, but so far it has been much less direct and decisive."

of knowledge alternatively called "peace research," "sociology of war and peace," or "psychology of international relations." Their concerns lie very much in the same policy areas as those of the civilian strategists (e.g., questions of national survival, international order, global conflict). In many ways they have tended to orient themselves toward the same high-level policy-making bodies as the civilian strategists. There are important differences, however. Through their affiliation with research organizations set up to service decision-making bodies, the civilian strategists have had ready access to policy-makers through such devices as briefings. The "peace researcher" whose concern with international politics in most instances have been extraneous to his academic activities has been forced to legitimize his interest in policy matters and attempt to gain access to decision-makers by referring to his roles as a spokesman for a profession or a concerned citizenry.

These two groupings often view themselves as opposing camps not only by virtue of their divergent policy preferences but also in light of the different modes of interpretation they apply to phenomena on the international scene. The sociologists and psychologists have thus in many instances tried to meet what they see as the excessively abstract, logical, and hence "dehumanized" methods of analysis used by civilian strategists with behavioralistic concepts and theories which rest on other, usually implicit normative bases. The frequent interactions between these groups undoubtedly stem from these actual or perceived differences of opinion which have led their members to seek each other out as opponents in debates and discussions.

These networks can be viewed as forming the upper parts of a pyramidical structure when they are viewed in terms of the "size" of the policy issues with which they are concerned or of the level of the decision-making bodies which they have or would like to see as their audiences. As we move away from these, the policy issues involved tend to be fractionalized and the audiences become specialized departments and agencies, usually with operational as well as policy-making functions. On these levels it becomes much harder to establish clearcut networks. All we can hope to do here is to sketch some of the configurations that have been important in the postwar period.

Among the groupings that have had the military as their audience we find a number of social scientists engaged in producing knowledge with some relevance to the operations of U.S. military forces abroad. Most easily identified are those social scientists whose primary interest and skills lie in "area studies," in this case in those areas in which U.S. military forces are operating or may come to operate. An example of the type of knowledge that social scientists have produced for use in military operations abroad would be the Area Handbooks prepared for the Army. Although the major work on the handbooks was done in the Army's "captive" research organization, Special Operations Research Office (SORO), each handbook draws upon the knowledge of a particular "area community" whose members in most instances can be found in academic institutions.

Many social scientists with an area specialization, however, would not regard the particular "area network" to which they belong as their "primary reference-group." Instead, the area identification often becomes subsidiary to the overlay of conceptual schemes used in studying foreign areas, or to the operational problems on which the research is designed to throw light. The increasing prestige of "behavioralist" scientistic and quantitative approaches has made us particularly likely to talk about foreign area research as being "elite studies," or "cross-cultural communications research" rather than "Burmese studies" or "Vietnamese studies." But even among pursuers of more traditional forms of scholarship, we have seen ready abilities to switch from East

European specialization to studies of the Far East or Latin America when the latter areas gained greater topicality.

Among the networks that orient themselves toward military audiences, there are in addition and as an overlay to the area communities, a number of groupings engaged in research on the social, political and psychological aspects of certain types of military operations. The psychological warfare activities which have come to be regarded as an adjunct to military operations have been the focal point of a broadly based community which traces its roots back to the research activities of social scientists in government during the Second World War. The interest and skills that tie this community together lie in the field of communications research, propaganda analysis, and the techniques of persuasion and attitude change.

In most recent times "counterinsurgency" operations or "unconventional" warfare have emerged as labels for research activities covering a wide variety of subject matters. To a considerable extent, the social science interest in these topics stems from a concern with "lower levels of warfare" as alternatives to nuclear war. To the extent that research in this area has been designed to support planning and operations, it has concentrated on historical examples of insurgency and the processes and mechanisms whereby insurgency develops and is contained. The "counterinsurgency" label, however, has also provided a justification for research on such questions as how countries threatened by insurgency can be guided toward peaceful change and "stability" through the development of social and political institutions.

Among other networks with military audiences we find, also, the "military sociologists" who are concerned with the role of armed forces in society, not only in the United States but abroad as well. That the identification of so much of this work is with "sociology," rather than, say, with political science, reflects the occasional dependence of networks on the agency of one or two luminaries. The "military sociology" network in large measure owes its form, its growth and its close identification with the sociology discipline to the social and intellectual leadership of one individual. His identification with the field, in turn, is probably derivative from his early association with a leading political scientist. The latter would also figure centrally in a genetic tracing of several other important networks in the field of policy studies, as indeed, with the very term.

Specific methods, such as simulation or gaming, have formed the focal point of other groupings. In the military, simulation activities have centered on the Joint War Games Agency of the Joint Chiefs of Staff. In a survey of the use of simulation in the federal government, Bailey (IV.3, 1967: 9) finds that the exercises conducted by the agency mentioned above have had impact "on the highest levels of government and the greatest number of different agencies involved in international affairs."

A network which perhaps has entered into the most direct relationship with a military audience is represented by psychologists active in the field of "human engineering." Although there may be some overlap, the "human factors" researchers form a grouping apart from the foreign area research networks with which we are dealing here primarily as a result of their "man-machine" orientation. The decisions at which their research is aimed are the very "small" ones in the sense that they have little or no bearing on policy. Organizational connections between personnel and policy studies, however, have led to an occasional transfer of specialists between them.

Leaving military departments and agencies aside and looking instead at the Department of State and its various "satellites" (AID, ACDA, USIA, etc.), we find that these, with some exceptions, do not perform the same role as the military when it comes to guiding and stimulating social scientists specializing in foreign area research. The State Department's limited role in this respect has often been explained by the insurmountable difficulties it faces when trying to secure funds for a contract or grant research program. Much social science knowledge emanating from the academic community has certainly been pulled into the department—through the activities of the Office of External Research, for instance—but on the whole, its various research-oriented offices have not contributed significantly to the building of new networks or the restructuring of existing ones.[1]

Most of the social science knowledge that is taken into account by staffs of the State Department, therefore, must stem from sources such as those discussed earlier. Here we may surmise that the knowledge used by the Department of State has been primarily area knowledge of a more "traditional" type. By this we mean less of an emphasis on studies that use a behavioral framework to explain or interpret events on the international scene and more of a historical-descriptive type of analysis. To take specific examples, this would be the difference between George Kennan's writings on the Soviet Union and the Harvard University study on "How the Soviet System Works" sponsored by the Air Force.[2]

In this context, it seems desirable to establish some distinctions between the area knowledge produced through "intelligence research" and that emanating from the social sciences. Using the audience as a point of reference is not of much help here as the bodies that use the products of the social science community would in many instances also be users of intelligence reports. This is the case with the State Department, for example, where these two types of knowledge are merged in the organization—the Bureau of Intelligence and Research—charged with the "input" of knowledge in policy-making and operations.

As a general rule it seems that some distinction between research and intelligence can be established on the basis of methods and modes of analysis. On the whole, it would seem that the stress on explicitly defined systematic methods of observation and the use of concepts denoting generalized relationships which characterizes social science research is not characteristic of intelligence work. More important, however, the two communities are separated by institutional barriers which mark off the domain of intelligence. One of the difficulties that has faced government-supported research in foreign areas in the postwar period has been the effective limitation of studies that, because of their subject matter, have been considered as "intelligence" and hence outside the jurisdiction of governmental research agencies with social science programs. The most important distinction between the two communities is, of course, the nonpublic character of much of the work of the intelligence community and the fact that its products are rarely presented publicly for professional examination.

A grouping in the nonmilitary sphere which perhaps has been somewhat less visible in recent years as compared to the earlier part of the postwar period are the communications specialists engaged in gathering knowledge about foreign public opinion, especially as it relates to the United States policies and programs abroad. The major sponsor of this type of research has been the United States Information Agency. This agency is also the main audience for research evaluating the impact of American information and propaganda activities abroad. USIA polls, however, are used in

---

[1] See the discussion in the Editors' Introduction (p. 14) of the significance of the CIA in limiting the connections of the State Department with the research world.

[2] A very useful discussion of the community of "Sovietologists" which suggests structuring according to the approaches or the modes of interpretation used by writers in this field is found in Bell (V.2, 1962).

many other departments and agencies concerned with international policy and operations. The placement of the foreign interviewing survey responsibility of the government in its information agency may have severely hampered the extension of clienteles in this network. This possibility is suggested by imagining domestic interviewing surveys having remained the primary property of the mass media during the past 25 years (as they were at the time when polls were first used), rather than, as has been the case, their having expanded to where they are the most broadly used tool of the social sciences.

In important ways the "international communications" network has gone beyond the task of studying foreign public opinions. In the early postwar period there was considerable interest on the part of the members in this group in linking the study of international communications—not limited to mass-media but also taken to include "exchanges of persons" in the cultural, educational and scientific fields—with the reduction of world tension. This, for instance, was the thinking behind the large-scale UNESCO project on "Tensions Affecting International Understanding" initiated in 1947. In this respect, the "international communications" network may be viewed as one precursor of the "peace research" community which has appeared on the scene in recent years.

The main impetus for the upsurge of research activities in the field of "political warfare" in the fifties was the feeling among government officials that it was necessary to follow Communist propaganda activities closely and, if possible, find ways of counteracting them. By the same token, the leveling off of activities on the Communist propaganda front in recent years may be one of the reasons for what appears to be the diminishing role of this type of research. Another explanation may be a tendency on the part of the East-West conflict to evolve around issues or areas (e.g., the problem of deterring "wars of national liberation") where mass public opinion either does not exist or is not considered a major factor.

Let us finally make a brief reference to the network that has been formed around the problem of socio-political development in "underdeveloped" areas. This again is a group which draws heavily on the knowledge and skills of the various "area networks." It has emerged as a superstructure to a host of "area networks," however, as a result of its focus on the common problem of building socio-political institutions in these areas. To a significant degree the development of this area of research can be traced to a conscious decision on the part of one organization—the Committee on Comparative Politics of the Social Science Research Council—to support the development of knowledge in this particular field.

In summary, what makes us able to identify these networks in terms of audiences and operational problems? For one thing, an interest on the part of governmental planners or policy-makers in a certain area of research brings about a convergence of many disparate interests and strands of research in this general area. In the general field of communications research, for instance, we can notice how the label "psychological warfare research" came to be used as an "umbrella" covering a wide range of research activities and interests. We do not want to give the impression, however, that the relationship of government and the social science community is a unidirectional one with the social scientists on the receiving end. On the contrary, interest on the part of governmental agencies in a certain subject matter often stems from "missionary" activities by social scientists.

The existence of an audience in government for a certain type of knowledge often leads to the establishment of networks of communication between social scientists who otherwise would not be in contact with each other. Government interest and support leads to the creation of new forums in the form of symposia and seminars organized to facilitate interchange between social scientists and government officials. Often, however, the major function of these gatherings has been to promote contacts among social scientists. Bibliographies in the area of interest are also compiled and inventories of relevant research conducted. There is a need for social scientists who have received funds for research in the area and for those who are seeking support to keep in touch, if for no other reason than to avoid apparent duplication in their research efforts. In a very real sense, this is what makes it possible for us to talk about the formation of networks around certain problems of policy and operations.

ORGANIZATIONS PRODUCING RESEARCH

Researchers, Scholars and Policy Makers: The Politics of Large Scale Research

PETER H. ROSSI

INTRODUCTION

The campus of a major university was once marked by definite borders, on the one side of which were the distinctively academic buildings—dormitories, classrooms, libraries, laboratories and administrative buildings—and on the other side, the motley architecture of the town . . . . The concept of a Campus on which all academic activities take place within the distance that can be spanned easily on foot by students and professors has given way to a more diffuse spatial pattern in which classrooms, dormitories and libraries are still at the center[1] but in which the periphery occupied by institutes and centers is vaguely defined and discontinuous . . . .

The physical marginality of the new academic organizations reflects their academic marginality. Traditional university tables of organization lose their branching symmetry in attempts to place them in their proper places in chains of command, and university officials sometimes ignore them in the planning of university expansion, perhaps in the hope that if ignored they will vanish. Academic departments or schools to which the research centers may be attached are somewhat at a loss to deal with them, for the personnel of the centers and institutes are hard to assimilate into the rank and privilege systems of academia. The personnel of the centers are not quite sure of their identity, for on the one hand they are members of the university community, while on the other their major commitments are not to the teaching and training functions which are at the center of the university's activities.

. . . . In the modern sense . . . centers were first established by the natural sciences with the astronomical observatories representing the first of the structures to be physically separated from the central campus. In the empirical branches of the social sciences, . . . the precedents for research centers are now being established. Social science research centers are connected with almost every one of the major universities, the density varying from the proliferation on the Berkeley campus . . . to the sparser distribution at Johns Hopkins, where there are only one or two . . . .

The major concern of this paper will be with some of the organizational consequences of the development of research centers within the university environment. Properly to deal with this topic would require a breadth of knowledge which has yet to develop about how such centers are

---

• *Daedalus*, Vol. 93, No. 4: The Contemporary University: U.S.A., pp. 1142-1161. Reprinted by permission of the American Academy of Arts and Sciences, Boston, Mass., and the author.

[1] Classrooms and dormitories also mark the center of the spatial distribution of prestige, with research centers and institutes marking their importance to the university by how close they are to this center.

organized in a wide variety of fields.[1] I will be concerned primarily with the newer social science research centers, bringing in such information on other types of centers as is available in the very sparse literature on the organization of academic research, from direct knowledge of the few such research centers I have been able to visit and from the excellent survey of social research centers conducted by P. F. Lazarsfeld (III.1, 1961).

* * * * *

I. WHY RESEARCH CENTERS EVOLVED

The major missions of the first-rank university include both training and research. Since the establishment of graduate study in America and its diffusion to the major centers during the early part of this century, training has come to include both undergraduate and graduate instruction, and research has included both scholarly and laboratory activities.

There is no doubt that the amalgamation of training and research in the professorial role is an alloy at the same time beneficial to both activities, while tension-producing . . . .

The tensions between the somewhat contradictory activities of teaching and research have several sources. Within the professorial role the tensions are produced partly by the different phasings of the two activities: teaching demands that a set schedule of classes, seminars, etc., be met, while research has variable and unpredictable time demands . . . .

Within the organization of the university at the departmental level, the tensions are produced by other mechanisms. The allocation of authority within a department need only be extremely rudimentary as far as teaching goes. The basic unit of activity is the course, for which a professor is responsible and which is conducted essentially without supervision. The division of labor within a department centers around the curriculum in which responsibility for courses is allocated among department members . . . .

In contrast, research activity which involves more than the minimum division of labor between a scholar and his acolyte graduate students produces continual organizational tensions. Decisions have to be made continually, responsibilities for particular activities have to be allocated to different persons, men have to pace their work to the paces of others. There are strong strains to produce a bureaucratic organization for research activities in which there is a much more clear line of authority than is necessary for the teaching activities of a department.

The evolution of research centers can be seen as one attempt to solve by segregation the tensions between teaching and research: research institutes were to be the proper place for research and the departments to remain the proper place for teaching . . . .

Not all research activities lead to the establishment of centers and institutes. Research and scholarship in the more humanistic fields typically have not led to the establishment of centers and institutes, and those established have not been very long-lived . . . . The example of the humanities underscores the organizational imperatives that give rise to research centers in other fields . . . .

II. RESEARCH CENTERS IN THE SOCIAL SCIENCES

In the social sciences a good illustration of the organizational impetus toward the establishment of research centers is provided

---

[1] A literature concerning research centers has just started to develop, stemming in part from the needs of foundations, government agencies and universities to understand the intellectual implications of this organization of scientific activity. See, for example, Vollmer (VI, 1962).

by the development of sample surveys in the last two decades. One of the major research developments in the empirical social sciences has been the set of techniques which has enabled social scientists to gather their own data on a broad enough scale to make statements about significant segments of large scale societies at relatively reasonable costs....[1]

Properly accomplished, a sample survey is a large scale enterprise involving a fairly elaborate division of labor and using a considerable amount of resources. This is best exemplified in the two major academic survey centers, the Survey Research Center at the University of Michigan and the National Opinion Research Center at the University of Chicago, as well as the survey activities of the Bureau of the Census or some of the better commercial firms. It takes a combination of skills, ordinarily not residing in a single person, to conduct a large sample survey properly. Even smaller surveys (involving perhaps the sampling of a small city or neighborhood) can be carried out by a single person only in an inefficient manner.

* * * * *

Properly to conduct a survey, one needs to assemble at a minimum the following skills: (1) sampling; (2) questionnaire construction (an art perhaps rather than a skill); (3) interviewing; (4) data processing; and (5) statistical analysis. All of these would be needed to conduct a survey of an area larger than a small city or neighborhood.[2] To sample survey a population to which one ordinarily wants to generalize implies skills at a high enough level to require specialization. Furthermore, a large scale sample survey is expensive. Properly conducted national surveys (or for that matter, regional, state, or metropolitan surveys) collecting about 2,500 interviews of about an hour's length can cost anywhere between $50,000 and $125,000. Surveys of special populations (for example, chiropodists or college students) can cost more or less depending on the existence of reliable sampling frames for the populations in question.

Survey research did not develop initially within universities but was grafted onto them after it had passed through the critical periods of infancy. The National Opinion Research Center is still an independent corporation affiliated with the University of Chicago. Michigan's Survey Research Center was set up initially by a group of researchers who had worked together in a survey organization run by the Department of Agriculture during the forties....

Large scale research in the social sciences is no exception.... Large scale survey research in the universities is conducted by institutes and centers whose organizational principles involve a hierarchy of command and a distinct division of labor. Indeed, the larger the scale of research, the steeper the hierarchy and the more elaborate the division of labor. Thus the two university-affiliated centers which conduct national surveys (Michigan's Survey Research Center and Chicago's National Opinion Research Center) have more complex structures than that of the Bureau of Applied Social Research at Columbia or the Institute for Social Research at North Carolina, the scope of whose work is more restricted in scale.

Characteristically, institutes and centers have "directors" while departments have "chairmen," expressing in the titles of their chief administrative officers the greater authority of the one as compared with the other. Because of his greater authority the director's role is more critical to the proper functioning of a research center than a chair-

---

[1] For example, about one-third of the articles in the most recent two years of the major professional journals in sociology were based on surveys, outstripping by a good deal the employment of other methods.

[2] Institutionalized populations (e.g., students or soldiers) can be reached more easily, and hence surveys of such populations are favored by the social scientist working on his own.

man's role is to the prosperity of a department. A research center functions best when its director provides both intellectual and administrative leadership. It may have been the pious hope of university administrators as they allowed and in some cases fostered the establishment of research centers that the departmental organization and the institute organization could be integrated very closely. Indeed, the ideal pattern in some ideal sense might be one in which the personnel of a department and the personnel of an institute would be one and the same, and that while teaching courses, sociologists, for example, would run themselves along departmental organizational lines, and while doing research they would run themselves according to institute lines. In fact, this has never occurred. Rather, either the department has restructured itself along the hierarchial lines of the center (as was the case for Columbia's Department of Sociology) or the center never developed a good division of labor (as was the case for North Carolina's institute) or the two structures remained side by side with some overlap of personnel (as in the case of the Survey Research Center and the National Opinion Research Center) but with considerable tension between the two.

The strains against the amalgamation of these two types of organization arise out of the relatively greater demands for precise timing and phasing of activities that result from an elaborate division of labor . . . . Thus, within the institutes has developed a set of persons whose primary task is research, whose position within the academic community is ambiguous because they have only "courtesy" rank within the instructor-to-full-professor hierarchial order, and whose freedom to control their own activities is considerably less than those of departmental members.

* * * * *

There is little doubt that being a professor is more prestigeful than being a researcher. Tenure— . . . has not generally been extended to the institute personnel except on the highest level. Researchers' salaries have been generally higher for persons of the same age and academic accomplishments, but professors can and often do supplement their salaries from outside sources. Drawing a balance, it appears as if the professor has the edge; he has the higher prestige, the greater security, the greater freedom, and sometimes, through his outside activities, the greater income.

In fact, it now appears that there have grown up two distinct career lines—that of researcher and that of professor—with relatively little interchange between the two occupations. If one follows the researcher line, one ends up a second-class citizen in the university community; if one follows the professor line, one ends up a first-class citizen but restricted in the scope of the research in which one can engage. This accounts for much of the low quality of research reported in the professional social science journals. The individual scholar working on his own cannot command the kinds of skill that make for a first-rate piece of research. This also accounts for the oft-noted tendency on the part of academicians to start up their own research centers to increase their scope and power while looking upon the similar activities of their colleagues as academic imperialism.

Although the full-time personnel of a research center may not have the same psychic and sometimes monetary rewards of the members of the professoriat, there are advantages to full-time membership which in time may outweigh disadvantages. At its best functioning, the research center can multiply by some factor the efforts of a researcher, raising his work productivity as well as its quality. More than one better-than-average social scientist has been raised to the level of first-rank social scientist because he has had at his command the facilities and organization that a large scale research center represents . . . .

Although the community of social scientists does not yet have the extensive character reported by Holton (VI, 1962) in which collaboration in the writing of an article may be the joint work of as many as ten different individuals from several institutions and two or three countries, social science research is beginning to take on more and more of a cooperative slant. I surmise that the advantages of collaboration and close contact will become more obvious when the social scientists have more in the way of specialization in knowledge. At the present time, there is hardly a subfield of sociology and social psychology in which a good social scientist could not pick up as much detailed knowledge as the prime experts in that subfield to write an acceptable proposal to a grant-giving agency. When almost everybody knows as much as everyone else (or could know it easily) the benefits of collaboration are not as obvious as in the case when knowledge from one subfield could materially advance the progress of work in another.

III. THE FINANCING OF LARGE SCALE RESEARCH

Large scale research in any field is expensive whenever it requires an extensive division of labor (as is the case for most social science research) and/or large capital investments in equipment. Unlike research in the humanities, in which continuing support is provided by the capital investment represented by a library collection and by regular allocation provided in the university budgets, other types of research tend to be financed on a project-by-project basis.

In empirical social research the *ad hoc* nature of financial support has important implications for the kinds of research that can be conducted and the kinds of personnel who can be attracted to research centers. Surveys on any appreciable scale are quite expensive. Furthermore, such research has grown increasingly expensive as its technology becomes more complex and as survey researchers demand more and more precision from their data . . . . (Price, VI, 1963.) For example, the best known of the National Opinion Research Center's studies, the 1947 study of the prestige of occupations, cost a little more than $9,000 to conduct. We are presently conducting another study on this topic for which we have received a grant of more than $150,000 . . . .

. . . . One of the important consequences is that few individual researchers can command enough in the way of resources to mount an extensive survey operation . . . . In departmental research courses, graduate students are being taught how to do research in ways which their teachers themselves are unable to follow. Professors eye with some envy the large project budgets of the research centers, which are put at the disposal of persons often junior to them in status.

The most important implication of the high cost of surveys is that there are only a limited number of sources from which sums on this scale can be obtained, and the purposes for which such funds are given are limited in a peculiar sense . . . . Hence large scale survey research is generally "applied" social research; that is to say, the grantor is convinced that the results will have some immediate bearing on policy formation. The high cost of social research has meant a close tie with the machinery of policy making.

Some specific examples may help to illustrate dramatically what this implies for large scale research. At NORC we have developed a fairly strong program of research into the related areas of manpower and higher education, support for which comes primarily from the National Science Foundation and the National Institutes of Health. One of our studies involves a longitudinal study of the June, 1961 graduating classes of American universities and colleges. In 1961 we sampled that year's crop of new Bachelors for the purpose of studying how this group found their niches in the occupational world. The interest of the sponsoring agencies, in this case the National Institutes of Health, the National Science Foundation and the Office of Education, was quite clear and direct: they were concerned about the impact of federal scholarship and fellowship policies on postgraduate training and how such policies might be changed to channel more of the talented into postgraduate training leading into critical scientific and professional niches. Spread over a period of five years, the total sum allocated to this project is half a million dollars. Two of these agencies are supporting a replication of this study on June, 1964 graduates, and I predict that we may be conducting such studies on a periodic basis in the future. . . .

. . . . [T]he initiative for the[se] studies came from the sponsors and they have taken a strong interest in their outcomes. The consequence of this pattern of research support is that if one wants to study a particular subject, one has to find some foundation, agency or person with a direct interest in the outcome of the study and with some understanding of and concern with social research. . . .

. . . [Not] all of the work of the large scale survey centers is applied. . . . Each manages to get some projects sponsored which are of no particular applied interest whatsoever, although it must be admitted that this happens infrequently and usually involves research on a lesser scale.[1] At least as important is the process of broadening applied interests to cover research topics of considerable intensive interest but only indirectly related to each applied interest. For example, there are probably no funds available to study directly the supply of humanists mentioned earlier. NORC did get a considerable amount of money to study recruitment to the physical, biological and social sciences, engineering, medicine and education. However, we are *also* studying recruitment to the humanities because we were able to convince the clients that it was more expensive for technical reasons to restrict the research only to those who might go into the "hard science" fields . . . .

What I have just described might be called passive "robinhooding"—as some researcher facetiously named the broadening of objectives of a policy-oriented sponsor to include concerns which are of intrinsic interest but for which no funded (or vested) interest is likely to be found to supply support. There is also the active type of robinhooding, in which one starts out with an objective of some intrinsic interest and then fits it to the applied interest of some agency or foundation. NORC's study of the career plans and aspirations of the June, 1961 graduates grew in part out of a long standing interest in measuring the productivity of colleges and universities as affected by their organizational characteristics. Robinhooding in both its passive and active forms leads to considerable tension between the policy maker and the researcher. On the one hand it looks as if the researcher is hoodwinking the policy maker; on the other hand it can be viewed as a process of bargaining in which the research center agrees to do something in return for support to do something else in addition. Incidentally, it often turns out that in the end the policy maker is quite pleased with the results of the extended study, perhaps more than he would be if he were given only that which he wanted originally.

In the negotiations between the researcher and the policy maker, there is an important weapon in the hands of the researcher—his technical expertise often puts the policy maker at a disadvantage. In the end, technical considerations must override other considerations if research of any great scientific stature is to appear. Indeed, one of the major reasons why government agencies come to the universities rather than to the commercial firms is that we are more con-

---

[1] In recent years, the establishment of a Social Science Division within the National Science Foundation and behavioral research study sections within the National Institute of Mental Health has increased considerably the amount of funds available for basic social research.

cerned with technical purity than are the latter. Incidentally, when the market researchers and the advertising agencies want to have something that literally will stand up in court, they also come to the academic research organizations.

* * * * *

The financing of large scale social research has put a distinct advantage into the hands of those social scientists who have affiliated themselves to the social research institutes. Foundations and government agencies properly conceive of such organizations as having better capabilities to carry through such research, and more of a sense of responsibility to carry them through. But there are disadvantages as well. Large scale social research is likely to have an applied emphasis, and worthy research endeavors may go unsponsored . . . .

IV. IMPLICATIONS FOR THE CONTEMPORARY UNIVERSITY

The basic structure of American universities scarcely has had a chance to react and accommodate to the great development of research activities within the university in the past forty years, and virtually no time at all to adjust to the growth of social science research in the two decades since World War II. The final pattern of accommodation has probably not yet appeared . . . .

* * * * *

It is hard to judge whether research activities unduly intrude upon the teaching function or whether it enriches teaching. Certainly the faculty member who is wrapped up in his research may not be able to spend the time necessary to prepare lectures which are of the highest quality, but his lectures may have the benefit of being more up-to-date and alive because his research is on the frontiers of the field in which he is teaching. Perhaps the most serious inroad upon the university arises out of the rise of research as an alternative to entering upon a career of academic statesmanship. Departmental chairmanships appear to be going begging and on occasion few candidates have appeared as contenders for deanships . . . .

The teaching of graduate students appears to me to have benefited considerably from the development of research in the university. No longer is the dissertation the sole research experience of the new Ph.D. . . .

It is more difficult to discern the trends concerning the roles of professor and of researcher. On the one hand there are strong trends toward the amalgamation of the two roles, with research institutes becoming more intimately parts of the university community. On the other hand, the trend toward research activities on larger scales and involving larger sums produces a strain toward the development of quite separate research organizations . . . .

It is hard to predict the specific form that the status of researcher will take in the evolving university structure. Perhaps the recent rashes of appointments of persons to "research professorships" presages the future position.[1] Or it may be the case that research institutes will develop into entities like departments, with complements of tenure positions to bestow. Whatever specific organizational forms will arise . . . the American university will be profoundly affected by massive changes in the definition of the professorial role and perhaps even in the definition of the goals of the university community . . . .

[1] The University of Chicago has evolved a new status—Professorial Lecturer—to be held by persons with primarily research appointments who are so senior in accomplishment that they cannot be left out of the academic rank system. However, this new status does not involve the critical issue of assimilation of researchers into the university, their participation as voting members in departmental decisions.

Values and Organization in a University Social Research Group

WARREN G. BENNIS

The structure of social research has undergone some remarkable changes, especially since the end of World War II. Research organizations have grown up in which teams of social scientists from varying disciplines work on common problems.... Accompanying the development of large-scale and programmatic research, there has been another, though perhaps less obvious change, a shift of values among social scientists toward acceptance of a purposive orientation which has broadened the social role of the man of knowledge. Nothing testifies to this change better than the contrasts in criticism between social critics of the 1930's and present day writings on methodology and aims in social science.[1]

* * * * *

These developments have created fairly significant changes in the role and values of the modern social scientist, and it is the main task of this paper to suggest some of the consequences of these developments.

The present study was undertaken in the belief that a start should be made towards analysis of the special problems of the research social scientist by a careful study of an organized group which has as its special function the production of new knowledge. Hence, for a period of fifteen months, a social science research organization located at a university and financed largely by a foundation was examined intensively. Each of the social scientists—twenty economists and fifteen "behavioral scientists" (psychologists, sociologists, and political scientists)—was interviewed by the author at least twice and co-operated in filling out various questionnaires and cartoon completion tests. One of the chief goals of the research organization, which will be called "the Hub," was to offer social scientists the opportunity to influence the nature of U. S. foreign policy by analyzing problems strategic to our government's role in world politics. Thus its main activity centers around international affairs and economic development. The case approach, of course, limits the degree of generality that can be made for the study....

THE HUB SOCIAL SCIENTIST

A Fortune magazine survey of 104 "top scientists" showed that 75 per cent of the sample felt "scholarly training and status carry with them a responsibility to be particularly well informed on world affairs"; and 75 per cent thought that only 1 or 2 per cent of present day scientists were as uninformed as Oppenheimer was during his

• *American Sociological Review*, Vol. 21, 1956, pp. 555-563. Reprinted by permission of the American Sociological Association and the author.

[1] For the difference between the 1930 worldview on the application of social sciences and the present, see Lynd (I, 1948: 6-7); and Parrington (VI, 1930: xxvii). For recent criticisms see, among others, Hacker (VI, 1954); Lee (VI, 1954); Riesman (VI, 1951: 101); Rose (VI, 1954).

younger days (Bello, VI, 1954: 143). These data corroborate the general sentiment found among Hub social scientists: a firm involvement with world issues and policy. For example, to the question, "Was there a specific interest or incident which drew you to your field?" ten of the thirty-five staff members mentioned the 1930 Depression and/or improving world conditions. (Over half of the Hub personnel were adolescents during the years of the Depression.) And when asked their opinion about the following statement, "As a social scientist you will soon welcome—as facilitating scholarship and reflection—the customary isolation of the American scholar from responsibility and policy," only 13.3 per cent considered it a valid statement. If political activity can be judged an index of social consciousness and responsibility, all but 8.8 per cent of Hub staff members considered themselves as followers of a political point of view: 53.3 per cent Democrats, 32.4 per cent "Independents," 2.9 per cent Republicans, and 2.9 per cent Progressives.

In addition to this purposive orientation the Hub social scientist is a participating member of an organization. Involvement in an organization commits the Hub scientist even further to the "real world," for an organization manifests loyalties, competition, hierarchies, co-operation, conflicts, and above all a web of complicated relationships among individuals . . . . [H]e seems to be involved in three worlds, a set of concentric circles: the academic world with the traditional demands of scholarship and detachment, an organizational world which includes loyalties and attachments, a policy world which includes action-research and a purposive orientation.

In order to cope with this complex of problems, the Hub social scientist has had to emulate, to some extent, the businessman. This is due partly to the nature of the research undertaken, as well as to the diverse relationships the Hub has to maintain with important organizations, such as the users of research, sponsors, the university, other research organizations, etc. The Hub researcher is a particularly busy man and, unlike his forebears in social science research, cannot relax in the "armchair." His main research concerns foreign lands in delicate balance vis-à-vis the United States and with functioning organizations of all kinds, e.g. government bureaus, factories, newspapers, etc. Interpersonal responsibilities are a part of the daily routine. One project, for example, spends 10 per cent of the average work-day "taking care of visiting firemen." About 25 per cent of the time is spent on non-task matters for the entire staff, while the project directors divide their time equally between direct research and organizational and administrative matters. This past year a good deal of time was spent preparing research proposals for the Foundation. Here the research man had to balance budgets, predict whether or not County X will be under one or another party influence at a certain time, choose personnel, and come up with a financial request.

As has been indicated, the social scientist has to engage in an interpersonal windmill partly because of the nature of research. A good deal of research entails subject-interviewing. Here he has to "establish rapport." At times the research cannot begin until a foreign country has, so to speak, "warmed up to it" . . . . [G]ood research may even hinge on favorable relations with foreign representatives. For example, a staff member spent several days in Washington for the express purpose of developing a favorable relationship with members of a foreign delegation.

These pressures have a direct effect on the social scientist . . . . As one project director put it:

"I confess to slight neglect of my own staff for my own administrative needs. It isn't only directing a team, but this peculiar organization has to develop public relations and persuasion . . . particularly with X government, its delegation in New York and Washington, the FOA, X country's desk at State, with other research organizations, with big business interested in X country, with the Chamber of Commerce, with the Colombo Plan organization, all of which individually make quite good sense, but putting them all together, it's extraordinarily time-consuming. There is no other problem equal to the organizational demands made on your time."

Another effect of this large-scale approach to social science research has created a new type of academic contribution. In many seminars one or two members will play the "contact" man or "big operator." They will say, "Now I know where we can get two people working on that and it won't cost us a penny. They're working on a problem similar to ours for X Foundation, and they'd be happy to do that for us if we asked a couple of questions on our questionnaire for them" .... Thus, the "contact" man attains status and makes a contribution on a non-theoretical, but nevertheless, important academic level.

That the Hub placed enormous and complex demands on the researcher was shown in response to the first question on the interview schedule, "As you see it, what are the three main problems of research here at the Hub?" The following table summarizes the responses in terms of five categories.

"What are the three main problems?"

Organizational	53
External	52
Substantive	29
Bureaucratization	27
Interpersonal	25
Total problems	186

1. *Organizational problems* include items on leadership, interdisciplinary research, and organization of research.

* * * * *

2. *External problems* consist of items such as "financing," "stability of Hub," and other diverse exogenous demands from the Foundation or other research organizations. Examples of this response are:

"The main problem is the *ad hoc* year-to-year financing which kicks continuity in the pants.

I would say that in our project we have to slowly cultivate good public relations in order to obtain data. We have to operate in the public relations area."

3. *Substantive problems* include items such as formulation of the research problem, availability of data, library facilities, etc. An example of this response is the following:

"My main problem is no one at the Hub is interested in X area. Consequently I have to go to X University or use correspondence which is usually unsatisfactory. Thus I don't go to seminars or meetings very often."

4. *Bureaucratization problems* are those factors dealing generally with the constriction of research creativity as a result of organizational sanctions. The following is an example:

* * * * *

"The basic problem here is how to administer an integrated program of research so it forms a complete mosaic and design without restricting the freedom of each man to pursue the ideas that are important."

5. *Interpersonal problems* consist of statements on communication, lack of autonomy, too much secrecy, low morale, bad relations with project director and/or colleagues. The following is an example:

"Any organization which has grown as rapidly as this suffers from a lack of communication. No one cares about my work—the air of coziness and 'how is your work coming along?' is completely gone. The organization has changed completely and I deplore the present size. It's grown too fast and big."

We can see from the above table how the problems of the Hub personnel are reflected in a variety of areas. A frequency distribution of the number of personnel selecting various categories shows that over 60 per cent of the personnel mentioned at least one organizational problem; about 47 per cent, academic and substantive matters; and under 40 per cent, interpersonal affairs. The new role of the social scientist then, is the product of divided loyalties and sometimes conflicting institutional demands. In view of this, let us ask two interrelated questions: How does the social scientist perceive the route to success? How does he propose getting there?

WHICH WAY IS UP

There are at least three institutional paths of mobility at the Hub: academic, government, and organizational. To get some idea of the desired aims of the staff, the following question was asked in order to force individuals to choose one, and only one, career pattern:

If you had to restrict your choice to one, which of the following careers would you choose? (Assume all these jobs are available; assume the salaries are the same.)

1. Top administrative job in government
2. Top executive job in industry
3. Professorship in first rate academic institution with no research opportunities
4. Senior research appointment in first rate institution with no teaching opportunities
5. Director of intellectual organization with no teaching, but an admixture of administration and research

Table 1 shows the results. Notice first that the construction of choices was so frustrating for four respondents that, against

TABLE 1. Restricted Choice of Careers* in Percentages†

	N	Total (34)	Age Groups			Economists (18)	Behavioral Scientists (16)
			20-34 (16)	35-39 (10)	40-54 (8)		
Professor in first rate academic institution with no research opportunities		38.2	37.5	50.0	25.0	33.3	43.7
Senior research appointment in first rate academic institution with no teaching opportunities		26.5	25.0	20.0	37.5	22.2	31.3
Director of intellectual organization, no teaching but mixture of administrative research		23.5	31.2	10.0	25.0	33.3	12.5
Combination of research and teaching		11.8	6.3	20.0	12.5	11.2	12.5
Total		100.0	100.0	100.0	100.0	100.0	100.0

* "Top administrative job in government" and "Top executive job in industry" were not chosen.
† No differences are significant at the .05 level. This, of course, is to be expected with so few cases.

instructions, they felt compelled to write in "Combination of research and teaching." No one at the Hub could be tempted by a top administrative post in government or industry. A Professorship in a first rate institution appeared to be the choice of almost 40 per cent of the Hub staff with votes split between Director of intellectual organization and Senior Researcher. Notice that the behavioral scientists were less enthusiastic about the former (the Directorship) with only 12.5 per cent choices compared to 33.3 per cent economist choices. Also 25 per cent of the 40-54 age group chose Director of intellectual organization as compared to 10 per cent of the 35-39 age group. In addition, 50 per cent of the 35-39 group checked Professorship compared to the Hub mean of 38.2 per cent.

These facts hold meaning for much of what follows. First, the age group 35-39 is generally at a crucial career phase. A professorship, tantamount to a permanent university post, remains the single most important goal. Charles Morris, the University of Chicago social philosopher, made the following statement after analyzing "Paths of Life" data on the Hub staff:

". . . Your results for the age 35-39 group are interesting. Psychologically that is a very stressful age. The person is old enough to know what he can do in the work he has chosen, and yet must decide if he is content to settle down in that work for a lifetime. There is often a tendency to rebel (at least inwardly) and to wish to relax and enjoy life more."[1]

[1] David Riesman's adaptation of Charles Morris' "Ways to Live" was used here. This consists of seven ideal types of living based on specific philosophic and religious doctrines. They range from hedonism to Buddhism. Each Hub social scientist was asked to rank them in order of the kind of life "you personally want to live." These data were compared with a sample of more than 2000 college students collected by Morris. See Riesman (VI, 1952: 181–184); and Morris (VI, 1948: Chapter IV).

Second, the behavioral scientists tended to be less enthusiastic about a Directorship—an administrative or policy position—than the economists. We can say with some degree of certainty that the economists, as later becomes more evident, are willing to engage in active policy work for extended time periods. Again quoting Charles Morris' interpretation of the "Paths of Life" data:

"I found the comparison of economists and non-economists of greatest interest. The economists seemed to be definitely more conservative, group oriented, control-oriented than the non-economists—who show more inwardness and self-direction, and who are much more sympathetic with persons as persons but less group oriented."

Table 2 is a compilation of responses to

TABLE 2. Goals: What Do You Expect To Be Doing in Five Years?

	Number of Responses
1. Job	
Government—contribution to public life	6
Teach plus some research	11
Do research plus some teaching	3
Teach	4
Write alone	2
Other	4
Total	30
2. Intellectual	
Merge economic development and human welfare	5
Make solid academic contribution	4
Other	3
Total	12
3. Organizational	
Field work and travel	7
Want to be in academic environment	11
In New England or California	2
Good economics department	2
Sizeable amount of money for research	2
Other	1
Total	25
Total responses	67*

* Thirty-four members of the Hub responded to this question with one or more goals.

the question, "What do you expect to be doing or want to be doing five years from now?" Note that thirty of these goal responses deal with *actual jobs* such as "contribution to public life" (government), twelve with *intellectual goals* such as "combining social psychology with international relations," and twenty-five responses on *organizational prerequisites* such as "provides field work and travel."

How can these data be interpreted in view of the ideas set forth earlier concerning the role ambivalence of the Hub social scientist? First, there is less emphasis on intellectual goals *per se,* more on organizational and job prerequisites. Second, virtually all individuals desire the combination of teaching *plus* some research. Third, all six individuals who chose government service were economists, which suggests again that this professional group has less conflict about work in the public policy area. As one economist put it:

"The kind of career I want is one where I can apply the best analytical thought process to economic policy. We haven't an elite in our society. We, as intellectuals, have to translate and communicate to the action-man."

In large part this response was typical of other economists at the Hub.

* * * * *

Perhaps due to the great influence of economists in government planning and availability of career opportunities in national and international economic organizations, their adaptation to a policy-making role is the least difficult.[1]

Whether or not the Hub itself was viewed as the specific organization destined to fulfill member five-year-goals was shown in response to the question, "Do you expect to be here in five years?" Most generally the answers were related to age. Nine individuals looked upon the Hub as a permanent post, i.e. they had no immediate plan for looking elsewhere. All of these subjects were either project directors or senior researchers, mostly in the 35-39 age group. On the other hand nine individuals (all in the 20-34 age group) viewed the Hub more transiently as a place where they would have time to write or finish their doctoral dissertations. Corroboration of this last point appears in responses to a cartoon completion test used in this study.[2]

Of the seventeen individuals who completed the speaker's statement in Cartoon 1 [(". . . in the past year, three of our young men have . . .")],* only three implied that the young man would remain at the Hub. Ten of the total responses designated that the way up is getting out of the organization. This supports other data on physical research laboratories which show that the university laboratory was used as a training center, a sort of "supergraduate school," helpful for many young men as a stepping stone for their careers (Shepard, VI, 1954). The Hub appears to fulfill this function for many of its younger staff members. Seven individuals responded that "three of our young men" have published articles or obtained a professorship, etc.; i.e. the way up is seen through the typical academic and in-

---

[1] Perhaps Lord Keynes represents the "ego ideal" for the economists. To a question on "heroes," a significantly greater proportion of economists chose men-of-action relative to the behavioral scientists. The triumvirate of Lincoln-Churchill-Roosevelt captured well over 50 percent of the total choices for the economists. Keynes, incidentally, was selected by seven of the economists. Heroes of the behavioral scientists included more

introverted or aesthetic or "altruistic" individuals. Ghandi, Einstein, and Schweitzer received the bulk of the non-economist choices. Lincoln received the highest number of choices from the entire Hub with a total of fourteen.

[2] Eighteen cartoons, two of which are shown here, were used in the larger study.

* Cartoon 1, omitted here, shows an older, bespectacled executive sitting at his desk, talking to a young man—presumably a prospective new member of the staff—and telling him about the opportunities the organization offers. *Eds.*

tellectual channels; six individuals mentioned industry as a source of advancement.

* * * * *

WHAT DOES IT TAKE TO GET UP?

In order to elicit the Hub researchers' attitudes toward the strategy of getting ahead, the following question was asked, "What words of advice or counsel would you give to a young Ph.D. just beginning his or her career?"[1] In Table 3 we see the results categorized into four rubrics: Intellectual and Task Skills, Personal Values, Strategic Skills, and Job Orientation.

TABLE 3. Words of Counsel

1. Intellectual and Task Skills	
Interdisciplinary skills	9
Learn math and/or physics	6
Study, read, get facts	4
Work hard	4
Combine fact and theory	3
Other	4
Total	30
2. Personal Values	
Be adventurous, take chances	4
Self-fulfillment	3
Broad outlook	2
Be kind, humble, respect others	2
Talk straight, forget jargon	2
Be objective, analytic	2
Intellectually honest	2
Other	2
Total	19
3. Strategic Skills	
Publish	6
Know right people	4
Social skills	2
Other	1
Total	13
4. Job Orientation	
Teach	5
Specialize	3
Other	3
Total	11

The need for interdisciplinary skills, as Table 3 shows, was considered highly important: "interdisciplinary skills," "combining fact and theory," and "broad outlook" make up about 20 per cent of the total (73) pieces of counsel. Second, notice under the Intellectual Skills category that six individuals emphasized the learning of mathematics or physics. With one exception, they were all economists.

* * * * *

The Hub staff member frequently had considerable and understandable difficulty in response to this question. He invariably felt that the "words of counsel" would differ, depending upon the individual. Consequently, the responses were often made in terms of two types of individuals: advice for the bright one and the mediocre one, for the theorist and the empiricist, etc.

Responses to Cartoon 2 corroborate the themes observed in the "words of advice."[*] Here the emphasis is on the determinants of colleague respect.

Of the total twenty-seven categorizable statements, sixteen dealt with *interpersonal relations,* nine with *intellectual* task concerns, and two with *organizational* matters. The following are examples in each category:

Interpersonal Relations:
That you can't criticize the boss even behind his back. Everything always gets back to everybody.
To communicate, co-operate, and be less suspicious.
To be a good joe, take a coffee break like everybody else, relax.

Intellectual-Task:
Know something more about the problem-setting which characterizes other disciplines than his own. It's really difficult for him to undertake criticism of work outside his field,

---

[1] This question was based on one which was asked of all living presidents of the American Sociological Society. See "Presidential Advice to Younger Sociologists" (VI, 1953).

[*] Cartoon 2, omitted here, shows three men having coffee, with one of them saying, "Yeah, but he'll never gain the respect of his colleagues until he learns. . . ." *Eds.*

as he does, until he gains some understanding of what these other disciplines are trying to find out—on what techniques and assumptions they are based.

Organizational:
To organize and delegate the work.

In the interpersonal area the chief response was a combination of "talking too much" or "too soon" and "dogmatic in approach." This response accounted for 56 per cent of the total. The main factor in the intellectual-task area (55 per cent) was the need for careful economic analysis and rigor.

Thus, the "words of counsel" and Cartoon 2 underline the multi-responsible role of the new social scientist as we have observed him at the Hub. In order to gain success, he must perform a juggling act of prodigious difficulty: the balancing of rigorous intellectual skills with political skills, important personal values with a practical job orientation.

We have seen in the past two decades, and particularly since World War II, the rise of a new social organization: groups of social scientists from varying disciplines at programmatic work on practical and urgent problems. And when a project is undertaken by a group rather than an individual, methodologically appropriate rules of social behavior have to be found and formulated. The modern man of social knowledge, if the Hub is at all typical is grappling with these new norms and demands and, ultimately, values. Historically, the scientist has been responsible to one audience: a body of colleagues who represent an intellectual reference group. Today, the Hub social scientist is like a three-headed Janus facing outward: to the intellectual audience, which makes ever more elegant demands in terms of the current trend toward precision and positivism; to the research organization which imposes on the social scientists the need for interpersonal skills; and lastly, to the public, users and sponsors of research whose support is desperately needed if the social scientist is to continue his quest for a better world.

The Utilization of Social Scientists in the Overseas Branch of the Office of War Information

LEONARD W. DOOB

Many social scientists employed by the government or in the armed services during the war found their research and scientific wisdom not eagerly accepted, wisely interpreted, or sensibly followed by policy-makers. Unlike some of the old-line departments, the war agencies had no established procedure for utilizing social science. Social scientists had a place on the ever-changing organization charts, sometimes merely because it was somewhat vaguely felt that all kinds of brains, even academic, were necessary to win a total war. Often they had to carve out for themselves the specific rôles they wished to play. They functioned, not in accordance with the charts, but within . . . informal organizations of their own making.

In many situations, there was a discrepancy between what social scientists thought they could do and what the policy-makers were prepared to let them do. Some sought deliberately to bridge the gap by promoting and marketing their disciplines and themselves. Like their colleagues in the natural sciences, they wished to be consulted when problems involving their own expertness were involved.

The informal techniques that social scientists employed in behalf of social science

• *The American Political Science Review*, Vol. 41, 1947, pp. 649-667. Reprinted by permission of the American Political Science Association and the author.

and themselves are worth recording because certainly similar ones must often be utilized whenever social scientist meets policy-maker . . . .

What follows in this article is a necessarily abbreviated case history of the writer's experience in one war agency. It is deliberately somewhat autobiographical, so that the raw materials may be presented as concretely as possible. Naturally, the social-science demands of the Overseas Branch of the Office of War Information were not typical, nor does this writer—a psychologist —claim to represent anyone except himself . . . .

I. TYPES OF RESEARCH

By executive order, the Overseas Branch of the Office of War Information—as distinguished from the better known but smaller Domestic Branch—was the government agency charged during the last war with responsibility for transmitting official American propaganda to enemy countries and for disseminating "information" in the name of the United States to allied and neutral countries outside the Western hemisphere. Within an active theater of operations, this responsibility was shared with military and naval authorities and sometimes taken over by them. Every conceivable vehicle of communication was employed, extending from a short-, medium-, or long-wave radio program to a lecturer on American literature in one of the British Dominions, or from a slick magazine to a greeting from the American people printed on a soap wrapper. Concealed or "black propaganda" (like rumor-spreading) did not concern the OWI, since all of its "white propaganda" and information were clearly labelled as coming from this country.

In the accepted jargon of government, a sharp distinction was drawn and actually existed between policy-makers and operators. A policy-maker contributed to the formulation of a propaganda directive or criticized propaganda output before or after its dissemination. Propaganda directives of the OWI were written in Washington with or without the help of other government agencies, but they became official government policy only after being approved by the Department of State and the War and Navy Departments. An operator, on the other hand, "implemented" the directives through one of the communication media. At all times his production was "controlled" —or was supposed to be controlled by policy-makers or their representatives.

Research in the Overseas Branch was divided into three types: policy, operations, and background. Policy research, which was almost always classified as secret or confidential, consisted of facts and generalizations which helped policy-makers write directives for countries that were, or might eventually be, reached by the OWI's propaganda. The "state of morale" in Germany and Japan, for example, was frequently assayed; obviously, it was said, one kind of propaganda is needed for people with a high morale and a different kind for those whose morale is sinking. Operational research, which was never classified, contained facts or pseudo-facts of interest to operators. If a directive commanded that the people of one country be told that Germany's morale was high or low, a research group uncovered items allegedly demonstrating the Reich's mental state. Background research, which was either restricted or not classified at all, fell somewhere in between, but generally strove to increase the insight of operators.

The research resulted in reports that varied in length from a sentence to a volume. The size of an obscure town or the latest propaganda line employed by Radio Tokyo was determined in response to a face-to-face, telephoned, teletyped, telegraphed, cabled, or radioed request. At the other extreme were weekly reports analyzing significant events inside a country, often with the aid of tables and graphs indicating the frequency with which a given propaganda theme was being employed on the radio, in the press, or by both. Then facts were merely assembled in a form convenient for operators; for example, there was a daily publication listing, under convenient rubrics, quotations from foreign journalists and newscasters which could be incorporated into feature stories or radio scripts. Some intricate research also was carried on, such as an anthropologist's attempt to delineate the character structure of a few countries on the basis either of prisoner-of-war interrogations or of interviews conducted with scattered informants residing in the United States.

The OWI's research cannot easily be classified as belonging to one rather than another social science. In fact, it may be seriously questioned whether much of it had anything at all to do with social science, unless social science be defined broadly as simple fact-gathering about people. From a social-science viewpoint, the problem for policy research was real enough, since it was always a variant of one of the following questions: what is happening inside a particular country, what are the people doing and thinking, what are the leaders plotting and planning? The answers to such questions, however, required adequate data before any social science could be systematically employed. Such data were lacking. Often fairly important reports existed, but, because they were of necessity highly classified and/or came from other agencies and governments with which effective liaison was gradually established, they could be distributed only to a few key researchers. The OWI never developed its own intelligence-gathering facilities overseas, even in countries where the people themselves could have been studied. Other agencies asserted that this was their function, although they seldom discharged it satisfactorily.... One top social scientist was able to recruit an excellent staff to do research in one of the liberated countries, but soon after he had completed some first-rate reports a quarrel with the commanding officer of the military group under whom he worked in that theater brought the entire project to an end. In a sense, too, the OWI's inability to secure the information it needed resulted from the scattering, both in Washington and abroad, of research related to propaganda and information and of competent personnel.

By and large, therefore, it can be said that the data at hand secured all the analysis they deserved. Sometimes, in fact, the analysis was too refined and represented a deductive leap into the unknown, motivated by the social scientist's desire to use his social science or by his impulse to compete with journalists on their own terms. Far too many risky and dogmatic inferences concerning the state of morale in enemy countries, for example, were made on the basis of radio transcripts and newspapers simply because these data were at hand by the train-load. What was seldom done was to pool the available data and information of all experts in order to determine systematically—in terms of social-science principles—how people might respond to propaganda. Instead, the easier and quicker solution was simply to consult one of the self-styled or recognized experts concerning the desirability of the propaganda innovation. This was a hit-and-miss approach in a situation in which no one except an omniscient deity will ever know in detail what hit and what missed. The social scientist could not protest, inasmuch as his own position was too vulnerable; if he talked in terms of principles or theories, he ran the risk of being called a "professor" and of delaying fast-moving operations.

II. ADMINISTRATIVE ORGANIZATION

Research was permitted within the Overseas Branch because each policy-maker and operator in his own way paid lip-service to "facts" and was convinced that someone ought to collect and perhaps analyze them. Journalists, cooped up in an office or an army establishment, were worried because the conditions of war prevented them from running down the facts; they looked upon research workers as glorified, if not qualified, "leg-men" for a city editor. Men from the fields of advertising and radio had previously grown accustomed to some type of market research to bolster their intuition and they claimed they needed a substitute. There was always the feeling that the OWI, young and lusty though it was, deserved its own research organization equally with its occasional rival, the Office of Strategic Services, or like the big, mature respectable agencies of State, War, and Navy....

Almost every kind of organization plan for research was tried. During the existence of the Overseas Branch, there was a research group at each level of the agency, and the various groups had administrative and functional responsibility to all imaginable policy-makers, operators, and administrators. At one time, it is fair to say, only the fiscal office and the janitor did not have to worry directly about the kind of research being conducted or the promotion of a bilingual clerk. A central Bureau of Overseas Intelligence in Washington contained approximately one hundred people who concentrated on policy research, and who also wrote background and operational reports. For administratively obscure but politically evident reasons, the principal policy-makers in

Washington were permitted to have their own research staffs or did research themselves. The large operating offices in New York and San Francisco had sections called Operations Intelligence and other research groups which supplied implementing materials to operators. Yet here again some of the operators had their own research staffs or trusted no one but themselves to carry on the work. Similarly, the outposts located throughout the world and the combat propaganda teams functioning close to enemy lines collected intelligence which might or might not be sent back to the United States. Some of these groups, though inadequately staffed, prepared their own policy and operational reports.

* * * * *

III. RESEARCH PERSONNEL

In the Overseas Branch, it was by no means thought that social scientists alone had the ability to make sense out of heterogeneous data; journalists, with their traditional "nose for news," were frequently considered better equipped to piece the facts together. In some instances, less capable journalists and radio men, who did not quite live up to the Branch's standards in their profession, were sentimentally retained but farmed out to research. The conviction existed that a national, almost regardless of what his previous training had been, was *ipso facto* an authority on the nation from which he had come or fled. His expertness might be questioned if he showed bias one way or the other regarding, for example, the issue of communism, but otherwise he tended to be accepted as a one-man panel truly representative of the millions in his homeland with whom he might have had no contact for years. It was amazing to observe that such individuals were sufficiently courageous or foolish to dare foretell in detail precisely how an entire nation would respond to a propaganda appeal. Nationals of a foreign country, of course, had to be employed for purely linguistic reasons, but very quickly many of them—too many of them, in this writer's opinion—were permitted to transcend their rôle as translators, announcers, or clerks. In addition, there were a few individuals—approximately five or ten per cent—who would be recognized as social scientists inside or outside any academic community; and they tended to occupy the most prominent and important research positions.

This policy of mixing social scientists, journalists, and nationals was not necessarily deplorable. The snap judgment of the journalist could not be dismissed or ignored by the social scientist who felt himself intellectually paralyzed by the paucity of reliable or unreliable data. In such a situation, he excelled only as a critic. His training tended to make him less subjective, less ethnocentric, less prone to generalize from biased data, and—all in all—less likely to be dogmatic. A critic is seldom popular, and the research race in the OWI tended to be won by the swift and the glib. In a competition between shrewd or wild guesses and scientific hypotheses or theories, the social scientist ordinarily has or should have an ace up his sleeve: verification. Verification during the war was generally out of the question, or at least consisted of ambiguous or out-of-date sense-perceptions. The OWI, in large part through no fault of its own, was definitely not a good testing-ground for social science or social scientists.

IV. RESEARCH MORALE

As in any organization, the research worker's morale fluctuated as a function of personal circumstances and the *esprit* he had established with his immediate associates. Three factors, however, seemed to affect almost everyone. In the first place, an individual was happier if convinced that he had access to "inside" information, which almost always was classified intelligence originating in another government agency (especially the Department of State) or an OWI outpost. Then the completion and circulation of a report brought satisfaction . . . . But, most important of all in wartime, was evidence that operations or policy, or both, had been affected by a report.

Only by examining actual output could an individual determine whether or not operational material provided by him, or one of his general propaganda suggestions, had been utilized. The enormous production of the OWI, however, never permitted a complete survey . . . .

The writer of a policy report, on the other hand, could always determine whether or not his contribution had been influential by consulting the weekly directive. Although these directives were classified as confidential, they were made available to most of the research workers, and the principal one —called the Central Directive for the entire organization—was read aloud and discussed at weekly meetings. Many of the directives, moreover, contained not only a list of "do's" and "don'ts," but also a concise background summary of trends and events which gave a partial explanation for the propaganda policy, and which might contain research materials.

Some individuals inside the OWI tortured themselves with another thought, which then affected their morale: was the dissemination of propaganda or information itself an important contribution to the war effort? . . . . Such soul-searching naturally was not confined to research workers, but often pervaded the Overseas Branch. It was sometimes stimulated by congressional or newspaper attacks upon the OWI. Or it occurred when the individual himself felt guilty because his was an intellectual job and not a task in a combat area—the way to win a war, the phrasing went, is through bombs and not words. The OWI and the individuals themselves, therefore, provided a set of justifications, few of which were rationalizations. If psychological warfare could shorten the war only by a few minutes, it was said, thousands of lives would be saved, and so every propagandist's superego could feel at ease. Evidence concerning the effectiveness of propaganda (such as the number of prisoners carrying surrender leaflets or the enemy's effort to refute an American propaganda line), moreover, was frequently at hand and widely displayed.

Social scientists, in addition, faced a morale problem of their own. Most of them quickly realized that for the reasons already outlined, they could not function as specialists. Why, then, did they remain in the Overseas Branch if they had little or no opportunity to use their talents? Each man and woman no doubt had his own answer. Some did move into other agencies whose research fields looked greener, or returned to their colleges and universities. Others wanted to move, but were persuaded to continue. Those who remained—and the writer has the impression that many more remained than left—were simply intrigued by the OWI . . . . A few kept hoping that some day or week or year they would be permitted to collect the data they required. Still others felt the challenge of trying to make as much of social science as possible work under unfavorable circumstances. There was always the thrilling possibility of being sent overseas . . . . Anyone interested in propaganda as such was able to meet propagandists and to observe, perhaps, what made them tick and fail to tick . . . .

V. PROMOTION OF RESEARCH

As chief of the Bureau of Overseas Intelligence, the writer realized that social-science research, especially projects requiring execution overseas, had to be promoted. He knew that the administrators were sympathetic toward bright and sound ideas within budgetary limits. He never convinced himself, however, that additional policy research was basically either necessary or feasible.

For one thing, he concluded that research could play only a negligible rôle in the formulation of OWI directives which were so dependent on the country's political policies and so constantly affected by military and naval clamor regarding security. By and large, it must be said, the propaganda implications of political and military policies were seldom considered. What the OWI was usually compelled to do was to justify or propagandize in favor of decisions already made. The policy of unconditional surrender for Germany, which may have stiffened German resistance, was perhaps a wise one in the long run, but here it need only be suggested that no research could be carried out in the OWI to estimate its wisdom in advance, and none could be tolerated to ascertain the desirability of publicizing its existence, since the OWI obviously had to conform to the wishes of the President. Similarly, the appeals to be employed by combat teams in calling upon a particular group of enemy soldiers to surrender required no systematic research; instead, only a few elementary facts about the conditions of those troops were required, and these were obtainable from Combat G-2. Policy-makers were correctly convinced that propaganda had its best opportunity to be effective during a military or political lull; but the directives written at such a time stemmed almost exclusively from common sense and not from research, and, in addition, they were bound by general American policy and security considerations.

The OWI's propaganda principles, consequently, tended to be unsubtle and elementary, with or without research backing. The usual procedure was not to obtain the psychological facts, but to psychologize concerning the situation at hand. It was quite possible to conceive of genuine research on a social-science level which might or should affect policy, such as the state of public opinion in a country as measured by a refined survey; yet such research, as has been pointed out, was not permitted . . . . Under these circumstances, the writer eventually abandoned research and during the last year of the war became Policy Coördinator of the Overseas Branch.

While in charge of research in Washington, however, the writer did manage to overcome his paralyzing inhibitions and to promote research. He found himself most successful among policy-makers whose respect, or at least affection, he had won through means not at all related to the research itself or social science in general. Specifically, this meant being liked personally by the policy-maker, humbly pointing out that the research would not be an encroachment upon the individual's own empire of assistants, forcefully indicating that the results could improve the directive and thus redound to his credit, etc. Certain background reports were sent to the OWI outposts, and the ensuing letters of thanks and approval were then employed as proof that research was necessary. In addition, responsible and capable section chiefs within the Bureau were encouraged to cultivate working relations and friendships with the policy-makers of their areas. In this way they acquired an awareness of the policy-makers' problems on a day-by-day basis.

[*Editors' Summary*. Similar deliberate promotion of research was carried out with operations, staffed by journalists, with headquarters in New York. Attempts to assuage the existing friction and hostility, intensified by geographical separation, rested primarily on personal efforts, with weekly visits by at least one member of the research staff to the New York office. A useful service performed by research for operations was the censorship and alteration of selected classified material to the extent that it could be used safely by operations.]

VI. MARKETING OF RESEARCH

It is difficult to say in general whether or not research was eagerly accepted by the OWI's policy-makers and operators . . . . Information with the highest prestige originated outside the Overseas Branch, and it produced submission simply because it came from another agency. Hardboiled journalists in the OWI frequently knew perfectly well that a report from State, War, or Navy was essentially worthless, but they could not disregard the logical or illogical conclusions drawn therefrom for fear of offending the agency involved and, as a result, of having the OWI hauled up before the Joint Chiefs or the Secretary of State. Within the Overseas Branch, there was a tendency to give more credence to research carried on within one's own section than to that produced by another group.

Policy-makers were more than eager to be guided by research findings when a report seemed, or could be employed, to justify one of their own propaganda ideas, and especially when the respectable departments were opposed to the idea. At a crucial meeting, for example, the representative of the War Department might say that he considered the directive proposal "bad propaganda," a phrase which naturally meant absolutely anything or nothing. The OWI official could reply by saying that "the boys in research have some dope which shows that this is what is needed" . . . .

Whether or not policy recommendations were made by research workers depended on the policy-maker involved. During an early period of the Overseas Branch, the top policy-maker—in this writer's opinion, a most capable but erratic man—believed that only he had the brilliance to formulate policy . . . . His two successors did not believe that they alone possessed all the propaganda wisdom inside the OWI, and therefore suggestions from the Bureau were acceptable and frequently utilized. As time went on, the chief of the Bureau was invited to attend most of the important policy meetings. There he could determine some of the areas of ignorance among policy-makers and later make an effort to have his Bureau supply a relevant report.

At these meetings, too, he could advance suggestions for the new directive. The suggestions he made might have their origin in research, in some principle of social science which he happened to consider applicable to the problem at hand, or simply in common sense. If he had research to buttress his argument, so much the better. But he successfully affected policy by pitching into the discussion and succeeding or failing on the basis of what he said. Whether or not in this rôle he was functioning as a research worker, a social scientist, or just a more or less intelligent human being, is a purely academic question. Research and social science, in short, were the excuse which enabled him to get into the policy discussions in the first place. This point must be clearly understood. Expressed differently, it suggests that in some situations, where social science data are inadequate or where social science itself can provide only principles or a way of approach to a problem, the social scientist must hurl himself into the debate, participate on an equal or unequal footing with men and women who are not social scientists, toss some of his scientific scruples to the winds, and fight for what seems to him to be valid or even good . . . .

A question of social or scientific ethics, however, arises in this connection: should the social scientist attempt to add prestige to his argument by always representing himself as a social scientist? The reply each individual gives is obviously a function of his own conscience. The solution of the writer was clear-cut if somewhat self-righteous. When he argued from data, he indicated their nature as well as their limitations. When principles seemed to give rise to his point of view, he named the principles, suggested how valid they were generally thought to be by his colleagues, and never stated that the propaganda universe would collapse if these dicta were disobeyed. When he spoke from what seemed to him to be common sense, he unequivocally and appropriately labelled his thoughts. This procedure did not necessarily make him sound verbose or pompous, for a simple phrase could convey the distinction.

"According to reports we have . . . ," "psychologists generally believe that . . . ," or "in my personal opinion . . ." managed, it was hoped, to specify the esteem he merited . . . .

There was no way to force an operational report into a story, script, motion picture, or some other medium. The operator was the technician whose judgment had to be accepted if not respected. One could argue and argue, but the only convincing challenge was, "If you don't use this, then how are you going to implement the current directive?" The operator even then might use different material, or perhaps claim that the directive could not be implemented with the type of information available. If an operator, for whatever reason, once employed research material which he himself has not collected, and if his product won approval within the office, then of course he was more likely to trust the research group in the future.

One of the frequent complaints of operators in the New York and San Francisco offices was that the policy directives would prescribe a propaganda line for which there was no operational material. Representatives of research were able to help alleviate this difficulty. As each new directive was being discussed, they indicated whether or not the propaganda line was feasible in terms of available material. Often they also suggested that a propaganda theme be adopted for the reason that non-classified material was at hand. If the theme became part of the directive, then the operators were more or less dependent upon research for implementation. In fact, during the last few years of the OWI's existence, a list of reports from the Bureau which had been compiled, or which would be ready by an indicated deadline, was attached to the Central Directive; thus the week's research could be planned in terms of the Directive and the operators could depend on the Bureau for implementing material.

Reports had to be tailored to the readers, their interests, and their peculiarities. In general, brevity was almost always desired. Most policy-makers and operators had neither the time nor the training to examine long reports whose conclusions were indecisive, and whose factual information was surrounded by verbal hedging. A concise summary at the beginning sometimes helped. After some experimentation, it was found that few research workers could write a satisfactory report. The style of social scientists, for example, tended to be wordy and too involved. As a result, a small group of editors in the Bureau of Overseas Intelligence assumed the functions of translating first drafts into simple English and, if necessary, into "journalese"; of studying the research and stylistic requirements of the different groups in the Overseas Branch; and of distributing copies of the reports to the most appropriate people. No report could coast along on the prestige of social science, first, because social science had little prestige, and second, because—in the nip-and-tuck of war, empire-building, and the public relations of the OWI—coasting led nowhere.

VII. OUTSIDE OBSTRUCTIONS TO RESEARCH

The difficulties and problems facing the research worker in the Overseas Branch so far have been confined to those originating inside the agency. There were, in addition, some nuisances from the outside . . . . First of all, social scientists from academic institutions sometimes breezed into the offices of policy-makers not familiar with social science for the purpose of making a proposal which they considered sensational and important. They had to be treated politely for the sake of the OWI's budget and reputation. Generally this was a waste of time . . . . What these consultants failed to realize was a simple, mundane matter: research could not be superimposed on the working organization from the outside and, if it was, someone inside the agency had to assume the unattractive responsibility of sticking the nose of the relevant officials right into the report . . . .

VIII. PERSONAL ADJUSTMENT

Service in the Overseas Branch as a research worker was trying for the writer in innumerable ways. Most of all, he found it difficult, as the phrase would have it, to be diplomatic . . . . He had learned the valuable lesson, as frankness increased his frustrations, that he would be more useful as a social scientist and happier as a human being if he treated almost every individual like a psychiatric patient who had to be understood in the gentlest possible fashion before he could be expected to swallow the pill of research. In the Overseas Branch, this meant being pleasant to what seemed to be millions of people—which, for this writer, was quite a strain. The adoption of a psychiatric approach, it should be parenthetically added, was fruitful in ways related and unrelated to the performance of duty. In trite but very meaningful fashion, it was possible to like some people when they were better understood, and the subsequent perception that the feeling was reciprocated proved gratifying. By and large, moreover, the members of the OWI were very highly motivated, worked exceedingly long hours, were productive to the extent that their talents and the organizational set-up permitted, and represented as decent if heterogeneous a group of individuals as anyone might ever meet. Under such circumstances, the strain of removing egocentrism, the ethnocentrism of social science, and a heavily reinforced system of personal habits in social relations could be tolerated. A similar problem faced the writer when he worked exclusively on the policy level. Then he learned that you could lead an operator to a directive, but you could not make him implement it—no matter how strict the system of controls—unless he understood it, approved of it, and/or had trust in the policy-maker.

*   *   *   *   *

GOVERNMENT ORGANIZATIONS USING RESEARCH

Political-Development Doctrines in the American Foreign Aid Program

ROBERT A. PACKENHAM

It is becoming increasingly evident, if it is not clear already, that one of the most critical problems in the overall modernization of the developing countries is political development. In South Vietnam, in the Congo, in Brazil, in Indonesia—all over the underdeveloped world—the capacity of countries to cope with their problems and, consequently, the stance of the United States toward these nations, turns in varying degrees on the successes or failures of their *political* systems.

All over the world today inadequate performance by political systems is impeding the attainment of a major, often stated goal of U. S. foreign policy: to contribute to the creation of a "community of free nations cooperating on matters of mutual concern, basing their political systems on consent and progressing in economic welfare and social justice" (U. S. Agency for International Development, VI, 1963. 1). Given this goal, political development in other countries is an appropriate concern of American foreign policy.

It would seem to follow that the creation and utilization of a comprehensive political development strategy would not be considered merely idealistic, utopian, or naively humanitarian but would, instead, be considered quite pragmatic and necessary to advance the national interest. Thus the expectation would be that efforts have been made to evolve such a strategy based on available knowledge and to have it widely utilized in implementing foreign policy.

To what extent does the United States, in fact, have an explicit doctrine or strategy of political development? The study reported here is an attempt to answer that question, primarily in terms of a related one: What approaches to political development are embodied in one specific instrument of foreign policy: economic and technical assistance?

This study deals primarily with economic and technical assistance programs in the United States during the one-year period from the spring of 1962 to the spring of 1963, as they were carried out by the government agency primarily responsible for them—the Agency for International Development (AID).

The study methods consisted in (a) a survey of a large volume of published documentary materials about the purposes and accomplishments of the programs, (b) a series of 54 formal interviews with officials involved in aid policy, the interviewees being selected from the Administrator's Office, Regional Bureaus, Program Coordination Staff and Office of Human Resources and Social Development of AID, which preliminary investigation revealed to be the major

● This is a slightly revised and substantially shortened version of an article which appeared in *World Politics,* Vol. 18, 1966, pp. 194-235. Reprinted by permission of *World Politics* and the author.

decision-making units and (c) dozens of informal talks with AID officials and others concerned.

These methods facilitated the main strategy of the study, which was to ascertain (a) the degree to which policy-makers conceptualize the relation of aid to long-term, broad-scale political change in recipient countries and (b) the approaches to political development—explicit and implicit—used by the officials who make aid policy.

The basis for ordering, and evaluating, the approaches to political development used by the officials (which approaches we call "doctrines") is the knowledge contained in the scholarly literature. Knowledge in this field, although far from adequate, is much greater than it was fifteen years ago, when large-scale aid programs began. It is known to be specific, that political development usually depends not only upon changes in the economic system, but also upon alterations in social structure, administrative capacity, and that set of attitudes and expectations which has come to be called "political culture." Aware of these dimensions, one can better evaluate the adequacy of the doctrines of political development actually found in the foreign aid program.

This literature is very briefly summarized here. Scholars have been much more attentive to and precise about the conditions of political development than about defining the dependent variable itself, i.e., the phenomenon of political development. Thus our standard derives from these conditions—the independent variable—more than from the dependent variable, political development itself. But we shall discuss both to facilitate comprehension of the whole field.

Dealt with at greater length are the doctrines of political development as they are revealed in the stated views of the AID policy-makers. The differences between the scholars' knowledge and the operators' doctrines have important short- and long-range implications for the AID program, as does the variance in views between AID and State Department officials.

I. THE NOTION OF POLITICAL DEVELOPMENT IN THE ACADEMIC LITERATURE

Scholars writing on political development have tended to stress five conditions as the prime correlates or determinants of political development.

A *legal-formal constitution* prescribing such features as equal protection by the law, the rule of law, regular elections by secret ballot, federalism, and/or the separation of powers (Theodore Woolsey, Woodrow Wilson, John W. Burgess, most comparative government textbooks).

A level of *economic development* sufficient to serve the material needs of the members of the political system and to permit a reasonable harmony between economic aspirations and satisfactions (Marx, Beard, Millikan and Rostow, Lipset, Coleman, Wolf).

The *administrative capacity* efficiently and effectively to maintain law and order and to perform governmental output functions rationally and neutrally (Weber, Brzezinski, Pauker, Wriggins).

A *social system* that facilitates popular participation in governmental and political processes at all levels, and the bridging of regional religious, caste, linguistic, tribal, or other cleavages (Deutsch, Lipset, Scott, Weiner, Kornhauser, Almond).

A *political culture*—that is, fundamental attitudinal and personality characteristics—among the members of the political system such that they are able both to accept the privileges and to bear the responsibilities of a democratic political process (Almond, Beer, Leites, Inkeles, Lasswell, Parsons, Banfield, Lerner, Pye). (Packenham, V.2, 1964.)

These determinants, excepting possibly

the first, are not just hypotheses. A substantial body of literature, ranging from reports of intensive, mostly qualitative, studies of single countries to extensive quantitative surveys of several or more countries, exists to support the economic, social-system and political-culture approaches. Studies to support the administrative approach are less plentiful, but not wholly lacking.

In fact, their validity is sufficient to favor their use as a standard for evaluating aid political-development doctrines, and also as a source of ideas for an American political development strategy. They serve both purposes here.[1]

As to the dependent variable—the phenomenon of political development itself—when not ignored or evaded, it has been handled with little precision and considerable uncertainty. Most of the concepts and indices used have been "rough and subjective."[2] And when rigorous indices have been attempted, they have tended to be formalistic and unrealistic.

A small but growing group of writers has begun to think in terms of a dynamic theory of political development. Still another current of thought insists on leaving the dependent variable "open-ended" in order to allow for the perception of evolving, and possibly radically different, patterns.

Halpern (VI, 1964) avoids some of these difficulties by viewing political development not as a list of characteristics or qualities but as a dynamic relationship among a few key variables. His approach stresses the "interaction among three elements: the *imbalances* existing within and among the systems of a society (e.g., the disparity between population and resources, between educated men and the jobs available for them, between modern problems and theories relevant for understanding them) and the *will* and *capacity* of a society (especially the political system and its leaders) to transform these imbalances so that it may generate and absorb continuing transformation" (p. 179). The modernizing state by his definition is one that has a "persistent capacity for coping with a permanent revolution" (p. 177).

Lasswell and Huntington recently have urged relatively more stress on the political aspects of political development and relatively less on its societal aspects. Both, moreover, deal with a much neglected area —political decay—and both posit the influential relationship of domestic (national) and international systems to each other in the matters of development and decay.

Huntington (VI, 1965) makes a most significant contribution through his conception of political development as the "institutionalization of political organizations and procedures." He considers the role of input structures, such as political parties, in dealing with social mobilization far more than other scholars, thereby giving us the best statement to date of the need to harness, control, organize and put to work the processes of social change. He, moreover, takes more responsibility than others have done for making concrete policy proposals based on his work, such as that "American policy should be directed to the creation within modernizing countries of at least one strong non-Communist party" (p. 429).

Such a proposal, if accepted as a U. S. objective, would present formidable difficulties in application; for example, in countries like Ethiopia and Brazil which have no strong party. The alternatives would not

---

[1] As noted, our standard is necessarily a rough one. Given the small amount of attention to political development in the aid program, however, it is entirely adequate to our task. The measuring instrument need be only about as refined as the phenomenon to be measured. A full-blown strategy of political development is unnecessary to see the state of U. S. political-development doctrines.

[2] The phrase is used by Everett Hagen with reference to his own classification of political systems ["A Framework for Analyzing Economic and Political Change," in Robert E. Asher et al. (VI, 1962: 4) but it has wider applicability.

seem so simple as he suggests, nor American influence so great.

Lasswell (V.2, 1965: 301) offers fewer policy suggestions but makes a significant contribution by stressing the crucial importance of "the contextual principle." In other words, there is no panacea for the political ills of developing countries; the search for a single solution is futile.

The theorist's problem is to find a model that leaves room for *varying* patterns of political development and a typology of developing political systems that suggest *different categories* of specific policies and programs appropriate to the various system types.

Halpern's dynamic-relational approach seems by far the most promising. It provides a simple yet meaningful model that embraces all political systems without abandoning the contextual principle and without adopting a single-instrument strategy that is bound to be sometimes or often inappropriate.

Yet because the emerging nations are evolving in many and possibly unique ways, open-ended political-development models undoubtedly are the most appropriate approach at present. At the same time, "open-ended" should not be interpreted to connote "meaningless." Some political systems are more developed than others, even if we have not yet specified the concepts that satisfactorily formalize that intuitive knowledge. Pye (VI, 1963) points out that observers in both developed and developing societies are uncertain before the very notions of "underdeveloped," "advanced," or "backward," and that some of this uncertainty stems from lack of knowledge about the similarities and differences in the two kinds of societies. Yet, he concludes, "everyone seems to sense that some forms of differences are acceptable, while others are not." (p. 14.) Open-ended models or a combination of models may be the means by which we can arrive at one or a number of concepts that allow formalization of the intuitive knowledge we already possess.

II. TOWARD A POLITICAL-DEVELOPMENT STRATEGY FOR AMERICAN FOREIGN POLICY

Despite the need for them, there have been few studies of any kind dealing with ways in which foreign policy can influence political development, and fewer still that use the now formidable number of works on developing areas to derive guidelines useful to the foreign policy-maker.[1] An attempt is made here to translate the results of the most important study findings into some rough guidelines, the thesis being that existing knowledge is sufficient to allow some responsible policy decisions to be informed by it.

Two considerations are fundamental in the creation and use of a political development strategy. The first is the level and nature of points of access to the process of political development. Through nonclandes-

[1] Among the exceptions to these generalizations is the report of a Brookings Institution Study Group (VI, 1961). Many of the main conclusions of this study group appeared in Haviland (VI, 1962). In the same issue of the *AID Digest* see Rustow (VI, 1962) and Wriggins (VI, 1962). To show how one aid instrument—technical assistance programs in labor—might be used to foster political development, an excellent study is Millen (VI, 1963). Of the large number of studies of the process of political development and modernization in general, many of course make occasional observations about what their findings might mean for foreign policy. While unsystematic, many of these insights are well worth considering, as in the following volumes: Pye (VI, 1962) and (VI, 1963); McClelland (VI, 1961). Almost all the items just cited attempt no more than speculations about what might be done. Reliable studies about how aid, or any foreign-policy instruments, has actually been used in relation to political development are practically nonexistent. This appears to be no less true in government research and evaluation organs than among nongovernment researchers, at least so far as unclassified material is concerned.

tine instruments—our primary concern—the United States has access to the central government of other countries through diplomacy, and to the total society through economic, military and technical assistance and information programs. The second consideration is time span; what effects a political development strategy would have immediately, and also the medium- and long-range effects. Both points of access might be utilized in a U. S. policy of political development.

One possible U. S. strategy at the level of the central government would involve giving consistent support to those governments showing ability not only to maintain their political systems in the face of continuing transformations but to generate and absorb transformations, as suggested by Halpern. This implies attention to the administrative, economic, social and political-culture bases of political development.

At the level of the total society, valid instruments could be derived from any one or an appropriate combination of the conditions for political development; for example, the economic approach might mean rigorous economic criteria for aid projects, such as those currently employed: capital-output ratios, cost-benefit ratios, rate of marginal saving, rate of export expansion, foreign-exchange position, and the like. The administrative approach would suggest the whole range of technical-assistance activities in public administration and other fields that could improve the recipient governments' output capacities at all levels of government. The social-system approach would suggest use of labor unions, local communities, private cooperatives, professional and trade associations, newspapers, and the whole range of civic, educational, economic, and other *groups* that constitute a differentiated social infrastructure. The political-culture approach would suggest political education institutes; political education handbooks; in-service training schools; and politicization of "people to people," participant-training, education, information, and other programs to inculcate democratic values, teach bargaining skills, and in general foster a democratic political culture.

The use of such instruments in specific instances would depend upon a wide variety of factors, such as other demands of foreign policy and—scarcely to be minimized—the experience and intuition of officials on the foreign scene and in Washington about the wisdom of the measures. But the scholars' findings seem sufficiently solid today to be used as guides to suggest policy alternatives. At the very minimum they indicate some crucial new *dimensions* of the conditions of political development—dimensions that are not just economic and administrative but profoundly social and psychological, and that cannot be ignored by the policy-maker.

III. POLITICAL-DEVELOPMENT DOCTRINES IN THE UNITED STATES AID PROGRAM

The remainder of this article describes, and frequently evaluates, political-development doctrines embodied in the United States economic and technical-assistance programs primarily during the period from the spring of 1962 to the spring of 1963.

While the political-development doctrines to be described here appear similar in many respects to the political-development doctrines of other time periods, agencies, and aid activities, note that the specific scope of the current study is limited mainly to 1962-63 and the Agency for International Development (AID). Other caveats are that this is a study mainly of doctrines, not actions; of Washington, not the field; of public, not private, aid activities, and of overt, not covert, aspects of U. S. foreign policy.

A. Political Development: A Purpose but Not a Policy

A dominant doctrine, especially among the highest officials, is that the overriding goal of aid, as of all instruments of American foreign policy, is the creation of a "world community" of free and independent nations, "each free to work out its own institutions as it sees fit, but cooperating effectively in matters of common interest." This goal should not be obscured even by important short- and middle-range considerations, such as the Cold War, which "we should keep . . . in perspective as only one element in our continuing effort to achieve a viable world order." To the objection that such a goal is beyond the capacity of the U. S. alone to achieve, the doctrine provides that "the United States must nonetheless play the leading role in shaping the history of our time in that direction. This is both the burden and opportunity of our generation in this country." (Rusk, VI, 1962: 100.)

The political-development content is even clearer in other official declarations of basic purpose. In his 1962 Foreign Aid Message, President Kennedy said, "Our new aid policy aims at strengthening the political and economic independence of developing countries," and that it reaffirms "our nation's basic interest in the development and freedom of other nations." The President also declared, in his second State of the Union address, that the main goal of foreign aid is to help create ". . . a peaceful world community of free and independent states, free to choose their own future and their own system so long as it does not threaten the freedom of others."

The significance of this doctrine should not be minimized. Official U. S. aid statements do not have to stress such values as world community and independent, democratic (i.e., based on consent) states. This doctrine is a result of a conscious choice— some argue an altogether utopian choice. (Banfield, VI, 1963: 61-65.) Nor has the government always argued the case for aid in these terms. During the period from the outbreak of the Korean War until 1960, under the Mutual Security Act of 1951 and its successors, there were few such statements (Legislative Reference Service, VI, 1959: 48). This doctrine is not meant to be mere rhetoric. It is a serious and constantly repeated goal of United States foreign policy.

Yet these declarations bear little clear relation to specific aid objectives and programs. The approach to political development that is most often relied upon to achieve these objectives is economic; and even it is only implicit. True, there is some reference to the social, psychological, and even legal-formal aspects of political development among top-level elites. Secretary Rusk (VI, 1962), for example, includes among the objectives of foreign aid relating to the broader goal of world community such abstractions as "free institutions," "human dignity," "self-reliant nations," and "vigorous and vibrant societies" (*passim*). He also speaks of "ideas" as "our strength and our defense against aggression" (p. 110), and observes that the peoples of developing countries should be allowed to "discover that . . . economic and social advances can best occur under free institutions with a mobilized effort of peoples acting by consent, and not through direction from an authoritarian society" (VI, 1962: 45). *But these abstractions seldom are given specific content, as are references to economic abstractions.* While laudable goals, as guides to specific objectives and programs these concepts are not important because they are not meaningful in concrete, specific terms.

The interview data reveal this gap still further. At least ten of the respondents spoke of the broad, overall objectives of aid, citing, in substance, the goal of a "world community of mutually independent and democratic nations." Six of these ten took the line that to achieve this goal the best course is "to pursue economic growth consistent with democratic institutions." But they had not a single criterion, other than economic measures, that could serve as an instrumental guide or intellectual tool with which to achieve this goal. Of the other four cases, two illustrate the fundamental ambiguity resulting from the statement of political-development goals at the abstract level and the absence of objectives, concepts, and instruments with which to implement them at the specific level. The chief planning officer in one of the AID regions said, "You know, one thing I've never been clear about is what our fundamental policy is on the question of whether we're trying to promote democracies or not."

The second statement is from an office director in the Latin American region: "We're somewhat schizophrenic here. We want governments that are free and independent, but also non-Communist. I suppose this makes our posture that we like them to be free to choose any type of government that won't ally with the Communists—preferably a democratic one."

These two officials have put their finger on a widespread phenomenon in AID: the absence of a clear connection between the goal of the high-level policy statements and the real goals that they themselves, as operators, pursue. These two respondents have articulated this gap more than have the others, but it is there, in some measure, in almost every instance.

B. Meanings of "Political Development"

Not surprisingly, AID officials understood the term "political development" in various ways. This had been anticipated, but even so the meanings attached to the term were different from those expected.[1]

One of the most common responses was, in effect, that political development is anti-Communist, pro-American political stability. According to this interpretation, aid for political development is aid for short-term political purposes. Examples are aid to shore up a crumbling, pro-American government, or aid as a bribe for a military installation, or as a means of meeting a deficit in the country's balance of payments. These uses take little or no account of the economic development plans of the country, which are so dear to the hearts of many AID officials. In fact, they may hurt economic development.

Another meaning is, in effect, economic development. When asked for a reaction to the notion of political development, the respondents approve, and then talk as if we were asking about economic development. A striking example of this was an official who said the Soviet Union was politically developed. When I pursued the point, it turned out he meant that the Soviets have a high standard of living. "Political-development function" means, in these cases, long-term rather than short-term aid; but it also means political development only in the sense of a purely economic approach.

AID stands for "Agency for International Development." The concept of "development," we would argue, should include but not be limited to economic development. Yet for a majority of respondents the real meaning of "development" is "economic development." For them, the two terms are interchangeable; AID is, in effect, "Agency for International Economic Development."

Thus "political development" usually means either "short-term political," or "economic development." Nearly all AID officials see the uses of aid primarily in terms of this dichotomy.[2] As a result few officials

---

[1] It was explained that what was referred to was long-term, broad-scale political change. But this explanation usually did not prohibit the respondents from giving their own understandings of the term.

[2] An example of the dichotomization, and some indication of why it developed, is the following piece of testimony by then Under Secretary of State Douglas Dillon regarding the establishment of the Development Loan Fund: "The purpose of the [economic] criteria is to make clear that all these loans will be made only where we think that they contribute to economic development of the less-developed countries, and will not be used for political purposes or short-term political objectives. That has been one of the troubles in the past, as your committee found—the intermingling of purposes. The reason for these criteria is to single out

even conceive of a third alternative, namely, *political development*.

In addition, many AID administrators find it very difficult to think about society-wide political change systematically and analytically (as they often can about economic development). Those interviewed also found it almost impossible to deal conceptually with the question of how aid instruments might be used to effect "broad-scale political change." They had a strong tendency to limit the meaning of political development entirely to leadership elites in the existing central government or to those elites, immediately surrounding the existing government, who might succeed it. Elites in other levels of government (provinces, local areas), nongovernmental elites, and non-elites were usually not considered part of the process of political development. All of these tendencies continued even after it was indicated to the respondents that what was meant by political development was long-term, broad-scale change in the political system.

C. Explicit Attention to Political Development

The number of places and persons in the aid establishment that are explicitly concerned about political development is not very large. However, it was possible to identify three loci of such attention: some very high-level elites; research and planning units in the Department of State and AID, and a minority of the largely middle-level elites in AID interviewed for this study.

1. Highest-Level Foreign Policy Elites. One locus of explicit attention to political development is found in a few individuals at the highest level of the U. S. foreign-aid policy elite. Secretary of State Rusk, for example, urges that aid be used to help establish "free institutions . . . and . . . development of the individual and family status and dignity."[1] Former Assistant Secretary Edwin Martin says that the U. S. should support and work with groups who cherish democratic values and constitutional government. . . ."[2]

There are still others who could be mentioned. But they are a small minority. By and large the high-level officials do not give attention to the analysis of political development prior-to-events rather than *ad hoc* in response to events; nor do they recognize, again prior-to-events, "the importance of political advancement as a central [or even a peripheral] aspect of foreign policy and operations."[3]

2. Research and Planning Units. At least three research and planning units in the Department of State and AID devoted attention specifically to the question of political development. The Bureau of Intelligence and Research (INR) of the Department of State had several papers prepared on the subject of political development and the relation of U. S. policy instruments toward it. Papers done for INR in 1962 by Richard Neustadt, Thomas McHale, Chester Bowles, and one unnamed author were circulated restrictedly in the executive branch in the fall of 1962; the paper done anonymously, "Creating Allies for Socioeconomic Progress with Political Stability in Latin America," was, by our standards, very good. It said that the military, the labor unions, and the universities and secondary schools are potential allies of the U.S. for "progress with political stability," and that therefore the U. S. might well try to strengthen them by channeling financial assistance through them.

Neustadt effectively argued the case for

very sharply this Fund as only a development fund that would be based on economic development" (Committee on Government Operations, VI, 1960: 11).

[1] Testimony before Committee on Foreign Relations (VI, 1962: 22).
[2] Testimony before Committee on Foreign Relations (VI, 1962: 404).
[3] The phrase quoted comes from Brookings Institution Study Group Report (VI, 1961).

more attention to political development, but did not do much else. McHale restated the familiar notion that there are fundamental social and attitudinal differences between "folk" and "urban" cultures. Bowles's piece fairly pointed out that most of the developing countries are primarily agricultural. INR also commissioned at least two social scientists to do case studies of political development in individual countries.

The Policy Planning Staff of the Department of State has also been interested in political development. One member of this staff has written on the subject and was perhaps the man most often identified by aid personnel as a responsible government official who was interested in and knowledgeable about political development. However, he himself was not sanguine about the amount of influence that aid can have on political development. Moreover, like most State Department personnel, he had a strong proclivity to view political development in terms of short-term rather than long-term political change, in terms of elites only rather than the political system at large, and to consider only specific political development activities rather than the maximization of the political-development implications accompanying all assistance activities.

In AID, a major point at which a political-development concern was in evidence was the Program Coordination Staff (PCS), especially its Policy Planning Staff. The *Program Guidance Manual* (1962) for FY 1964 has some general statements in the text to the effect that political development ought to be a consideration in planning the aid program for each country. Multiyear planning is encouraged. The *Manual* sets out a framework for the development of "LAS's" (Long Range Assistance Strategies) for twelve countries, some elements of which are to be applied to all countries, in the "CAP's" (Country Assistance Programs) and "GP's" (Goals Plans). Attention to political development is considerably greater here than in other manual order material we saw. The *Program Guidance Manual* (PGM) asks that, when planning country programs, current U. S. objectives and policies be analyzed to see whether economic and political objectives are coincidental; whether these objectives are the same for the U. S. as for the countries' leaders; and if they differ, whether the U. S. should try to change them. It then asks that certain kinds of analyses be made of trends in the country—not only economic, but also social, political, and administrative analyses. (U. S. Agency for International . . . , VI, 1962: 1022. 2, 3.)

The *Manual* affirms the importance for effective long-range assistance strategy of encouraging "forward-looking" elements in and out of governments, to promote the growth and change of institutions. One annex to the *Manual* suggests a framework far in advance of similar guidelines for appraising conditions and trends in a given country, and lists specific questions as aids in making the appraisal. These are outlined here with selected excerpts:

1. Survey of broad social, political, and administrative characteristics of the country.

 (a) What are the broad social characteristics?
  (1) attitudes toward change
 (b) What are the general political characteristics of the country?
  (1) relationship between political leadership and important segments of the population
  (2) political recruitment and competition
  (3) articulation of popular demands
 (c) What are the general administrative characteristics of the country?
  (1) How adequate to development tasks is the basic administrative organization and procedural set-up?
 (d) What are the country's major social and political goals within the next few years or decade?

2. Statement of LAS social and political goals and their relation to total country strategy.

> (a) Within the context of the survey outlined above, what should U. S. strategy view as the most important social and political goals in the country?
> (1) political and social goals
> "Identification of desirable social and political goals for another country and culture inevitably requires making some value judgments. . . . Since judgments of some kind are essential, it is preferable that they be systematic, considered, and prior to events rather than *ad hoc* in response to events."
> (b) What is the optimal balance for the total country program between more immediately productive types of economic investment, and use of resources to promote social/political goals which may have only indirect and long-run economic impact?

Another annex to the *Manual,* entitled "Analysis of Self-Help and Social Development," lists the following "standard political and social items" to consider in determining a country's level of political development, and elaborates each briefly: land and income distribution, taxation system, elementary and general education, welfare programs, and political organization and popular participation.

Most of these questions in this guidelines manual are asked for the first time. Before this document was published nobody, either in the field or in Washington, had much guidance on questions they should be asking or concepts they could or should be using. Regarding his experience in Thailand, Neustadt wrote: "What of Washington? To judge from questions asked, reports requested, through the various channels to our Mission staffs, your town *had not, as of December last, given much guidance on or voiced much interest in political analysis beyond the range of plots and personalities.* As one official put it: 'We don't get many inquiries from any quarter: we pretty much have to guess what they want.' This certainly is not conclusive on the frames of reference held in Washington. But it is rather suggestive." ("Memorandum . . . ," VI, 1962: 9.)

Because the PGM appeared in August 1962 (after "December last," i.e., 1961), one may hope that there has been some improvement in the situation Neustadt characterized. However, at the conclusion of this study there was considerable reason to believe that there is still not "much guidance" or "much interest" in political development from Washington. Even within the Program Coordination Staff, the office which produced the PGM, it is doubtful that the importance of political-development guidelines was fully accepted. The specific political-development concepts and lists of criteria elaborated at length in the full-length (several hundred pages) PGM (1962) are nowhere visible in a condensed (forty-nine pages) version of the *Manual* distributed for Agency and public use. The absence of these concepts is significant because the condensation is presented as a "summary statement . . . of the principles which guide U. S. economic assistance programs" (U. S. Agency for International Development, VI, 1963a: i). Political-development concepts are almost totally absent from the factors that the Program Coordination Staff said in May 1963 determine official aid strategies and types of economic assistance (U. S. Agency for International Development, VI, 1963b). An AID official in a position to know informed us that the inclusion of Annex B and the other political-development questions in the full-length PGM reflected the interest of a very small group of PCS of "perhaps a half-dozen." Thus, to have the questions in the *Manual* is one thing; to have them accepted by all of the planning staff is another; and to have them used by AID/Thailand and even AID/Washington is still another, and very distant, matter.

3. Middle-Level Elites: The Interview Sample. The third locus of attention to political development is found in the interview sample. Among these fifty-four officials, nearly all of whom are middle-level elites, a minority of seventeen—not quite one-third—may be said to display some attention to political development. These are officials who give some indication of having thought about political development sufficiently that it might influence some of their aid decisions. These seventeen display doctrines corresponding to approaches to political development in the following proportions: legal-formal, none; economic, six; administrative, nine; social-system, seventeen; political-culture, thirteen.

It is notable that the legal-formal approach is nowhere in evidence. Thus among not only the academicians but also these operators, legal-formal concepts of political development are not regarded as useful. It may be observed here that there is little evidence in this entire study that Banfield's (VI, 1963: 59-60) charge, "Our faith that democracy can regenerate the world without coercion has led us to try one legal or institutional gadget after another," is accurate with respect to the attitudes of AID administrators. The vast majority of our evidence suggests little tendency to try to achieve political development by legal-formal means.

The administrative approach is expressed primarily in the stress on stability. This doctrine is found equally among generalists and public administration specialists—often more vehemently and with less sophistication among the former than the latter.

Given the demands put on administrative apparatuses by social mobilization, it can well be argued, as Brown (VI, 1964: 67-77) does, that the quantity of aid resources should be increased rather than decreased. First, however, other weaknesses of the administrative-approach doctrine should be corrected. One weakness is that programs of public administration are no more part of a strategy of political development than are most other technical-assistance programs. This should change. Moreover, the general stress on order and stability for their own sakes should give way to a more adequate political-development strategy, such as one that helps political systems to cope with *and* generate continuing transformation.

Expressions of the social-system and political-culture approaches are primarily at the level of (a) *group* life (e.g., development of alternatives to existing political power groups, land reform, institution-building, support of groups fostering democratic values and constitutional government), or (b) attitude change among *adults* (e.g., the Political Education Institute in Costa Rica, diplomatic pressure urging military juntas to hold elections, as in Peru in 1962 and Guatemala in 1963). A third possibility—childhood, especially schooltime, socialization—does not appear to have been tried. Perhaps it cannot be tried because this area is too sensitive and politically dangerous for U. S. foreign policy to become involved in it. Yet in light of the apparent importance of political socialization for political development, the mere existence of this lacuna is significant. For it means either that an important dimension of political development is inaccessible to influence by the instruments of foreign policy, or that an important opportunity for such influence is not being used.

D. Concentration and Typologies: Political Development Policies?

Some aid officials and others in the government grant that there has been a lack of attention to political development in the *content* of aid programs in any given country, but argue that such attention has been expressed through the *timing,* the *amount* of aid, and the *choice* of the country that receives it. They argue that aid is directed to countries doing a good job of democratic nation-building: Greece, Israel, and Nationalist China are cited as examples. Thus, goes the argument, the policy of aid concentration constitutes an aid political-development policy.

In fact, the policy of concentration has not been a political-development policy at all. In the selection of countries on which to concentrate, economic-development criteria have been dominant, while explicit political-development criteria have very little in evidence.

Concentration of aid efforts in a relatively few countries was introduced as an Agency policy in 1960. In testimony before the Senate Appropriations Committee (VI, 1960: 35-36), the Director of ICA said that new emphasis was being "given to selecting and developing free world *economic* strong points, or 'Islands of Development.'" He added that three countries— Taiwan, India, and Pakistan—had "been singled out for special consideration and concentration of assistance." An examination of the criteria of aid assistance in these three countries would reveal that they were almost strictly economic and short-term political.

The Director of the Program Coordination Staff developed a "concept of successive concentration." This is the notion that aid should be concentrated in those countries where the rate of marginal savings and the rate of export expansion are high. In effect this means countries that are closest to "takeoff" into self-sustaining economic growth. When the country reaches the takeoff stage, aid can be transferred to other countries.[1] The criteria for concentration are rigorously economic. Except in terms of an implicit economic approach, political-development criteria are entirely absent from this concentration concept.

Related to—perhaps part of—the concentration theme, and related also to a desire to refine the theoretical underpinnings of aid, are several efforts to set up categories of aid recipients. The most widely publicized of these was the so-called "Bowles Memorandum."[2] Others in the Bureau of Intelligence and Research and the Policy Planning Staff of AID, have produced similar typologies, not all of which were made public.

None of these typologies gives much attention to political development as a criterion. One of them stated, "The most important factors that distinguish aid strategies in different countries are: (i) the nature and extent of U. S. interest in the country; (ii) the country's present stage of development and potential over the next decade; (iii) the country's development policies and the extent of self-help, present and prospective; (iv) the availability of other sources of external financing; (v) external or internal threats to security and political stability. Variations in these elements lead to [three] principal types of U. S. assistance strategy."

The three principal types of assistance strategy cited are (a) "Development-Oriented Strategies," (b) "Stability- and Security-Oriented Programs," and (c) "Limited-Objective Strategies" (U. S. Agency for International Development, VI, 1963b; 1963a: 1-7). Of the five "most important factors" or "elements" that distinguish aid strategies, the only one that comes close to specific mention of political development is "external or internal threats to security and political stability." Of the three strategies, only the first, "Development-Oriented Strategies," has anything resembling an explicit reference to a political-development standard: "democratic traditions" is mentioned as one of five characteristics that make a recipient country "relatively important to the U. S."

One is forced to the conclusion that

---

[1] For another version of an aid strategy of concentration, see Etzioni (VI, 1962: Chapter 10).

[2] "The Need for More Specific Criteria . . . , (VI, 1962). This memorandum was not widely distributed to the public; for good summaries in the press, see the *New York Times,* October 8, 1962, and the *Wall Street Journal,* October 4, 1962.

political development is wholly absent as an explicit-criterion for establishing the categories of the typologies. Concentration in terms of economic and security criteria is truly an agency-wide and agency-deep doctrine.

E. Implicit Approaches to Political Development

Since explicit attention to political development is slight, implicit political-development doctrine becomes important.

Among those thirty-seven respondents who showed little or no attention to political development, no fewer than thirty-three exhibited clearly the implicit economic approach. These are officials who had not thought about political development beforehand and who, when asked about it, indicated that they could think of no better way to achieve it than by taking the same steps and using the same criteria as they use to achieve economic development. *This doctrine is, by a wide margin, the most widespread approach to political development in the Agency.*

Indeed, it could hardly be otherwise in an agency in which most officials see the economic development of other countries as the organization's primary operational goal. A forthright statement by Assistant Administrator Gaud illustrates the point: "What is our objective in this program? It is very easy to state. . . . Our objective, to put it in a few words and perhaps to over-simplify it a little, is to achieve sound economic development in these countries with those countries making the maximum practical contribution to their own development. In other words, foster and further their economic development but insist that they do what they can in partnership with us" (Committee on Foreign Affairs, VI, 1962: 579).

There are numerous other ways in which this approach is expressed. As noted earlier, the very name of the Agency reflects the goal of overall "development"; yet the interviews disclose that "development" most often means "economic development" only. The same may be said of "long-term development plans," which are advanced as an "ultimate objective"; upon examination, they are plans for *economic* development. Repeatedly the goal of the Agency is stated as the development of "self-sustaining economies." The *Program Guidance Manual* (1962) states, under "Basic AID Policy," that "aid as an instrument of foreign policy is best adapted to promoting economic development." Criteria for aid, except when they are short-term political, tend most often to be economic criteria, such as cost-benefit ratios and prospective contribution to GNP. Among the officials interviewed, and in the hearings, typologies of recipient countries tend to be based primarily upon the country's economic-development situation. Even where more elaborate criteria are stated, political-development standards are almost wholly lacking. In the interview material the officials frequently make an analogy between the relationship of the U. S. to the recipient country and that of a banker-lender to his client.

The tendency to rely on the economic approach, and the near-blindness of so many to the sociological and psychological dimensions of development, are alarming when we consider what is known about development and the stage at which many developing peoples find themselves today. Whereas the past decade was one of rising *expectations*, the one coming has the potential to be one of rising *frustrations*. As Daniel Lerner (VI, 1963) observes, economic growth without psychic satisfactions produces "'the insatiable expectations of politics' that lead ultimately only to frustration . . . . Short-sighted politicians," he argues, "have been sowing a storm they may not be able to harvest" (p. 350). To the extent such channels are ignored, however unwittingly and with whatever good intentions, is it not possible that aid officials too are "sowing a storm they may not be able to harvest"?

IV. CONCLUSIONS

Our examination shows that while the declared purpose of American foreign aid is to help create "a community of free nations cooperating on matters of mutual concern, basing their political systems on consent and progressing in economic welfare and social justice," the doctrines of AID and aid administrators in other agencies indicate little explicit attention to political development. What accounts for this gap between purpose and policy? In these remaining paragraphs we shall suggest some factors that seem to us most important, and shall try to evaluate their validity as inhibitors of an explicit U. S. political-development policy.

It is clear that one element in the explanation is the administrators' doubt that aid is a strong enough instrument to affect the course of long-term, broad-scale political change in the recipient countries. Far from being utopian, they are most cautious in their estimates of the potential influence of aid in building viable political systems. Their caution stems in large part from uncertainty about the relation of aid to development. This uncertainty is, of course, not unfounded. No one knows with confidence how much influence the United States has on the recipient countries. Another factor that helps explain the current doctrine, therefore, is scarcity of knowledge. The current AID Administrator (then Director of the Budget Bureau), David E. Bell (VI, 1961: 14), spoke for the vast majority in AID when he said, "Until we understand better how to bring about the kinds of political development that [are] needed and will work in the developing countries, we are necessarily limited in the advice and help we can give them."

Yet it is important to distinguish between knowledge of the conditions of political development, and knowledge of ways and means of bringing these conditions about, especially by the instruments of foreign policy. We know a good deal about the former—not so much as we would like (do we ever have that?), but enough to improve the quality of policy decisions. We know very little about the latter. The few studies we have are primarily speculative. In addition to more of these, we very badly need empirical studies of the actual and potential impact of U. S. foreign-policy instruments on the economies, the social systems, and especially the politics of these countries. Not only the academies but also the government research and evaluation organs have practically ignored these questions. As late as 1962–63—after fifteen years in the aid business—there was still (with the possible exception of economic studies) no effective government organ for systematically gathering, storing, cataloguing, and analyzing the wealth of data generated during that experience.[1] As a result, although useful studies are still possible, much of that data is lost forever.

Such studies, and continued experience

---

[1] In July 1960, John Ohly concluded, after a careful assessment of aid agency research needs, "The Executive Branch in general, and this agency in particular, have been seriously derelict in failing long since to initiate a large and systematic research and development program. This failure is tragic, and may prove exorbitantly costly as we progressively reap the consequences of our own negligence . . ." ("Research and Development in the Field of Foreign Economic and Technical Assistance," International Cooperation Administration Executive Secretariat Note 3, July 22, 1960, mimeographed, p. 10). In 1961, for the first time, a research unit with a separate identity and its own budget was established in the aid agency. But it did not achieve much in the first two years. It could not find personnel. It became lost in the total AID reorganization of that period. Worst of all, questionable contracting practices got it into serious hot water with the Congress. By 1963 it had made little organizational progress, and had few if any research results in hand. Its morale was poor, and its prospects were not bright. See Walsh (VI, 1963).

with aid programs, could tell us more about aid as a tool for manipulating political change. In the meantime, as Professor Mason reminded us, foreign aid "is not the only area in which action—or inaction—has to be undertaken on the basis of inadequate knowledge of the consequences." Whether or not aid does in fact have a substantial impact on the course of development in the recipient countries, the underlying assumption of aid is that it does. Thus it is incumbent on aid officials as well as on outside critics to consider that impact more carefully—and to consider not only the economic but also the political system.

Another part of the explanation is the strong tendency—shown by over half our interview sample—to separate politics and technology. At the broadest, most abstract level of verbal justifications of aid all the respondents regard it as political—that is, they say that aid is an instrument of foreign policy, that it cannot be considered simply a means for the U. S. to express its humanitarianism. At this level the *sine qua non* justification of foreign aid is national interest. However, at the instrumental level of day-to-day decisions, aid is seen as properly separate from politics. Aid can best promote the national interest if it contributes to economic development, according to rigorous economic criteria that are separate from political considerations. According to the modal tendency, political aid—a politically charged instrument designed to maximize and consciously direct its effect on the political system—is bad; technological aid—a politically neutral instrument whose effects on and relations with the political system are constantly minimized—is good. The characteristics associated with political and technological aid by the majority of the AID administrators are as follows:

ADMINISTRATORS' VIEWS OF POLITICAL AND TECHNOLOGICAL AID

Political Aid	Technological Aid
dangerous	safe
unmeasurable	measurable
invisible, intangible	visible, tangible
skills, values, techniques unteachable	skills, values, techniques teachable
deals with abstract ideals	deals with concrete realities
not transferable	transferable
complex	simple
disorderly	orderly

This pattern is reinforced by another element in the situation—the continuing institutional battle between AID and the Department of State. AID has a strong bias toward strict economic criteria and is therefore constantly threatened by the Department of State, whose criteria tend to be short-term political.

The long, intense, and often bitter debate —or, often more accurately, shouting match —between these two points of view has inhibited consideration of still another alternative, political development. For the economically oriented group in AID, "political development" tends to be evil because it is "political"; for the politically oriented group in the Department of State, it is naive because it is "developmental." It is small wonder that political development is not considered as a realistic alternative or complementary policy.

Still another factor militating against the formation of a political-development policy is the fear of involvement in the internal affairs, especially the internal political affairs, of the recipient nations. The administrators accept the inevitability of involvement in the economic systems of the recipients, but not in the political systems. Some writers have suggested that it is cultural relativism that inhibits U. S. aid administrators from coming to grips with problems of political development, but this was definitely not the case in the interview sample. One inhibitor seems to be the traditional diplomatic doctrine of nonintervention. However inappropriate some aspects of this venerable doctrine may be as a guide for the use of foreign aid in the contemporary world, it still is highly respected by the aid administrators. A second and even more important inhibitor is the fear of politics—the apprehension that involvement in politics in the recipient country is dangerous for U. S. interests. The contrary view, that "noninvolvement" carries with it its own very real set of dangers, is not widespread in AID.

The American historical experience with political development is possibly a sixth factor. We were "born free," Hartz (VI, 1955: *passim*) rightly reminds us; and Pye (VI, 1964: 8-9) has pointed out that the American society and economy developed before the government, whereas in most of the world, governments are trying to pull societies and economies up after them. Therefore it is not surprising that the American experience has produced an attitude of disdain toward the idea of a possible "technology of political development" or "technical assistance for political development."

Among a majority of the aid administrators, the sociological and psychological dimensions of political change are not perceived or are not salient factors in their implicit models of political change.[1] Among the academics, the importance of these dimensions has passed speculation and hypothesis and arrived at a point of demonstrated fact. Hence it seems clear that the findings of the researchers are not being communicated to the operators. For example, American political scientists were recently asked to name the members of their profession who they thought had "made the most contributions to the discipline since World War II" (Somit & Tanenhaus, VI, 1963). Of the six men named, all were "behavioral" political scientists but one, Hans J. Morgenthau. Interestingly, Morgenthau is the only one of the six whom the aid administrators mentioned as useful or even said they knew about, despite the fact that the others (especially Lasswell and Dahl) also deal with themes that would seem to be of comparable interest to men trying to build a world community of stable, democratic nations. Now it may be that that which political scientists think a contribution does not in actual fact help us to understand our world. Or, more likely, academic contributions *can* help us but *do* not because most operators are very little aware of these research findings. That the findings of the social and behavioral sciences be better employed in the quest for solutions to problems of public policy is not a new plea; however, it still seems to be a very relevant one.

Finally, it is evident that an important reason why these findings are not meaningful to the operators is that their implications for the instruments of foreign policy are not clear. We have already noted that many studies, of various types, are needed. Some conscious experimentation to see what can be achieved with aid instruments might well be in order.[2] If political development is a

---

[1] Our evidence confirms McClelland's (VI, 1963) observation that "Often travelers, technical advisers, or 'old-hands' from a given country return with tales of how disorganized, dishonest, or untrustworthy the people are; but once the tales have been told, everyone settles down to a theoretical description of, or plan for, the economy of that country which does not take into account in any formal way the psychological characteristics of the people just described. Experts are informally convinced that people differ and that these differences should be taken into account somehow, but they have as yet discovered no way to include such variables in their formal models of economic and social development" (p. 152).

[2] McClelland (VI, 1963) recently dared to suggest, "Nowadays many nations as a matter of public policy, and both national and international organizations, are trying to help underdeveloped countries to achieve either rapid economic development or political stability. Why would it not be

worthwhile objective, the creation of an instrumental doctrine for policy-makers is a most important task. It is a crucial next step if world community—at present only a hope— is to be made a truly meaningful objective.

We have argued in this article for a more

possible to persuade one of these organizations to choose two countries that are matched in every way possible and to try, for example, to raise the achievement level in one, while the other is treated in more traditional ways, to see which of the two countries develops more rapidly economically? . . . With so many countries in the world currently seeking rapid modernization, and with so many different agencies trying to help them, it should not be impossible to find a way to carry out such an experiment over a five- or ten-year period." (P. 181.)

explicit and sophisticated political-development policy in the U. S. aid program and in U. S. foreign policy generally. No one can say with certainty that such a policy—more calculated and, perhaps, more ambitious than the current posture—would be successful. The uncertainties are many and the cost of missteps could be high. But our present course has uncertainties as well, and there may be substantial hidden costs in opportunities foregone. We have tried to point out some serious weaknesses in the reasons adduced to defend the present stance; other justifications are less yielding. On balance, the wisdom of a political-development strategy is still debatable, but at the least it deserves much greater attention than it has received.

The Soldier and International Relations

MORRIS JANOWITZ

By custom, law, and political necessity, the professional soldier must be nonpartisan in domestic political affairs. Yet it is clear that the professional officer requires considerable sensitivity to the political and social consequences of military operations. At each step in the graduated application of force, threatened or actual, to the control of international relations, political and social factors are completely intertwined with what has been called military considerations. In varying degrees this has always been the case. But today military administration permits a very small margin of political and social miscalculation. Assuming an effective form of civilian supremacy, the implementation of military policy is so complex that important political and social tasks tend to adhere to the military even in peacetime. The relations between troops and native civilians in overseas areas, the conduct of counter guerrilla warfare, the management of foreign assistance programs, the implementation of military alliances, and negotiations for arms control, are as much political and social arrangements as they are military operations.

Military leaders in the United States over recent decades have developed a concern for the political and social implications of their behavior. Their concern for these problems does not imply that they have the tradition, knowledge, or the resources at their disposal, to act on the basis of their concerns. Hence, there is little evidence that the American military elite corresponds to the stereotype of a power elite bent on a secret conspiracy. The military elite over the past two decades, like the civilian elite groups, has had to broaden its horizons to include the entire spectrum of international relations. . . . It would be in error to describe this process as "designed militarism" . . . [which] involves the modification and destruction of civilian institutions by military leaders acting directly and premeditatedly through the state and other institutions.

Equally significant, and more likely to account for crucial aspects of contemporary American problems, is "unanticipated militarism." Unanticipated militarism develops from a lack of effective traditions and practices for controlling the military establishment. . . . Under such circumstances a vacuum is created which not only encourages an extension of the tasks and power of military leadership but actually compels such trends. . . .

Nevertheless, the concern of professional officers with the political and social aspects of military operations—in particular with the limitation on force—is likely to continue, for better or for worse. One can say for better, since it could contribute to a rational foreign policy; for worse, because politically sensitive military leadership could be less responsive to civilian control. . . .

● Morris Janowitz, *Sociology and the Military Establishment*, New York: Russell Sage Foundation, 1965, pp. 115-129. Reprinted by permission of the publisher and the author.

Political indoctrination in the American military establishment has, of course, been a continuous problem. The essential requirement of maintaining a position of neutrality toward issues with partisan implications is especially difficult in a political democracy. One effect of this requirement has been a restriction of topics discussed to those which have been resolved by consensus and removed from public debate. Such topics are then of such a general and abstract nature that instruction is difficult and produces an apathetic response. But basically, there has been a profound and complete rejection by the military—both officers and enlisted personnel—of political indoctrination.

* * * * *

New Professional Perspectives

The changed character of international relations presents the professional soldier with the necessity of a new conception of the appropriate means of employing force. The general trend may be described as one of reverse escalation. The prospect of total war dominated the military concept of international relations for a brief period following the explosion of the atomic bomb. With increased recognition of equal enemy capability, a concept of mutual deterrence developed. Limited nuclear warfare was then briefly proposed as an alternative, but the risk was so great that it might develop into unlimited nuclear warfare that it proved to be only a transition back to conventional warfare.

Meanwhile, a decision to employ conventional warfare involved the corresponding risk that it might develop to the point that nuclear weapons would be employed. This restraint provoked concern with the development of such methods of limited conventional warfare as irregular warfare, armed subversion, and resistance by counter-subversion. While such subconventional methods continue, the persisting threat of nuclear warfare has produced extensive discussion of the strategy and tactics of mutual warning, inspection, and disarmament. At this point, political and social—rather than military—considerations predominate. As a result, changes in doctrine and self-conception of the military profession are required. Janowitz (IV.2, 1960) suggests:

"The use of force in international relations has been so altered that it seems appropriate to speak of constabulary force . . . continuously prepared to act, committed to the minimum use of force, and [which] seeks viable international relations, rather than victory, because it has incorporated a protective military posture . . . (p. 418).

* * * * *

The effect of these trends is already apparent in the changing organizational experience of the professional officer. Numerous senior officers have combined achievement in both spheres of the military establishment as a result of their experiences in World War II and the Korean Conflict. Even at lower levels of military organization, activities have grown beyond the traditional categories of platoons, regiments, and staff sections. An entirely new vocabulary of structures has developed, including teams, missions, and projects, as well as boards, committees, and directorates. Officers are likely to spend less time with their own organizations and an increased amount of time in extra-organizational activities. Such activities provide the officer with an area of initiative outside of specific hierarchical control, and involve evaluations by colleagues on the basis of diversified professional situations. He is thus required to develop a new set of skills in the form of committee behavior, resembling those of the political leader: evaluating the relative weight of the recommendations of various staff sections, mustering support and answering counter-arguments, and sensing an incipient consensus.

A similar trend modifying hierarchical organizational conceptions in the Army is apparent in the structure of the "Reorganization Objective Army Division." This formation consists of multiple small specialized and standardized units, designed for flexible and variable alignments within the larger organization. . . . Hierarchical arrangements are consequently functional and transitory, thus reducing the emphasis on domination and substituting lateral patterns of communication for the traditional vertical pattern.

From the long-range perspective of a career, however, important points of tension persist. Strains are especially prominent in the transition from the emotional and technical requirements of a combat officer assigned to duties at sea, with tactical ground units, or with air crews, to the requirements of higher command. . . .

An alternative dichotomy of career development is emerging which may separate leaders with broad managerial orientations toward their tasks from those who are primarily concerned with the technical development of new weapons systems. An increasing number of senior officers are now following scientific and technical careers . . . . With an assured position in the hierarchy and steadily rising prestige in scientific matters, they are frequently permitted to pass judgment on broad professional issues for which their specialized technical experiences have not adequately equipped them. This trend produces new strains in the military establishment and may impede the development of broader perspectives.

Research into career lines and career development in the military establishment is continually required to understand these trends and their consequences. Such research must be broader than personnel selection research and must focus on organizational change. One interesting approach is the analysis of sponsored military literature, as reflecting changes in the professional self-image of the services. In such an analysis, Feld (IV.2, 1964) concluded that both Army and Navy have moved from a traditional "primitive self-conception" to a competitive or managerial one. However, there appeared to be a significant divergence between these services: "The Navy has followed a pattern of increased professionalization by stimulating conformity to existing patterns while modifying them slowly. The Army has engaged in a drastic and unstable search for new bases of professional identity." (p. 188.)

CONSEQUENCES OF FORCE

Thus far the focus of this study has been on the internal structure of the military establishment as a social system and as a reflection of the larger society. To speak of the consequences of military behavior—the political and social outcomes—requires a broader frame of reference. The military specialist thinks of force as a factor in international relations in absolute quantitative and physical terms—manpower and firepower. The sociologist must assume that military force is but one of several means that a nation state has at its disposal for influencing international relations; others are economic, cultural, and political media, diplomatic negotiation, and mass persuasion. Of crucial importance to the sociologist is the particular organization of these various means, for the same instruments differently organized have different consequences.

For example, military occupation by American forces carrying their own logistical support has had very different political consequences from those resulting from occupation by Russian troops who exploit the local resources. The performance of American military government, from Germany to Korea, was deeply influenced by not only the political directives under which it operated but also by the fact that military government organization was kept strictly parallel to tactical military organization. Consequently, as the front expanded, specific localities were administered by as many as four different units, each having to rebuild its own local contacts. Even after stabilization, or where military government took over major areas directly as in Japan and Korea, the channels of command were unduly complicated by their articulation with occupational units. The arrangement tended to emphasize administrative efficiency at the expense of social and political objectives.

The utilization of a sociological perspective by the military establishment has been limited chiefly to those functions which the military in the past has considered to be secondary functions—political and psychological warfare, military government, and troop indoctrination. With the exception of economics which has emerged as a powerful tool of management, the use of the theoretical and technical capabilities of social scientists in dealing with military problems has been sporadic and infrequent at best, although notable instances can be reported by social scientists. Perhaps the most marked and dramatic shift has been the introduction of sociological materials, especially about the military profession, into the general education of military officers.

The relevance of sociological thinking is not limited to the analysis of consequences of particular military operations. It has a broader relevance for understanding the potentials and limitations on the use of force in all its dimensions as a factor for influencing international relations. Such dimensions include strategic and operational planning, the direction of operations, the consolidation of outcomes, and the assessment of effects . . . .

In the past, the political and sociological assumptions that military planners have made either remained implicit or were limited to their stereotypes as to how soldiers of specific nationalities behaved in battle . . . . But as warfare grew to require total involvement of the population, the problem extends well beyond the scope of professional military thinking. The U. S. military services entered World War II unprepared to handle such estimates in their strategical planning. During the course of the hostilities, the evaluation of strategic intelligence was developed to the point that highly sophisticated estimates of the probable behavior of German and Japanese social systems under attack were developed . . . .

Many of these estimates were developed by civilian social scientists in uniform and were often the results of self-generated assignments, which ultimately developed some organizational legitimacy.

Since the end of World War II, the necessity for strategic political and social intelligence for guiding national security policy, including military policy, has been generally accepted. The armed forces even played a role and continue to be active in subsidizing university-based social research on foreign social systems, as for example, the Russian research program of the United States Air Force at Harvard University. By contrast, strategic political military intelligence in the Korean Conflict did not reach the same levels of analysis, because of the difficulties of mobilizing specialized civilian personnel in a period of limited hostilities. While there has been a marked proliferation of country and area type studies concerning the new nations, the systematic analysis of civil-military relations, and the sociology of war and revolution in these areas is only gradually emerging. The theoretical dimensions and practical requirements of strategic intelligence for foreign policy is a topic that evokes strong and passionate opinions among experts, especially in a period of difficult foreign relations, since it is easier to declare that intelligence was faulty than to reevaluate policies.

However, the sociological analysis of total societies is not yet adequately developed to clarify these basic issues. Current sociological analysis tends to view violence in a social system as a form of disorganization or as deviant behavior (Parsons, VI, 1951). It is also important to note that such an orientation is prevalent among social anthropologists, even though a major source of social change among nonliterate social systems has been warfare....

Given the present state of sociological theory, one feasible approach to a more systematic understanding of the role of force in social change is the comparative sociological study of military organization; that is, all types of military organization, including paramilitary forces, guerrilla units, and resistance movements. A model for such research can be found in the analysis of the guerrillas in Malaya by Lucian Pye (VI, 1956). An alternative frame of reference is to focus on military elites as a social grouping and to analyze their social composition, career lines, and indoctrination as an index to military behavior (Pool, VI, 1955). In *The Military in the Political Development of New Nations* (Janowitz, VI, 1964), a series of propositions are presented to account for the role of the professional soldier in the politics of some fifty emerging countries....

The patterns of "armed forces and society" in western Europe have been studied to some limited degree on a comparative basis as part of the effort to understand military professionalism and civil-military relations in advanced industrial countries. These studies indicate a broad pattern of uniformity in that the military do not operate as partners of the political leadership, but as pressure groups. At the same time, there are important differences from country to country in the influence of the military as a pressure group and in their professional objectives ("Armed Forces and Society . . . ," VI, 1965).

* * * * *

As long as the military concept of warfare focused on atomic warfare, the official stimulus for research was on the social and psychological aspects of disaster rather than on political and psychological warfare. Most available civilian disasters have been carefully investigated and important observations systematized by Martha Wolfenstein (VI, 1957). With the reemergence of limited warfare concepts, questions about the social consequences of military operations are more pertinent. What situations of the past and the present are likely models to clarify future contingencies? The nature of limited warfare since the end of World War II involving Communist forces has obscured the distinction between conventional military operations and police duties. Even the United Nations forces operating in the Israeli-Arab conflict found that more conventional police organization was required to maintain an unstable equilibrium....

The analysis of the sociological consequences of limited warfare cannot be understood within the categories now used by the American military establishment. In an effort to accommodate itself to political needs, a number of specialized auxiliaries have been incorporated as staff agencies: psychological warfare personnel, military government specialists, guerrilla warfare teams and special forces. Personnel are also trained for military assistance operations. The effectiveness of these specialists depends on U. S. national policies. The concept that these specialists perform separate technical functions, however, has been a fundamental weakness in their support of military operations. Research on the successes and failures of these politico-military functions in the recent past continues to be essential. This involves an understanding of how American social structure has influenced the development of our military institutions and how military organization adapts to and resists change....

The impact of military operations in South Vietnam has been significant in the extent to which these activities have required a modification of organizational doctrine for dealing with the problems of limited war and guerrilla operations. While there is yet no major social science synthesis of these events or their impact on the armed services, it is clear that the consequences will pervade the United States armed forces in the decades ahead. The dramatic responses to the new requirements range from the creation of Special Forces to deal with guerrilla warfare, to the emergence of the civic action concept in which the military seek to be agents of social change by using their resources for economic and social welfare activities . . . . But sociological writing on insurrections and counter-insurgency is much too diffuse and relatively unconcerned with organizational realities.

The traditional experience of the professional officer has fostered a mechanistic conception of society which recent trends have shown signs of modifying . . . . [B]ecause of the systematic rotation of assignment and residential seclusion in military installations . . . few professional officers have had opportunities to participate in social action which has been generated by local events. The "bargaining" component of the local political process is rarely encountered. Tasks assigned to the military usually imply that the political process has been exhausted, and frequently the professional officer only has an awareness of the political process after there is evidence that it has failed. Hence, he is prone to believe that the political process can be eliminated, or that the same result can be achieved by a more direct method.

The lack of local involvement of the professional officer also cultivates a conception of the political process in its most highly visible aspect: the electoral campaign. As a result, in foreign areas he places an exaggerated reliance on mass communications techniques such as radio and leaflets. The conception of the welfare state as a "vote-getter" rather than a demonstration of the regime's recognition of a social need leads to sporadic distributions of food or demonstrations of modern medical healing in villages which cannot support such services from their own resources . . . . Such techniques at times have the effect of sharpening a sense of deprivation and accelerating aspirations beyond the capacity of the native regime to satisfy them.

In the present state of international relations, the military establishment persists in thinking mainly about the implications of future hostilities, insurgent, limited or total. But there is an immediate impact of the worldwide U.S. military system on international relations and worldwide politico-military affairs. The official doctrines of the U.S. military establishment have had important consequences in fashioning Soviet strategy and tactics in the nuclear age (Garthoff, VI, 1958). The stationing of troops in allied countries and the creation of new elites and counter-elites by military assistance programs are equally important aspects of military operations . . . .

The United States trains large numbers of foreign military personnel, especially in the borderline areas of the control of guerrilla warfare and para-military operations. More recently, new programs of civic action are being launched, especially in South America, where the American military seek to stimulate their local counterparts to engage in economic development and nation-building. In all of these areas, the military are active agents of social change or can become factors resisting social change.

Some public opinion polling has been conducted on the attitudes of allied populations toward the American troops stationed in their countries. The work of staff members of the Social Science Division of The Rand Corporation has been a notable example of a sustained research contribution to these problems. Research studies from this group include Hans Speier's (VI, 1957) on reactions of German military elite to remilitarization, and the case study by W. Phillips Davison (VI, 1958) of the classic use of the military establishment in the cold war, *The Berlin Blockade: A Study in Cold War Politics*.[1]

But sociologists and members of related disciplines have not accepted the responsibility for the systematic study of the impact of the military, as a social system in being, on international relations. Under these circumstances it is understandable that the military has not developed a profound interest in these research matters. Moreover, it would be most undesirable in a democracy if the locus of concern were exclusively or even mainly with the military. If social change, at home and abroad, is a central theme of sociological analysis, the implications are obvious.

---

[1] The Social Science Research Council has established a Committee on National Security Policy, under Professor William Fox, which stimulates and reflects the interest of historians and political scientists in the analysis of the backgrounds of military policy.

The Social Sciences in the Foreign Policy Subsystem of Congress

PAUL DE FOREST

INTRODUCTION

In the complex political system that is American government, foreign policy develops as a result of mutual adjustment and accommodation among many actors—the Executive, Congress, interest groups, other nations and the public. The requirement that the demands of many actors be considered means that foreign policy can never be prescribed. Instead, it is evolutionary, developed in a never-ending chain of successive comparisons of policy alternatives. These alternatives emanate from analysis and evaluation of popular demands, foreign actions, possible ends and available means, and the impact of previous policy. It is in conjunction with this evaluative process that social scientific expertise can contribute to the making of policy.

This "model" of the decision-making process can be applied not only to the overall governmental system but also, by analogy, to each of its parts.[1] When we examine the actors who participate in the policy making process, it is apparent that nowhere is the fragmented and disjointed nature of this process more pronounced than in Congress. The variety of actors, interests, and settings which characterizes Congressional decisions necessitates a high degree of mutual adjustment and accommodation within the Congressional social system, preliminary to Congress' confrontation with the Executive.

Under these conditions, policy will be coordinated not so much as a result of the acts of a central authority or by individual decision makers adhering to common schemes of thought and action as through the multiple instances in which a given policy is analyzed and evaluated. According to Lindblom, this increases the likelihood that available information and intelligence are brought to bear on a given problem, that decision makers are made aware of the values and interests of different groups in relation to the issues at stake, and that policy alternatives are explored (Lindblom, II.3, 1965: Chapter I; Braybrooke & Lindblom, II.3, 1963: Chapter V).

In Congress this function of analysis and evaluation is performed by Congressional staffs, members of executive departments and agencies, representatives of interest groups appearing before Congressional committees, extragovernmental experts and also, above all, by Congressmen themselves. In this article we shall concentrate on a segment of this overall grouping—social scientists whose primary occupation is research or teaching—and its contribution to Congressional evaluation and analysis of foreign

• The article was written for this volume.

[1] For a theoretic statement on decision-making through mutual adjustment, see Lindblom (II.3, 1965).

policy.[1] Here it should be pointed out that we understand the role of the social scientist in this area as being not only that of the expert who furnishes Congressmen with the tools, techniques, or facts for policy analysis but also that of the advocate of certain policy positions or alternatives. As an advocate, he may speak as a member of the social science profession or step out of his professional role and act as an individual or a citizen.

While there has been a number of studies of interest groups and their relation to Congress, Congressional use of extragovernmental experts, whether they be scientific, social scientific, or other, is an area which has remained largely unexplored. Although some information of this type can be culled from case studies of Congressional decisions or decision-making procedures, such as Hammond's study of defense budgets or Dahl's of the role of Congress in foreign policy making, we know of no study dealing exclusively with the use of outside expertise.[2]

As to social science expertise, the lack of interest can probably be explained by the commonly held notion that the social science contribution is so limited that it does not warrant systematic study. This view is evidenced in the writings of social scientists who, when discussing these matters, have commonly taken a "missionary" stance, their major objective being that of "selling" Congress on the use of social science.[3]

Whether the gloomy picture drawn by social scientists is a valid one is a question which can only be answered by studying the relations of Congress and the social science disciplines over a period of time. Since this article constitutes a first attempt to deal with these matters in an analytic rather than a prescriptive fashion, it is important to clarify some of the methodological issues raised by such a study.

First it is important to recognize the dual roles that most Congressmen play in relation to social scientists and social science. Congressmen are either "users" of social science knowledge or participants in the processes whereby government research programs in the social sciences are formulated and controlled. Without a clear distinction between the two, it is easy to assume, as social scientists have often done, that the negative attitudes of certain Congressmen toward government support of social science research means that they are opposed to social science research as such. Opposition to government social science research programs often derives from other factors, such as an attempt to control government spending or an aversion to expansion of the governmental sphere.

Another, and related, issue is the distinction that has to be made between the attitudes of Congressmen toward social science and the use they actually make of social science products. Many Congressmen react to the words "social science" rather like a bull to a red flag; it evokes a whole set of negative attitudes summed up in words such as "socialistic" or "manipulatory." These same Congressmen may, however, frequently and often unknowingly use social science techniques and findings, as is the case, for instance, with public opinion polls. Since attitudes are not a very good indicator of use, they will have to be supplemented by other, more objective measures, such as the frequency with which social scientists are called as witnesses before Congressional committees or employed as staff members

---

[1] Our definition of "social scientists" is a very broad one. It includes all with formal advanced training in the fields of political science, international relations, economics, psychology, sociology, and anthropology who, at the time of their contact with Congress, were professionally attached to a university or research organization.

[2] See especially Dahl (VI, 1964: Chapter X); Hammond (VI, 1962). See also Carroll (VI, 1965); and Dexter (VI, 1963).

[3] See Alpert (III.2, 1958); Bailey (VI, 1955); Halperin (III.3, 1960); and Likert (I, 1957).

and consultants, or the extent to which social science concepts and findings are incorporated in committee reports.

Before putting these indicators to use, however, we will explore more broadly some characteristics of Congressional decision making and decision makers that we feel may have an effect on the use made of social science. These are important as a means of guiding us to the points in the Congressional system where social scientists are most likely to gain access. In some small measure such decision-making characteristics may also provide an explanation for our findings in this study.

CONGRESS AS A SOCIAL SYSTEM

While it is accurate to refer to Congress as the legislative branch of the federal government, it is simplistic, even misleading, to consider its only function to be the proposal, consideration, and passage of law. Congress is far more than a lawmaking body; it is charged with representing the electorate, it appropriates the funds by which laws are executed, it oversees the administration of the laws, and it contributes to the formation of policy in areas which legislation cannot reach.[1]

These functions are performed by a variety of actors, among whom the Congressmen themselves, in a formal sense, are the key figures. The limits on their time, however, and the pressure of other responsibilities force them to depend on their assistants or committee staff members to gather background information, analyze legislative proposals, and draft bills. In studying the social scientists in relation to Congress, we have to take into account not only their contacts with the Congressmen themselves but, also, with these other actors whose contribution, largely informal, to Congressional decision making often is highly significant.

In addition to the variety of functions and actors, the Congressional system is also characterized by a diffusion of power. While the House and the Senate share power equally, both usually accept the recommendations of their committees without change. Likewise, committees usually defer to specialized subcommittees, and often also to the expertise of individual members. Considerable influence may also be exerted on a particular committee by Congressmen who, although they are not members, speak authoritatively on matters within its domain (Huitt, VI, 1961). Another contributing factor is the existence of informal groups such as the Liberal Study Group or the Wednesday Group, the former composed of liberal Democrats and the latter of moderate Republican Congressmen.

These three characteristics—a variety of functions and of actors, as well as a diffusion of power—suggest that for analytic purposes Congress is best viewed as a complex, decentralized social system. What are some of the implications of adopting this view in a study of the role of the social sciences in Congressional decision making?

The variety of actors and the diversity of their backgrounds and interests, for instance, mean that we will find considerable differences in the ability and willingness of individual Congressmen and their staffs to use social science knowledge. It is hardly surprising that former professors and teachers of social science, such as Senators Fulbright, Morse, and now Vice-President Humphrey, have gained a reputation among social scientists for being sympathetic listeners and supporters. Going beyond personalities we may hypothesize that receptivity to social sciences and scientists is definable in terms of a "local"-"cosmopolitan" scale. Contributions to a "local" orientation are all those factors that make a Congressman more interested in the prob-

[1] A broad discussion of the legislative function can be found in Lasswell and Kaplan (VI, 1950: 195-196).

lems of his constituents than the broad issues of national policy.

The use made of social science knowledge, however, is not only a function of background and orientation but also of the opportunity of Congressmen to exert influence in areas which have a "social scientific" character. This is often dependent on securing membership on particular committees, which, as a rule, depends more on seniority than on experience and interest. But there are important exceptions to this rule: in committees concerned with foreign policy, as will be shown later, experience seems to carry some weight in selection for membership.

As to the diffusion of power, the decentralized nature of the system is such that there are a large number of points at which outside groups, such as the social scientists, can gain access. Since the aim of many Congressmen is to create individual positions of influence and power, it can be assumed that they welcome the aid of outside groups who are able to furnish them with policy proposals and intelligence. Some evidence for this hypothesis is found in a study by Bauer, Pool, and Dexter (VI, 1963: 197-198) of interest groups concerned with foreign trade policies. This study showed that Congressmen were considered considerably more receptive to suggestions for changes in trade policies than were members of the Executive Branch.

This one study, however, can hardly be used as a basis for generalizations regarding the receptivity of Congress to policy proposals from outside groups. Many of these groups, as is often the case with the social scientists, have policy views and maintain ideological positions which are much less acceptable to the average Congressman than are those of interest groups concerned with foreign trade. Rather than attempting to generalize regarding the effect of the "openness" of the Congressional social system, therefore, it becomes important to try to find answers to questions such as "open to whom," "under what conditions," and "with what limitations." A series of case studies of individual groups, such as the social scientists, and their relations to Congress would undoubtedly provide answers to some of these questions.

The diffusion of power may also limit the ability of Congress to stand up to the other branches of government and guard its decision-making prerogatives. Such a possibility has obvious implications for the role of the social scientist in Congress. If it is true, as is often maintained, that Congress has lost its initiative in foreign affairs and that the Executive alone has the information and the ability to act decisively in this area, then it may not be surprising that social scientists should regard executive agencies and departments as more promising audiences when it comes to the application of social science to the making of policy.[1]

The assumption contained in statements such as these, however, are only partly correct and in many ways misleading. First they are misleading because they fail to take into account the distinct nature of the Congressional role in the formulation of policy. Whereas the Executive has primary charge of both the formulation and the execution of decisions, Congress retains an important and distinct role in both. During the formulation process it investigates and evaluates executive bills, provides a forum for support or opposition of interested publics, and perhaps proposes alternative policies. In the administration of legislation and the conduct of executive policy, it reserves the right to criticize, caution, and penalize with all the instruments at its command.

Second there are the variations found in the way Congress performs its decision making role in different areas of national concern. Looking at the overall field of international affairs, for instance, we find consid-

---

[1] Other explanations, for example, policy congeniality and availability of research funds, may, of course, be more important.

erable differences in Congressional influence over national defense policy, on the one hand, and foreign policy on the other—these being roughly defined as the respective areas of responsibility of the Departments of Defense and State. As was pointed out by Dexter (VI, 1963:306), Congressmen "have little tendency to raise and consider questions of military policy in terms of its meaning for some national or international political objective or goal." Rather they are concerned with structural details and emphasize the "sacred cow" of the itemized budget as a means for detailed control over the implementation rather than the formulation of defense policy. Here, as a rule, they tend to rely heavily on the military, scientific, and technical expertise provided by the Department of Defense and the armed services (Carroll, VI, 1965: 165 ff.).

In the field of foreign policy, Congress appears much more anxious to play an active role and has jealously upheld its right to be heard. This is evidenced, for example, by the practice, among those committees concerned with foreign policy matters, not only to carry out far-ranging reviews of policies and decisions emanating from the Executive Branch but, also, to put forth their own policy proposals. In doing so they seem to rely on a wider range of expertise than that provided by executive departments and agencies. In the following we will examine the role played by social scientists in what might be termed the foreign policy subsystem of Congress.

THE FOREIGN POLICY SUBSYSTEM

The foreign policy subsystem, like its parent Congressional social system, is characterized by a multiplicity of functions and actors and a diffusion of power. A measure of the diverse character of its involvement in foreign policy matters is found in Table 1 which gives a categorization of hearings published by eleven committees of the House and Senate, respectively, and two joint committees during the period January 1959 to June 1966.

This table points up two factors of interest in studying the role of extragovernmental experts. First it shows that the Senate and the House in important respects share equally in foreign policy decision making. Although the Constitution gives primacy to the Senate through the provision that it must participate in the ratification of all treaties, the importance of this function has been reduced over the years by the growth of executive agreements. As a consequence only nine important treaties were considered by the Senate Foreign Relations Committee during the period 1959–1965. Concomitant with the decline of this function, Congress has come to perform an increasingly important role in areas where the House and the Senate have roughly equal power: legislation, appropriations, and the review of foreign policy decisions and proposals. There may well be differences between the two in the application of social science knowledge to foreign policy but, in terms of structure

TABLE 1. Congress and Foreign Policy, January 1959–June 1966: A Categorization of Published Committee Hearings[a]

Category	House	Senate	Joint
Legislation	78	85	3
Authorizations and Appropriations	35	33	0
Background and Review Studies on Independent Congressional Initiative	59	70	17
Resolutions and Treaties	5	11	0

[a] Excluded are those hearings which lasted less than a full day, which were concerned exclusively with Presidential nominations, or which were devoted to very minor or obscure legislation (especially certain tariff bills).

and powers alone, the Senate and House are equally promising audiences.

The second factor revealed by Table 1 is the large number of background and review hearings undertaken by both the Senate and the House (70 and 59, respectively). Included in this category are hearings dealing with foreign policy undertaken on the independent initiative of the house or committee concerned, but not hearings dealing with executive bills or proposals. Background and review hearings provide the prime focus for this article because they can be considered as readily accessible examples of Congressional policy initiative, and the most likely platform for those experts giving advice as *professionals* rather than as members of interest groups.[1] Almost half of these hearings were undertaken by two committees, Foreign Relations and Foreign Affairs which, as the nucleus of the foreign policy subsystem, will receive most of our attention. But equally significant is the large number of such hearings conducted by other committees. Although on the periphery of the foreign policy subsystem, they, along with the Appropriations committees, form an important part of it.

The frequency with which background and review hearings are being conducted suggests the possibility that these committees may be actively attempting to evaluate executive policies and develop possible alternatives of their own. This, however, is only tentative, since we know very little about the extent to which information and suggestions developed in such hearings are taken into account by Congressmen or the frequency with which they lead to action in the form of legislation. More important for our purposes are their informative-evaluative character and the wide variety of topics. These characteristics make it likely that we will find all types of "social scientists," strictly or loosely defined, appearing as witnesses.

The background, training, and experience of the actors operating within the foreign policy subsystem provide us with another measure of the receptivity of the system to a contribution from the social sciences. Of primary interest are the members of committees. Table 2 shows the familiarity of the membership of these committees with social science disciplines through education, training, and professional activities (i.e., teaching or research). For comparison we have included committees dealing with both foreign and defense policy matters. Listed in Table 2 are Congressmen and Senators serving at least one session on any of these committees during the period studied.

The table shows that the number of committee members with training or experience in the social sciences is very small, indeed. This is not surprising since law traditionally has been and still is the most common form of higher academic training for members of Congress. Yet a background in social science is probably more frequently found among members of these committees than in Congress as a whole. Although we find, in the House, little difference in the backgrounds of members on committees concerned with defense policy, on the one hand, and foreign policy, on the other, the Senate Foreign Relations Committee has a significantly higher ratio of members with training in the social sciences.[2]

---

[1] Those giving advice based on interest rather than professional competence, will be likely to concentrate on hearings where actual bills are being considered—e.g., businessmen on tariffs, church groups on the Peace Corps, and minority groups on immigration. Social scientists may, of course, have an *interest* in a particular policy. If their interest is professionally based, they are classified as social scientists; if it stems from their appearance as spokesmen for church groups, political action groups, or minority groups (there were a number of such cases at legislative hearings) they are classified as members of such groups.

[2] Our data supports the findings of Donald R. Matthews (VI, 1960: 155), for the period 1947-

TABLE 2. Social Science Background, Members of Committees and Subcommittees with Major Role in Foreign or Defense Policy, January 1959–June 1966

	Membership Total	Number of College Graduates	Graduate Training in Social Science	Advanced Degree in Social Science	Professional Experience in Social Science
House					
Appropriations[a]	39	33	6	4	1
Armed Services	64	53	6	5	2
Government Operations[b]	12	10	1	1	0
Foreign Affairs	54	47	4	3	2
Judiciary[c]	13	13	0	0	0
Senate					
Appropriations[d]	30	26	3	3	1
Armed Services	26	21	2	2	1
Government Operations[e]	19	17	4	3	1
Foreign Relations	25	20	9	8	5
Judiciary[f]	18	17	1	0	0
Joint					
Joint Economic Committee	23	23	6	4	3

[a] Defense, State, and Foreign Operations Subcommittees.
[b] Foreign Operations Subcommittee.
[c] Subcommittee on Immigration and Naturalization, 1959-1962. Subcommittee number 1, 1963-1966.
[d] Defense and State Subcommittees.
[e] Subcommittees on Reorganization and International Organizations, National Policy Machinery, National Security Staffing and Operations, and Foreign Aid Expenditures.
[f] Permanent Subcommittee on Immigration and Naturalization. Special Subcommittees on Internal Security, Refugees and Escapees, and Trading with the Enemy Act.

Most members with advanced degrees or professional experience are either political scientists or economists. Of the five members on the Senate Foreign Relations Committee with professional experience, three had taught government; one, history; and one (Senator McCarthy of Minnesota), sociology. The House Foreign Affairs Committee presents a somewhat different picture: of the two members with professional experience, one had taught and the other had practiced psychology. In the first case, however, the member's major academic training was in law. In the second case the position was in the field of vocational psychology and social work. Furthermore, since there were only three members with advanced training in social science, they could hardly have affected the work of so large a committee in any concerted manner.

Another category of actors influencing the extent to which social science expertise is brought into the foreign policy subsystem are the staff members of committees. For almost twenty years students of Congress have attempted to correct the inadequacies of the Legislative Reorganization Act of 1946 by calling for greatly increased professional staff assistance to enable Congress to examine independently and in detail executive policy proposals and appropriations requests.[1] The decision to increase staff size,

1957 in the Senate. "Among the college professors, Foreign Relations is by far the most desirable of the top committees, and there were over three times the proportion of them on Foreign Relations as in the Senate as a whole."

[1] For the most recent example, see the proposals of Alfred de Grazia and Heinz Eulau in Alfred de Grazia (VI, 1966).

however, rests essentially with the legislature itself. And, for a number of reasons, Congress has deliberately chosen to keep its staffs small. Despite the extremely small size of the staffs of the Foreign Relations and Foreign Affairs Committees, even by Congressional standards, they still manage to assist greatly in committee operations, by providing background information,[1] evaluating executive proposals, selecting and screening witnesses, and writing committee reports. If social scientists are to provide advice in the field of foreign policy, one of the readiest means of access may be through staff members, who are either themselves trained in the social sciences or else sympathetic to the kind of expertise social scientists can provide.

The only previous study of membership on committee staffs, covering a period ending fifteen years ago, found social scientists to be scarce relative to lawyers. The explanation the author gave for this was that the latter were more flexible and better able to generalize and, thus, made more useful aides to Congressmen (Kofmehl, VI, 1962: 83-88, 92 ff.). This may be valid—although it deserves a more conclusive test. It is true that in the period 1959-1966, only three professional staff members on the Foreign Relations Committee and two on the Foreign Affairs Committee possessed advanced degrees in the social sciences—all, moreover, in political science, public administration, or international relations. A better explanation for their scarcity, however, may be that fewer social scientists apply for staff positions. There would seem to be nothing to prevent social scientists who work for Congress from being as flexible and as unbiased as lawyers. Moreover social scientists appear to be successful staff members out of proportion to their numbers—a political scientist has headed the staff of the Foreign Relations Committee for about two decades and an international relations expert now ranks second on Foreign Affairs.

PROFESSIONAL SOCIAL SCIENTISTS IN THE FOREIGN POLICY SUBSYSTEM

The contacts between social scientists affiliated with universities or research organizations and the actors in the foreign policy subsystem vary widely. According to a simple typology, these may be categorized as follows:

1. according to the points within the system at which they take place (with individual Congressmen or committee staffs, appearances before Congressional committees, relationships with informal groups such as the Liberal Study Group);

2. according to the types of social science inputs (solicited or unsolicited, contributing policy advice or policy intelligence, theoretic concepts or tools, etc.).

Our preliminary investigation of the contacts between the foreign policy subsystem and outside social scientists during the past seven years shows very few instances of social scientists engaging in formal research projects sponsored by Congressional committees concerned with foreign policy matters. The Foreign Affairs Committee has done no studies of this type in the past and apparently has no intention of undertaking any in the future. There are only a few examples of such commissioned research by the Foreign Relations Committee: a series of studies carried out by thirteen research organizations in 1958-1959; an analysis of Latin America in 1958; and a recent attempt to grapple with the issue of neutrality in Southeast Asia (*United States Foreign Policy,* VI, 1961; *Neutralization in Southeast Asia,* VI, 1966). In this area Congress differs markedly from the Executive Branch, where commissioned or contract research probably is the major form of contact with

---

[1] The Foreign Relations Committee staff, for example, undertakes a large number of staff studies yearly, many of which are "limited print," i.e., for the use of the committee members alone.

the academic community. Congressional committees, however, have had neither the funds nor the inclination to sponsor research of their own, choosing instead to rely on their own staffs, to draw on research undertaken for executive agencies or departments or, when neither of these has been considered sufficient, to call in outside experts on an individual *ad hoc* basis.

In the large majority of cases where the advice or knowledge of social scientists is brought to bear on foreign policy matters, access is probably gained through informal contacts with Congressmen or their staffs. This seems to be a realistic assumption considering the individualistic attitudes of both Congressmen and social scientists and the decentralized nature of the Congressional social system. It must remain an assumption, however, until the frequency and nature of such contacts can be studied in detail. At present, next to nothing is known about this important form of interaction.

A third type of contact is the appearance of social scientists as witnesses at hearings conducted by committees concerned with foreign policy matters. In addition to being the most visible form of contact, these hearings possess the advantage of being easy to study. Their limitations as a measure of social science input into the system are obvious. Among the most serious of these is the incomplete and distorted picture the text of a committee hearing may give of what actually transpires; incomplete because testimony in executive session is not included in the record; distorted because such appearances are often primarily formalistic, with the printed statement giving no indication of the extent to which the knowledge or advice presented receives consideration. Testimony at hearings does mean, however, that social scientists are gaining access to the system, and may hence be viewed as the first lap of the obstacle course that runs from access to acceptance to influence over the formulation of policy.

Two categories were used for the analysis of the frequency with which different kinds of social scientists appeared as witnesses at foreign policy hearings during the January 1959–June 1966 period. The first included hearings held on legislative proposals introduced either by the Executive or by individual Congressmen. From the large number of such hearings conducted during the period, nineteen were selected for analysis.[1] The second category consisted of hearings dealing with reviews of foreign policy or the development of "background" for new legislation. Since these latter reflect policy innovations by Congress and also are of a nature that favors a social science contribution, it was decided to do a fairly intensive analysis of the hearings of this type conducted by the Senate Foreign Relations and the House Foreign Affairs Committees. While a large number of other committees engaged in background and re-

[1] The sample was biased in the direction of the foreign policy committees and included those legislative hearings where social science contributions were presumed to be most likely. The committees and hearings included are as follows. Senate Foreign Relations: Foreign Service Act Amendments (1959); ACDA (1961); AID (1961); Fulbright-Hays Act (1961); Peace Corps (1961); Foreign Affairs Academy (1963); Test Ban Treaty (1963); Foreign Aid (1965). House Foreign Affairs: ACDA (1961); AID (1961); Fulbright-Hays Act (1961); Peace Corps (1961); East-West Center (1962); Foreign Aid (1962). House Judiciary: Immigration Amendments (1964); Immigration Amendments (1965). House Un-American Activities: Freedom Academy (1965). It is recognized that foreign policy alternatives may be proposed in hearings dealing with specific legislation. The case where the dividing line is perhaps most difficult to draw is the Foreign Relations Committee hearing of January-February, 1966, which began, in Fulbright's words of January 28 "to consider S. 2793, which would authorize an additional $415 million in foreign economic aid for the current fiscal year . . . $275 million for Vietnam," but by February 17 had as its primary purpose ". . . to inform the American people, the members of the Committee and the Senate as fully as possible about the implications of the war in Vietnam. Whether our country is to continue to enlarge, to continue on the present basis, or to settle this war . . ."

TABLE 3. Witnesses Testifying at Legislative Hearings Dealing with Foreign Policy, January 1959–June 1966

	Number of Hearings	Total Number of Witnesses[a]	Social Scientists	Physical Scientists	Other Professionals	Congressmen	Government Officials	Interest Groups	Political Action Groups
Presidential Proposals	11	357	3	10	14	21	168	106	29
Legislative Proposals	6	111	6	0	31	42	20	9	2

[a] Includes seven unclassifiable witnesses.

view studies, these were selected because they accounted for nearly a majority of the total number of such hearings conducted by Congress over the seven-year period.

Our limited analysis of legislative hearings gave evidence for the view that extragovernmental social scientists play a very minor role at this type of hearing. As shown in Table 3, witnesses were primarily of two kinds; on the one hand government officials having an interest in the proposed legislation and, on the other representatives of broadly-constituted interest groups, e.g., AFL-CIO, SANE, or the Liberty Lobby, appearing as advocates for or against the proposed measure.

The failure of social scientists to appear at legislative hearings may be explained by a limited need for professionally-based intelligence and advice. The primary purpose of legislative hearings is to give the proposers a chance to justify their requests and to allow interest groups to present their views. As a consequence there is little room for a contribution from the independent professional, something which is evidenced by the scant representation not only of social scientists but also of physical scientists and "other" professionals, such as businessmen, educators, or lawyers. The emphasis on advocacy rather than analysis is further demonstrated by the few social scientists who appeared, the majority of whom spoke as supporters or opponents of the proposed legislation.

Although, as is shown in Table 4, government officials and representatives of interest groups remain in the lead as witnesses at background and review hearings, this group of hearings has a larger proportion of extragovernmental professionals (approximately twenty-five percent of all witnesses compared with ten percent in the legislative group). A more striking difference between these and the legislative hearings, however, is that social scientists at these former hearings outnumbered all other categories of extragovernmental professionals. At the same time it should be pointed out that they made up a very small portion of the total witnesses appearing before these two committees (eighteen percent for the Senate Foreign Relations Committee and ten percent for the House Foreign Affairs Commit-

TABLE 4. Witnesses Appearing at Background and Review Hearings Dealing with Foreign Policy, January 1959–June 1966

Committee	Number of Hearings Analyzed	Number of Witnesses	Executive Branch	Legislative Branch	Social Scientists	Physical Scientists	Other Experts	Interest Groups	Political Action Groups	Other
Foreign Relations	27	185	57	16	33	6	17	27	22	7
Foreign Affairs	26	345	88	82	35	3	31	66	28	12

tee) and, perhaps more important, the total number of background and review hearings at which even a single social scientist appeared was very small, indeed (thirteen out of fifty-three).

What types of social scientists appear at background and review hearings and what roles do they perform in connection with such appearances? As was noted in the introduction we included in the "social sciences" the behavioral sciences (psychology, sociology, and anthropology), economics and political science, and the interdisciplinary fields of international relations, foreign policy, and area studies. We also assumed that in their contacts with Congress, the representatives of these various fields would perform a variety of roles ranging from that of the scientific expert who furnishes empirical data or scientifically tested generalizations to that of the "wise man" who bases his advice or predictions on "experience" and personal observations.

Table 5 shows the disciplinary or other specializations of social scientists testifying before the two committees studied. Not surprisingly we find that the fields of political science and economics are the most heavily represented; international relations and area studies follow close behind. By comparison the behavioral scientists form a definite minority, more so, in fact, than appears in the table since three of the psychologists came from a singe hearing—Congressman Fascell's investigation of the United States ideological effort entitled "Winning the Cold War"—and both anthropologists are the same man (Melville Herskovits) testifying at two separate hearings. The question of whether behavioral scientists have contributed much at this level is academic, therefore; they hardly ever appear. Among the other categories, primarily the political scientists and international relations experts, not more than a handful could be considered to have a behavioral orientation.

Our examination of the roles performed by testifying social scientists sheds some further light on the particular kind of policy-oriented social science with which we are dealing here. In Table 6 we have classified the testimony of each witness by two major categories:

1. The advocacy of particular policy proposals and alternatives of a non-professional nature, through which the testifying social scientists perform a role similar to that of representatives of interest groups; and

2. Professionally-based policy advice, process advice, or intelligence. The policy advice may be of two kinds: a clarification of policy alternatives or an evaluation of and choice among different policies. Process advice relates primarily to procedural, organizational, or administrative matters. Intelligence can be given in the form of "raw"

TABLE 5. Testifying Social Scientists—January 1959-June 1966: Categorized by Field[a]

Field	Foreign Relations	Foreign Affairs	Total
Total	33	35	68
Political Science	11	14	25
Economics	5	4	9
International Relations and Area Studies	11	14	25
Sociology	2	0	2
Psychology	2	3	5
Anthropology	2	0	2

[a] By number of appearances rather than number of persons. A total of 58 social scientists have appeared at least once before one or both of the committees. Twenty-nine have appeared at least once before the Foreign Relations Committee and 35 at least once before the Foreign Affairs Committee.

TABLE 6. Testimony of Social Scientists at Background and Review Hearings January 1959–June 1965: by Category of Advice[a]

Category of Advice	Foreign Relations	Foreign Affairs	Total
Advocacy	3	3	6
Policy Advice	27	7	34
Clarification of Policy Alternatives	3	1	4
Evaluation of Policy Alternatives	24	6	30
Process Advice	1	4	5
Intelligence	26	28	54
Providing Information	6	7	13
Evaluating Information	20	21	41
Total	57	42	109

[a] Only primary categories of advice are included. Many witnesses provided advice in more than one primary category.

background data only or added to it can be a professional or personal interpretation. The testimony of each witness was categorized according to its primary thrust, although there were difficulties because the lines of demarcation between the criteria were not always clear. Since many witnesses stressed more than one area in their testimony, it was necessary, in some instances, to place a given testimony in more than one category.

Table 6 shows that social scientists were most often called upon to give intelligence, that is, to provide and evaluate information. The intelligence sought referred almost entirely to social, political and economic development in foreign countries. Furthermore, of the 68 testimonies mentioned in Table 5, 29 dealt directly with Communist affairs; these were given by 14 international relations experts, 11 political scientists, and 4 economists. For the most part, what the committee members wanted and what the witnesses provided were not so much the facts as a professional evaluation of facts, interpretations of past events, predictions of future developments, and the like. The same emphasis on evaluation rather than mere clarification was found in the "policy advice" category.

The emphasis on evaluation does not necessarily imply an abandonment of the role of the scientific expert by the testifying social scientists. According to prevalent norms of the academic community, evaluations are an integral part of scientific expertise if based on empirical data or arrived at through scientific generalizations. In the testimonies analyzed, however, the evaluations given were, in most instances, of a personal or professional rather than a scientific nature. Conceptual or explanatory schemes, even of an untested prescientific nature, were noticeably absent, one exception being a discussion between Max Millikan, Director of the Center for International Studies at MIT and Senator Symington of the concept of "take-off" in economic development. This tendency to avoid observations and evaluations based on scientific generalizations was a dominant feature in the testimony of representatives from the Brookings Institution, the Washington Center of Foreign Policy Research, and other policy research organizations.

More surprising, perhaps, is that a similar tendency was shown by many "pure" academicians, some of whom have contributed significantly to the development of international relations theory (e.g., Hans Morgenthau and Quincy Wright).

As is shown in Table 6, the elaboration and evaluation of policy alternatives was most often found in the Senate Foreign Relations Committee hearings. There are a number of possible explanations for this, the most obvious one being that this committee has a greater tradition of policy participation than does the House Foreign Affairs Committee. A second possible explanation may be the different procedures of the two committees. The Foreign Relations Committee usually gives witnesses more time for testimony, provides questions formulated by staff members to guide testimony, and directs it to matters of policy during the considerable interaction that takes place between witnesses and Committee members. The Foreign Affairs Committee falls behind in all these areas, although some use has been made of seminars in which a number of witnesses in similar areas, after giving short prepared statements, are questioned together as a group by Committee members.

Finally more policy pronouncements may be made by witnesses at the Foreign Relations Committee hearings because these are, in fact, closer to the policy making arena, which usually means the Executive Branch. A rough measure of support for this hypothesis is that 10 out of 29 social scientists and international relations experts testifying before the Senate Foreign Relations Committee held policy positions in the Executive Branch either prior or subsequent to their testimony, compared with 7 out of 35 witnesses before the House Foreign Affairs Committee. Another measure of support is the number of witnesses who were members of the Council on Foreign Relations (17 out of 29 in Foreign Relations hearings compared with 14 out of 35 in Foreign Affairs). This organization's ties to federal agencies, notably the State Department, led Kenneth Galbraith to describe it as a major meeting ground for "the foreign establishment."[1]

The presence of such witnesses indicates that Congress may be attempting in its background and review hearings to increase its participation in the "foreign policy consensus" and, simultaneously, to broaden the base of that consensus. The presence of certain other witnesses, however, gives some support for the opposite view—that in these hearings Congress is attempting to delineate an independent position in foreign affairs, often a position in opposition to that of the Executive. Evidence for this may be found in the sharp, often hostile, cross-examination of social scientists testifying in a professional capacity at legislative hearings on executive proposals. Their appearance is usually at the request of the executive departments, and their testimony usually in support of executive positions. Other evidence may be found in background and review hearings, for which witnesses are usually selected by the committees and whose selection may depend on their presumed support for Congress in its struggle with the President. Certainly a prime example is the Foreign Relations Committee investigation of the "Psychological Aspects of International Relations" conducted in May 1966, when the questioning made it obvious that Charles E. Osgood was invited to testify more for his views on foreign policy than for his psychological expertise. Furthermore not all of the members of the Council on Foreign Relations who appeared (e.g., Hans Morgenthau) would support the Executive in a policy confrontation with Congress. No conclusions regarding these matters can be reached, however, without a closer examination of the policy views of the witnesses and the factors involved in their selection.

CONCLUSIONS

The general findings of this study—that social scientists have not been used by Congress to any great extent in foreign policy areas, that behavioral scientists are used least of all, and that even when used they have rarely provided new and different kinds of policy alternatives—must remain tenta-

---

[1] Address to the annual convention of Americans for Democratic Action, Washington, D.C., April 22, 1966.

tive until specified or modified by further research. At the same time, some explanations will be offered for these findings, even though they, of necessity, must go beyond the data.

First, to what extent are our findings accounted for by the attitudes of social scientists? Social scientists, according to David Apter (VI, 1964: 35-38), are trained to keep ideology and politics as distinct as possible, an orientation which many of them extend to the advocation of a total separation between "science" and politics. They often adopt an elitism and an intellectualism resulting in, to some degree, alienation from politics. This is expressed alternately by bemoaning their lack of influence in government and by the accusation that those social scientists who do participate in government are "selling out" for power, prestige, or monetary reward (Hofstadter, VI, 1966: 396-397). This attitude is far more prevalent among behavioral scientists than among political scientists, economists, and international relations specialists. The second group seems to gain access a great deal more readily than the first.

Second, what kind of environment maximizes the utility of social scientists at background and review hearings? The answer would seem to be, where specific future remedies and policy alternatives are sought, where the areas of inquiry are subject to definition by the committee, but the inquiry itself and the proposals put forth are guided primarily by the professional expertise of the witnesses. It is our opinion that this "ideal" environment rarely exists. Most of the hearings were found to be of two types: *propagandistic,* investigating areas with minimum policy results but maximum political advantage for the committee members; or *partisan,* reviewing the "mistakes" of executive policy and pressing for previously determined Congressional policy alternatives. The first type was found more often in the Foreign Affairs Committee which, despite its increasing prestige, still does not play a very significant foreign policy role. The Foreign Relations Committee, befitting its more powerful policy position, has held more *partisan* hearings and has offered a greater number of policy proposals. Yet these often have been sacrificed when they have outlived their partisan usefulness. A good example is the concept of long-term foreign aid financing, proposed by Massachusetts Institute of Technology in a study undertaken for the Committee in 1959. For years the concept was enthusiastically championed by the Committee as a whole, but the Committee eventually reversed its position. (*United States Foreign Policy,* VI, 1966: 1165-1269.) It was shelved seemingly not because of any inherent lack of administrative merit but because some members of the committee had become disenchanted with the entire concept of foreign aid as an instrument of American foreign policy. There are only a few cases, such as the Fascell subcommittee hearings on the Cold War and the Foreign Relations Committee reviews of foreign policy in 1960 and 1961, where the ideal model is rather closely approximated.

Third, to what extent can the disinclination of Congressmen to use social science, especially of the behavioral variety, be explained by some form of hostility toward it? Congressmen are not entirely unjustified in attributing to social scientists a distinct ideology which is often political in nature, revealing itself, they feel, through the scientists' siding with the Executive in its conflicts with the legislature and criticizing established Congressional procedures.

Another source of Congressional opposition to social scientists may be hostility to their intellectualism. The anti-intellectualism found in Congress is refined and complex. Opposition to physical scientists, for example, is mitigated by their indispensability. Social scientists are not so obviously essential. Congressmen often express resentment when social scientists challenge their professional competence and object to their belief that knowledge can be a substitute for experience in politics.

This opposition may stem not so much from hostile Congressional attitudes as from a more basic dichotomy between the two groups arising from what might be called "generalized mind sets," the elements of which include professional background, training, orientation, and role. Most Congressmen are lawyers by training and profession, which imparts a tendency to see policy in terms of legal rather than social issues. Their high regard for procedural rules and their reluctance to resort to legislation gives them, as a rule, a marginal incrementalist view toward policy change. The academic orientation of most social scientists leads them to examine policy from a doctrinal rather than a procedural standpoint. They feel much less need to accommodate change with tradition, to compromise the future by the past. This dichotomy must be regarded as true only in very general terms. The exceptions on either side may be regarded as facilitators for the access of social science to legislation.

Fourth, to what extent is a lack of readiness by Congressmen to make use of social science explainable by what they feel is a failure of social science to be useful to them? Of the three types of assistance which social scientists provide—intelligence, tools, and policy proposals—only some tools have been found very useful, most notably public opinion polls. Both groups level charges of misuse at each other: the social scientists, against Congressmen for using public opinion polls for partisan purposes; and Congressmen, against social scientists for misusing government research funds, featherbedding, emphasizing areas of research with little utilitarian value, and attempting to interfere with the making of policy rather than limiting themselves to policy advice. The negative experiences of both groups make constructive contacts more difficult to achieve.

Finally, what factors may bring about an increase in the use of social science in legislative policy making? One solution might be the permeation of social science, the incorporation of its concepts and indicators into the policy mainstream, so that they become a part of a Congressman's legislative repertoire. Of great assistance in this process would be the successful divorce of products and producers, and the removal of the "red flag" of "social science." This may have happened already to the economic concepts introduced by Lord Keynes; it is almost certainly the case with public opinion polls.[1] But permeation is at best a long-run solution, requiring initial access by other means, extensive translation, and an extended period of successful use. In the short run other means are needed to overcome the widespread feelings of mistrust and antipathy.

One hopeful sign may be that the hypothesized mind-set dichotomy between social scientists and legislators may bear closer resemblance to a continuum. Between the two extremes, there are individuals on both sides who can serve as facilitators or translators, such as "cosmopolitan" Congressmen and staff members with social science training, and social scientists who have participated in background and review hearings. Our findings indicate that social scientists probably should be considered as three distinct groups: (a) psychologists and sociologists, rarely found as witnesses and on staffs in the foreign policy subsystem, seem to possess the lowest awareness of legislative needs and to engender the greatest hostility; (b) foreign policy experts have the advantage of needing little translation to be of direct legislative use but the disadvantage of being often incapable of translating from the more behavioral social sciences; (c) "process specialists"—political scientists

---

[1] Robinson (IV.1, 1964) found that between 25 and 30 percent of the members of the House in the 85th Congress used polls on some occasions, but none volunteered the opinion that social scientists were of any use in their work.

and economists—may be the most fruitful source of translators. They are more intimately aware of Congressional needs and, at the same time, are becoming increasingly familiar with the behavioral social sciences. The increasing use of "process specialists," through such means as the American Political Science Association's legislative intern programs and their direct employment on Committee staffs, may provide an index of the future potential of social science in legislative policy making.

CHAPTER III

The Affairs of Social Scientists with the Affairs of State

The tendency to formulate the policy roles of the social sciences in normative terms gives the literature in this area much of its special flavor. Over the years with predictable regularity, the same general questions are posed. Should social scientists be involved in governmental affairs? What should be the contribution of social science knowledge to policy making? How can social scientists reconcile the role of scientist with that of participant in the policy-making process? These questions figure as prominently in writings by Durkheim, Mannheim, and Weber early in this century as they do now in panel discussions at professional meetings or in letters to the editor of the *American Sociologist* or the *American Psychologist*. While many prominent social scientists have at one time or another written or spoken on these issues and while those who have done government research have shown the particular concern of a group with special interests, the debate has by no means been restricted to the elite and the involved. Social scientists who cherish disinvolvement have perhaps even more frequently sounded off on these questions.

This chapter includes writings on the issues and problems of the policy roles of the social sciences as perceived by social scientists of various inclinations at different points in time. Our purpose is not to try to solve the problems raised here, if, indeed, these are problems with potential solutions. Nor do we want to dwell on the specific arguments contained in these articles. Instead we want to view them as source materials for work on the sociology of social science. As such they reflect both the different perspectives which have been applied toward the role of social science knowledge in policy making and the different positions in which the social sciences have found themselves vis-à-vis government at various points in time.

THE INFLUENCE OF NORMATIVE PERSPECTIVES

In their concern with the desirable rather than the actual and the specific issues raised and argued, the debates carried out in this country in the past few decades show the influence of the formulations advanced by German social scientists of an immediately preceding generation. Echoes of Mannheim and Weber resound with particular strength.

The starting point to these discussions has been a traditional insistence on the separation of political and scientific values and on the necessity for intellectuals to remain "unattached" and unencumbered by political commitments. The straight and narrow path from this starting point leads directly to prescriptions emphasizing the virtue of "pure" science and the pursuit of knowledge as an end in itself. While many influences which we shall discuss later have led most social scientists to move out of its narrow confines in greater or lesser degree, this orientation nonetheless continues to exercise a powerful hold over their professions.

In their emphasis on *Wertfreiheit,* Mannheim and Weber reflected the situation in German universities during their time and earlier. The conditions and doctrines prevailing in nineteenth century Germany gave little opportunity for scholarly involvement in governmental affairs, or even for the development of a social science oriented toward the political problems of the day. Their formulations, despite their efforts to give them a philosophical and ideal base, were dictated by existing realities.[1] But the high level of abstraction, which characterizes the writings of Mannheim in particular, was also functional for a writer in this environment:

it preserved a certain distance between him and his highly political subject matter. This same characteristic gave Mannheim's ideas wide applicability—to different times, problems, and countries—and may explain his continuing influence.

Although the doctrine of *Wertfreiheit* may have served the interests of the German university as an institution at that time by strengthening its neutrality and independence, it often conflicted with the highly *engagé* bent of many German social scientists and intellectuals. The solutions they proposed to the dilemma of trying to reconcile value-free social science with some political participation have become important elements of the cultural norms of social science. While the specific conditions under which the social sciences have developed in this country have made these norms lose some of their original thrust, the formulations found in several articles in this volume remain in loose accord with those proposed by Weber, in particular. Implicit in them are one or more of the following resolutions of the potential conflicts between science and social action involvements:

1. Formulations stressing the different rights and responsibilities of the social scientist acting as a scientist or professional and as a citizen. In the latter role he can express value-preferences provided he makes explicit that he is speaking as a private individual.[2]

2. The view that social scientists *qua* scientists cannot set the ends of public policy but can examine critically the internal consistency of ends and of means to ends, their compatibility with larger goals and the value premises on which they rest (Weber's concept of *Wertrationalität*).[3]

3. Formulations in which social scientists become technicians solely concerned with calculating the means necessary to reach given ends (*Zweckrationalität*).

---

[1] In a recent analysis by Ben-David and Zloczower (II.1, 1962: 60) the doctrine of *Wertfreiheit,* and the situation that gave rise to it were characterized as follows: "It was the doctrine best suited to the maintenance of the delicate balance in a situation where free, non-utilitarian inquiry was supported and given high status by an absolutist state; and where free-thinking intellectuals taught students usually sharing the autocratic views of the rulers of the state and preparing for government careers as civil servants, judges, prosecutors and teachers." Neither this point nor our discussion of the historical articulation of the efforts of Mannheim and Weber reflect on the philosophical or existential validity of their formulations.

[2] See e.g. Osgood in this Chapter, pp. 166–167.
[3] See e.g. Hauser in Chapter IV, p. 249.

4. Formulations, those of Mannheim in particular, in which social scientists are seen as members of the "unattached intelligentsia," primarily concerned with charting the broad goals forming part of "democratic planning."

PROMINENT ISSUES IN THE DEBATE

The debate on the policy roles of the social sciences reflected in some of the writings in this chapter shows the influence of conditions peculiar to the postwar relationship of government and the social science community. Two trends in particular are responsible for many of the conflicts that have surrounded these relationships. First the emphasis on empirical social research and costly fieldwork in particular has led to a reliance on the federal government as the main source of funds for large-scale research. During most of this period such funds were most readily forthcoming when the research could be linked to the symbols of national and international security. Within the military establishment social science programs often had to be rationalized in terms of a general utilitarian value or an ability to contribute to the solution of specific problems of military policy and operations. During the entire period 1952 to 1960 the Department of Defense was either the largest or the next to largest sponsor of social science in government. In two of these years—1952 and 1953—it spent more for social science than all other sponsoring agencies and departments combined. (*Federal Funds . . .*, III.2, 1952 through 1960.)

Second the urgency of the problems that have dominated the postwar international scene—Communist and reactionary dictatorships, the threat of nuclear obliteration, poverty and misery in the underdeveloped world—awakened in many social scientists a desire to become engagé and to commit the intellectual positions of their disciplines to the solution of these problems. The particular positions they took on these issues, however, frequently placed them in opposition to postwar administrations.

These general considerations are reflected in the specific issues posed in the postwar debate on the role of social science in the making of foreign and military policy. Put in simple terms, those participating in the debate can be placed along a continuum of goal orientations. At one extreme are those who have assigned prime importance to influencing the values and goals contained in postwar foreign and military policies. At the other extremes are writers whose prime consideration has been the use of research in policy or operations regardless of the values the knowledge comes to serve. For the individuals between the two poles, the relative importance assigned one consideration over another has varied depending on such matters as the organizational context in which they were viewing the issues or the particular set of policy issues to which they were orienting their comments. In many instances these considerations have been intermingled with yet another—the enhancement of the social science institution or individual social science disciplines.

The general rationale with which an individual approaches social science participation in the affairs of state has had a lot to do with determining what he perceives as the concrete issues raised by such participation. While the individuals at both poles wish to increase the influence of social science, those with an end-value orientation, such as Osgood or Horowitz, wish to exert this influence to further specific views or policy proposals. Influence is sought either from the outside by social scientists performing roles of social critics or through participation in government research programs. In the former role social scientists have had considerable influence, despite their disposition to feel weak, semi-ostracized, and relatively ineffectual. The article by Osgood and the attention received by the "peace research" movement as a whole illustrate the ready access and hearing, as well as considerable deference, accorded university experts when they advance policy alternatives. Even when their proposals are extreme relative to official policy, they are accorded respectful attention if the exposition is well-reasoned and involves a proper degree of abstraction.[1]

The view that participation in government research programs affords ready access to policy makers and policy-making bodies has made many social scientists regard such programs as effective means of influence. The urge to influence coupled with the possibility of enhancing a research specialty (in this case, problems of social change in developing nations) are both cited by Horowitz, for example, as important elements of the decision by some social scientists to participate in the Army-sponsored project on counter-insurgency (Project Camelot) launched in 1965.

A number of the more prominent issues in the debate concerning social science and public policy arose when research programs were seen as subserving foreign and military policies to which many prominent social scientists were opposed. The key problem raised by social scientists' participation in such research is exemplified by the following statement by Horowitz: ". . . in the process of addressing major problems, the autonomous character of the social science disciplines . . . should not be abandoned."[2] In Horowitz's view social scientists can preserve their integrity while participating in government activities whose end-value is questioned by setting the conditions for such participation. The Camelot researchers, for instance, should have had "complete command of the right to thrash out the moral and political dilemmas as . . . they saw them."[3]

Other social scientists have had misgivings about the feasibility of setting conditions for participation by bargaining directly with sponsors and clients. For such scientists the question of the organizational relationships that would guarantee the autonomous position of social scientists becomes more important. Interest in these issues in the late 1960's also stems from the degree to which the acceptance of sponsorship has come to be regarded as connoting support of the overall policies of the sponsoring agency. Military sponsorship became particularly troubling.

Social scientists also often exhibit concern regarding the effect of sponsorship on one's relations with colleagues and subjects. The debate over what constitutes "clean" and "dirty" money in research reflects these concerns. In the intricate system by which the attractiveness of various kinds of government sponsorship is evaluated choices have frequently rested on the degree of support that exists within the colleagueship for the policies and goals represented by the agency in question. Crawford (III.4, 1966) has described scholars' attitudes toward agencies supporting research on international affairs:

"On the whole, government money is considered more 'holy' than industrial money but less 'holy' than foundation money, which is 'holiest' of all. Of government money, CIA money, when identified as such, is the least 'holy,' defense money, if given for unclassified research, somewhat, but at present not much, more acceptable, ACDA money considerably more 'holy' and NSF money on a par with lower prestige foundations. Although the strength of the sentiments underlying these prestige rankings vary, they still seem to be so

---

[1] Their proposals must be sufficiently abstract so as not to reject specific measures favored by much of their audience and so as not to give offense to concrete symbols their audience holds sacred. At the same time the proposals have to be sufficiently specific, even if only by use of illustrations, to appear responsive to the concerns of policy makers and, indeed, to be grasped at all.

[2] Horowitz, p. 180.

[3] *Ibid.*, p. 181.

strong that currently defense and [transparently] CIA sponsored research may be getting done mainly, on the one hand, by those of such high professional repute that they are not threatened by status-loss through the sources of their support and, on the other, by those so lowly in status that they have very little to lose (p. 144)."

A high degree of consistency in the colleagueship toward the policies and goals of a given sponsoring agency has also helped minimize the transparency of conflicts with the value-free stances of many social scientists.

Rejecting sponsors who do not meet criteria of politico-ideological cleanliness has in most cases been an individual reaction of social scientists (Orlans, III.4, 1967). When collective solutions have been proposed—by officials and committees of professional associations, for instance—the problems of participation in applied or policy-oriented research are seen as an overdependence on government funds or too close an identification with aversely regarded policies. When the collective perspective is taken, proposed solutions most frequently involve basic changes of the system for government support of social science research. One favored measure is attempting an institutional separation of different kinds of government-sponsored research: "mission-oriented" research which involves closer identification with the goals of the sponsoring agency would be conducted in the government's own research organizations (in-house or "captive") whereas "basic" research or research exploring different policy alternatives would be conducted in the universities or university-affiliated institutes.

The most ambitious of these attempts to date has been the effort to establish a National Foundation for the Social Sciences (Subcommittee on Government Research III.4, 1967). Prompted to a large extent by the "Camelot affair" and the ensuing drive for the "civilianization" of government social science, the bill to establish a NFSS envisages a separate agency which would support "innovative" and "controversial" social science research, initially at the rate of 20 million dollars annually. As of early 1968, however, the prospects for rapid Congressional approval of the bill appeared dim.

In contrast to the writers with an end-value orientation, for those whose primary concern has been the effective use of social science and social scientists within a framework set by organizational goals, the issues of policy-oriented social science are generally of a more pragmatic and practical nature. As exemplified by the articles by Croker and Cottrell, they raise such questions as the following:

1. How research projects in support of military missions should be organized and conducted (in in-house laboratories, under contract with academic institutions, or nonprofit research organizations)?

2. How the federal government can attract highly talented social scientists who can work together with operators and operational planners, particularly given the difficulties arising from security regulations, Civil Service classifications, and rules concerning publication?

3. How to achieve coordination and establish lines of communication between research, planning, and operational functions in the military and civilian agencies?

4. How to plan and conduct research in support of governmental missions in the foreign field (e.g., programs aimed at creating a climate of opinion favorable to the United States) for which there is no centralized direction and planning?

5. How to organize research in support of long-range planning in the field of foreign policy?

The decisional problems raised by these questions are not essentially different from those of other areas of management and administration; that is, they concern the most effective use of funds and personnel, problems of inter-and intra-organizational communication, and the ways in which specialized activities such as research can serve general organizational goals. Those debating these matters have frequently had considerable experience as research administrators or as members of research planning groups and review boards. The many reports and memoranda issued by these groups and panels constitute a particularly rich source of knowledge and insight concerning the questions raised.[1]

In the final analysis the contribution of social science to policy rests not so much on the ways in which the activity can be organized to meet criteria of organizational effectiveness or on how the autonomy aspirations of social scientists can be satisfied, as on the substantive knowledge and tools provided decision-makers by different social science disciplines. The debate concerning the applicability of different social science methods and materials has been carried out continuously over the years.[2] Three articles in this chapter (Farber, Free, Davis) discuss the relevance to international affairs of a different research specialty or methodological orientation. They are presented here in rough correspondence to the sequence with which these intellectual products had prominence at various points in time. National character studies were particularly influential during World War II. After the war, surveys of foreign public opinion became an institutionalized part of the government's information and propaganda activities. In the 1950's and early 1960's problems of strategic deterrence and advances in computer technology made for more frequent use of such techniques as simulation, game theory, and systems analysis for studying international influence processes.

In discussing the relevance of their concepts and methods to problems of policy and operations, social scientists have most frequently and quite understandably employed the same criteria as they use to evaluate the scientificality of their products. The limited applicability of abstractly defined concepts and models to complex international situations confronting decision-making has been regarded as a key problem. The discussions in this chapter by Farber and Davis are examples. A scientist, preoccupied with this special concern, however, frequently fails to see that the scientific weaknesses of the products of social science do not necessarily impede their use by policy officials. National character theory is perhaps the best example of a social science research specialty which achieved considerable currency among foreign and military policy officials, despite its being frequently criticized for methodological and substantive weaknesses (Almond, V.2, 1950). The popularization of national character theories through such books as those by Benedict (VI, 1946), Gorer (VI, 1948), and Mead (VI, 1942) certainly contributed to their widespread acceptance within and outside government.

POLITICAL AFFINITY AND DISAFFECTION

In the postwar period, despite their frequent disposition toward a highly pragmatic and instrumental stance, social scientists have rarely disregarded the political and ethical issues raised by their involvement with foreign policy and military agencies

[1] See e.g. Bray (V.2, 1962); Lybrand (V.2, 1962); and Pool (V.2, 1963).
[2] See Biblio. Part V, Sections 2 and 3.

and departments. A considerable degree of affinity between one's own political and ideological beliefs and the course of government action has often been the basis for decisions to enter or continue government research activities. In the Cold War period the orchestration of government activity in the foreign field subordinated specialized policies and programs (including research) to the overall objective of "winning the Cold War." This created a climate of opinion in which participation in government research came to require agreement not only with the specific policies or programs which the research was designed to test or facilitate, but with more general and basic foreign policy goals as well. Involvement with military and foreign policy agencies could thus be regarded as entirely unproblematic primarily by those social scientists who were in general accord with the policies of the Cold War.[1]

While broad ideological affinities were an important factor in determining which categories of social scientists could be recruited for government research activities at this time, it was by no means the only one. The variety of considerations that entered into these decisions is reflected in the many associations, often loose and temporary, that have been formed between academic social scientists, many of whom were opposed to Cold War policies, and foreign affairs and military agencies. These associations arose out of such varied historical contexts as: (a) patterns of cooperation established in World War II (the wartime involvement of anthropologists such as Mead, Benedict, and Kluckhohn was continued in the Navy in a program of "national character" studies); (b) events on the international scene (liberal social scientists have moved closer to government in times of crisis—the Korean War, the Berlin blockade, the Cuban missile crisis); (c) events on the domestic scene (the advent of the Kennedy administration, the threat of a Goldwater); (d) intra-governmental strife (at the time of "Project Camelot" many academic social scientists sided with the State Department against the Department of Defense).[2]

In the past few years such facilitating contexts have not been sufficient to bridge the gap of politico-ideological disaffection that now separates the academic part of the social science community and the foreign affairs and military policy establishments. Many members of the scholarly community have come to regard defense research, whether because of its presumed secret nature or because of its value context, as antithetic to professional and ethical norms. Partly as a result of this opposition, although there were other more influential circumstances, defense support of research in social science has declined absolutely and, of course, relative to total government spending for social science research. In 1967 it accounted for less than five percent of those federal obligations classified as being for research in the social sciences (Research and Technical Programs Subcommittee, III.2, 1967: 33).

The disengagement of the social science professions from the military has to be seen in the overall context of the erosion of the consensus surrounding national foreign and military policy. The de-Stalinization campaigns in the Soviet Union, the easing of the Soviet hold over the Eastern European countries, and the general "thaw" in East-West relations have removed from the military-political context much of such consonance as existed between world political outlooks prevalent among social scientists

---

[1] Those who were extremely out of sympathy with such policies, of course, were also either frightened away or repelled by security and loyalty clearance practices.

[2] The hearings conducted by the Subcommittee on International Organizations and Movements (III.3, 1966) of the House Foreign Affairs Committee in 1964 and 1965 illustrate some of the strange configurations of actors and settings in which the views of social science have been heard. Here we find high-level representatives of the Department of State voicing the left-opposition of academic social scientists to defense-supported foreign area research in a set of hearings and reports entitled *Winning the Cold War: The U.S. Ideological Offensive*. The work of the subcommittee has been referenced often and approvingly by social scientists who have written critically about governmental foreign area research programs. Almost invariably, however, they find it expedient to omit the title of the hearings from their citations.

and evident in national military policy during the Cold War.

Increasingly, counteracting "wars of national liberation" in the developing world has become the focus of attention in military and foreign policy. This has introduced a host of new elements of value-dissonance into the relationship of the military and social science institutions and further widened the area of disagreement. Much of this hostility toward the involvement of the United States in Latin America and toward military intervention of the Dominican type, was reflected in the opposition to "Project Camelot."

In the late 1960's the war in Vietnam made disaffection more widespread and intense than ever before. While the conflict has come to play a dominant role on the domestic as well as on the international political scene, it has not so far posed the security threat or had the ideological resonance that made the Korean War, for instance, evoke a positive response from many social scientists. Further, for most social scientists, the situation seemed to have passed the point where meliorist, marginal, and relatively noncontroversial contributions to policy, such as they had been wont to make in the past, could be seen as potentially useful and constructive. Unlike the Korean period, when studies of negotiation processes, communist authority patterns, or prisoner-of-war handling were regarded as at least of potentially marginal usefulness to successful termination of the conflict, nothing short of a major alteration in policy could be viewed by most scholars as a way of avoiding disaster in Vietnam; and, further, large numbers of the profession were at a loss even with regard to what such a change might be.[1] Basing their opposition heavily on moral considerations, academic social scientists have largely refrained from visible involvement in research activities contributing to the war effort. At meetings of the sociological and anthropological associations during the period of major escalation of the Vietnam war, for example, the war played hardly any role in papers reporting the results of research but figured prominently, instead, as an issue requiring political action by these professional organizations.

THE ISSUES OF THE FUTURE

The disengagement from the military institution has been facilitated by the shift in emphasis in government social science research programs from national and international security to domestic welfare. Given their closer accord with the diverse opinions of social scientists regarding desirable and appropriate involvement with governmental bodies, domestic welfare activities could emerge as an important new base in government for social science research. This was particularly the case for research with an academic orientation.

[1] See, for example, the "Report on Viet Nam Survey" (VI, 1967) a survey by the American Sociological Association of its membership. Only 12 percent of the voting members of the association approved of the policy of the administration.

In some areas—housing, transportation, and economic development, as examples—social scientists are participating in the role of "social technicians," providing the survey data, the techniques for analyzing complex systems, or the knowledge about the functioning of such systems, and performing additional tasks that comprise an important part of "technical" decision-making. In other problem areas—poverty, community action, education and training of disadvantaged citizens, or equal rights—where the programs involve choices between complex and often conflicting political, ideological, and humanitarian factors, social science involvement was facilitated, at least initially, by affinities in the goals of government agencies and the ideological beliefs of academic social scientists. Overall the growth and spread of government social research programs will probably bring into focus many new types of relationships of government and social science. Instead of being based on the polarization of interests characteristic of the Cold War, these will probably involve much more varied and specialized concerns, often of a more technical than ideological nature.

POLITICAL AND PROFESSIONAL ISSUES

The Psychologist in International Affairs

CHARLES E. OSGOOD

I am going to divide this essay into two parts. The first . . . will be a personal report which I hope will be informative and perhaps encouraging to my colleagues. The second part will deal more directly with the ifs, hows, whens, and wheres of what most people call "peace research."

PERSONAL

What ingredients are required to make an ordinary self-satisfied experimental psychologist—with more scientific jobs planned than his life can encompass anyhow—into a "peacenik" who spends nearly half of his time writing, lecturing, consulting, and doing research aimed at reducing international tensions? One ingredient is felt concern about the significance of the problem; a second ingredient is felt efficacy; a third is having something to work for, a new alternative, an idea; and the fourth ingredient, I guess, is some ability to run uphill.

Felt Concern

If one has a modicum of intelligence coupled to a modicum of imagination, it is not difficult to get concerned about the present world situation. No one who looks at the evidence and thinks about it can deny: (*a*) that never before in history have so few been able to destroy so many and so much in so short a time—indeed, there is no physical reason for not building a weapon that would radiate the entire surface of the earth (and some say we must do this because the Russians might); (*b*) that nuclear weapons are almost entirely offensive, not defensive, in nature, and therefore the continuing arms race produces less, not greater, security; (*c*) that the only "defense" against the use of such weapons lies in mutual fear of annihilation—a pretty fragile defense, indeed, humans being human.

Yet, how many intellectuals have lifted their brilliantly plumaged heads up out of the sand and looked fully into the face of a nuclear holocaust? How many have asked themselves the traumatizing question—of what value is present work if this larger problem is not solved? . . . Some psychologists, being only human and subject to the laws of cognitive dissonance, will cease reading this at this point. Yet they cannot deny that almost instant elimination of everything they consider valuable is now possible in a way it never has been before in human history.

*   *   *   *   *

[I]n my case, at least, felt concern had another source as well. This was an intense devotion to rationality—I cannot think of any better way to say it. Annoyance with human irrationality has been a constant in my make-up (except, of course, when it is myself that is irrational!); I'm sure my children suffered from this when they were little. For the first 30 years or so of my life this was not directed in any way toward the political behavior of the human animal. I couldn't have cared less about national and international affairs. I didn't even bother to vote.

In 1945, while I was working on the training of B-29 gunners at the Smoky Hill Army Air Force Base in Kansas, came announcement of our first use of a nuclear bomb against Hiroshima, then soon after announcement of our second use against Nagasaki. I considered these acts both immoral and stupid—and I still do. I suppose I should have asked myself what I was doing training B-29 gunners, but I didn't.... I even joined the ADA (Americans for Democratic Action) to work on a special committee of the New Haven chapter for internationalizing control over nuclear energy and weapons. But when it became obvious that nothing along these lines was going to be accomplished in a hurry, I went back to being a struggling young psychologist.

And then McCarthyism struck home to me. When he began attacking academic freedom . . . when he began destroying people with irrational smear techniques . . . I began *reading* the newspaper, including columns and editorials, rather than just glancing at the headlines and enjoying my favorite comics. This just jangled my rationality factor all the more. Occasionally I would get so mad that I would write a letter to the editor! . . . But finally McCarthy picked the wrong target, got his "comeuppance," and went the way of all flesh. And I went back to psycholinguistics, still muttering and growling at what I saw in the newspapers and on TV.

Felt Efficacy

Concern over the irrationality of man, and the extraordinary danger of such irrationality in a world of competing nation states armed with nuclear weapons, is not enough. One must also feel capable of doing something about it. This comes partly, I think, from personal self-confidence and security in one's own profession; it comes partly from the conviction that one's special knowledge is in some way relevant; and it comes partly from the discovery that some people, at least are willing to listen . . . .

In 1958 I had my chance to spend a year at the Center for Advanced Study in the Behavioral Sciences . . . . I went out there to write a book on psycholinguistics; I never wrote a word of it. I hardly opened the 20 or so fat flolders that contained materials for its various chapters. I did a variety of minor scholarly jobs, but the main reason the book didn't get written (it still isn't) was that I found myself in the next office to Jerome Frank, a psychiatrist from Johns Hopkins. Jerry shared my concern—but more, he was busily and effectively doing something about it. He had already written an article for *Harper's* that had great impact and was preparing to serve as a witness before the Humphrey Subcommittee on Disarmament.

This was the catalyst I needed—but hadn't been looking for . . . . For years I had been crying "What can I do?" as a means of convincing myself that I couldn't do anything— . . . . Yet here was a constant reminder that one could do something relevant and even get people to listen. The more I looked at my own special areas of competence in psychology—in human learning, in the dynamics of human thinking, and in human communication—the more relevance I began to see. More than this, I convinced myself that the psychological factors in international relations, while by no means the whole story, were particularly significant precisely because they were so largely unrecognized.

New Alternative

The kind of action into which one is thrust by the combination of felt concern and felt efficacy depends upon what one is . . . . It is most likely to thrust the scientist or scholar into *his* characteristic problem-solving activities—reading, talking, researching, and writing. So we set up a weekly seminar at the Center, on Social Science Aspects of Policy in a Nuclear Age; it included lawyers, economists, sociologists, anthropologists, a few political scientists, and almost every foreign scholar resident that year. We read the literature, talked to each other informally, wrote papers and read them to each other, and, since a wide spectrum of policy opinion was represented, occasionally became embroiled in heated debate.

I began as an ardent unilateral disarmer. It seemed perfectly logical to me that if one side threw away its weapons, the other would soon follow suit. Just as we would not leap to destroy a disarmed Russia with nuclear weapons, neither would they leap to destroy us. I felt confident that we could win the real war for men's minds by nonmilitary means in a disarmed world. In fact, I believed that the conditions of a nonthreatening, economically healthy, and openly communicating environment would gradually serve to strengthen democratic as against totalitarian ways of life, both at home and abroad. I still believe these things.

But now we come to the hardening of this peacenik. When I sat down to write out my ideas for presentation to this seminar . . . and kept trying them out on my colleagues over coffee in the California sunlight, it became perfectly clear that, logical or not, ordinary unilateral disarmament simply wasn't viable. My own arguments about the irrationality of human thinking under stress —mechanisms like denial, semantic remoteness of concepts, projection, psycho-logic, and stereotypy in perceiving alternatives— which I used to characterize the cold-war mentality also offered apparently insurmountable obstacles to acceptance of any nonviolent resolution of international conflict. I became obsessed with the criterion of *feasibility*. The problem became to devise and justify a strategy that could move us toward a more peaceful world and reduce the likelihood of nuclear weapons being used, yet operate within reasonable limits of national security as perceived by people in decision-making positions.

The original paper introduced the basic ideas of graduated and reciprocated initiatives in tension reduction (which, in the way of such things, is now usually referred to as GRIT). It met solid criticism from participants in the seminar and from others to whom I sent it—but it also generated interest as a somewhat novel policy idea. So I went back to the drawing boards again to tighten it up and try to meet the main sources of criticism. The next major version was published in *The Liberal Papers,* edited by James Roosevelt (VI, 1962), and was entitled "Reciprocal Initiative." The book was seized upon by the Republican National Committee as campaign material; they called it "the Democratic plan for surrender," and my particular contribution "surrender on the installment plan" . . . .

This book, coupled with distribution efforts of my own, began to bring these ideas to the attention of hard-nosed but equally dedicated and concerned people both in and out of government. (It also brought my correspondence to a level where it couldn't be handled.) I discovered that once one gets his nose up into that atmosphere, it serves as a lightning rod, attracting all kinds of things—good and useful things (like lecturing opportunities and consulting activities) but also some bad and wasteful things (like letters from crackpots and invitations to too many redundant conferences). These experiences and contacts gave me an even clearer idea of the weaknesses and strengths of my own proposal, however.

* * * * *

Ability to Run Uphill

I know this sounds like patting oneself on the back, but I cannot claim to have gotten very far up. An ant at the bottom of a teacup has no place to go but up. The flat fact of the matter is that when you have an unconventional idea in a political area of intense feeling, and you must get the idea moving through the complex and curious mass media, you have an uphill battle on your hands. You try to reach the minds of key people in the decision-making process (decidedly uphill) while at the same time, by writing paperbacks and giving lectures all over the place, you try to reach the general public. With one hand you do research, or support research, that you believe has critical bearing on the major issues, while with the other you act more like a lobbyist and apply what you think you already know. You are simultaneously impelled by the urgency of the issue and restrained by the necessity (if you are to be effective) of maintaining your balance and dignity as a scientist and scholar.

I am often asked questions like: "Are you getting anywhere?" "Are your ideas having any influence in Washington?" . . . . For one thing, it is easy to overestimate your own influence, to indulge in wishful thinking; when a pattern of events, like the handling of the Cuban Crisis and its aftermath, looks like what you have been suggesting, it is only too easy to assume that your advice has been taken—when, in fact, the advisors are many and the possible reasons for actions multiple. For another thing, I suspect that even if unconventional policy ideas are to eventually be successful, they will become so in a fashion analogous to "sleeper effects" in attitude change studies; that is, they will have their first effects quietly in the minds of men, and only when enough people are thinking differently and the time is ripe will the unconventional approach achieve public acceptance . . . .

PROFESSIONAL

It may be professional myopia, but I think psychologists as a group have been more actively involved in "peace research," and over a longer period, than any other behavioral or social science. For a long time we have had SPSSI (Society for the Psychological Study of Social Issues) whose members have done research and written about problems in areas of public concern like race relations, civil rights, and peace and war. More recently in 1960, beginning with a working group under Roger Russell, a continuing committee for the profession as a whole on Psychology in National and International Affairs was established . . . . Most recently, through a grant from the Marshall Fund we have been able to support a full-time person, Lawrence Solomon, in Washington to work on the Committee's tasks.

Why should it be so—if indeed it is—that psychologists have gotten themselves involved in this area earlier and more deeply? Perhaps it is because psychology had about the right "distance" from public issues—close enough to have developed a scientific conception of man and his behavior, but not so close as to have become intimidated. Perhaps the fact that psychology is more like the physical and biological sciences in methods and in quantification created a feeling of security and efficacy . . . . Or perhaps it is the outward reaching tendencies of psychological theories about behavior, which may have their moorings in the Skinner box, the tachistoscope, or the therapeutic interview, but are generalized as widely as possible.

* * * * *

The psychologist working on public issues may wear any one of three hats, but he should be aware of which hat is appropriate for which occasion. On some occasions he may legitimately don his "professional" hat —when he speaks as a psychological scientist on the basis of hard facts and generally accepted principles. On other occasions he should wear his "specialist" hat—when he speaks as an individual psychologist who, by virtue of his special training and experience, may claim a higher probability of correct insights and opinions in certain areas than others not so trained. On yet other occasions, he must explicitly display his "citizen" hat —when he speaks his opinions, expresses his attitudes, and takes his stands on matters where neither his science nor his expertise gives him any obvious advantage over other equally intelligent citizens.

* * * * *

It is not always easy to maintain these distinctions, and some will argue that, with an issue so urgent as avoiding a nuclear war, trying to maintain them is a delicacy verging on the ludicrous. The answer, I think is that to fail to make these distinctions is to destroy whatever potential contribution we can make as psychologists.

There are two other caveats I must make before saying something about action and research on international affairs. One concerns what we mean by "peace" . . . . It is the opposite of "war," which we're all against, and there surely is a good feel to it. But do we mean peace in the no-war sense? In the no-nuclear-war sense? In the complete disarmament sense? In the permanent tranquility sense? In the sense of establishing and observing the rule of international law? In the sense of peaceful (competitive) coexistence? In the Pax Americana sense? How one answers this question will determine what he would include under "peace research," how much effort he will put into short-term versus long-term action programs and research programs, and so forth. The controversy that is now going on between the "arms management and control" proponents and the "general and complete disarmament" proponents in part reflects differences in what kind of peaceful world people have in mind.

The other caveat concerns our own stereotypes and intolerances. Being merely human, psychologists are prone to the same cognitive dynamics they study in others. In our own striving for a simplified, comprehensible world, it is easy for us to set up Bogey Men of our own—in the Pentagon, in Congress, in the mass media, in the defense industries and so forth. Here are the war mongers here are the evil men who, for selfish and aggressive motives, are deliberately risking all our lives. There probably are a few such people, but I have yet to meet them. I have yet to find a person in government, in industry, in the media, in the military or elsewhere, who did not profess to desire peace (on his own terms) as ardently as I did (on mine) . . . . I do not want what I have just said to be misinterpreted: I am convinced that there are many people in the institutions we are discussing who are misguided, who have dangerous misconceptions about the nature of the world today and the nature of the people who inhabit it, and who are following policies that have a high probability of eventuating in the destruction of everything we hold valuable—but as a social scientist I cannot consider them evil and I must consider them modifiable.

Action

By "action" aimed at moving toward a more peaceful world I refer to the whole spectrum of endeavors to change people's minds, and thereby their behaviors, through utilizing what we know (or think we know) as psychologists and as intelligent citizens. It involves all the skills we have as individuals in interpersonal relations, in persuasive communication, and in problem solving. It means trying to inject psychological insights and skills wherever they are relevent—and often the first, and more difficult, step is to convince others of their relevance.

One type of action is, frankly, *lobbying* in the best sense. And by "best sense" I mean trying to influence decision making in government for altruistic rather than selfish ends . . . . The Committee on Psychology in National and International Affairs, . . . has been trying to develop and maintain effective contacts with relevant government agencies and activities . . . as well as with members of Congress. One side of this activity is of necessity educational—it is surprising how nonpsychologists, both in government and in the public at large, see us *only* as clinicians in and competent with personality problems! Another side of this activity is predictive—trying to anticipate public issues just over the horizon and prepare for them. Yet another side of this is a mediating role—bringing into fruitful contact the public official with a problem and the psychologist with maximally relevant skill and experience.

* * * * *

Yet another type of action is playing the role of devil's advocate—questioning assumptions which are generally taken for granted. Examples of such assumptions would be; that our opponent (whoever he may be) is motivated by aggression and hatred while we are motivated by insecurity and fear; that we must maintain military superiority in order to be secure; that our nuclear deterrent is nothing more than that (it is also a security base from which to take limited risks); that credibility of our deterrent requires that we present the face of implacable hostility to an opponent; that prior commitment from both sides via negotiation is a prerequisite for tension-reducing action by either; that we can have unlimited national sovereignty and unlimited international security at the same time. It is precisely because such assumptions are often implicit and largely taken for granted that they must be questioned and raised to the level of public debate.

* * * * *

Research

Psychologists are as prone to fads as anyone else. . . . Although a great deal of research that has been going on steadily in social psychology, communications, cognitive processes, and many other areas is clearly relevant, "peace research," under that name at least, certainly is not prestigeful in our profession. However, the pulling power of a research area depends both upon the stature of the senior people who work in it and upon the availability of funds for doing it (which are not independent factors, incidentally!) and the situation seems to be becoming more favorable. . . .

Action-Oriented Research. Some research is designed to produce dependable information that can be transmitted directly into action programs. This is particularly characteristic of research oriented toward public issues. One illustration is the monograph on "Psychological Factors in Peace and War"—being prepared by Shel Feldman, Joseph de Rivera, and myself. . . .

The general purposes are to make available to behavioral and social scientists in a readily digestible form the existing evidence relating to psychological propositions explicitly or implicitly made in the literature in this field, the hypotheses that need investigation, and the available personnel in terms of contributions and interests. Another example would be the production of what might be called "instant public opinion" on foreign issues and assumptions. . . . The point is that decisions are often made on the basis of assumptions about "public opinion" that may well be invalid. If such informed opinion could be collected in synchronized fashion over a broad sample of the population, it could have impressive impact.[1]

* * * * *

Understanding-Oriented Research. What we usually refer to as "pure" or "basic" research is directed toward increasing our understanding of human behavior without any immediate concern for social action. What impresses one when he starts searching

---

[1] I once had the fantasy that there was a huge map of the United States on a building near the White House. Above the map, a flashing sign announced the "issue of the day." With each county in each state represented by a small panel that would be turned to either black or white depending on the responses obtained there, the whole map would represent, by shades from white through grey to black, "instant public opinion" on the issue as well as regional variations. . . .

the literature for material relevant to the present topic is the fact that—if one forgets the particular substantive material—almost everything we are investigating has some relevance. A William McGuire does ingenious experiments on susceptibility to, and immunization to, persuasion; the persuasive materials may be counterarguments to unquestioned assumptions about the value of brushing one's teeth! But they might just as well have been counterarguments to the unquestioned assumptions about national security listed earlier. The point is that there is much that we are doing already just because we want to find out more about human beings . . . that could be made directly relevant to the crucial issues of our time by a minor shift in materials, in subjects, or emphasis.

Some will argue that it is impossible to be truly objective when the topics under investigation are policy relevant, are emotion laden, or involve the investigator himself. I think this is sheer nonsense. As soon as one has become wound up in his own theory, his mentor's theory, or even his own previous findings, he is equally liable to subjective bias. The whole purpose of our training in rigorous, objective, and quantitative methods is to protect ourselves from such bias, and objective methodology will protect us if adhered to.

Merely by way of illustration, here are some areas of understanding-oriented research that I think are particularly relevant: the simulation of complex human decision making processes, whether by computers (e.g., Herbert Simon's work) or by people (e.g., Harold Guetzkow's internation simulations); studies on the dynamics of human perceptions or cognitions as they affect choice behaviors of all types (e.g., extending and refining the theories of Heider, Festinger, and others); research on interperson, intergroup, and internation communication (e.g., the problem of multiple audiences receiving the same message, the problem of information restriction because of the structure and function of the mass media); cross-cultural and cross-linguistic studies of psycholinguistic and other cognitive phenomena, both as a means of quantifying what might be called "subjective culture" and as a means of specifying cultural similarities and differences more rigorously.

The principles and tools developed in the course of such understanding-oriented research could be transferred rather directly into "applied" research that is needed by society. Take for example internation simulation (which is not too different from the "war games" played by the military): if the validity of such simulations can be demonstrated and they can be shown to reduce uncertainty in policy decisions significantly, one can imagine a massive program of such research designed to simulate and thereby anticipate critical decision points in the constantly expanding "near future." Our present transportation and communication technologies make cross-cultural tests of hypotheses and international surveys entirely feasible—we no longer need be provincial in the behavioral and social sciences. Indeed, many of our hypotheses require testing against a cross-cultural and cross-linguistic matrix, in order to distinguish that which is culturally and linguistically unique from that which is common to the human species. Research on this scale would require a great deal of money, to be sure, but no more than is thrown away every time an experimental missile or space vehicle plops into the ocean as a failure.

The Peace Research Game

MARTIN OPPENHEIMER

Within the past decade a group of "New Civilian Militarists" has arisen to supply the Establishment with some natural and social scientific armor—Teller, Kahn, Kissinger, many others. Slowly a counterforce to the NCM has been growing on the American campus, too. The *Bulletin of the Atomic Scientists* and the Society for Social Responsibility in Science were among the first to move in this direction. Now the body of social scientists concerned with the prevention of war has become respected and relatively sizable, so much so that many have voiced a fear at its overly rapid institutionalization and absorption by the very Establishment it criticizes.

There are more than 100 institutions in the U.S. doing research related to peace and disarmament. They range from the U.S. Naval Ordnance Test Station at China Lake, California, to privately sponsored groups such as the University of Michigan Center for Research on Conflict Resolution (and its *Journal of Conflict Resolution*). One of the key figures in this development, economist Kenneth Boulding, has termed it a "peace research movement." Boulding and other social scientists, notably economist Emile Benoit, management engineer Seymour Melman, sociologist Amitai Etzioni, and psychologists Charles Osgood and Erich Fromm, have assumed increasingly important roles in the peace movement because of their writings and their participation in such academic groups as the Councils for Correspondence.

The Peace Research Movement has to a certain degree become a vested interest because foundation and government funds are involved. This has created an informal but nevertheless useful counterweight in government circles to the New Civilian Militarists and their more saber-rattling allies. But some negative consequences, too, follow from the Peace Research Movement's presently respectable status. Peace research output, based as it is on the present academic establishment (both for its theoretical roots and its financial support), shares the assumptions of that establishment. Most social scientists in this country tend to see society as a functioning whole, beset from time to time by minor dysfunctions. Hence social change is viewed as a series of minor adjustments, and not as a dynamic historical process. Since no basic structural change is envisioned, the instruments of such change, namely masses of people, do not play much of a role in the analyses of most peace researchers. Rather, the dominant concern is with influencing the status quo and its present decision-makers, both East and West. Even when the masses are subjected to study, as in public opinion work, it is with a view to seeing how their opinions can be brought to bear on decision-makers, rather than how they can be brought to intervene themselves, as people.

This has led the vast bulk of present

● *Dissent,* Vol. 11, Autumn 1964, pp. 444-448. Reprinted by permission of the publisher and the author.

peace research to focus upon three problems: decision-making of elites (including the effects of public opinion on this process), communication between elites (including some national character studies), and the construction of utopian models (formal and mathematical or adapted to such purposes as planning economic alternatives to arms production). The replacement of present elites, the elimination of basic problems which give rise to international "misunderstandings," and the processes by which societies get to the point where the models might work are generally not considered.

Glancing through the pages of one of the chief organs of peace research, the *Journal of Conflict Resolution,* one runs across research concluding that "legislators with economic or personal ties to the other country are more likely to be responsive to the needs or the other country than are legislators lacking those ties." Presumably, therefore, in order to improve the techniques of crisis control (rather than resolve the causes of crisis) all the K's should intermarry. This might be termed the "beyond the hot-line" theory of conflict control. Another study falling into the same school suggests a formula by which we may analyze a foreign government's policy statements for their hostility content. When they get too hostile we can take appropriate steps to reduce the hostility, the assumption here, as elsewhere, being that hostility is due to misunderstanding or misjudgment. The *Journal* is filled with elaborate mathematical models based on game theory (used by peace and "war" researchers alike) to analyze such phenomena as the number of war dead related to the number of frontiers and the density of population along them; or the results of escalation under conditions where one nation attacks another in order to get it to attack a third, ... "It is therefore imperative," concludes the model-maker, "that constructive alternatives to deterrence through retaliation be found," a point not exactly startling in originality.

The psychologists of the peace research movement are primarily interested in communications-perceptions problems. Charles Osgood, perhaps the leading spokesman for peace-research-oriented psychologists, has summarized the problem as he sees it: "Surely, it would be a tragedy, a cause for cosmic irony, if two of the most civilized nations on this earth were to drive each other to their mutual destruction because of their mutually threatening conceptions of each other—without ever testing the validity of those conceptions." So it is conceptions which have created the Cold War! Osgood believes, apparently, that if the conceptions were tested they would be proven false, and, in happy understanding, the two "civilized power blocs, now enlightened, would live happily ever after. But suppose the "conceptions" turn out to be accurate? What then?

Osgood's contribution to peace theory (see his essay in *The Liberal Papers*) is termed Graduated Reciprocation in Tension Reduction, which is a fancy way of saying unilateral initiatives. With his program one cannot quarrel very much. It is his assumptions about the nature of the Cold War, and the increasing popularity of these assumptions, that give one pause. These theories take up a good deal of the time of peace researchers. In the *Journal of Conflict Resolution* one writer recently put it this way: "Clearly, as long as decisionmakers on either side of the Cold War adhere to rigid images of the other party, there is little likelihood that even genuine 'bids' [note the gamesmanship terminology—M.O.] to decrease tensions will have the desired effect." True enough, but is it images that create tensions, or are tensions created by other factors, and reinforced by images? Shall we treat symptoms, or causes? Another *Journal* writer, moving into the tricky field of national character, suggests, "If several of the leading nations of the world were to undertake a careful study of their national myths and the extent to which these myths influence policy, the cause of international understanding would be greatly advanced." True again, but this is rather like suggesting to a psychotic that he take hold of himself and look at the world rationally.

This view is, after all, only the other side of the Soviet apologists' line that international exchanges of the youth Festival type will somehow solve international problems. It has been taken to its conclusion by psychologist Morton Deutsch who, in his presidential address before the Society for the Psychological Study of Social Issues, suggested that peace requires "attitudes which consciously stress mutual acceptance, mutual welfare, mutual strength, mutual interest, and mutual trust." These attitudes are to be generated through UN sponsorship of "a series of periodic international contests which would enable the different nations of the world to reveal their achievements . . . ." So a leading spokesman for American social science and peace research recommends (or at least implies) that we cease our criticisms of unpleasant features of other regimes and channel the social, political, and economic drives of imperialism (a word which is very rarely seen in peace research, by the way) by staging olympic games, fairs, and ballet festivals. A discouraging level of analysis indeed.[1]

Boulding, Benoit, Melman and Etzioni have succeeded in popularizing another assumption of peace research: that the conversion of the world's war industry to peacetime uses can be accomplished without "serious dislocation, unemployment, or checks to economic growth." Melman puts it this way; ". . . economic conversion under disarmament can be carried off in fine style, especially if reasonable advance planning is done." Etzioni, who is slightly tougher-minded, still basically agrees: "It seems safe to conclude that if we investigate the problems involved and plan ahead for them, the transition to a peacetime economy can be eased . . . ."

Models of such a transition are not difficult to construct—see, for instance, Melman's *A Strategy for American Security,* or the U. S. Arms Control and Disarmament Agency's *The Economic and Social Consequences of Disarmament*—particularly if one remembers that most of the peace researchers assume a gradual, staged disarmament lasting upwards of ten years. But there are serious political obstacles. In a recent *New York Times Magazine* article Benoit admitted that a course of economic recovery more oriented towards federal spending for welfare "would encounter serious obstacles. Even in the unlikely event that Congress would approve a doubling of Federal nondefense programs, this would offset only about one-quarter of the probable net cutback in defense expenditures."

It would be foolish to argue that what Benoit believes to be difficult is technically impossible. It is *possible* for government to step in and produce the kinds of goods and services required to make up the difference between defense production and what private enterprise is willing to substitute for it, even adding in the multiplier effect, continuing automation, and a growing labor force coming out of the schools each year. It is *possible* that the private sector will submit to the degree of planning soon to be required to maintain the economy under [present defense circumstances] and it is even possible that it will submit to the greater degree of control which will be necessary under disarmament. But it is not probable.[2] It would therefore seem that the problem is not so much alternative ways of spending money, but rather methods of achieving the political and social changes which are the

---

[1] Pachter (V.3, 1963) makes a similar criticism, but does it from a view that peace researchers don't understand the Russian Menace, and strongly suggests that to be "realistic" one ought to back NATO. Two unrealities, however, do not make a reality.

[2] See the fine discussion of this point in Brand (VI, 1962).

prerequisites for making such alternatives operational.

Such a focus, however, would fly in the face of the assumptions of most peace researchers, namely that only minor economic alterations are needed, not major social changes. For them, mass movements are not required (and may even be embarrassing); hence the emphasis on trying to convince the present leadership of the Establishment through lobbying, personal contacts, and "education." At the very moment when the peace organizations of the nation are beginning to recognize the ineffectiveness of pure-and-simple lobbying, at the moment when they are beginning to wet their feet in mass politics—including the labor and civil rights movements—along come the researchers to place the focus of action once again upon the mechanisms of helping the elite adjust the system. We are diverted from attention to the real roots of international conflict, and, with the aid of psychologists, are informed that the only thing stopping disarmament is that the leaders don't understand strategy and don't understand each other.

The peace researchers seem determined to undermine the more traditional radical view, which is that the arms race stems from the inherent socio-economic and political natures of capitalist and Soviet societies, since both of them generate imperialist drives which, when they collide, threaten to break out in violent conflict.[1] This traditional view seems at once clearer, yet more complicated, than the "reformist" views of the peace research groups. It is clearer because it does not bog down in the confusion of elitist decision-making and decision-changing. It is more complicated because it requires a grasp of the underlying dynamics of social systems, and how to change them. And it requires attention to the social forces which are needed to make such changes—the millions of Americans who must be recruited into peace and other movements if those changes are to take place.

There are a few peace researchers who understand this need, and who argue a more radical position. Anatole Rapaport in his *Strategy and Conscience* helps to lay bare the assumptions of strategic thinking. Mulford Sibley, Sid Lens, and Irving Horowitz have recently contributed to a series, "Beyond Deterrence," published by the American Friends Service Committee. Some of the research reported in the *Newsletter* of the Councils for Correspondence seems to be pointing in a new direction. Radical economists are receiving a wider reading. Criticism of the basic assumptions of peace research is growing. These are hopeful signs. But the chief paradox of the peace research wing of the American peace movement still remains: what is required is a movement concerned with the dynamics of at least political if not yet social change. We are moving in that direction, but very slowly. Perhaps as the civil rights movement becomes more and more involved in the multitude of social problems with which it must deal, the movement of both peace and civil rights forces towards political change will accelerate and intersect. Peace research should be pointing the way. Instead, it drags behind, encumbered by the traditional, static thinking of the academic community.

---

[1] An amended view, also radical, is that both the U.S. and the U.S.S.R. form a high-level system together, which is in fundamental conflict with revolutionary developments in the third world. The exploitation of the third world by this system, as a root cause of conflict, is almost totally neglected by the mainstream of peace research.

The Life and Death of Project Camelot

IRVING LOUIS HOROWITZ

In June of this year—in the midst of the crisis over the Dominican Republic—the United States Ambassador to Chile sent an urgent and angry cable to the State Department. Ambassador Ralph Dungan was confronted with a growing outburst of anti-Americanism from Chilean newspapers and intellectuals. Further, left-wing members of the Chilean Senate had accused the United States of espionage.

The anti-American attacks that agitated Dungan had no direct connection with sending US troops to Santo Domingo. Their target was a mysterious and cloudy American research program called Project Camelot.

Dungan wanted to know from the State Department what Project Camelot was all about. Further, whatever Camelot was, he wanted it stopped because it was fast becoming a *cause célèbre* in Chile (as it soon would throughout capitals of Latin America and in Washington) and Dungan had not been told anything about it—even though it was sponsored by the US Army and involved the tinderbox subjects of counter-revolution and counter-insurgency in Latin America.

Within a few weeks Project Camelot created repercussions from Capitol Hill to the White House. Senator J. William Fulbright, chairman of the Foreign Relations Committee, registered his personal concern about such projects as Camelot because of their "reactionary, backward-looking policy opposed to change. Implicit in Camelot, as in the concept of 'counter-insurgency,' is an assumption that revolutionary movements are dangerous to the interests of the United States and that the United States must be prepared to assist, if not actually to participate in, measures to repress them."

By mid-June the State Department and Defense Department—which had created and funded Camelot—were in open contention over the project and the jurisdiction each department should have over certain foreign policy operations.

On July 8, Project Camelot was killed by Defense Secretary Robert McNamara's office which has a veto power over the military budget. The decision had been made under the President's direction.

On that same day, the director of Camelot's parent body, the Special Operations Research Organization, told a Congressional committee that the research project on revolution and counter-insurgency had taken its name from King Arthur's mythical domain because "It connotes the right sort of things—development of a stable society with peace and justice for all." Whatever Camelot's outcome, there should be no mistaking the deep sincerity behind this appeal for an applied social science pertinent to current policy.

However, Camelot left a horizon of disarray in its wake: an open dispute between State and Defense; fuel for the anti-American fires in Latin America; a cut in US Army research appropriations. In addition, serious and perhaps ominous implications for social science research, bordering on

• *Trans-action,* Vol. 1, November-December 1965, pp. 3-7 and 44-47. Reprinted by permission of the publishers and the author.

censorship, have been raised by the heated reaction of the executive branch of government.

GLOBAL COUNTER-INSURGENCY

What was Project Camelot? Basically, it was a project for measuring and forecasting the causes of revolutions and insurgency in underdeveloped areas of the world. It also aimed to find ways of eliminating the causes, or coping with the revolutions and insurgencies. Camelot was sponsored by the US Army on a four to six million dollar contract, spaced out over three to four years, with the Special Operations Research Organization (SORO). This agency is nominally under the aegis of American University in Washington, D.C., and does a variety of research for the Army....

Latin America was the first area chosen for concentrated study, but countries on Camelot's four-year list included some in Asia, Africa, and Europe. In a working paper issued on December 5, 1964, at the request of the Office of the Chief of Research and Development, Department of the Army, it was recommended that "comparative historical studies" be made in . . . [twelve Latin American countries plus a few countries in the Middle and Far East]. "Survey research and other field studies" were recommended for Bolivia, Colombia, Ecuador, Paraguay, Peru, Venezuela, Iran, Thailand. Preliminary consideration was also being given to a study of the separatist movement in French Canada. It, too, had a code name: Project Revolt.

In a recruiting letter sent to selected scholars all over the world at the end of 1964, Project Camelot's aims were defined as a study to "make it possible to predict and influence politically significant aspects of social change in the developing nations of the world." This would include devising procedures for "assessing the potential for internal war within national societies" and "identify(ing) with increased degrees of confidence, those actions which a government might take to relieve conditions which are assessed as giving rise to a potential for internal war." The letter further stated:

"The US Army has an important mission in the positive and constructive aspects of nation-building in less developed countries as well as a responsibility to assist friendly governments in dealing with active insurgency problems."

Such activities by the US Army were described as "insurgency prophylaxis" rather than the "sometimes misleading label of counter-insurgency."

Project Camelot was conceived in late 1963 by a group of high-ranking Army officers connected with the Army Research Office of the Department of Defense. They were concerned about new types of warfare springing up around the world. Revolutions in Cuba and Yemen and insurgency movements in Vietnam and the Congo were a far cry from the battles of World War II and also different from the envisioned—and planned for—apocalypse of nuclear war. For the first time in modern warfare, military establishments were not in a position to use the immense arsenals at their disposal —but were, instead, compelled by force of a geopolitical stalemate to increasingly engage in primitive forms of armed combat. The questions of moment for the Army were: Why can't the "hardware" be used? And what alternatives can social science "software" provide?

A well-known Latin American area specialist, Rex Hopper, was chosen as Director of Project Camelot. Hopper was a professor of sociology and chairman of the department at Brooklyn College. He had been to Latin America many times over a thirty-year span on research projects and lecture tours, including some under government sponsorship. He was highly recommended for the position by his professional associates in Washington and elsewhere. Hopper had a long-standing interest in problems of revolution and saw in this multi-million dollar contract the possible realization of a life-long scientific ambition.

THE CHILEAN DEBACLE

How did this social science research project create a foreign policy furore? And, at another level, how did such high intentions result in so disastrous an outcome?

The answers involve a network spreading from a professor of anthropology at the University of Pittsburgh, to a professor of sociology at the University of Oslo, and yet a third professor of sociology at the University of Chile in Santiago, Chile. The "showdown" took place in Chile, first within the confines of the university, next on the floor of the Chilean Senate, then in the popular press of Santiago, and finally behind US embassy walls.

It was ironic that Chile was the scene of wild newspaper tales of spying and academic outrage at scholars being recruited for "spying missions." For the working papers of Project Camelot stipulated as a criterion for study that a country "should show promise of high pay-offs in terms of the kinds of data required." Chile did not meet these requirements—it is not on the preliminary list of nations specified as prospects.

How then did Chile become involved in Project Camelot's affairs? The answer requires consideration of the position of Hugo G. Nutini, assistant professor of anthropology at Pittsburgh, citizen of the United States and former citizen of Chile. His presence in Santiago as a self-identified Camelot representative triggered the climactic chain of events.

[*Editors' Summary.* Nutini, in Chile on other academic business, had been given a temporary assignment to Project Camelot to determine informally the possibilities of obtaining the cooperation of Chilean scholars. Despite the limitations placed on his role he managed to convey the impression that he was an official of Camelot with authority to make proposals to prospective Chilean scholars. At about the same time Johan Galtung, a Norwegian sociologist—then in Chile and associated with the Latin American Faculty of Social Science (FLASCO)—was invited to participate in a Camelot planning conference. Galtung turned down the invitation for several reasons, the major one being that he could not accept the US Army as a sponsoring agent in a study of counter-insurgency. Galtung had voiced concern over the project to several of his colleagues and had also shown them the memorandum of December 5, 1964, mentioned earlier. The public controversy broke when Professor Fuenzalida, a sociologist at the University of Chile, in a meeting between Nutini and university officials, made public the sponsorship and military implications of the project by referring, among other things, to the memorandum. Simultaneously the authorities at FLASCO turned over the matter to their associates in the Chilean Senate and in the left-wing Chilean press. The most immediate consequence of the furor that arose in Chile and in Washington was the cancellation of Project Camelot. Hearings were also promptly conducted by, among others, the House Foreign Affairs Committee. A development with long-term consequences for the relationship between social science and government was a letter issued by President Johnson to Secretary Rusk on August 5 which stipulated that: "no government sponsorship of foreign area research should be undertaken which in the judgment of the Secretary of State would adversely affect United States foreign relations]."

The State Department has recently established machinery to screen and judge all federally-financed research projects overseas. The policy and research consequences of the Presidential directive will be discussed later. . . . How will government sponsorship of future social science research be affected? And was Project Camelot a scholarly protective cover for US Army planning—or a legitimate research operation on a valid research subject independent of sponsorship?

Let us begin with a collective self-portrait

of Camelot as the social scientists who directed the project perceived it. There seems to be general consensus on seven points.

First, the men who went to work for Camelot felt the need for a large-scale, "big picture" project in social science. They wanted to create a sociology of contemporary relevance which would not suffer from the parochial narrowness of vision to which their own professional backgrounds had generally conditioned them. Most of the men viewed Camelot as a bona fide opportunity to do fundamental research with relatively unlimited funds at their disposal. (No social science project ever before had up to $6,000,000 available.) . . .

Second, most social scientists affiliated with Camelot felt that there was actually more freedom to do fundamental research under military sponsorship than at a university or college. One man noted that during the 1950's there was far more freedom to do fundamental research in the RAND corporation (an Air Force research organization) than on any campus in America . . . .

Third, many of the Camelot associates felt distinctly uncomfortable with military sponsorship, especially given the present United States military posture. But their reaction to this discomfort was that "the Army has to be educated." . . .

Fourth, there was a profound conviction in the perfectibility of mankind; particularly in the possibility of the military establishment performing a major role in the general process of growth. They sought to correct the intellectual paternalism and parochialism under which Pentagon generals, State Department diplomats, and Defense Department planners seemed to operate.

Fifth, a major long-range purpose of Camelot, at least for some of its policy-makers, was to prevent another revolutionary holocaust on a grand scale, such as occurred in Cuba . . . .

Sixth, none of them viewed their role on the project as spying for the United States government, or for anyone else.

Seventh, the men on Project Camelot felt that they made heavy sacrifices for social science. Their personal and professional risks were much higher than those taken by university academics. Government work, while well-compensated, remains professionally marginal. It can be terminated abruptly (as indeed was the case) and its project directors are subject to a public scrutiny not customary behind the walls of ivy.

* * * * *

THE INSIDERS REPORT

Were the men on Camelot critical of any aspects of the project?

Some had doubts from the outset about the character of the work they would be doing, and about the conditions under which it would be done. It was pointed out, for example, that the US Army tends to exercise a far more stringent intellectual control of research findings than does the US Air Force . . . .

Another line of criticism was that pressures on the "reformers" (as the men engaged in Camelot research spoke of themselves) to come up with ideas were much stronger than the pressures on the military to actually bring off any policy changes recommended. The social scientists were expected to be social reformers, while the military adjutants were expected to be conservative. It was further felt that the relationship between sponsors and researchers was not one of equals, but rather one of superordinate military needs and subordinate academic roles. On the other hand, some officials were impressed by the disinterestedness of the military . . . .

Another objection was that if one had to work on policy matters—if research is to have international ramifications—it might better be conducted under conventional State Department sponsorship . . . .

There seemed to be few, if any, expressions of disrespect for the intrinsic merit of the work contemplated by Camelot, or of disdain for policy-oriented work in general. The scholars engaged in the Camelot effort used two distinct vocabularies. The various Camelot documents reveal a military vocabulary provided with an array of military justifications; often followed (within the same document) by a social science vocabulary offering social science justifications and rationalizations. The dilemma in the Camelot literature from the preliminary report issued in August 1964 until the more advanced document issued in April 1965, is the same: an incomplete amalgamation of the military and sociological vocabularies. (At an early date the project had the code name SPEARPOINT.)

* * * * *

POLICY CONFLICTS OVER CAMELOT

One of the charactiristics of Project Camelot was the number of antagonistic forces it set in motion on grounds of strategy and timing rather than from what may be called considerations of scientific principles.

- The State Department grounded its opposition to Camelot on the basis of the ultimate authority it has in the area of foreign affairs. There is no published report showing serious criticism of the projected research itself.
- Congressional opposition seemed to be generated by a concern not to rock any foreign alliances, especially in Latin America. Again, there was no statement about the project's scientific or intellectual grounds.
- A third group of skeptics, academic social scientists, generally thought that Project Camelot, and studies of the processes of revolution and war in general, were better left in the control of major university centers, and in this way, kept free of direct military supervision.
- The Army, creator of the project, did nothing to contradict McNamara's order cancelling Project Camelot. Army influentials did not only feel that they had to execute the Defense Department's orders, but they are traditionally dubious of the value of "software" research to support "hardware" systems.

* * * * *

[*Editors' Summary.* In the following, the author discusses the opposition to Project Camelot voiced in the Departments of State and Defense, in Congress and among social scientists. In the case of the former groups (State, Defense, Congress) he links the response to Camelot to the larger issue of civilian vs. military control over foreign policy. In the latter case the issues are professional and ethical. Since this is our primary concern, in this section we are focusing on the response of the social scientists.]

* * * * *

One reason for the violent response to Project Camelot, especially among Latin American scholars, is its sponsorship by the Department of Defense. The fact is that Latin Americans have become quite accustomed to State Department involvements in the internal affairs of various nations. The Defense Department is a newcomer, a dangerous one, inside the Latin American orbit. The train of thought connected to its activities is in terms of international warfare, spying missions, military manipulations, etc. The State Department, for its part, is often a consultative party to shifts in government, and has played an enormous part in either fending off or bringing about *coups d'état*. This State Department role has by now been accepted and even taken for granted. Not so the Defense Department's role. But it is interesting to conjecture on how matter-of-factly Camelot might have been accepted if it had State Department sponsorship.

Social scientists in the United States have, for the most part, been publicly silent on the matter of Camelot. The reasons for this are not hard to find. First, many "giants of the field" are involved in government contract work in one capacity or another . . . . Second, most information on Project Camelot has thus far been of a newspaper variety;

and professional men are not in a habit of criticizing colleagues on the basis of such information. Third, many social scientists doubtless see nothing wrong or immoral in the Project Camelot designs . . . .

The directors of Project Camelot did not "classify" research materials, so that there would be no stigma of secrecy. And they also tried to hire, and even hired away from academic positions, people well-known and respected for their independence of mind. The difficulty is that even though the stigma of secrecy was formally erased, it remained in the attitudes of many of the employees and would-be employees of Project Camelot. They unfortunately thought in terms of secrecy, clearance, missions, and the rest of the professional nonsense that so powerfully afflicts the Washington scientific as well as political ambience.

Further, it is apparent that Project Camelot had much greater difficulty hiring a full-time staff of high professional competence, than in getting part-time summertime, weekend, and sundry assistance. Few established figures in academic life were willing to surrender the advantages of their positions for the risks of the project.

One of the cloudiest aspects to Project Camelot is the role of American University. Its actual supervision of the contract appears to have begun and ended with the 25 percent overhead on those parts of the contract that a university receives on most federal grants. . . . No official at American University appears to have been willing to make any statement of responsibility, support, chagrin, opposition, or anything else related to the project. The issues are indeed momentous, and must be faced by all universities at which government sponsored research is conducted: the amount of control a university has over contract work; the role of university officials in the distribution of funds from grants; the relationships that ought to be established once a grant is issued. There is also a major question concerning project directors: are they members of the faculty, and if so, do they have necessary teaching responsibilities and opportunities for tenure as do other faculty members.

The difficulty with American University is that it seems to be remarkably unlike other universities in its permissiveness. The Special Operations Research Office received neither guidance nor support from university officials . . . . If American University were genuinely autonomous it might have been able to lend highly supportive aid to Project Camelot during the crisis months. As it is, American University maintained an official silence which preserved it from more congressional or executive criticism. This points up some serious flaws in its administrative and financial policies.

The relationship of Camelot to SORO represented a similarly muddled organizational picture. The director of Project Camelot was nominally autonomous and in charge of an organization surpassing in size and importance the overall SORO operation. Yet at the critical point the organizational blueprint served to protect SORO and sacrifice what nominally was its limb. That Camelot happened to be a vital organ may have hurt, especially when Congress blocked the transfer of unused Camelot funds to SORO.

* * * * *

WAS PROJECT CAMELOT WORKABLE?

While most public opposition to Project Camelot focused on its strategy and timing, a considerable amount of private opposition centered on more basic, though theoretical, questions: was Camelot scientifically feasible and ethically correct? No public document or statement contested the possibility that, given the successful completion of the data gathering, Camelot could have, indeed, established basic criteria for measuring the level and potential for internal war in a given nation. Thus, by never challenging the feasibility of the work, the political critics of Project Camelot were providing backhanded compliments to the efficacy of the project.

But much more than political considerations are involved. It is clear that some of the most critical problems presented by Project Camelot are scientific....

The research design of Camelot was from the outset plagued by ambiguities. It was never quite settled whether the purpose was to study counter-insurgency possibilities, or the revolutionary process. Similarly, it was difficult to determine whether it was to be a study of comparative social structures, a set of case studies of single nations "in depth," or a study of social structure with particular emphasis on the military....

In one Camelot document there is a general critique of social science for failing to deal with social conflict and social control. While this in itself is admirable, the tenor and context of Camelot's documents make it plain that a "stable society" is considered the norm no less than the desired outcome. The "breakdown of social order" is spoken of accusatively. Stabilizing agencies in developing areas are presumed to be absent. There is no critique of US Army policy in developing areas because the Army is presumed to be a stabilizing agency. The research formulations always assume the legitimacy of Army tasks—"if the US Army is to perform effectively its parts in the US mission of counter-insurgency it must recognize that insurgency represents a breakdown of social order...." But such a proposition has never been doubted—by Army officials or anyone else. The issue is whether such breakdowns are in the nature of the existing system or a product of conspiratorial movements.

The use of hygienic language disguises the anti-revolutionary assumptions under a cloud of power-puff declarations. For example, studies of Paraguay are recommended "because trends in this situation (the Stroessner regime) may also render it 'unique' when analyzed in terms of the transition from 'dictatorship' to political stability." But to speak about changes from dictatorship to stability is an obvious ruse. In this case, it is a tactic to disguise the fact that Paraguay is one of the most vicious, undemocratic (and like most dictatorships, stable) societies in the Western Hemisphere.

These typify the sort of hygienic sociological premises that do not have scientific purposes. They **illustrate** the confusion of commitments within Project Camelot. Indeed the very absence of emotive words such as revolutionary masses, communism, socialism, and capitalism only serves to intensify the discomfort one must feel on examination of the documents—since the abstract vocabulary disguises, rather than resolves, the problems of international revolution. To have used clearly political rather than military language would not "justify" governmental support. Furthermore, shabby assumptions of academic conventionalism replaced innovative orientations. By adopting a systems approach, the problematic, open-ended aspects of the study of revolutions were largely omitted; and the design of the study became an oppressive curb on the study of the problems inspected.

This points up a critical implication for Camelot (as well as other projects). The importance of the subject being researched does not *per se* determine the importance of the project. A sociology of large-scale relevance and reference is all to the good. It is important that scholars be willing to risk something of their shaky reputations in helping resolve major world social problems. But it is no less urgent that in the process of addressing major problems, the autonomous character of the social science disciplines—their own criteria of worthwhile scholarship—should not be abandoned. Project Camelot lost sight of this "autonomous" social science character.

It never seemed to occur to its personnel to inquire into the desirability for successful revolution. This is just as solid a line of inquiry as the one stressed—the conditions under which revolutionary movements will be able to overthrow a government. Furthermore, they seem not to have thought about inquiring into the role of the United States in these countries. This points up the lack of symmetry . . . .

In discussing the policy impact on a social science research project, we should not overlook the difference between "contract" work and "grants." Project Camelot commenced with the US Army; that is to say, it was initiated for a practical purpose determined by the client. This differs markedly from the typical academic grant in that its sponsorship had "built-in" ends. The scholar usually *seeks* a grant; in this case the donor, the Army, promoted its own aims. In some measure, the hostility for Project Camelot may be an unconscious reflection of this distinction—a dim feeling that there was something "non-academic," and certainly not disinterested, about Project Camelot, irrespective of the quality of the scholars associated with it.

THE ETHICS OF POLICY RESEARCH

The issue of "scientific rights" versus "social myths" is perennial. Some maintain that the scientist ought not penetrate beyond legally or morally sanctioned limits and others argue that such limits cannot exist for science. In treading on the sensitive issue of national sovereignty, Project Camelot reflects the generalized dilemma. In deference to intelligent researchers, in recognition of them as scholars, they should have been invited by Camelot to air their misgivings and qualms about government (and especially Army sponsored) research—to declare their moral conscience. Instead, they were mistakenly approached as skillful, useful potential employees of a higher body, subject to an authority higher than their scientific calling.

What is central is not the political motives of the sponsor. For social scientists were not being enlisted in an intelligence system for "spying" purposes. But given their professional standing, their great sense of intellectual honor and pride, they could not be "employed" without proper deference for their stature. Professional authority should have prevailed from beginning to end with complete command of the right to thrash out the moral and political dilemmas as researchers saw them. The Army, however respectful and protective of free expression, was "hiring help" and not openly and honestly submitting a problem to the higher professional and scientific authority of social science.

The propriety of the Army to define and delimit all questions, which Camelot should have had a right to examine, was never placed in doubt. This is a tragic precedent; it reflects the arrogance of a consumer of intellectual merchandise. And this relationship of inequality corrupted the lines of authority, and profoundly limited the autonomy of the social scientists involved. It became clear that the social scientist savant was not so much functioning as an applied social scientist as he was supplying information to a powerful client.

The question of who sponsors research is not nearly so decisive as the question of ultimate use of such information. The sponsorship of a project, whether by the United States Army or by the Boy Scouts of America, is by itself neither good nor bad. Sponsorship is good or bad only insofar as the intended outcomes can be pre-determined and the parameters of those intended outcomes tailored to the sponsor's expectations. Those social scientists critical of the project never really denied its freedom and independence, but questioned instead the purpose and character of its intended results.

It would be a gross oversimplification, if not an outright error, to assume that the theoretical problems of Project Camelot derive from any reactionary character of the project designers. The director went far and wide to select a group of men for the advisory board, the core planning group, the summer study group, and the various conference groupings, who in fact were more liberal in their orientations than any random sampling of the sociological profession would likely turn up.

However, in nearly every page of the various working papers, there are assertions which clearly derive from American military policy objectives rather than scientific method.

* * * * *

In conclusion, two important points must be clearly kept in mind and clearly apart. First, Project Camelot was intellectually, and from my own perspective, ideologically, unsound. However, and more significantly, Camelot was not cancelled because of its faulty intellectual approaches. Instead, its cancellation came as an act of government censorship, and an expression of the contempt for social science so prevalent among those who need it most. Thus it was political expedience, rather than its lack of scientific merit, that led to the demise of Camelot because it threatened to rock State Department relations with Latin America.

Second, giving the State Department the right to screen and approve government-funded social science research projects on other countries, as the President has ordered, is a supreme act of censorship. Among the agencies that grant funds for such research are the National Institutes of Mental Health, the National Science Foundation, the National Aeronautics and Space Agency, and the Office of Education. Why should the State Department have veto power over the scientific pursuits of men and projects funded by these and other agencies in order to satisfy the policy needs—or policy failures—of the moment? President Johnson's directive is a gross violation of the autonomous nature of science.

We must be careful not to allow social science projects with which we may vociferously disagree on political and ideological grounds to be decimated or dismantled by government fiat. Across the ideological divide is a common social science understanding that the contemporary expression of reason in politics today is applied social science, and that the cancellation of Camelot, however pleasing it may be on political grounds to advocates of a civilian solution to Latin American affairs, represents a decisive setback for social science research.

ORGANIZATIONAL ISSUES

Some Principles Regarding the Utilization of Social Science Research within the Military

GEORGE W. CROKER

WHAT THIS MEMORANDUM IS ABOUT

In an era when conflict is a way of life, one of the agencies sorely pressed to cope with the changes demanded of it is the United States Air Force. In addition to the overwhelming demand for continuous adjustment to technical changes that is implicit in its primary mission, the Air Force has been required in less than a decade to adjust to two other changes, different in character, but each of substantial magnitude. First, it won its "fight" for independence and in 1947 became a Department. From a secondary, supporting arm of one service during an era when military affairs and civilian affairs of government were relatively discrete, it was suddenly "on its own" as a co-equal with the Army and Navy in an era when policy and power were no longer brothers, but Siamese twins. Then, before completing its first deep sigh of pride and uttering its first groan of responsible despair in this capacity, it was forced to assume an even greater responsibility: the role of the primary military arm.

Hence there is logic in using the Air Force as a "laboratory" in which to examine the process of change. In a general, modest way this memorandum will attempt to do so. Specifically, it will direct attention to problems that are confronted in the utilization of social science research within a military setting, that of the United States Air Force. Its ultimate purpose is to draw from experience some hypotheses, or principles, that appear to underlie, or govern, the utilization process—if not social change itself. To do this, there will be first, a discussion and analysis of four research projects (selected primarily for their illustrative characteristics) conducted under the aegis of the Human Resources Research Institute (the Air Force's social science research agency from 1949 until 1954, hereafter in this memorandum referred to as "HRRI," the short title by which many came to know it), and second, a discussion of some general aspects of the problem of utilization of social science research within a military setting.

SOME ESSENTIAL BACKGROUND

It should be made clear that in the Air Force research is controlled to a large extent and in many aspects by individuals not trained in a scientific discipline. This is particularly true of social science research, especially during the planning and utilization phases. In this memorandum the generic term, "operator," selected because it is the term used by the military itself, will be used to refer to this representative of "management." He may come from one or

● Charles Y. Glock et al., *Case Studies in Bringing Behavioral Science into Use,* Stanford: Institute for Communication Research, Stanford University, 1961, pp. 112-125. Reprinted by permission of the publisher and the author.

more of the following functional areas: "policy," "plans," "command," "personnel management," "training," or from "operations" itself. In the social order of the Air Force he is supreme. He controls the "purse strings" and is promoted faster and in greater numbers than his research brother. In brief, he "runs the show."

He first enters the research process in the "requirements" phase, during which the question: "Does the Air Force *need* the research?" is theoretically answered. He has to state—or agree in those cases in which the scientist himself suggests a research study—that the Air Force requires the research proposed. Or, if the study has passed the early test of "being required," he can cancel it simply by eliminating the "requirement." Implicit in many instances is the demand placed on the "operator" to admit either that he or someone in the hierarchy is incapable of coping with the problem stimulating the research, or that some aspect of the system has been mismanaged and help is needed. Moreover, it is implicit that sponsorship or acceptance of a research project means that the "operator" understands the dimensions and nature of the problem researched—or, where no definite problem is involved, the relation of the research to the Air Force's mission—as well as the manner in which the research can be of assistance to him or the Air Force.

In the utilization phase, additional forces are present that work on the "operator." Now he is confronted with a need to change something: a procedure, a policy, an organization—perhaps even eliminate all or part of his own function or area of responsibility. At this point the reluctance of an individual to change his behavior is accentuated and becomes as crucial to the social process as does the necessity for him to understand in the first place the problems and the relation of the research to the totality of the situation.

Example I. The Ethics Project

While bold and visionary in its approach to the solution of its new problems and responsibilities, the Air Force, like a person newly come to power and position, was sensitive about the manner of its performance. One manifestation of this concern is of interest to this account. Shortly after the close of World War II, some leaders of the Air Force became worried about the high incidence of dissident behavior among its officers and were led to the conclusion that a set of explicitly stated behavior standards, a "Code of Ethics," would lessen the degree of "bad" behavior.

The first attempt to develop such a standard, or code, was made within the Air Staff (the staff of the Chief of Staff of the Air Force). A board was created in 1947 and given the task of writing a Code of Ethics for Air Force officers. Several months of unproductive effort led to the delegation of responsibility for the task to the Commander of the Air University. This action led to the establishment of HRRI.

On the staff of the Commander of the Air University at that time were two colonels: X, a senior Chaplain within the Air Force, and Y, one of its outstanding combat commanders of World War II. While obtaining his doctorate, X had added understanding and appreciation of social science research methods to a professional and deep personal interest in the causes of human behavior. Y's intense combat leadership experience had convinced him that there was a pattern in the affairs of men, and that such affairs could be conducted better if it were known. They both deplored the guesswork that often characterized the management of Air Force personnel.

The Ethics Project was assigned to them.

While exploring methods of undertaking the task assigned them, these two officers learned of the Committee on Human Resources of the newly created Research and Development Board of the Department of Defense. Under the broad guidance provided by this Committee, the Air Force was to have an integrated human resources research program; in fact, two agencies concerned primarily with psychological research—the Human Resources Research Center ("HRRC") and the Human Resources Research Laboratory ("HRRL")—already had been established. There remained a need for a social science research agency. Initial inquiries by X and Y concerning ways to evolve a Code of Ethics led to a broader question: Should the Air University fill this need? The answer was "yes"; consequently in June of 1949 HRRI was established at the Air University and given the mission of conducting research in these substantive areas of concern to the Air Force: Officer Personnel, Officer Education, Manpower, Human Relations, Psychological Warfare, and Strategic Intelligence Methods. Y became its first Director, and X the Director of the Ethics Project. The author was assigned to HRRI and the Ethics Project in August 1949.

Planning for the study was completed and data for the first phase collected shortly after the establishment of HRRI. The design of the study was as follows: Using Flanagan's Critical Incident Technique, a sample was obtained of approximately 1,000 incidents of "good" (ethical) and "bad" (unethical)) behavior on the part of Air Force officers. These "cases," obtained from officers of the rank of major, lieutenant colonel, and colonel, were then subjected to qualitative analysis for the purpose of determining the ethical "themes" implicit in the judgments made by the officers providing the cases. The rationale was that "real life themes," as distinct from ones philosophically determined, were a logical step toward a Code of Ethics.

The Project staff was unanimously in accord that the implementation of the research results was as important as the research itself. Consequently, a great deal of planning and effort was devoted to the "Utilization" phase. For example, numerous attempts were made at communicating interim findings to Air Force officers through lectures and seminars in various schools of the Air University. Such efforts had a feedback effect on the Project staff in that they contributed both to preparation of the Project report and to sharpening the insights of the staff during the final stages of the analysis phase. In addition, an explicit effort was made to inform all "operators" within the Air Staff (e.g., "Personnel" and "Training") who might affect the utilization of the research results and of the progress status of the project. Activities such as these brought the project to the attention of several key commanders of the Air Force. Among them was General Curtis E. Lemay, Commander of the Strategic Air Command, who considered the project to be of great potential worth in solving a major problem—that of moral leadership—in his command.

By early 1950 the analysis of the first-phase data was complete and steps were under way to obtain additional data to complete the project as originally planned. However, several factors entered the picture that affected the conduct of the study and the utilization of the research results. Late in 1949, a civilian had succeeded Y as Director of HRRI. After he had been on the job for a brief period, he voiced disapproval of the Project on the grounds that (a) it was not scientific enough, and (b) it was not possible to study "ethics" except in terms of the total "community." (The reader might note that the American Psychological Association used a study similar to the Ethics Project to evolve its own ethical standards.)

The specific effect of the new Director's position on the utilization phase of the project was to alter significantly the character of the Project Report. In fact, X was given to understand by the new Director that it would be the better part of wisdom on his part if "he would forget the whole thing," and that "in no case would an official report from HRRI be issued on the Project." However, X possessed an obstinate character when such was needed. He simply refused to permit over two years' work to be side-tracked.

Widespread and profound interest in the study by the thousands of officers who had come to know it through his lectures and seminars fortified his desire to publish a record of the inquiry. As a compromise, 45 mimeographed copies of an "Interim Report" bearing no "official sanction" by HRRI was published. No "official" distribution of the report was ever made.

Thus, the Ethics Project was "concluded" short of its original goal: To create a Code of Ethics for Air Force officers. Yet it came close to attaining the essence of its purpose, if not the letter, for in June of 1950, the Chief of Chaplains of the Air Force arranged for a personal briefing on the study for his immediate superior, the Deputy Chief of Staff for Personnel, Headquarters, United States Air Force. The latter's response to the presentation is indicated by a comment he made in a discussion afterwards: "This is the most important work going on in the Air Force today." He followed this remark with instructions to prepare a program of moral leadership for the entire Air Force *to be implemented personally by its major commanders,* and to be based on the findings on the Ethics Project. To understand why this program was not undertaken one needs only to know the date on which the presentation occurred: 25 June 1950. The invasion of South Korea by the North Korean Army diverted the interest of Air Force leaders to more pressing problems!

But to understand fully the broader impact of the Ethics Project one has to take a brief journey to two events in later history. For the first, let us rejoin Colonel Y in the Fall of 1952, more than two years after he transferred from HRRI to General Lemay's Strategic Air Command (SAC). Now commander of an important SAC base in the middle west, Y is as enthusiastic as ever regarding the use of the social sciences in helping solve Air Force human problems.

* * * * *

To pursue further his sharp interest in and insight into the patterns of human behavior, Y instituted a management school at his base. To help him in this endeavor, he sought the assistance of HRRI. A team of social scientists was made available to help Y in his program. The "tangible" results of this work was a set of procedures for improving the operation of an SAC base while effecting a considerable reduction in personnel required for the task. Moreover, the study became well known and stimulated similar studies at other SAC bases.

* * * * *

. . . The Ethics Project [meanwhile] had come to the attention of the Commander of the United States Air Force in Europe (USAFE). As a result, he requested that a study be made of the standards of behavior of Air Force Personnel in the European area. This study was completed in the fall of 1952, but its usefulness was seriously impaired as a result of two errors of judgment by the staff of HRRI:

1. Too great an insight into, and ability to use, the final report was attributed to the Air Force "operators" in Europe. This conclusion resulted in omission from the report of "suggestions for action," a major failure in this instance.

2. An Air Force Chaplain should have been included on the research team. Failure to do so offended the Chief of Chaplains and his representatives in Europe.

Notwithstanding these serious shortcomings, the report made on this study was the basis for some worthwhile policy decisions in the United States Air Force in Europe.

Now what apparent principles of effective utilization can be derived from the Ethics Project? The first—perhaps most important—is one that characterizes progress in any field of science: The products of scientific inquiry are often used for purposes other than those contained in the original goal of the inquiry; i.e., they may be applied to the solution of a different problem, or form the basis for further inquiry which in turn leads to new knowledge or ways of doing tasks simpler or better. The Ethics Project did not attain its goal of a Code of Ethics for Air Force officers; yet, its findings had a number of effective uses, only two of which are related in this account: Y applied them in operating a base of a Strategic Air Command, and the Commander of the United States Air Force in Europe used them as a basis for further exploration of a related practical problem. Elsewhere in the Air Force they were used as a basis for a course in leadership in the Air University, and as a "stepping-stone" to a manual on discipline for the Air Force.

Second, the Ethics Project illustrates the effect of a "negative" position on utilization that can occur in the military .... In the Ethics Project, the disapproval of the civilian Director seriously decreased the possibility of attaining the Project's initial goal. In the "Standards of Behavior" study in Europe, the negative position of the Chaplains affected detrimentally the utilization of the report of the study.

Third, the Ethics Project illustrates the principle that effective utilization of social science research will depend often (especially where pervasive or controversial changes are involved) on the addition of a force or influence on the part of persons not immediately identifiable with the social situation in which the change must occur. The presentation of the briefing to the Deputy Chief of Staff for Personnel on the Ethics Project Interim Report was arranged personally by the Chief of Chaplains of the Air Force. Had the Project staff been responsible for arranging it, the briefing would not have occurred.

* * * * *

Example II. The Air University Far East Research Group (Social Science Research in Combat)

If the Air Force fails in its primary mission—that of deterring war— them it must fulfill its secondary mission—to be maximally effective when war occurs. Combat effectiveness of course is a function of the combination of machines and men. To study this relation, as well as to look into other aspects of the human elements in the war, HRRI sent a group of social scientists to Korea and other areas of the Far East in the fall of 1950. A unique opportunity existed in the substantive areas of psychological warfare research and strategic intelligence methods research, for in South Korea there existed for the first time a "laboratory" in which the "products" of sovietization could be studied firsthand.

Specific recommendations that HRRI study the human aspects of the Korean war came from a Planning Group of eminent social scientists who met at HRRL during the summer of 1950 for the purpose of outlining broad areas of research which they felt were appropriate guidelines for an Air Force social science research program. (The late Prof. S. A. Stouffer, who directed the morale studies conducted by the War Department during World War II, was Chairman of the Group. It is interesting to note that one segment of the report dealt with the subject of "research into methods of utilization of research.") Except for the utilization aspects of the study, the planning and execution of this project was essentially without fault . . . . Participation by HRRI's sister agencies, HRRC and HRRL, made it an integrated Air Force effort in the field of human resources research.

The group was comprised of 14 social scientists and two officers, of which the author was one. A majority of the group came from various universities and the remainder from the staffs of the permanent agencies. Meeting at HRRI some time before departing for the Far East, the group completed the planning originated by the in-service staffs of the HRRI, HRRC, and HRRL. Two "teams" were formed: A Personnel Research team of 10 scientists and one officer, and Psychological Warfare Research

Team of 4 scientists and one officer. Tentative methods of approach and design of interviews and questionnaires were completed. A name, "The Air University Far East Research Group," or "AUFERG" for short, was chosen.

The Personnel Team devoted its attention to such subjects as attitudes toward the war and toward Koreans, leadership, job satisfaction, and other human relations aspects of the war. It gathered its data in the form of structured interviews and questionnaires from five different combat units, 2 of which were in Korea, 2 in Japan, and one on Okinawa. Several thousand questionnaires and over one hundred and fifty intensive interviews were obtained. No analysis of the data was attempted in the Far East.

An account of the study conducted by a sub-team of a unit in Korea will illustrate the nature of the Personnel Research Team's task. The unit, a fighter Wing comprised of approximately 1800 men and 75 aircraft, was engaged in intensive combat operations at the time the sub-team arrived at its base. From the outset, the Wing Commander indicated that his regard for the study was not high. He "didn't see its purpose," and had his permission been sought, the study of the Wing surely would not have occurred. However, he did nothing to obstruct the research.

The two civilian scientists, (Dr. Floyd L. Ruch of the University of Southern California, and Mr. Dan Camp of HRRI), both superb practitioners of human relations, immersed themselves in the social climate of the Wing and established remarkable rapport in a very short time. The interviews were conducted and the questionnaires obtained, of course, during non-combat periods.

As the research progressed, certain marked changes occurred in the behavior pattern of the personnel of the Wing, as well as in the attitude of the Wing Commander toward the research team. The normal earmarks of a fighter-type unit—which might be described by the phrase, "boisterous exuberance"—became less noticeable. Instead, a conservative climate became normal. The Wing Commander became friendly and approachable in contrast to the distant attitude he had displayed initially.

* * * * *

. . . [A]fter the return of the Group to the United States, it became clear that insufficient thought had been devoted to the analysis of the data of the reports pertaining to the work of the Personnel Research Team. Months passed before a single report was published, and many of the reports originally intended for publication never reached that stage.

By comparison, the Psychological Warfare Research Team was a model both of how to carry out research in an overseas theater and of effective utilization. Despite the bitter Korean winter and amidst the confusion of a badly confused war, the Research Team not only completed its data-gathering, but coded it, transposed it to IBM cards, and completed a partial analysis while still in Korea. (Note: If the reader wonders about the availability of IBM equipment in Korea at this particular time, he may be consoled by the knowledge that so did the author.) Within four weeks after the return of the Team to the U. S., its report was completed, and within two months, printed and distributed. But of more importance, those who could use the report were kept apprised of its nature with the result that it was used widely.

As a result of the work of the original AUFERG, and in light of the broad social science mission assigned it, HRRI decided to establish a permanent detachment in the Far East. This action was taken with the personal knowledge and approval of the Vice Commander of FEAF, Maj. Gen. (later Lt. Gen.) L. E. Craigie. The Rand Corporation agreed to provide one scientist to work in cooperation with the permanent AUFERG.

One of its first projects was a morale study of Chinese and Korean prisoners of war. By the time of the Korean Armistice negotiations, the analysis phase of the project had advanced sufficiently to permit an interpretation by the Rand representative, Dr. Herbert Goldhammer (who had provided major guidance of the research). His conclusions had such import that they were brought to the attention of the truce team. By then, Gen. Craigie had become the first Air Force member of the truce team. His knowledge of AUFERG's work prompted him to invite Dr. Goldhammer to visit Panmunjon, where he remained for over four months as a major advisor to the team.

What principles can be derived from the experience with AUFERG? First, it demonstrates that effective utilization of social science research depends to a large degree on planning for such utilization at the same time that plans are made for the research itself. Little or no attention was paid by HRRI planners to the subject of utilization of the research findings of the Personnel Research Team. Primarily for this reason, the results were not forthcoming in time to be of real use . . . . Conversely, because *utilization* was planned for, the findings of the Psychological Warfare Research Team were produced and distributed with dispatch. As a result their usefulness was greatly enhanced.

Another principle of utilization (and one closely related to the preceding one) is that effective utilization must take into account the dynamic, changing nature of social situations. Again, this principle may seem so obvious as to not warrant mentioning; however, in altogether too many instances researchers have foreclosed on the possibility of effective utilization of their efforts by attempting overrefined analysis. Failure by HRRI to recognize this principle was a major factor in the ineffective utilization of the findings of the Personnel Research Team . . . .

Effective utilization must recognize that a research endeavor tends to affect the very situation which it has under study: this is the third principle illustrated by this project. The members of the fighter Wing knew that it was being observed by scientists; this knowledge affected their behavior. The change in the Wing's behavior impressed the Wing Commander, whose attitude toward the research was affected . . . .

The final principle illustrated by this Project is that effective utilization usually will depend on an operator possessing insight into, and knowledge of, how the social sciences can be utilized in solving problems of policy and management . . . .

Example III. Project Repair (A Study of Repatriated Prisoners of War)

As early as 18 months prior to the return of the first U. S. prisoners of war which resulted from the end of fighting in Korea and subsequent negotiations, HRRI attempted to establish a research project designed to reveal the character and nature of a problem that later was to assume large dimensions. It was felt that prisoners who had been subjected to intensive Communistic propaganda and brainwashing presented a problem, the solution of which could be helped by social science research, and that to be maximally effective, research should begin at the time the prisoners were first liberated. However, the effort to establish a requirement for such research was not successful.

As a result, it was not until the fall of 1953 that the POW problem was perceived by the Air Staff as having aspects in which social science research could be of some help. Even then, the requirement that led to HRRI's participation emanated primarily from the understanding of the potential contributions of social science to the solution of the problem by the Commander of the Air University at that time, Lt. Gen. (now General and Commander of the North American Defense Command) Lawrence Kuter, rather than from the formal organizational entity of the Air Force responsible for determination of requirements. In fact, the Air Staff apparently perceived the problem successively from four aspects prior to the initiation of any research: first, as a psychological warfare problem (i.e., what would be its effect on public opinion); then as a problem of medical rehabilitation of the returned prisoners; next, as a security problem; and finally, as a punitive problem (who should be punished, what should the punishment be, what should it cost). At the latter point, HRRI began its research.

An interdisciplinary team of psychologists, psychiatrists, sociologists, anthropologists, and statisticians conducted the research. Data were obtained from a number of sources, including a vast body of written material obtained by agencies other than the project staff (such as intelligence interviews), psychiatric interviews with a number of the prisoners, and a comparative study of historical and legal information. From the operator point of view, the research was to provide suggestions on these aspects of the problem:

1. Punitive.
2. Policy.
3. Training.

Completed in the fall of 1954, the report on REPAIR (together with a number of periodic briefings by members of the project staff for the policy board established at the Air Staff level to deal with the problem) was a major influence in the formulation of Air Force policy governing treatment of returned prisoners of war . . . .

What principles of effective utilization can we observe in this project? Project REPAIR, both from a research as well as the utilization point of view, was one of HRRI's finest hours. It was conceived by a senior ranking general officer of the Air Force (one who has a singularly broad understanding of the political and social responsibilities of the Air Force), and the utilization process was considered an integral part of planning for, and conduct of, the research study itself. Explicit effort was made to tell each operator concerned with the ultimate policy formulation how the work was progressing —in his language. In fact, whatever success the project had was due in large measure to the effective performance of two key operators on the Air Staff, one who had been in HRRI before his assignment to the Pentagon and the other a social scientist turned operator.

Example IV. The "Working Model" of the Soviet Social System

In the summer of 1950, HRRI initiated its largest and most important project: An Analysis of the Soviet Social System. The project was carried out entirely by contract with the Russian Research Center of Harvard University, the late Prof. Clyde Kluckhohn, Director. Since a final report of the project is to be published in the near future, only a brief explanation will be provided in this memorandum. The project consisted of the analysis of a large body of data in the form of interviews, questionnaires, and clinical tests gathered in Europe during 1950-51 from Russian émigrés. The objective of the study was to formulate a set of descriptive principles about the Soviet system from which depictions could be made about how it would react to a given set of conditions. Original written material about the project described this set of principles as a working model.

While the analysis of the data was underway in the summer of 1953, the project was brought under attack in the Congress. Senate interest in it was stimulated by lack of understanding as to how one would make a model of such a thing as a social system. It should be noted that both HRRI and the Russian Research Center had earlier recognized that the use of the term working model was likely to create misunderstanding in the minds of operators, but the budget cycle being as it is, there was no chance to remove this term from the materials included in earlier budget presentations.

As a result of the inquiry by Congress,

tremendous pressures were brought to bear within the Air Force to cancel the project. Only the intervention by individuals high in the government prevented the project from being abandoned. (It should be noted that much if not all of the congressional criticism could have been avoided had there been a representative of the Air Force present at the hearings who was knowledgeable of its responsibilities as a social and psychological factor in the conduct of national affairs.)

While this project illustrates a number of principles of effective utilization (e.g., that sometimes effective utilization will depend on the intervention of someone not immediately identifiable with the situation), the project best illustrates perhaps the most important of all the principles of utilization: That effective utilization depends on the manner in which the research results are portrayed with symbols understandable to the operator.

From a practical point of view, communication between the scientist and the operator is the most difficult aspect of the utilization of social science research. The difficulties resulting from the use of the term, working model, epitomizes the troubles that can result from failure to consider the importance of this principle. To take another example of this important principle, let us go back to the Ethics Project. The use of the word "ethics" was a source of great difficulty, for it has almost as many meanings as there are people who use it. This meant that the project staff often received arguments instead of responses.

SOME GENERAL COMMENTS ON THE UTILIZATION OF SOCIAL SCIENCE RESEARCH

. . . [M]any aspects of the utilization problem are missed, overlooked, or incorrectly appraised by scientist and operator alike. First, and transcending all other aspects in importance, is that in the social sciences, utilization of research is inseparable from the conduct of the research itself. To say this another way, utilization must begin when the research begins and must continue throughout the life of the research, and even far beyond in many instances. It cannot be taken for granted, or treated passively. It must be supported adequately. It does little good, for example, to spend $250,000 on a research project only to have publication of the results prevented by lack of $10,000.

In the second place, effective utilization will always depend on recognition of the total situation that can affect, or can be affected by, the results of the research. This would appear at first glance to be so fundamental as hardly to warrant comment. However, many fine research studies have been allowed to gather dust through failure to understand their importance. All too often the scientist or operator fails to take into account the relation to the total situation that characterizes the particular segment which is the focus of a specific study. For example, the research results of an outstanding study sponsored by HRRI and directed toward improving the career management of Air Force officers was vitiated through failure by HRRI to recognize the necessity for including in the planning phase of the study the key member of the Air Staff who was responsible for Career Management at that level.

Third, . . . effective utilization of social science research which is designed to aid top policy-makers must take into consideration the unitary nature of the total process of national security preparation. The scientist or operator responsible for social management aspects of the top echelons of the Air Force must consider these two things: One, the strong interrelationships among the major functions (e.g., between policy and logistics, and budget and personnel) involved in managing the Air Force itself, and two, the even stronger relations between the total Air Force mission and other major functions of national security preparation.

For example, a research study of Korean and Chinese prisoners of war should have been explicitly and intentionally related to truce negotiations rather than have occurred fortuitously.

Fourth, effective utilization of social science research is often handicapped by the operator's failure to understand its nature, which in turn stems from an implicit comparison of the measuring devices of the physical sciences to those used by the social sciences . . . .

A fifth and vital aspect of utilization often overlooked is that it seldom works on a "shot-in-the-arm" principle. Rather, in most instances positive and continued effort must be exerted to accomplish the changes that research would indicate. There is a need to understand that a decision by a policy-maker seldom if ever in itself accomplishes a change. Between the decision and the change there is a time interval and a need for overt effort to make the utilization effective.

Sixth, until a time comes when there are professional social engineers to implement the products of social science research, the best avenue to effective utilization in the Air Force will be through use of officers as quasi-social engineers rather than the use of trained social science research personnel for such a purpose. This, of course, is a matter of relative emphasis—both should be used if necessary. Two factors lead to this conclusion: One, it simply takes less time and effort to provide an officer with the necessary skills and insights to be an effective social engineer than it does to educate a competent scientist and then indoctrinate him with the complexities of the Air Force; and two, the symbols important to effective utilization favor the officer—i.e., he's already a member of the "in" group.

Finally, there is a need for comment on the importance of the utilization process. Both as a member of HRRI and later as a student and faculty member of a senior, joint-service school (the Industrial College of the Armed Forces), I was privileged to witness the formation of policy at high levels of government, both in and out of the Air Force. As a result, I became convinced of the truth of the statement made easily today: That the most important problems of the nation—if not mankind—are those the solution of which (if one is to be found at all) lies in the social sciences. Too often, however, social science research falls short of making real contributions simply because the utilization phase is not given adequate attention, particularly by the researcher. For some time to come, the latter must assume at least partial responsibility for the utilization of research results, if for no other reason than that if he doesn't no one else will! For those who may be offended by this thought, there is offered the counsel that even physical scientists have come to realize some responsibility for their efforts.

Social Research and Psychological Warfare

LEONARD S. COTTRELL, JR.

[It is awkward to attempt] . . . to discuss a research program, the specific content of which cannot be mentioned because of security requirements.[1] However, this stumbling block actually turned out to be a stepping stone to something I have wanted to do for some time, namely, to discuss with a group of interested social scientists outside the government some of the problems of doing research in the fields indicated by my subject and to suggest what appears to me should be done about this field by highly qualified social scientists independently of the government programs.

. . . I think I can demonstrate that there are promising scientific opportunities and even urgent responsibilities for those fortunate enough to operate at some distance from the pressures of immediate action requirements within the government. But in order to do this it will be necessary for me to consider with you at some length the problematic as-aspects of the contexts within which government research in this area is planned and conducted, including certain embarrassing questions about the concept of psychological warfare itself which have complicated the situation . . . .

● *Sociometry*, Vol. 23, June 1960, pp. 103-119. Reprinted by permission of The American Sociological Association and the author.

[1] This paper was originally presented at the meetings of the American Sociological Society, Washington, D.C., September 2, 1955, as part of the session on *Social Research with Reference to Defense Programs*, chaired by Raymond V. Bowers.

PROBLEMATIC ASPECTS OF THE CONTEXT

1. The concept of psychological warfare itself presents handicaps. The productivity of research imagination and planning depends heavily on the conceptual climate within which it occurs. In this case the central concept itself has been in large part responsible for a number of mistaken expectations and decisions, as well as certain deficiencies in research planning and in specific research design. Because I wish to use the discussion of the inadequacies of the concept of psychological warfare as a point of departure for proposing some of the things scientists outside the government might do, I shall . . . come back to it later.

2. Under present conditions in Washington it is difficult, if not impossible, to plan a systematic, coherent research program in support of psychological warfare, largely because of the unsystematic and, to me, unintelligible allocation of responsibilities among the various agencies of the government. Administratively and policywise it may make sense to say, as we do, that communication with countries with which we are at war will be the responsibility of the military forces, otherwise it is to be in the hands of the State Department and related agencies like the United States Information Agency. Moreover, it is probably necessary for each of the three military services to have its own psychological warfare responsibility. Finally, it may be necessary for each

agency to have its own psychological warfare and intelligence research capability.

... [This fragmentation makes little sense, and the necessity for it is questionable to many in and out of government.] ... The processes and problems involved in communicating with the peoples of the world, interpreting our actions and intentions, persuading, cajoling, confusing, or threatening them, do not divide themselves readily in accordance either with the bureaucratic structure of the government or the ambiguous distinction between states of war and peace. Within the Department of Defense, it has always been impossible to have meaningful divisions of labor in this field between air, land, and sea forces.

Some progress has been made by way of integration of effort through coordinating committees and boards at various levels. But it does not require a management engineer to see that the problem will remain a serious one until responsibility for this field is centralized in an effective agency directed from the top level of government.[1]

.... [T]he chaos I have hinted at seriously affects the planning and conduct of research .... If the process of communicating with the peoples of the world cannot be divided up logically among our present governmental agencies, even less so can the scientific study of these processes be so divided. The attempt to do this has been the source of much waste in men, time, money, and scientific progress. Here again, in my judgment, the government needs some centralization of research functions in this field, assuming of course that adequate safeguards are possible to prevent bureaucratic and nonprofessional stultification in such centralization. At the very least the fiscal officers of the government should recognize the necessity for, and encourage joint agency planning and conduct of, research.

[1] For an excellent historical study of the attempts of the United States government to organize its psychological warfare operations see Dyer (VI, 1959).

Many people will no doubt assert that all of this is being done. They are mistaken. There are paper plans and ineffectual organizations and some fairly promising starts. But we have a long way to go before this handicapping aspect of the governmental context is reduced to a minimum.

3. In any listing of what are, for research, important elements in the Washington context, there must be noted the hostility toward the social sciences, especially the so-called behavioral disciplines .... [Although] the actual extent of such hostility is not nearly so great as many suppose ... the confusion and ambiguity of role and responsibility among the agencies and the lack of a strong central leadership and direction in this field make it very easy for scoundrels and ignoramuses to threaten bureaucrats with budgets to defend. They are charged with misusing funds by stepping outside their proper responsibilities in doing research on this or that problem; or with boondoggling, by doing unnecessary research or duplicating the work of other agencies, and so on. I yield to no one in my admiration for the courage of our military men in the face of the enemy's fire, but there is a strange lack of guts when they confront a congressman, especially if he is a member of some investigating committee.

* * * * *

4. As if we didn't have troubles enough, the scientists and scholars themselves proceed to complicate the scene with their own internecine struggles. To me at least, the most repugnant aspect of the Washington scene is a scientist, and especially a social scientist, turned bureaucratic politician and little empire-builder. It not infrequently happens that the necessary interagency or interdepartmental cooperation in the development of a research program fails to materialize, not because of a recalcitrant administrative bureaucracy, but because of the professional jealousies and animosities of provincial academicians turned bureau-

crats. Progress in the application of the social sciences in a number of fields has been seriously delayed because some of these gentry, strategically placed, have operated on the assumption that the national interests are best served by maximizing the number of employees of their agencies who wear particular professional school ties, regardless of whether or not this policy makes the most efficient use of the full range of knowledge and skills required by the operational problems. It makes me unhappy to have to report that these people frequently have the backing and encouragement of responsible officials in their national professional societies. No one has yet estimated the loss in delays, inadequate theoretical structure, design, and methodology which this distorted value scale has produced. Several fields could be specified in which this kind of damage could be documented, psychological warfare being perhaps one of the more obvious . . . .

5. While the problems mentioned up to this point are difficult enough, a research director who is a good "operator," as we say, and who has patience, energy, and the willingness to devote the time to it can thread his way through the various hazards and keep a research program going, particularly if on occasion he is willing to throw caution to the winds and do some first-class broken field running. But I fear that the two problems I will now mention cannot be dealt with nearly so handily even by the most skillful improviser. They are not only more difficult, but more immediately relevant and vital to the possibility of proving the relevance and utility of research in the field under discussion. Unless they are recognized and effectively dealt with, we shall remain in limbo.

These two sources of embarrassment can be indicated by two questions: (a) Who are the consumers of research knowledge in this field? (b) Where are the middlemen? . . . .

When research programs are oriented to potential utilization of their products in some field of practical action, the situation usually involves some trained profession whose practitioners cast up concrete questions, and problems to which theory and research can be directed. Thus social scientists interested in research on problems in the medical and health fields, or social welfare, or theology, or military training and discipline, have recourse to a trained profession with an identifiable subculture, with values, skills, and identifiable needs for new knowledge which falls within the interests and competence of the social scientist. By any criterion, there is no profession of psychological warriors and even if we resort to a more general category and look for a profession of communications, there is still a substantial amount of ambiguity. At best there are some signs of professionalization of some parts of the communications field. What we must depend on for psychological warfare operators, of course, is a heterogeneous population of news reporters, journalists, writers, public-relations experts, advertising experts, radio and television announcers, entertainers, movie makers, poets, and others you can add to the list who have a gift of gab . . . . [T]hose who are engaged in the kinds of occupations mentioned are not distinguished by their regard for or reliance upon scientific research on human behavior, beyond perhaps a tendency to follow Hooper ratings and occasionally Gallup polls. They are the people of hunches, of bright ideas that will sell, and indeed frequently demonstrate that they are able to "appeal to the mass mind."

* * * * *

. . . [T]he research investigator in such a situation cannot expect to get much guidance as to salient problems for investigation which are of concern to a professional practitioner. Hence, if he is directed to do research in support of psychological warfare, he will necessarily define his problems in his own way, only later to discover, after doing his research, that his customer sees little or no relevance of his product for the operation in hand. The problem is greatly aggravated in the military services by the fact that there are no clearly marked career opportunities in this field, and officers accept assignment to psychological warfare branches as a kind of marking time or detour from their real career interests . . . . With his consumer such an uncertain quantity who possesses little capability for either defining problems on which research is needed or utilizing research knowledge when it is available, the reesearch investigator on psychological warfare problems stands doubly in need of a middleman to bridge the gap between research and the practical utilization of its results. Under such conditions we frequently find able research men having to turn into middlemen, if not into actual practitioners, and in the process losing their value as scientists.

Donald Young, (VI, 1955) in his presidential address to the American Sociological Society, has pointed out that to bridge the gap between a science and a profession requires personnel specially trained for this function. Under Dr. Young's leadership, Russell Sage Foundation has experimented in the development of such personnel perhaps more than any other organization in the country. Its attempts have been in the relations between the behavioral sciences and medicine, public health, psychiatry, education, social welfare, intercultural relations, theology, and certain types of government administration. Thus far the best results seem to come when a well-trained social scientist is made enough of a participant in the activities of the profession he is interested in to enable him to gain the perspectives and value orientations of that profession, and in that context see those problems for which, as a social scientist, he either has or can obtain the solutions.

. . . [D]eveloping such personnel as rapidly as possible . . . is a perfectly feasible possibility, which requires only that we enlist highly qualified social scientists and secure their full participation at all levels in the planning and operational agencies as operational rather than research personnel, but with the clear assignment to remain social scientists as well as become operators at least in part . . . .

THE CONCEPT OF PSYCHOLOGICAL WARFARE

. . . . [I]t has been my impression that far from being a clarifying concept which structures a field and guides action, to say nothing of research effort, the term "psychological warfare" is ambiguous and leads to confused thinking and action . . . .

In the first place, the term "psychological" naturally misled unsophisticated administrators into assigning primary research planning responsibilities to psychologists. Now the best psychologists in the government are in the physiological, clinical, testing, selection and training, and human engineering fields. They are by and large a well-trained and able group of men and women. But it is indefensibly unrealistic to ask those whose competence lies in these areas, and whose theoretical orientation is essentially monadic, and whose methods are primarily oriented to rigorously controlled laboratory experimentation on individual characteristics and learning, to plan or pass judgment on, or to supervise and defend research budgets for research in a field that is essentially communicative and interactional, requiring methods not appropriate to the conventional fields of psychology. As a result of just this sort of thing, research of a too limited conception was planned in many instances, or work in this area simply languished. It is gratifying to report that there has been steady improvement in this respect in the last few years; but much time and effort were required to educate agencies and officers to the necessity for a genuine interdisciplinary attack on the research problems of concern here. Let me note here that I recognize the importance of the role of psychological theory and research methodology for the area we are discussing. The strategic error the psychologists have tended to make, with notable exceptions of course, is that they did not rapidly move to supplement their own imaginations and skills with top quality competence in the other relevant disciplines, especially sociology, anthropology, social psychology, and political science.

In the second place, the term "psychological warfare" has encouraged a naive and only partly conscious assumption on the part of some in responsible decision-making positions that there existed somewhere a bag of slick tricks and black magic by which advertising psychologists and other modern spellcasters could put across ideas and beliefs in populations we wished to influence; that it was possible even to fight and win some wars with only words; and that somehow a lot of psychological warfare could be carried on in a vacuum with little or no relation to what was going on in the more tangible economic, political, and military aspects of international activity.

* * * * *

A third difficulty with the term "psychological warfare" is that the logic of the situation leads to responsibilities, action and requirements beyond the natural connotations of the term, and hence it has to cover too much for precise communication. Thus, while you wish to use communicational means to confuse the enemy and undermine his will to fight, you also wish to use such means to reassure and strengthen your friends . . . .

. . . [T]he problem is something more than a matter of esthetics and public relations. The natural foci of attention indicated by the term are enemies, and the natural, unconscious research tendency is toward a preoccupation with problems of communicating with a resistant target. Unless one is constantly on his guard, he may easily neglect the problem of communicating with allegedly friendly targets. I need not remind you that this sometimes requires a great deal of knowledge and skill, and is far more than a problem of mere access to mass media channels . . . .

[T]here is no research on the strengths and vulnerabilities of our own population, and your guesses as to the extent of our research exploitation of our present access to friendly peoples would be as good as mine. Even when we are dealing with a combat target, only a part of the psychological warfare effort is directed toward creating confusion, fear, panic, and similar negative conditions. Quite as much, if not more, effort is made to communicate credible news, to reason with the enemy, to persuade him, to convince him he is regarded as an intelligent reasonable human being who, given half a chance, would clean house and establish a decent government for his country, and so on.

. . . . [M]y own thinking about making more adequate use of social science in this field is greatly facilitated by regarding this area as *political communications* . . . . I might point to some gains, should it prove possible to take seriously the shift in orientation implied and to follow its implications.

1. Quite apart from the stimulus to a broader research perspective, some such term underscores the fact that a large proportion of that which we label psychological warfare falls well within what democratic cultures guarantee as an inalienable right—namely to convince other people that you are right and they are wrong. Indeed, we are committed to the technique of the free-for-all competition of ideas as a way of crystallizing our opinions on public issues . . . .

2. It places psychology as a contributing discipline instead of sole proprietor, and thus relieves it of the burden of an inappropriate role . . . .

3. It should help to dissipate any remaining implicit assumptions of magic and hocus-pocus.

4. It explicitly includes friends as well

as foes, self as well as other, as objects of interest and effort.

5. ... [I]t designates a field which social scientists can get hold of in terms of current theories and methods; and, what is more, they can work at this—mobilizing present knowledge, developing new theory, and doing new basic research without the hampering effects of security regulations.

6. All of this would seem possible and at the same permit, or indeed facilitate, the recognition of a substantial residue of operations and attendant research problems which can properly be treated as psychological warfare in a stricter and more precise sense, instead of having them confused by the broader operations and problems of political communications. There is potentially, if not actually, a body of doctrine and tactics for the military use of nonlethal weapons of light, sound, smell, taste, as well as of symbolic communication in either white (overt) or black (covert) operations to induce neutralization, defection, and surrender of enemy populations. Special research support of these operations is necessary, and most of it is and should be done under secure conditions just as any weapons research is.

To be sure, war is politics, and moreover, today it is total. Thus psychological warfare, in the more limited sense in which I have just used it, can and probably should be regarded as a special division of a more general area of political communications. Actually there are no sharp boundary lines here. But these considerations should on no account be allowed to obscure my main argument, that under cold war conditions, and to a substantial degree under hot war conditions, what has been called psychological warfare is better described as political communications; that the relevant research problems are better structured in that orientation; and that the major tasks of conceptualization and of basic research can better be done outside the handicapping context in which we are now working.

OPPORTUNITIES AND RESPONSIBILITIES OF NON-GOVERNMENT SOCIAL SCIENTISTS

This brings me then to the main point of my discussion, namely, to specify some opportunities and urgent responsibilities which I think are yours....

.... [A]lmost anything you would do in giving theoretical structure to the field of political communications, or in organizing present theory and substantive research knowledge into form for use in operations in this field, or in doing empirical research on the basic processes in communication in various types of interactional contexts would be pure gain.

From this assertion ... you may wonder whether there is any research done at all. The truly amazing thing is that there is.... [T]here has been and is now being conducted a substantial program within the government and on government contract. Some of it is of superior quality, and little if any of it could be regarded as of no value. One can get some idea of the quality of certain aspects of the research program by referring to the unclassified published reports from the Russian Research Center at Harvard University, the Center for International Studies of the Massachusetts Institute of Technology, and the Rand Corporation, forthcoming works from the Human Relations Area Files and associated subcontractors, and of investigators like Stuart Dodd, Paul Linebarger, Wilbur Schramm, Kingsley Davis, and their associates....

A large majority of the authorities ... would [probably] agree that, notwithstanding the claims of progress we can make, the following propositions can be accepted as true:

1. That the field of research in political communications requires a far more ade-

quate theoretical structuring than it has at present, even for reasonable advances in applied research;

2. That, lacking such a structuring, we have not yet formulated a rational program of basic research, to say nothing of research on pressing operational problems;

3. That the segmentation of political communications research responsibilities in the government, the legitimate pressures for quick *ad hoc* answers on day-to-day problems presented by the Washington situation, make it unlikely that the needed theoretical structuring and basic research planning will be done in the government programs alone; and

4. That this situation presents an opportunity and an unavoidable responsibility for competent social scientists to give some vigorous and sustained help.

Let us assume for the sake of discussion that agreement is sufficient at this point for us to raise the next questions of what to do and how to do it. What I have in mind can be accomplished in a variety of ways by many people working independently or in collaborative associations such as university seminars, committees, work groups, research centers, and the like. An organization like the Social Science Research Council or the National Research Council could undertake to facilitate coordination and exchange functions among the various interested people. A good deal of consultative help can be given by research personnel within the government without violating security regulations, though on this point I would be inclined to advise fresh looks at the field, with no compulsion to structure it in the way it has been done in the government programs. I am confident that good ideas and well-conceived plans of work in this field will get reasonable support from private sources, especially if they are shown how this problem requires independent as well as government-supported work. For that matter, good ideas can and will find some government support .... [A]rrangements for this latter type of support should preserve a maximum of freedom from pressure to phrase problems in the form the government agency may presently desire ....

1. I have already indicated the urgent need for theoretical structuring of the political communications field. This would involve systematization of the bits and pieces of relevant theory lying around, as well as novel formulations required by advances in empirical knowledge. While theorizing should not be hampered by reference to practical needs, it would be my guess that starting out to give theoretical structure to political communications problems in the context of practical questions about how to communicate effectively with a given culture or subculture will result in far more progress toward general theory than would be the case if we attempted to construct a general theory more or less in a vacuum ....

2. Efforts at theoretical structuring will of course necessitate organizing the findings of relevant empirical research .... [A] very vague and general focus or principle or organization will lead to results of little value to anyone. With a focus on answering practical questions in political questions in political communications, our needs will be better served, and I suspect more progress will be made toward valuable generalizations. With a focus on the required condition for effective political communications in various types of situations, areas of research which otherwise might not appear relevant become very much so. To illustrate, let me assert that nearly every topic listed in this program of the annual meeting has more than a tenuous relevance for our problems in political communications: .... [M]ost of the research reported in the papers in these sections probably has little immediate applicability to our problems here. But it would not be difficult for a competent social

scientist bent on orienting research knowledge to political communications purposes to select the considerable amount that is relevant and to point out research which would be of great value in the political communications field and which would be of general scientific interest as well....

3. We have a considerable number of area study projects in various universities, some of which have accumulated a great deal of information. We need exploratory efforts in organizing and focusing this information in such a way as to give maximum facilitation to political communications with any and all segments of a given society. Organizing the information in this way for a number of societies should yield a good foundation for a political-communications diagnostic outline, as a framework for asking the relevant questions and organizing information with more speed and efficiency than we now have. Something approaching this is presently being done in the writing of unclassified psychological-warfare handbooks on selected countries. I suspect they will be well done, but the further systematic treatment I am suggesting here will actually begin where these handbooks leave off. To put the problem another way, we might ask what information, organized in what way, is necessary to enable a political communications operator to take the roles of individuals located in different parts of a given society. It seems very clear that communication, if it goes beyond merely emitting messages more or less at random, requires that each of the participants be able to take the role of the other in reacting to the communicated material. Whether or not you accept this as proven, we can probably agree that messages are probably most intelligently phrased and controlled when we can most accurately predict the reactions of the recipient to them. This would then require of the operator in political communications a high degree of predictive accuracy about the reactive characteristics of his audience. What kind of information is necessary to give him this accuracy most economically? I put it in terms of role-taking. You can use whatever terms you like, but we need the practical answer.

4. As a matter of fact, why don't we include the test of this assumption of roles on the agenda of research tasks? This could be experimented with rigorously in terms that would be immediately relevant for deciding about essential training of operational personnel in political communications. Various amounts and kinds of information and training hypothecated as essential could be given to subjects who then could be tested for accuracy of role playing and predicting of reactions of target populations. Controlled study of reactions of this type of population to test messages by subjects of varying role-taking and predictive abilities could then be made. Results should be of great practical as well as theoretical value, especially if we take advantage of our own cultural heterogeneity and our access to a large number of potentially strategic foreign cultures in designing these experiments.

* * * * *

5. ... In keeping track of the shifting political alignments in the world, the intelligence agencies have to select the variables they regard as most diagnostic and interpret the way they behave in accordance with their best experience and judgment to make the best estimates of what is happening and what is likely to happen. The focus of concern is of course the drift toward and away from the current polar powers, the USA and the USSR. It would be of immense help if we could render their operations more economical and more precise. This involves identification of the essential variables, their interrelationships, and the proper weighting for the interpretation and prediction of trends. To me this suggests a large and difficult, but magnificently fascinating, multiple factor analysis of a large number of geographic, economic, political, military, demographic, cultural, social, and psychological

characteristics of a selected series of countries, tied to variables indicating tendencies toward or away from totalitarian governments, membership in the Soviet orbit, the neutralist positions, and active prodemocratic alignments. Such an analysis might reveal a certain limited number of underlying variables that could be indexed and used to keep track of the political weather of the world more effectively than we do now. If it did this successfully, it would not only be a boon to political intelligence agencies but help to identify more precisely the main themes of a political communications program, especially if combined with the detailed substantive knowledge derived from the qualitative cultural, social, political, and economic analyses.

* * * * *

Finally, let me repeat . . . my mention of the glaring need for highly talented social scientists to work closely with operators and operational planners, in order to become the all-important middlemen to bridge the gap between research and application. While this is a recruitment and training problem primarily, there are some interesting and important research possibilities on the problems of the dialectic between research and practice which should be explored. The specific problems concerning the gap between research and practice in political communications operations will probably have to be studied in the government situation, but we can get a good head start by compiling what we now know and by designing new research in kindred but less sensitive fields.

METHODOLOGICAL ISSUES

The Problem of National Character: A Methodological Analysis

MAURICE L. FARBER

Some six years have elapsed since Klineberg's (VI, 1944) pioneering article, among psychologists, dealing with the science of national character. Since then, there has been a burgeoning of investigation in this area, making it advisable, perhaps, on the basis of the additional perspective gained, to examine the salient methodological difficulties that have been revealed and to evaluate the prospects for future development.

The reasons for the expansion of this area constitute a problem for the sociology of knowledge, but one might speculatively suggest as a hypothesis the convergence during this period of the following trends: (a) the increased acceptance of the Freudian psychodynamics as an explanation of personality formation; (b) the development of projective methods of personality study with promise of intercultural adaptability; (c) the need, during the last war, for understanding the character of enemy and friendly nations, as well as our own, for the purpose of predicting and influencing morale; (d) a similar need, during the post-war period, for knowledge both leading to international understanding so that the possibility of war is mitigated, and, at the same time, providing ammunition for the current "cold war" or a potential future one, and; (e) the virtual exhaustion by cultural anthropologists of available un-described preliterate societies, with their subsequent turning to literate ones.

An interesting preliminary question is whether we are dealing here with pure or applied science. It is clear that the distinction is, in the social sciences, rather arbitrary. A nation represents one empirically observed type of human grouping and the character of such groupings may be studied as a problem in social organization in the investigatory spirit of pure science. On the other hand, if the scientist is primarily concerned in his research with the application of his findings to practical problems, such as international propaganda, then we are dealing with applied science. The distinction here would appear to revolve around the aim of the investigator, and these are rarely unmixed.

It should prove useful, at the outset, to examine the broad setting in which the problem rests.

A. NATIONS AND CULTURES

The problem of the measurement of differences between large groups of mankind is not, for social psychology, a new one. Psychological differences between the sexes, or among races, have been subject to researches for a good number of years. The demarcation of these groups, based upon anatomical differences, has been simple with regard to sex and not insurmountably dif-

• *The Journal of Psychology,* Vol. 30, October 1950, pp. 307-316. Reprinted by permission of The Journal Press and the author.

ficult, once the anatomical criteria have been decided upon, with regard to race.

Unlike sex and race, which are physiological-anatomical concepts, the concept of *nation* is essentially political-geographical. We are dealing, in the case of a nation, with *a sub-division of mankind living under a sovereign government and within a circumscribed geographical area.* Fairly frequently, to be sure, other properties characterize the people of a nation: blood-ties; common mores, language and religion; a sense of social homogeneity and common interest. None of these, however, is a *sine qua non.*

It is clear that such a grouping need not—and frequently does not—correspond with cultural groupings. And yet, *it is in relation to a particular culture pattern that one might expect to find a particular character structure.* Eastern Poles of similar culture may live in Poland or over the border in the Soviet Union; the Tyrolese of northern Italy are part of the same culture group as the Tyrolese just over the Austrian border, and were, in fact, under the Austrian-Hungarian flag until after World War I. The very formulation of our problem, then, immediately reveals rather awkward dimensions.

Not only do national and cultural boundaries often fail to correspond, but we are confronted with the further difficulty of nations containing several cultures . . . . A general statement about the character structure of the people of the Soviet Union . . . would have to include reference to Ukrainians, Letts, Armenians, Mongols, and a large number of other culturally diverse groups. A Canadian national character would need to include French and British Canadians, as well as, to an extent, Indians and Eskimos. It is dubious that any meaningful residuum of character structure could encompass such groups. It becomes clear that we cannot speak of a national character in multi-cultural nations, or stated positively, that the concept offers promise only in uni-cultural ones. It may be possible, to be sure, to speak of a nation having several subnational characters, but such a procedure appreciably modifies our present concept.

* * * * *

Then there are nations of a different type, rare perhaps, but worth mentioning for methodological reasons. Consider a new nation like Israel, consisting of a *mélange* of peoples from various countries of Eastern Europe, from Germany, from the United States, added to older native groups. No describable culture seems yet to have emerged and it would be pursuing a will-o-the-wisp to seek a national character in such a culturally unstructured nation. A period of historical continuity for a nation would seem to be necessary before uniformities in character might be expected.

B. THE INSTABILITY OF NATIONS

It has been objected by Fyfe (VI, 1946), for example, that the entire concept of national character is untenable because nations exhibit marked historical changes in behavior and attitudes. The national character . . . of the Japanese of 1850 is not that of the partially Westernized Japanese of today. There is every reason to believe that as a culture changes historically personality structure within it is concomitantly altered. In this connection, Kardiner and Linton (VI, 1949) have demonstrated, in a happily discovered "natural experiment," how an economic shift from a dry-rice culture to wet-rice culture apparently caused marked shifts in character structure in Tanala-Betsileo of Madagascar.

If we grant, then, this instability, what remains of our concept of national character? Clearly, we cannot insist upon descriptions that are true for all eternity: they are at best valid for only certain historical periods. If one were given a description of a national character, it would be difficult to state with certainty for how long that character had existed and impossible to state for how long it will continue to exist. Our concept is history-bound.

It must be pointed out that changes which are historically dramatic need not cause changes in national character structure. A nation may fight a war, suffer a change in government, or ally itself with a different power bloc without marked effect upon the character of its people.

There are, moreover, psychological aspects of nations that one would not want to include in the national character concept. Recently, for example, a trans-Atlantic plane crashed, killing a popular French boxing champion and plunging many French into a day or two of depression. It would be patently inadvisable to include "depression" as a component of the French character as it would be to ascribe "anxiety" to the Germans on the basis of their post-war state of mind. Short duration mood fluctuations, while they may well be related to character structure in the types of stimuli to which they are responses, for instance, or in the style of response, are not in themselves the psychological variables in which we are interested.

. . . The implied problem of precisely what levels of personality are optimally to be probed is beyond the limits of the present paper.

C. THE HETEROGENEITY OF NATIONS

Strictly speaking, there are probably as many personalities in a nation as there are individuals. Even if we ignore large areas of individual differences, we still find sharp differences between rural and urban dwellers, and among classes within a nation. Yet the concept of national character would attempt a single general description which covers the bulk of individuals as well as all classes. Consider, for example: "the French character structure" would need satisfactorily to include Leon Blum and Charles de Gaulle, peasants of Normandy and fishermen of Brittany, Communist auto workers of the Paris suburbs, the smart society of the Faubourg St. Honoré, inn-keepers of the Midi, and so on. Somehow, a lowest common denominator, or a modal personality must be extracted from this potpourri.

It has been suggested, indeed, that class differences within a nation may be greater than differences between given classes in different nations, for instance, that French and German industrialists might be more alike than are French industrialists and French peasants. This may well be true, though it does a certain violence by pulling out of context aspects of fairly integrated national constellations. . . .

There has been a tendency in some anthropological circles, particularly by Mead, to minimize this problem, apparently on the theoretical ground that every member of a nation necessarily exhibits the national character, so that it matters little which particular individuals one studies. To simplify, it is as if all members of a nation were envisaged as having been immersed in the homogeneous fluid of national culture, with the soaked-up fluid readily identifiable by a trained observer . . . .

A more scientific analogy would perhaps be with the Spearman theory of intelligence: though there are individual differences (s factors) there is a general national character (g factor) common to all.

Such a view would seem to the present writer untenable. There may well be little general factor of any consequence running through all classes and groups of a nation; class characters may be interrelated in complex, perhaps complementary, ways. Methodologically, how could one ascertain, by examining a few members of a given class, where their class characteristics ended and their national characteristics began? One could not, without sampling and inter-class comparisons.

The concept of "the basic personality structure" of Kardiner (VI, 1945) was designed for extremely broad cultural comparisons and not for the study of national differences. Kardiner maintains, for example, that the basic personality structure of Sophocles was essentially the same as that of modern Western man. Its possible applicability to the present problem, is, however, readily apparent, and Linton (VI, 1949) has indeed suggested its use with nations.

Substantially the same difficulties as encountered in connection with Mead's approach would seem to be involved here. One of the underlying postulates of the concept is "that the techniques which the members of any society employ in the care and rearing of children are culturally patterned and will tend to be similar, although never identical for various families within the society." Aside from the possibility . . . that child-rearing practices may be overstressed as cause, this postulate is certainly inaccurate for modern Western nations. Ericson (VI, 1946) has shown, for example, that there are important differences in child-rearing practices between social classes in the United States. Kardiner (VI, 1945: 365) . . . feels that the basic character in the United States is uniform and does not follow class lines. Thus he attempts to designate the basic personality structure of "Plainville," a rural American community, and to treat it as if it were the character structure of Western culture.

It would seem that approaches such as Kardiner's and Mead's run the risk of assuming what is to be proved by spreading a homogeneous semantic veneer over the cracks in the social structure of nations. There would seem to be no substitute, if we are to know the character of nations, for the laborious task of considering classes and other groupings within nations.

Kaldegg (VI, 1948) has recently compared English and German secondary school pupils, employing a projective test. While running the risk of failing to touch certain aspects of adult personality, this method, provided the social backgrounds of the student groups are comparable, would appear to be a useful one. Before generalizing about the entire nations, however, it would be desirable to sample students at several social levels.

The present writer has experimented with the method of comparing similar occupational groups in different countries, i.e., insurance clerks in England and the United States. While such a method appears to keep many factors constant, the greatest caution should certainly be employed in generalizing observed differences to "the British" or "the Americans" as nations. Other occupational groups may differ along quite other dimensions. Nevertheless, this method offers a preliminary approach to an admittedly baffling problem. . . . [T]here is a special problem concerning the relation of élites or policy-makers of a nation to the population at large.

. . . Can we generalize about the Russian character structure from the acts of the Politiburo? It would be extremely foolhardy, and yet some relation of considerable subtlety doubtless exists, for are these political leaders not Russians living in the context of a Russian culture? And do not their policy decisions in turn mold the institutions of Russia and thus modify the Russian character structure? As an élite, are their attitudes and behavior not imitated? Are their decisions, and more particularly the decisions of policy-makers in democratic countries, not limited by what "public opinion" will tolerate?

Let us keep in mind, on the other hand, that policy-makers are atypical members of a nation who have risen to their positions partially on the very basis of these atypical characteristics. Moreover, their governmental rôles expose them to different stimulus constellations as well as modify their motivational systems. Whatever their relation to the governed might be, it is certainly too complex to allow for easy transformation of descriptions between the two . . . .

Since policy is made by élites operating with a special psychological context, a pragmatic objection to the whole notion of national character arises from the viewpoint of applied psychology: that a description of a national character would be of little value in predicting the international political acts of a nation. Inkeles (VI, 1950) for example, has made this point.

... [T]his objection is a serious one to those more practically oriented. It would surely be perilous to predict whether a particular nation will attack by unannounced *Blitzkrieg* or only after a formal declaration of war, purely on the basis of national character data. Factors such as relative strengths, types of armaments, and geographical positions definitely are involved. Nonetheless, taken in conjunction with such variables, a knowledge of the national character would in all probability be of value.

Assuming, for instance, that Mead's (VI, 1942) "chip on the shoulder" description of the American character is valid, one would be more apt to expect the United States to fight only after it has been attacked or declared war upon, though it may possibly have maneuvered the opposing nation into a position in which it felt that it had to attack. Benedict's (VI, 1946) observations on the rôle of authority and hierarchy in the Japanese character have been useful in predicting the docility of the Japanese under occupation. In general, then, without insisting upon national character as the sole determinant of national policy, one can still insist upon its potential value when considered in conjunction with other variables.

E. PERSONALITY STRUCTURE OR SOCIAL STRUCTURE?

The term "national character" has thus far in this discussion been deliberately employed in a rather loose and undefined way so that various facets of it might be examined. A serious problem must now, however, be faced. Is it profitable to deal in this connection with personality structure in the narrowly psychological sense of an organization of traits? Or is it necessary, on a national stage, to employ a broader concept which includes personality together with descriptions of certain important social institutions of the nation?

Would it be meaningful, for example, to talk of the religiosity of the Spaniards without description of the officially monopolistic position of the church in Spain, or of the irreligiosity of the Russians without considering the attitude of the Soviet government toward religion? Would it not constitute a distorting removal from context to speak of American extraversion without reference to our market, pecuniary economy? Extraversion in Italy, for instance, would have quite a different meaning.

No sharp lines can be drawn here, but it would seem advisable, on the basis of such considerations, to include aspects of the national institutions and ways of life along with the more narrow description of psychological personality traits. That some of these institutions may contribute causally to the personality structure does not eliminate the necessity for their inclusion.

A recent development in research technique is relevant here. That is, the use of what Klineberg has called "cultural products," e.g., literature, art, and humor as an index of national character. McGranahan and Wayne (VI, 1948) have, for instance, compared the German and American character through analysis of popular plays. That the successful plays of a nation bear some relation to the national character is undeniable, but that this relation is sufficiently direct to allow easy inferences is another question.

Consider something of the life history of a successful play. It is written by a rare member of a nation, who selects and organizes certain aspects of experience based upon deep personal motives, yet in accordance with certain literary conventions. His work must convince a producer that its production will be profitable, and then it must in actuality attract certain publics who are willing to pay to see it. A series of selective processes is involved here, and the play succeeding in passing through them may reflect only narrowly and distortedly particular aspects of the national character. Plays may merely tell élite classes what they would like to hear, or mirror them as they would like to be. Plays may fail to touch upon huge segments of the national character because these are taken for granted in the nation, unverbalized, and not viewed as dramatic material.

Cultural products, then, must be analyzed with delicacy. If we can tease out something of the selective processes involved we may gain valuable insights into national character. McGranahan's stimulating findings indicate that there is rich material here. The difficulty is rather that cultural products may be too rich after passing through a series of social processes, furnishing at best hypotheses rather than verifications.

F. THE METHODOLOGY OF VERIFICATION

Investigators trained in a rigorously empirical, experimentalist tradition are apt to find themselves ill-at-ease and inhibited in confronting the problem of national character. Non-scientific writers, in contrast, have been relatively free of paralyzing cautions in their sweeping, impressionistic generalizations. Somewhere between these two extremes has been the recent work carried out in certain anthropological circles, best exemplified, perhaps, by Gorer's (VI, 1948) report on the American character. It should prove of value to examine methodologically this widely publicized book. . . .

At first glance the experimentalist is nonplussed by the total lack of the kinds of scientific controls he has come to consider necessary. There is no systematic method of investigation; no description of the numbers or kinds of people interviewed, if any; no quantification; no deductions that follow with necessity from particular arrangements of data. There are only stated conclusions, in terms, to be sure, of some ethnological and psychoanalytic sophistication, but in the final analysis essentially impressionistic.

And yet, the conclusions possess a certain plausibility, and even brilliance. There can be no doubt that the very experience of "plausibility" needs analysis. . . . In the present case, some of the material seems to correspond with the reader's own informal observations, but there is probably also another reason for the plausibility. That is, *that a single concept appears successfully to subsume a number of discrete social phenomena, or at least to interrelate them.* Specifically, Gorer relates to American rejection of immigrant fathers such characteristics as our contempt of Europe, of politicians, our dislike of military officers, of social planning, etc. In mature sciences, such subsumption is successful and precise. . . .

The problem here is first to ascertain whether Gorer's specific assertions are in the main true, and secondly to note whether his generalization succeeds in subsuming them. Unfortunately, . . . no firm evidence is adduced to indicate the extent, or indeed the very existence of the American characteristics he describes. On the other hand, . . . the general concept does succeed with a certain plausibility in subsuming and relating many of the specific descriptions of American character.

Methodological evaluation of this curious state of affairs is difficult. In the study of "the seamless web of culture," the method of plausible subsumptions may indeed be a valuable social science research tool. In the present case, one is, to be sure, disturbed by such considerations as the necessity for explaining the apparent dislike of authority in nations like France and Italy, where the causality could not be the same as in the United States. One would demand in addition, of course, evidence for the existence of the American characteristics as described. One is, moreover, *a priori* suspicious of the monolithic causal scheme presented. There is, however, no necessity for a dichotomous structuring which would either totally reject or totally accept Gorer's material or any other which uses a similar approach. There are provocative hypotheses here, which must be subjected to more rigorous test.

In conclusion, one can only point to the subtle and tenuous nature of the problem of national character. We are beset, particularly in this area of social research, by methodological riddles not easily susceptible of solution. We cannot plead, as is now being done, that the urgent need for results in a tense world justifies speedy but superficial work.

Is a science of national character possible? Yes, if we remain methodologically alert and are sufficiently un-compulsive to face the possibility that our laborious digging along this vein may never produce more than low-grade ore.

The Role of Public Opinion in International Relations

LLOYD A. FREE

The assumption that public opinion is somehow important in international relations is born out by the efforts of political leaders to woo it and by the practices of governments. Every major government in the world today, and many of the minor ones, spend varying amounts of time, attention and money on attempting to influence opinions on international matters among citizens of their own and other countries.[1] Oddly enough, judging from the colossal efforts they expend on propaganda at home and abroad, the modern totalitarian governments—from Hitler to Nasser to Communist Russia and China—are the most fervent believers of all in the idea that public opinion really counts.

In related vein, there has been a tendency in the case of at least some governments to give increasing attention to public opinion poll results, both domestic and foreign. Most of our recent American Presidents have been in the vanguard in this respect. Franklin D. Roosevelt was our first President to profit from really scientifically conducted polling. Particularly after the adverse reactions to his famous "Quarantine" speech, he was determined not to get too far out in front of public opinion concerning this country's participation in World War II—nor to stay too far behind. In this connection, he followed the polls with great interest, particularly trends of American public opinion charted for him by my associate, Hadley Cantril (VI, 1948).

Truman was much less oriented towards polls and polling; but I know from my own experience that President Eisenhower was deeply interested in the opinions of people in other countries. While working with Nelson Rockefeller in the White House as a Consultant to the President in 1955, we started a series of periodic reports to him on the psychological situation abroad, based chiefly on data gathered by the research branch of the United States Information Agency (U.S.I.A.) under the able supervision of Leo P. Crespi. On one or two occasions, after John Foster Dulles had given one of his masterful briefings, the President was heard to say: "But you forget the human side, Foster," pulling out one of my reports.

It was during the Eisenhower years that one of my privately-sponsored surveys scored a major success: a study in Japan covering not only public opinion, but attitudes of the four groups of greatest impor-

• A longer version of this article was delivered as a lecture at The Edward R. Murrow Center of Public Diplomacy, The Fletcher School of Law and Diplomacy, Tufts University. The original version will appear in the forthcoming volume of Edward L. Bernays Foundation Lectures edited by Arthur Hoffman, to be published by Indiana University Press.

[1] For books on the general subject of public opinion, see particularly Almond (I, 1950); Key (VI, 1964); and several related books by Alfred Hero. For an historical account of U.S. efforts to influence foreign opinion, see Sargeant (VI, 1965). For a broader treatment of international communications in general, see Davison (V.2, 1965).

tance in the power and influence structure. Later, I learned that my report had actually received consideration at the level of the National Security Council; and President Eisenhower's then special assistant for national security affairs told a friend of mine that it was one of the most useful documents the NSC had had available during the time of his service there.

John Fitzgerald Kennedy was, of course, a fervent believer in polling. He not only depended heavily on Louis Harris's finding about domestic opinion, but followed closely the U.S.I.A. data on opinion abroad. In the aftermath of the Bay of Pigs fiasco, U.S.I.A.'s findings that Castro was little known in Latin America and was generally viewed by the public with considerable allergy, contributed to the Kennedy Administration adopting a relatively low-keyed approach to Castro and Castroism.

When it comes to that great practitioner of "consensus," Lyndon Baines Johnson, the picture is the same. He regularly uses Oliver Quayle to poll in the United States on questions including international issues (Vietnam, for example), and keeps close at hand a thick, loose-leaf notebook not only of the latest surveys taken at home by Quayle, Gallup, Harris, etc., but also of polls conducted abroad.

Following the recent American intervention in the Dominican Republic, I immediately sent to the White House a report I had prepared in June of 1962 on the *Attitudes, Hopes and Fears of the Dominican People* (Free, VI, 1965). This showed that the Dominicans, as of then at least, were the most pro-American, anti-Communist, anti-Castro people we had found in any part of the world. Not only did President Johnson read the report, but the White House had it duplicated and distributed at the highest levels, and found it "very helpful." I have little doubt that it was one of the many factors which caused the Administration quickly to shift from an initial policy of exclusive support for the military junta to the later one of working toward a coalition solution.

Nor is this interest in public opinion surveys peculiarly American. Professor Stoetzel and Mlle. Riffault of the Institut Français d'Opinion Publique, for example, report that their results on political matters are regularly followed by President de Gaulle and the French Government. Professor Noelle-Neumann of the Institut für Demoskopie in West Germany says that their data are sent to the Federal Government about twice a month and have a steady influence on the way it reports in its press conferences. A number of the Ministries of the Indian Government, including External Affairs, are regular subscribers to the Monthly Public Opinion Surveys of Eric da Costa's Indian Institute of Public Opinion. The Japanese Government has conducted its own polls on diplomatic problems, mainly the China issue, normalization of relations with Korea, and the relationship with the Soviet Union. The West German, British, and Indonesian governments, among others, have commissioned various studies abroad.

FOREIGN OFFICE MYOPIA

There is another side to this story, however, much less pleasing to those interested in public opinion research. It has to do with the built-in "blind spots" toward the psychological aspects of world affairs exhibited by foreign offices and diplomatic corps the world over. For the most part, this includes our own State Department, and particularly most of its older officials high in the pyramid of power and influence. The late, great John Foster Dulles once remarked: "If I so much as took into account what people in other countries are thinking or feeling, I would be derelict in my duty as Secretary of State." More than one American ambassador has, explicitly or implicitly, echoed the words of one of their colleagues—a career man—who said, while serving in a country that is now in a state of acute crisis, largely because of the turbulence of its public: "To hell with public opinion and public opinion polls. I am here to deal with the government, not with the public."

In other words, many if not most of at least our older State Department officials and Foreign Service officers continue to believe, in their heart of hearts, that the game of diplomacy can still be played as it was in the days before World War I. They do not include in their calculations the degree to which the public all over the world has, in fact, got into the act; nor the extent to which propaganda, popular persuasion, and information and cultural programs have become major instruments of the new diplomacy.

This insensitivity sometimes leads to very pertinent public opinion research findings being either neglected or ignored. The most cataclysmic such "failure" in my own experience had to do with the Bay of Pigs invasion. A year before, I had managed by the skin of my teeth to get a public opinion study done in Cuba (Free, VI, 1960). This showed that Castro, at that time at least, was overwhelmingly popular among the Cuban people. There was a small opposition, but it was confined almost entirely to the City of Havana. Thus, whatever the expectations of those who planned the invasion, it came as no surprise to us that there was no popular uprising to assist the Bay of Pigs invaders. As with all of our reports, this study had been made available to the government, as well as to the public, and had actually been sent up to the White House by the bureaucracy. However, between the time our report was issued and the time of the attempted invasion, there had been a change of Administration when Kennedy came into the White House. And our findings were not called to the attention of the new President nor anyone on his staff when the question of invading or not invading was being considered.

DOES "WORLD OPINION" REALLY EXIST?

Not long ago, another of our great Secretaries of State, Dean Acheson (VI, 1965), claimed that Americans have a "Narcissus psychosis": "An American is apt to stare like Narcissus at his image in the pool of what he believes to be world opinion." After making the point that the only honest answer people in the world generally could give to questions on specifics of foreign policy would be a "don't know," he concluded; "World opinion simply does not exist on matters that concern us. Not because people do not know the facts—facts are not necessary to form opinion—but because they do not know the issues exist."

Thus, we practitioners of the art of public opinion research are faced with some very basic questions: Does such a thing as "world opinion" exist? Do people in various parts of the world really have meaningful opinions on international issues? If so, are these opinions of importance to international relations? Replying to these questions is difficult and complicated; in fact, few generalizations can be made. The real answer is, it all depends.

To start with, I must define in my own way some of the terms we will be talking about. An opinion, in my terminology, is simply an expressed attitude; an attitude that is communicated. An attitude, on the other hand, is really a form of perception—a way of looking at a given subject. In the course of our lives, we build up all sorts of assumptions through experience in attempting to achieve our purposes; and these assumptions vitally condition what we perceive as the realities of the world in which we live. Our attitudes spring from this "reality world" or "assumptive world" of ours; they are the resultant of an interplay of our assumptions, shaped and modified by experience. If I can use a term very much over-worked these days—"image"—an image is a rather fixed pattern of assumptions brought into operation by a situation in which one finds it necessary to react.

Hence, in a very real sense, if an individual has no assumptions learned from experience concerning a given subject or that can be related to that subject, he can have no attitudes—and hence no opinions, let alone anything that might be denominated an image. And any opinions an individual may express will be *meaningful* if, and only if, he in some way relates the subject at issue to his own purposes, no matter how narrowly individualistic or broad these may be. The range of his sense of purposes is again delimited by his "reality world."

Every non-psychotic individual on earth, no matter how primitive, has assumptions based on experience, and hence attitudes about *something,* even if they pertain only to his own personal life, his family, or his village. And he will relate many of these attitudes to his own purposes, so he will have a certain fund of meaningful opinions which he can express, if—and this is a very important "if"—*you ask him the right questions.* Conversely, every individual in the world has his "blind spots" of greater or lesser scope; that is, subject matter areas in connection with which he has *no* assumptions to bring to bear, and hence about which he has no attitudes.

THE ILLITERATES AND THE IGNORANT

Let me illustrate from a study our Institute did in Brazil a few years ago (Free, VI, 1961). When our interviewers asked rural Brazilians, most of whom are illiterate, about their *personal* aspirations in terms of their own lives, only 12 per cent could not respond. When the canvas was broadened to aspirations for their *country,* the "don't knows" jumped to one-third. The "reality worlds" of that proportion were not broad enough to extend to the nation as a whole.

The moment the inquiry shifted to the international scene, almost all of them were left behind. Eight out of ten could not name any country with which Brazil should co-operate. Ninety-five per cent were unable to identify the President of the United States. Under the circumstances, it would be an exercise in sheer futility to ask these people questions about the specifics of foreign policy.

And this is a situation of world-wide dimensions. As President Johnson pointed out not long ago: "Today, more than 700 million adults—four out of ten of the world's population—dwell in darkness where they cannot read or write. Almost half of the nations of this globe suffer from illiteracy among half or more of their people."

Lest Americans cockily assume that this problem of ignorance about international matters is confined to the underdeveloped countries, let me cite from a study, as yet unpublished, that I conducted here in the United States recently on the political beliefs and values of Americans. From some questions designed to test information and knowledge, it turned out, for example, that only 43 per cent of Americans could identify U Thant and only 15 per cent Sukarno; that 25 per cent had never heard or read of NATO; and that only 41 per cent knew that Russia is not a member of NATO.

Looked at in this perspective, one can begin to see the validity of certain aspects of Dean Acheson's views; and to question, as W. Phillips Davison (V.2, 1963) did in the *Public Opinion Quarterly,* the common assumption among Americans that if enough people are persuaded to adopt a given opinion, then the policy of their government will be affected, at least in a democracy.

PUBLICS: LIMITED AND MASS

Before we write off the importance of public opinion in international relations, however, let us introduce some other aspects of the problem. To start with, every country in the world, no matter how primitive, has *some* people, no matter how small the proportion, who do have meaningful opinions about international matters—at least in regard to issues they feel are related to their nation's purposes. This group in extreme situations of underdevelopment may be limited, to all intents and purposes, to those in the government who have responsibility for conducting the foreign affairs of their country. Usually, however, it extends at least to a broader educated elite, which may be of lesser or greater size.[1] We thus come to the concept of the "informed public." The fact that this elite may be small does not derogate from its power; we can meaningfully define "world opinion" in terms of the opinion of the publics which count in the particular situation, whether limited or mass.

Beyond this, however, the broader public, or elements of the public, can and often do get into the act, even in the underdeveloped countries. They may be "ignorant"; they may lack meaningful opinions on specific international issues. But at certain times and places, their broader basic or implicit assumptions or images may come into play in such fashion as to make a given issue, fraught with international consequences, a matter of *public* concern. Often this applies only to a minority of the greater public; frequently their concern is whipped up and organized for ulterior ends, whether by the Communists or by local leaders. But *react* they do; and often *act* they do.

This action may be as peaceable as signing a petition or writing a letter to one's Congressman or the editor. But increasingly, more extreme manifestations of public action in the form of demonstrations, picketing and rioting—reflecting strongly held attitudes by at least segments of the public—have become a phenomenon of worldwide scope. For example, rioting in Japan and Korea made it exceedingly difficult for the two governments to normalize their relations. Demonstrations and rioting in Panama were unquestionably instrumental in causing the United States—after a decent interval, of course—to agree to revise the Panama Canal Treaty. Anti-Communist violence in Indonesia strengthened the hand of the Army against the Communist Party in a struggle whose outcome has had the most profound international implications.

But the greater public also gets into the act in a more regular, generally more peaceable way, in the form of periodic elections in the democracies—and even some of the semi-democracies, if not the "guided" democracies. In such elections, international matters can, and often do enter as central issues of the campaign. In these election situations, public opinion polling is, of course, playing an increasing role, not only in the United States but in many other countries.

WORLD-WIDE CONSENSUSES

Having a bit ago given half of the pollsters' defense against Dean Acheson away by admitting that on a wide range of international issues the greater public does not have meaningful opinions, I must now take at least partial issue with his conclusion that "world opinion simply does not exist on matters that concern us." In general, this, no doubt, is correct; but in certain cases—admittedly rare—there *are* world-

---

[1] For one study of an American elite which undoubtedly was taken into account by U.S. policymakers in handling the Kennedy trade bill, see Bauer, Pool and Dexter (VI, 1963). Also Cohen's booklet (VI, 1959). One of the largest studies on elite opinion abroad is still being conducted by Daniel Lerner in Western Europe, having to do with attitudes of the elite toward European integration. When it comes to governmental elites, our own Institute for International Social Research has questioned cross-sections of national legislators in ten countries to date, the first series of which were recounted in Free (VI, 1959). Subsequent studies have been reported on in various of our monographs.

wide, or virtually world-wide reactions or consensuses on matters that do concern us.

One that comes to mind has to do with the Suez affair in 1956. I have little doubt that the well-nigh universal condemnation of the Israeli-British-French invasion of Egypt in the United Nations was supported by what can only be called a consensus of world opinion—a consensus shared by many people in the United Kingdom and France.

Another is the world-wide impact of Russia's launching of the first two Sputniks in 1957, followed by its subsequent achievements in space. These developments led to re-evaluations of the relative standing of the two super-powers, extending not only through official circles and elites, but to general publics as well (U. S. Information Agency, VI, 1963), which helped to contribute, along with other developments, to the idea that a nuclear stalemate now exists —a notion which has affected the foreign policies of most of the nations of the world.

Another, more recent example of a completely different sort was the universal reaction of horror and grief, among both high and low, set off by the assassination of President Kennedy. I would also maintain that there is a world-wide image of the United States, with many common elements, shared even by many illiterates.[1] In this connection, I would like to bring out a fact which may surprise most Americans and reassure what Dean Acheson calls their "Narcissus psychosis." The studies done by U.S.I.A., ourselves and others, show that the overall image of the United States abroad is eminently favorable at the abstract level of opinions about America. In fact, taking the globe as a whole, the United States is unquestionably the most popular major power in the history of the world, despite the evidence of sporadic anti-American demonstrations and the burning of U.S.I.S. libraries.

My final example is one of *potential* impact on what could only be called world opinion. I have no doubt that a truly worldwide reaction of great intensity would be kicked off against any power which first resorted to nuclear weapons anywhere in today's world.

REGIONAL AND NATIONAL CONSENSUSES

Short of these relatively rare global consensuses, there are certain basic attitudes so widely held in certain regions or areas of the world that they must be taken into account, both by the governments which rule there and by others dealing with them. The phobia in Latin America against "American intervention" is one example. Similarly, in almost all of Africa and Asia, basic attitude patterns opposed to "imperialism" and "colonialism" are deeply rooted. So, for example, is the anti-Israeli "set" of the Arab world; and, fortunately for us, the anti-Chinese bias in much of Southeast Asia.

In addition, there are many situations where there is a meaningful consensus of public opinion in particular countries, based upon common assumptions and attitudes in regard to certain issues the public has made matters of their own concern. One example is the widespread support for the United Nations by the Public in the United States.[2] Another is the almost universal aspiration

---

[1] U.S.I.A. has done a lot of research studying different aspects of the image of America abroad; a good deal of these data have by now been declassified. Dr. h.c. K. G. von Stackelberg reports that his Emnid-Institut in West Germany has done surveys about the German image in France, England, five Southeast Asian countries, and six Latin American nations for the use of the German press and information agency. See also "The Image of America Abroad" (VI, 1960); Pool and Prasad (VI, 1958); Joseph (VI, 1959); and Buchanan and Cantril (VI, 1953).

[2] My as yet unpublished American study, referred to above, shows that seven out of ten Americans agree that the United States should cooperate fully with the United Nations. Dr. Henry Durant,

of West Germans for the reunification of Germany. At present, too, I cannot help but believe that, despite their "ignorance," most villagers in India have very intense opinions about Pakistan, no matter how uninformed they may be about the specifics of the Kashmir issue. Then there is the fear and hatred of the Germans among most Russians and Poles, not to mention the anti-German bias of the public in the United Kingdom. Another example is the general opposition of the Japanese public to the full-scale rearmament of Japan.

DOMESTIC OPINION

The time has come to put this matter into some perspective. To start with, let us admit that, by and large, most of the time, public opinion, whether at home or abroad, has little relevance to the hundreds of day-to-day decisions on routine policy problems made by our Department of State and other foreign offices. Meaningful opinion on such specifics either does not exist, or, where it does exist, is usually so weak, either as to the proportion of the public holding a given view or as to the intensity of their feeling, that it has little significance. However, when it comes to the basics of a country's foreign policy and its international posture, government policy makers themselves live in a certain climate of opinion. They are members of their own society and they share many, if not most, of the common assumptions—and hence attitudes—on fundamentals involved in whatever consensuses exist in that society, if only among its elite. Beyond this, when the polls show that the public supports a given policy, the decision-makers will usually be reassured and feel reinforced in their pursuance of that line of action.

On the other hand, in any particular country, there are programs and policies

of the British Gallup Poll, reports similar support in the United Kingdom, which goes so far that 60 per cent would favor a United Nations police force, even if relatives of theirs had to serve in it.

for which no leader, no matter how popular or expert, can engender popular endorsement. In other words, the climate of opinion imposes limits, sometimes very broad, sometimes very narrow, on each government's area of maneuver. In the extreme, certain things are virtually taboo; in other cases, they are merely impolitic; in others, anything is possible, particularly where public opinion is either nonexistent, weak or divided.

Even totalitarian governments are subject to some restraints imposed by popular psychology. For example, the desire for a better standard of living among the Soviet people is now so strong that the last thing the leadership wants is another armaments race with the United States, which would divert more resources from butter to guns. This is almost certainly one of the reasons the Soviet Government agreed to the nuclear test ban treaty; and why Soviet policy has been generally unprovocatory since the Cuban missile flare-up.

Needless to say, strong leaders sometimes fly squarely in the face of domestic opinion. For example, President de Gaulle is pursuing policies opposed to the integration of Western Europe despite the fact that the French Institute of Public Opinion's figures have consistently showed overwhelming support for "Europe" at the public level. According to most observers, however, de Gaulle paid a price for this obduracy in the way of diminished popular support in the last presidential election.

FOREIGN OPINION

Even more often, governments do and, indeed, must fly in the face of public opinion abroad. This is particularly true of the United States as it plays its role of world leadership. In particular cases, this simply cannot be helped; everyone cannot be pleased. If we aid India to rearm against the Chinese threat, we are bound to incur the wrath of the Pakistani. We cannot assist

Israel without provoking an anti-American outburst from the Arab world, or vice versa. We cannot fight the war in Viet Nam without enraging the "doves" in many parts of the world.

No responsible critic of current practices that I have ever come across has maintained that our government, or any government, should slavishly follow foreign public opinion; nor that our foreign policy should be based, exclusively or primarily, upon courting momentary popularity abroad. Our position is a much more modest one. It is that, for the United States to be maximally effective in its role of world leadership, public opinion and other psychological data should be cranked into the overall intelligence appraisals of given situations; and that, at all levels of government, psychological factors should be taken into account, among other factors, in framing foreign policies and adopting and enunciating international positions.

You may well ask: "But isn't this so obviously desirable in today's world that it is already being done?" The answer is, not nearly enough; and, most emphatically, not *systematically* enough—even where public opinion data are available, which most of the time is not the case with the limited research efforts now being conducted.

THE RESEARCH POTENTIAL

Much more could be said; but, with apologies to Dean Acheson, I believe the point has been made that there *are* widely shared attitudes on international matters, whether global, regional or national, which governments simply must take into account and can ignore only at their peril. And the best way to find out about these with certainty and understanding, I would contend, is through public opinion research.

When it comes to such research, the sky is potentially the limit—or should I say the moon, once it has been colonized? Apart from political conditions which may make such an operation difficult or impossible, it is methodologically feasible by now, given the proper approach and facilities, to interview almost any type of people, anywhere on the earth today, from the most primitive to the most sophisticated. In addition to a number of international networks (of which the Gallup Poll and Elmo Wilson's International Research Associates are the leading examples), there are local research organizations, of varying degrees of competency, capable of carrying out opinion studies in many countries of the world today.[1] We pollsters even have our own international organization: WAPOR, the World Association of Public Opinion Research, with membership from more than 40 countries.

The need, however, is not only for *more* psychological data but for *better* psychological data. For research utilizing public opinion techniques to develop its full potential, it should go into matters more basic than "attitudes" and "opinions." It should investigate "reality worlds" in general and the assumptions, often latent or implicit, upon which attitudes and opinions are founded. It should look into the aspirations, preoccupations, values, frustrations and allegiances of the people studied. For deeper understanding, it should be carried forward on a trend basis to show changes systematically. For fuller meaningfulness, the findings should be interpreted against a broader background of social science data: studies of the power and influence structure in particular societies; of "national character," to use one of the older terms; of the "political culture," to refer to one of the newer concepts (Inkeles & Levinson, VI, 1954; Pye & Verba, VI, 1965).

---

[1] Working through local outfits, our Institute for International Social Research, for example, has been able to conduct surveys in some 21 countries in all parts of the world, including, incidentally, two Communist nations, Yugoslavia and Poland. Most of the results are analyzed in Hadley Cantril's *The Pattern of Human Concerns* (VI, 1965).

Especially if this is done, it is my belief that public opinion research can make a vital contribution—far more than it is presently contributing—not only toward the more effective conduct of foreign relations by the United States and other governments, but toward our broadest international goal: a more stable, viable, happier, democratically-oriented world, with greater mutual understanding between peoples, if not peace.

International Influence Process: How Relevant is the Contribution of Psychologists?

ROBERT H. DAVIS

Before the advent of nuclear weapons, it was possible to base national strategy on the defensive steps that might be taken *after* a war broke out. Today, the emphasis has shifted from defense, which is now technically infeasible in the case of strategic nuclear weapons, to deterrence, i.e., efforts to influence the decision to attack. This shift in emphasis has created an apparent opportunity for the psychologist to bring to bear on questions of national strategy the data and insights gleaned from literally thousands of studies. For, if the deterrence process is a matter of influencing the decision-making behavior of other human beings, surely the psychologist should have relevant and important observations to make on this process. Apparently many psychologists agree with this assumption, and some have devoted considerable effort to the problem.

Despite the psychological implications implicit in the concept of deterrence, it is not universally agreed that psychologists, as scientists, have an important contribution to make to this area. Probably the most vocal spokesman for those who feel psychologists do not have a useful role to play as scientists is N. Jordan (VI, 1963), who apparently believes that much of our professional effort has been, if not downright misguided and dangerous, then, at least, misspent. My purpose here is to take a look at the ways in which social scientists, in general, and psychologists, in particular, have tried to apply their skills and knowledge to the problem of influencing the behavior of other nations, and to try to assess the usefulness and validity of their efforts.

Although the deterrence problem is heavily weighted with psychological components, deterrence is not the only aspect of the international influence process toward which psychologists have directed or should direct their energies. Deterrence is essentially a negative concept; it is a strategy which threatens punishment in an effort to discourage certain forms of behavior. Because deterrence is based on threats, it seems reasonable to assume that it leads to increased tension. Clearly, there are other alternatives. Many believe that traditional diplomacy has emphasized discouragement through threat rather than encouragement through reinforcement. Charles Osgood (VI, 1962) has repeatedly stressed the more positive approach to influencing the behavior of other nations by advocating steps which would reinforce desired behavior and reduce international tension. Thus

● *American Psychologist,* Vol. 21, March 1966, pp. 236–243. This is a slightly modified version of a paper read as a Division 19 presentation at the annual meeting of the American Psychological Association, Los Angeles, September 1964. The author wishes to express his appreciation to Launor F. Carter of System Development Corporation and Robert Boguslaw of American University for their comments.

it is possible to distinguish two broad forms of international influence: deterrence, and what I shall call, for want of a better word, encouragement.

One way to assess the appropriateness of applying the science of psychology to this area would be to attempt to evaluate the contributions of individual psychologists. But psychologists have written and said so much about these problems in the past decade that an exhaustive review would be beyond the scope of this paper. Furthermore, when the contributions of individuals are evaluated, there is always the danger of lapsing into *ad hominem* arguments. A second approach is to ask: How have psychologists attacked this problem? What methods of analysis or research have they employed? To what extent have these provided useful and valid insights about the international influence process? And finally, what dangers characterize particular techniques?

At least four approaches can be identified: (*a*) Psychologists have devised models of the international influence process; (*b*) they have designed simulations or games and conducted research using these simulations; (*c*) they have drawn on the vast body of research which has been conducted on humans and lower animals to support arguments, models, and suppositions about national and international decision makers; and finally, (*d*) in the interest of completeness, there is a fourth approach, widely used today, which has not been the special forte of psychologists but which still deserves discussion, namely the game theoretic approach.

MODELS

It is a commonplace observation that the world we live in is extremely complex. We seek to unravel the simplest thread only to find that it binds together an enormously complex array of interdependent events. One of the ways commonly used to deal with this problem of complexity is through the construction of models. Models are simplified representations of some subject of inquiry. They help scientists and philosophers alike to visualize and determine how changes in one aspect of the model would influence other aspects or how such changes would influence the whole. All models presume some relationship to the more complex reality they are created to represent, and since they are less complex and are directly accessible to us, they can be manipulated more easily than the real world.

Men have been using models to organize and assist them in their understanding of the world for many centuries. Many of the models, used by social scientists to help organize and stimulate thought, have been derived from physical and mechanical systems. Descartes, for example, is identified with the rise of the mechanistic view of man —a view of man which, incidentally, he developed using as a model primitive automatons. Clark Hull's (VI, 1943) assumption that the brain acts as an automatic switchboard falls in the same mechanistic tradition.

Living organisms provide the basic analogue for a second class of models, organismic models. The organismic models stress the interrelatedness and integrity of a system as well as notions of growth and evolution, a point of view which has been developed in a very sophisticated form by the philosopher A. N. Whitehead (VI, 1950), but one which is also familiar to psychologists for its relevance to Gestalt theory.

One of the notions implied by the classic organismic model is purpose, which many social scientists still reject as unscientific. The modern discipline of cybernetics (Wiener, VI, 1954) has done much to define purpose in essentially mechanistic terms and it is now used quite widely as a model to explain individual, social, and political behavior (Deutsch, II.3, 1963). The computer, of course, has also stimulated new ideas regarding purposive behavior, particularly the development of computer program (Miller, Galanter, & Pribram, VI, 1960).

There are other kinds of models of interest to social scientists, including, of course, mathematical models; but if, for the moment, we ignore models inspired by game theory, which will be discussed under a separate heading, most of the models developed for studying the international influence process have been verbal. The complexity of the international influence process requires the use of multiple models as well as verbal material for their elaboration. It would be possible to represent, for example, some of the features of Osgood's model of the international influence process by a flow diagram (see Figure 1). Such a diagram is called an analogue model (Churchman, Ackoff, & Arnoff, VI, 1957). But, this flow diagram does not begin to represent the features of the process which Osgood presumably believes are crucial to an adequate description of the situation. Osgood has drawn extensively on experimental research in the area of perception to illustrate phenomena which are assumed to influence decision makers, and one might expand on the model shown in Figure 1 by constructing additional models to represent human psychological considerations.

David Singer (VI, 1962: 25-26), a political scientist, has chosen a probability-utility model to illustrate some of the perceptual problems of deterrence. This model has two axes: a utility-disutility dimension which has to do with a decision maker's assessment of the positive or negative value of any given course of action, and a subjective probability dimension representing the decision maker's estimate of the odds. Values attached to the dimensions of his model vary, of course, with the particular situation in which the decision maker finds himself. Although Singer provides no concrete guides for assigning values to these dimensions, he assumes that choice is a function of probability multiplied by success or failure.

To illustrate, the model shown in Fgure 2 is the deterree's estimated outcome and represents the ideal case from the point of view of the deterrer. Probability of success is low and the gain slight; probability of failure is high and the consequences relatively great.

Just as the model which was used to illustrate Osgood's approach was completely inadequate to encompass the complexity of the problem, the same may be said of Singer's model. Singer relies primarily on verbal material rather than the analogue model of

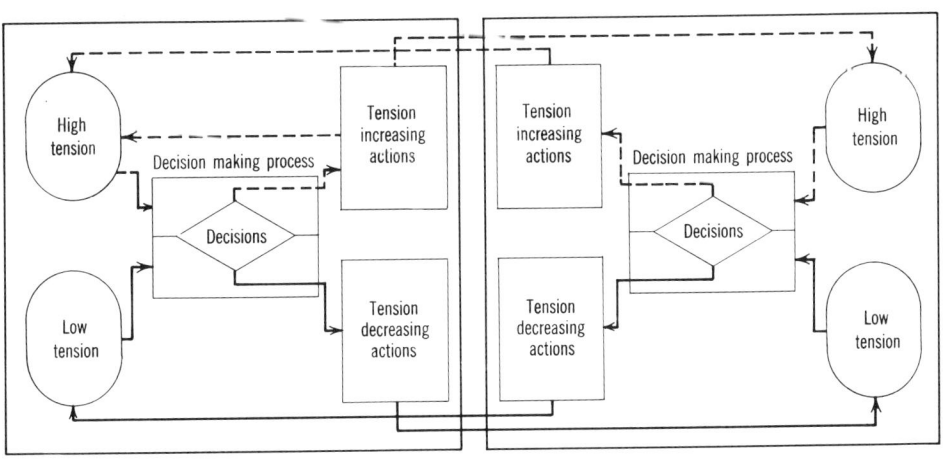

Figure 1. Model of an analog model. Schematic illustration of some of the features of Osgood's GRIT.

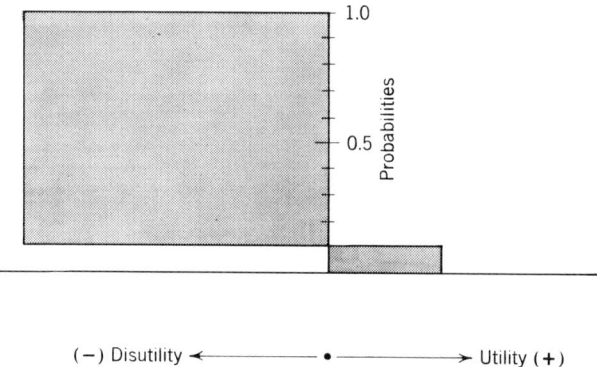

Figure 2. Deteree's estimated outcomes. Utility and probability of success are both low; disutility and probability of failure are both high. Rational deteree does not attack.

Figure 2, and Osgood has not, to my knowledge, ever attempted to create an analogue model of the strategy he has proposed.

There are dimensions of the problem which neither Singer nor Osgood analyzes in detail, and the requirement for multiple models is nicely illustrated by citing a third model, proposed by Karl W. Deutsch, to illustrate the flow of foreign policy information within a single government (see Figure 3).

Now it is clear that there is no end to the models which might be constructed by a shrewd observer of a process as complex as this. On the surface this may seem inconsequential, but the fact of the matter is, it is quite serious. In the absence of an agreement about models, all of the facts which might be relevant to the process seem equally important because there is no guiding paradigm. Data collection and even experimentation are consequently far more random than they would otherwise be. Thomas Kuhn (II.1, 1962) has recently argued most effectively that the near universal acceptance of a paradigm, providing research consensus, is an essential step on the route to normal science. Social science, in general, has been plagued by lack of consensus regarding fundamental paradigms—certainly no such consensus exists in the present case. Yet, the construction of paradigms and agreement regarding them is essential if we are to convert our philosophy into science. Thus, the enterprise itself is to be commended. The danger lies in premature assumptions about the validity of our models and the courses of action we recommend on the basis of them. Let me illustrate these points by a contrast and example with the physical sciences. Newton's *Opticks* provided the basic paradigm for research in optics in the eighteenth century; Newton assumed that light was material corpuscles. The fact that most scientists accepted the paradigm had a profound influence on their research strategies. Unlike early wave theorists, they began to search for evidence that light particles exerted a pressure by impinging on solid bodies. Their assumptions had little if any direct effect on humanity as a whole. If, on the other hand, social scientists were to accept and actively propose Osgood's model of the international influence process, the consequences would extend far beyond the bounds of our laboratories. When and if psychologists agree to do this, they must bear in mind that the name of the game is no longer psychology, or even science, but international diplomacy—an exceedingly complex and specialized game in which the stakes are unbelievably high.

In defense of the promotion of models de-

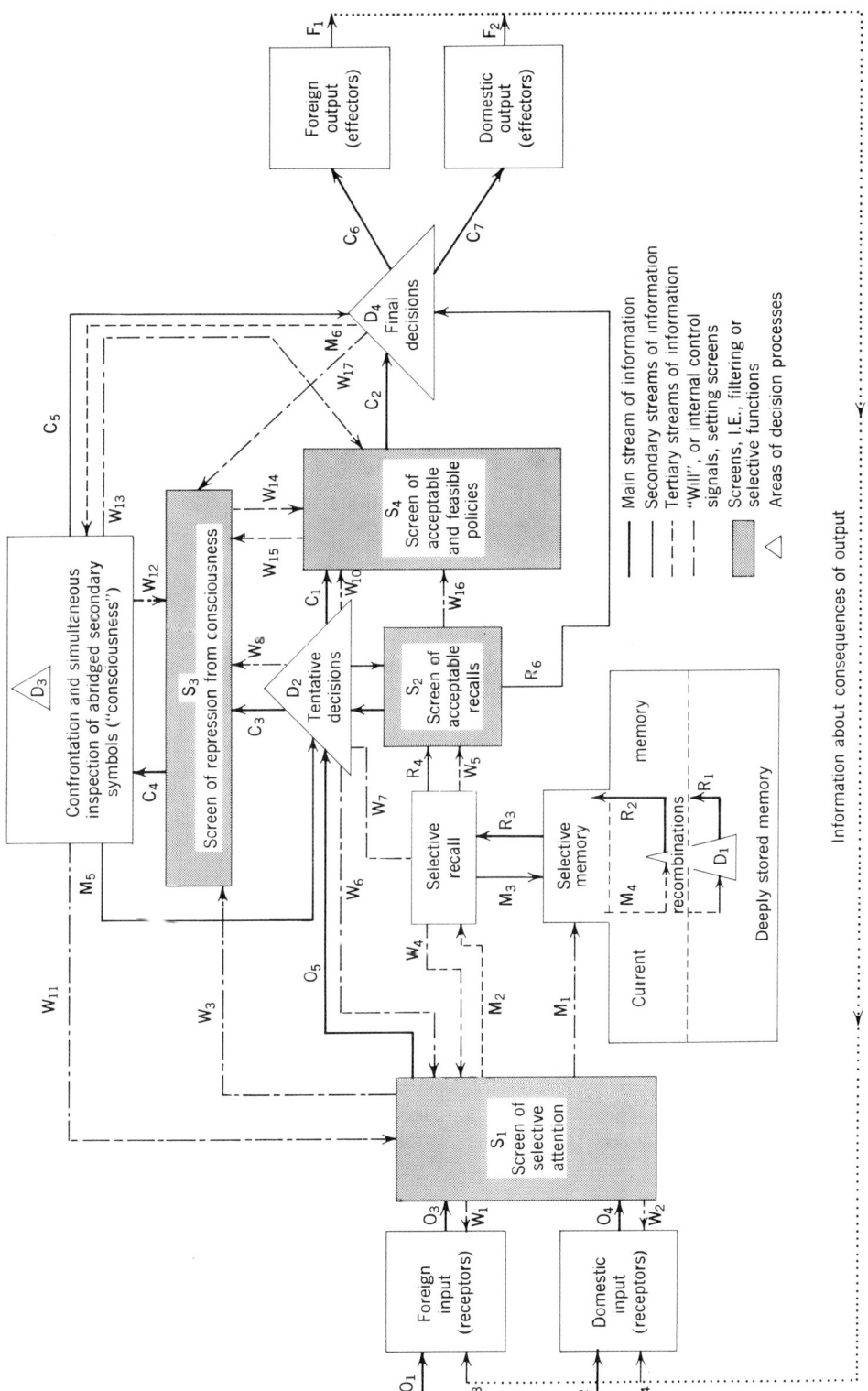

Figure 3. A crude model: a functional diagram of information flow in foreign policy decisions.

veloped by psychologists, it is only fair to point out that we are, unfortunately, living in a world in which many men will admit no bounds to their spheres of competence. All around us there are those willing to make the most blatant and unjustifiable generalizations about human behavior in support of their prejudices or preferred strategies of action. The conflict for the social scientist is clear. If he adheres to the rigorous canons of science, his voice may never be heard in the land. If he speaks out, as a social scientist, he will be criticized (generally by his own colleagues) for his lack of rigor. At the heart of the matter there is the question of purpose. A large part of our research has been directed at isolating fundamental laws of animal behavior; it may well be that our horizon has been too narrow. If we are to speak with authority on the larger issues which mankind faces, and be taken at our word, it may be necessary for us to define our objectives more broadly and utilize techniques which have greater face validity.

ENVIRONMENTAL OR OPERATIONAL SIMULATION

There is a class of research now being conducted which achieves a greater degree of face validity by stressing the simulation of content. Any international political situation may be characterized in terms of formal structure, content, or psychological essentials. Game theory stresses formal structure. Empirical research in the area of bargaining and negotiation has emphasized psychological essentials. Environmental or operational simulation stresses content.

There is apt to be some confusion over the terms "model" and "simulation" Both are extremely broad and inclusive terms, and it is possible to distinguish various categories of each. The two terms have in common the notion of an abstract representation of some subject of interest. They appear to differ primarily in terms of their static or dynamic connotation. Models are static, whether they be iconic, symbolic, or analogical. On the other hand, they need not be static; they can be "put into motion" and the effects of changes on them can be observed. When this happens, I prefer to use the term simulation. Thus, for example, there are *stochastic models,* which are essentially a set of assumptions about how probabilities are effected by some clearly recognizable time-ordered sequence of events. But there are also *stochastic simulations* which "set the model in motion" and enable the experimenter to compare theoretically predicted outcomes with observed outcomes. Such simulations may use digital computers or they may be done manually, but they amount to test runs of models under conditions which are determined by the play of emergent events.

The particular kind of simulation which bears most directly on the international influence process is environmental simulation, or operational simulation as it is sometimes called. Environmental simulation seeks to preserve the complexity of the environment rather than abstract it away. When using environmental simulation, the experimenter tries to maintain the richness and variety of the environment and allows human participants to respond to a situation which resembles as nearly as possible "real life." Both the more traditional social-psychological experiment and environmental simulation involve measuring human actions—one in an abstract environment which bears little resemblance to the real-life situation, the other in a more complete replica of its real-life counterpart.

There are a number of examples of this kind of simulation. Although modern day enviromental simulations frequently make use of digital computers, their origins can, nevertheless, be traced back to at least the seventeenth century and the development of early war games. Even today, some of the most critical political-military simulations, the so-called JCS Politico Military Desk

Games, do not require computers. These "games" are actually role-playing situations in which individual players represent the United States and foreign governments or factions within governments (McDonald, VI, 1964). The environmental simulation probably best known in academic circles is Inter-Nation Simulation, identified primarily with Harold Guetzkow (V.2, 1959) and his students. It has been used to study such problems as Osgood's Graduated and Reciprocated Initiative in Tension-Reduction Strategy—GRIT (Crow, VI, 1963) and some effects of the spread of nuclear weapons technology (Brody, VI, 1963). A description of one of the most complex and interesting simulations of this type has only recently become available in unclassified literature (Abt, VI, 1964). It is a man-machine game, called TEMPER, which is global in scope and permits up to 39 players.

Several characteristics of these simulations are worth noting. First, they are generally expensive to design and develop. Second, individual runs of the game often require large numbers of subjects—frequently subjects who have had prior specialized training. Consequently, the replications necessary to obtain the customary estimates of error variance are difficult and costly to obtain. Third, and perhaps more germane to the present discussion, is the fact that experiments using environmental simulation are, as a rule, not conducted to derive basic laws of international behavior or to test formal theory; instead, they are conducted for the purpose of producing certain specific phenomena under relatively controlled conditions and intervening in the process to observe effects. Whether the results can be extrapolated to the real world remains arguable. Generally, it is assumed that, as a minimum, simulations sufficiently representative of the real world will produce useful insights and add support to (or refute) arguments of an informal, less structured nature.

The emotional overtones which always characterize international crises can seldom —if ever—be simulated in the laboratory. A significant aspect of reality is thus virtually always missing from the environment of the simulated decision maker. Consider, for example, the startling results of a study reported by Shure, Rogers, and Meeker (VI, 1963). In their study, the operating environment of a SAGE battle staff, responsible for the air defense of a sector of the United States, was simulated in the laboratory. Four three-man teams of Air Force ROTC students (or specialists in air defense) faced various decision situations. One of these situations involved the choice of surrendering or continuing to fight after apparent defeat. That is, with their sector in ruins and information from the simulated Office of Civilian Defense indicating that Washington, D. C., SAC and ADC headquarters, many of the larger metropolitan areas, and military targets have been destroyed, *all* four crews decided to continue fighting. When one crew was advised that if they reevaluated the situation other cities might be spared, they still elected to go on resisting. Now it is perfectly clear that many factors may account for this dedication on the part of these experimental subjects, and the authors of this report discuss several possible explanations, including discipline, a lack of humanitarian values, and cognitive dissonance. A more compelling explanation may lie in a defect which characterizes all simulations of this kind, i.e., inability to capture the emotional overtones of the situation simulated.

GENERALIZING FROM TRADITIONAL RESEARCH

Presumably the vast body of literature and data collected by social scientists over the past several decades also provides valuable insights regarding the international influence process. Use of such data for this purpose requires a number of assumptions. First, one must assume that it is possible to generalize from the data of individual behavior to the behavior of nations. Decisions in international relations are, after all, made by individuals who are presumed to be subject to common psychological laws or principles. On the other hand, national decisions are made in the context of complex organizational structures which are characterized by internal conflict, inertia, and countless constraints on individual decision makers. Behind the formal organizational structure, available for convenient reference in the government manuals, lurks an informal structure with none of the tidy levels of responsibility or clear-cut lines of communication. Decisions affecting a nation's destiny are made daily by numberless individuals acting, reacting, or failing to act. Second, one must recognize that a very large part of the data of psychology comes from two highly select populations, the college sophomore and the albino rat. As a minimum, generalizing from animal studies to international relations presents formidable problems. With respect to the use of sophomores, Boguslaw, Glick, and I (Boguslaw, Davis & Glick, VI, 1964) have recently collected evidence which tends to indicate that for certain complex socioeconomic decisions, college students may behave very differently from mature, experienced scientists and administrators. Third, one of the characteristics of a controlled psychological experiment is the abstracting away of complexity. Special, highly artificial environments are required to elicit some of the perceptual and other psychological phenomena which have provided the basis for generalizations about the international influence process. Unfortunately, the frequency of interaction between political, social, and psychological variables is so great as to open to question the usefulness of this approach for extrapolating to real life.

Nevertheless, psychologists have generalized from such abstract situations to complex political problems. One need not look far for examples of such extrapolations of individual psychology from the laboratory to the world of international politics. Charles Osgood resorts repeatedly to this device in his many articles, making extensive use of perceptual studies. Ross Stagner (VI, 1961), Urie Bronfenbrenner (VI, 1961), and T. W. Milburn (VI, 1961) have found it useful to extrapolate from the data of individual psychology to the behavior of larger social systems. And I have done it (Davis, VI, 1963). Indeed, one suspects that a truly exhaustive list would include a very large number of psychologists.

A special case of generalizing from traditional research is the rapidly expanding use of mixed-motive games for the collection of empirical data about how humans behave in negotiating and bargaining situations (Meeker, Shure, & Moore, VI, 1964). The prisoner's dilemma is particularly useful for such studies and a number of variants of this game have been described by Pilisuk and Rapoport (VI, 1964).

GAME THEORETIC

For the purposes of this paper, it will be useful to distinguish two broad categories of games: the so-called zero-sum game and the non-zero-sum game. Zero-sum games are competitive and one player's gain is another's loss. Indeed, in such a game cooperation will always result in one player having a smaller payoff than he could have had without cooperation. Although this penalty for cooperation may appear to some to be so unrealistic a restriction as to completely eliminate it as a rational tool for the analysis of real life diplomatic situations, there are those who apparently believe that contemporary military and diplomatic policy is, in fact, one vast zero-sum game in which gains and losses do sum to zero. Mutual accommodation and the possibility of unilateral gain through cooperation are frequently deplored by those who see the world in these terms; total victory is extolled. In the zero-sum game, many of the most obvious features of international political bargaining and problem solving, such as bluffs, threats, promises, and similar psychological factors, are completely irrelevant. Indeed, the zero-sum game is in the domain of the strategy of pure conflict; there is no need for psychology in this domain, for its players are assumed to be perfectly rational and motivated by greed.

Clearly there are many situations in international negotiation in which one player's gain is not another's loss. Furthermore, both parties to a negotiation may, under some circumstances, gain by cooperation. Games which introduce these possibilities are called non-zero-sum. A class of non-zero-sum games called the mixed-motive game permits both competition and cooperation to occur. Unlike the zero-sum game, the mixed-motive game involves at least tacit communication between players, and the outcome depends upon the social interactions of the participants. Game theory, as it relates to the zero-sum game, treats the players as rational automatons, and since the criteria for their behavior are explicitly specified, their decisions can be deduced within the framework of the theory. The mixed-motive game, on the other hand, introduces great uncertainty about the player, his value system and his strategy. The mixed-motive game, in short, reintroduces psychology—but with it, as one might suspect, destroys the possibility of deriving a normative theory by analytic means. The study of mixed-motive games is therefore largely an empirical matter (Schelling, VI, 1960).

SOME CONCLUDING REMARKS

Decisions affecting the international influence process are commonly made in the context of a dynamic and complex environment. Frequently, the most critical situation, involving the effort to influence one's opponent or even one's allies, is one of a kind and requires a unique solution; action-relevant states of the system of international relations during an emergency such as the Cuban crisis cannot be specified or predicted in advance. Instead, the situation is emergent (Boguslaw, VI, 1961). In this sense, the real world frequently takes on the character of a problem-solving situation rather than a highly structured bargaining and negotiation situation.[1] In addition, foreign policy does not reflect a single will, intent, or purpose. Instead, it is the melding together of the hopes and aspirations, the motives and objectives of uncounted individuals, converging by processes only half understood on a few men who act or react or fail to act and thereby hurtle us to the brink of war or jerk us back to the sanctuary of an uneasy peace. To the extent that our destiny is determined by individuals, as Simon (VI, 1957) has observed, these individuals construct their own simplified models of reality and behave rationally with respect to that model, even though their "behavior is not even approximately optimal with respect to the real world (p. 199)."

Game theory, which is designed to deal with highly structured rather than emergent situations certainly is not directly applicable to the kind of world I have just described. Nor can we hope to substitute our models

[1] One aspect of the international influence process which appears to have been neglected by those who have emphasized the game theoretic approach, including those who have stressed the mixed-motive game, is problem solving. Because economists have done a great deal of original work in this area, *Homo economicus,* rather than man as a problem solver, has been emphasized. To psychologists who followed the Cuban crisis closely, for example, the problem-solving aspects stood out in bold relief. The effort to discover a satisfactory solution to the inspection problem, which included a number of interesting suggestions, such as the proposed use of the United Nations and the Red Cross, for this purpose, nicely illustrates its problem-solving dimensions. Almost daily exploratory suggestions by the United States, the Union of Soviet Socialist Republics, the United Nations, and other nations (and their rejection) created a dynamic and emergent environment. The formally structured aspects of classical bargaining were all but absent.

of reality for the decision maker's personal model, and it is not obvious that we should try since our models, too, are incomplete.

The problem is not to provide an invariant prescription for the ills of the world, but to enrich the decision maker's understanding of its complexity. We ought not to insist that decision makers adopt our model of reality, but that they expand their models by taking account of factors which we believe to be relevant. In this sense, the task is not to tell the decision maker what he ought to do, i.e., to formulate policy, but to help him understand an aspect of reality of which he may be unaware. The data from individual and social psychology are surely applicable in some way, but the transform equations are unknown, and we should not presume to know them. What we should aim to do with the tools, techniques, and data at hand is to help the decision maker formulate more complete models of reality.

CHAPTER IV

The Functions of Policy-Oriented Social Science

THE DESCRIPTIVE AND ANALYTIC STUDY OF FUNCTIONS

Implicit in many of the previous discussions in this book have been certain judgments concerning the utilitarian value of social science. Nowhere are judgmental and hortatory approaches to the social roles of the social sciences more evident than in discussions of the *functions* of policy-oriented social science. For, in these discussions, "function" invariably means *purpose* and the concern has been much more with what is "proper," "laudable," "feasible," or "scientific" in applied and policy-oriented research than with identifying and describing the objective consequences of specific research activities.

In the introductory pages we indicated more particularly our dissatisfaction with current formulations of the sociology of science as models for empirical study of the social roles of social scientists.[1] We had reason to question the common assumptions of a divine harmony between the philosophical, technical, and social-behavioral systems of science. Because they are affected by the intense, although nondistinctive, strivings of science for autonomy, we fear these models

[1] See, "Editors' Introduction," pp. 18–23.

of the sociology of science may introduce a special bias when applied to relations between scientific research and other institutions. Questions of the uses and usefulness of research are, of course, one class of such relations. Many other aspects of the extra-system relationships of research are interconnected with the actual and perceived usefulness of social science knowledge to specific clienteles and to society as a whole.

As was suggested in the Editors' Introduction, the empirical study of science would be improved by use of models that:

1. did not restrict delineation of the norms of scientific activity to principles derived from epistemic requirements;

2. did not assume that all normative and technical elements in the culture of science were logically consistent with one another or consistent with regard to the specific action they might suggest in any concrete situation —i.e., models that allowed for more room for alternatives and conflict;

3. payed greater attention to the requirements of viability of a system;

4. did not make exaggerated assumptions regarding the uniqueness of scientific activity.

SELF-IMAGES, PRESENTATIONAL IMAGES AND PERCEIVED IMAGES

In extrasystem relationships many of the operating assumptions that are implicitly accepted as bases for action within the group are open to questioning and challenge, defense and modification. In their interaction with publics and clienteles, professions and institutions develop "externalized-images" which are idealized, abstracted, and stereotyped. There are, in other words, ideal, presentational cultural images of an institution. These images do not correspond perfectly with the idealized in-group self-images which incorporate to a fuller extent complexities that are understood only by colleagues—understood both in the sense of comprehension and acceptance. The publicly perceived and accepted images, in turn, deviate from the presented images in that they include recognition of the presentational idea, but only as modified by a host of other influences among which are the experiences, interests, needs, and expectations of the perceivers.

Social science, of course, has suffered from particularly difficult problems of bringing about correspondence among its self-images, its presentational images, and those held by its publics and clienteles. A paper by Alpert (III.2, 1958) offers a succinct illustration of scientists' attempts to increase this correspondence. Writings in Alpert's vein, while explicitly addressed to the misperceptions of the public, frequently have colleagues as their audiences and serve to reinforce an ideal self-image. The following statements of what Alpert sees as the most common objections to the social sciences and his refutations of these were presented with special reference to support of social science within the National Science Foundation, but are seen as having wider implications:

"**Vagueness.** One cannot identify the social sciences or know just where and how far one is going in a social science program, since the social sciences are vague and indefinite. *Comment.* While the phrase 'social science' is used quite loosely in some quarters, it has been found possible to be both specific and concrete in identifying the precise areas of the social sciences which are included in a program of research support. This has been achieved by identifying the program in terms of recognizable and established academic disciplines.

"**Controversy.** The social sciences involve areas of public controversy which might jeopardize an agency's general growth and development. *Comment.* The social sciences unquestionably involve areas of public controversy, but the experience of the National Science Foundation and other government agencies has demonstrated clearly that reliance on scientific methods and the scientific integrity of investigators can insure freedom from involvement in controversial areas.

"**Soft Areas.** The social sciences include activities which are scarcely identifiable as science and are more concerned with considerations of ethics, welfare, and philosophical interpretations of man's destiny. *Comment.* The term 'social sciences' covers a wide range of activities. These activities may be thought of in terms of a continuum. At one end of the continuum lie the hard-core scientific studies of human social behavior. These include the use of experimental techniques, controlled experiments, laboratory studies, statistical and mathematical methods, survey design techniques, the development of measurement devices and instruments such as standardized tests and scales, the empirical testing of hypotheses and concepts, and other characteristic features of scientific research. At the other end of the continuum lie philosophical, ethical, and political studies and interpretations of human social conduct . . . . A social science program within the general framework of scientific objectives can properly be limited to the hard-core scientific end of the continuum.

"**Debasement of Human Dignity.** Social science provides powerful weapons for 'hidden persuaders,' 'brainwashers,' and other manipulators of human populations and permits them to direct and control human lives. *Comment.* The social sciences do not differ from the natural sciences in the utilization of scientific knowledge. The scientist provides fundamental knowledge. The objectives toward which that knowledge is directed are beyond his immediate control and are determined by a complex of societal forces. Whether the atom is used for peace or destruction, whether bacteria are mobilized for purposes of health or disease, whether knowledge of human motivations is used to provide happiness or to sell soap, are alternatives which the scientist as seeker of knowledge and truth cannot determine. It should also be noted that one of the best defenses against the manipulators of the human spirit is the understanding of their techniques and weapons which social science provides. . . .

"**Applied Research.** The social sciences are applied and practical and therefore have no place in a program dedicated to support of basic research and education. *Comment*. Like other scientific disciplines, the social sciences have an identifiable basic or fundamental component as well as an applied or developmental orientation. Although the line between basic and applied research is often difficult to draw in many scientific areas, experience over several years had indicated the possibility of a satisfactory operating division of labor between agencies supporting fundamental explorations of the unknown in social science and those whose major responsibilities lie in applied areas such as mental health, delinquency, marketing, social security, and illegitimacy (pp. 684-685)."

ENGINEERING FUNCTIONS

For presentational images, formulations of the uses of social science have largely followed a restricted model of functions that we will call *"engineering functions."*[1]

In distinguishing "engineering" conceptions from the other conceptions of the uses of research, we are considering six loosely-defined dimensions of possible variation. These dimensions can be applied to paradigms comprehending the production of knowledge as well as to the ways in which knowledge relates to purposive action; to the manner in which problems are presented to social scientists as well as to the manner in which social scientists address themselves to problems. "Engineering" conceptions are those that tend toward the low region defined by the following dimensions:

1. Number of variables embraced in the problem definition.
2. The degree of simplicity in the postulated means-ends relationships among the variables.
3. The number of possible parties whose differing interest standpoints are considered relevant.
4. The degree of system closure posited.
5. The extent to which historical or dynamic changes of system and environment are considered.
6. The degree to which variables are considered that are inaccessible to experimental or practical manipulation.

Since variation is possible along any of these dimensions independently of others, and since a broad range of variation in some of the dimensions is possible, a vast number of types of knowledge functions could be defined by possible combinations of position with respect to all six. We are positing a considerable tendency for correlated variation of paradigms along these dimensions,[2] and

[1] For general writings which explicitly or implicitly use the engineering model see, e.g., Alpert (III.2, 1958), Glock (I, 1961), Hauser (I, 1946), Likert (I, 1953 and 1957), Pfaffman (III.2, 1965); for examples of those relating it to specific cases of decision-making see, Bray (V.2, 1962), Kluckhohn (V.3, 1944), Myrdal (V.3, 1952), Windle and Vallance (V.2, 1964); for examples of writings dealing with the engineering problems of "conversion" and training of social technicians or "middlemen" see, Helmer (V.1, 1965), Herring (V.1, 1947), Lundberg (V.1, 1966); for critiques of the engineering model see Gouldner (V.1, 1957), Kecskemeti (I, 1952), Shils (I, 1961).

[2] There are some theoretical grounds for expecting that among scientists themselves there

we will focus on just three general regions or vectors.

That social scientists' conceptions subsumed in the engineering model are consonant with those of many clients may help explain its dominance as a definition of the functions of research. Many of those who see social science contributing to their practical purposes look to it for a "scientific" contribution; that is, they accept the similarity if not the identity of social and natural science. These administrators and practitioners are most likely to see social science contributing in the way which we have called engineering. Not only does this follow from the most common, lay cultural conceptions of what science is and what it can do, but it also derives from the way in which a practical problem is seen as potentially solvable by science.[1] This occurs when the problem already presents itself in terms of a few potentially manipulable variables and where a solution is seen as possible through finding an underlying principle which, to use a colloquialism, gives one a handle on them.

When thinking of the utilization of their work, social scientists have tended to use formulations that are consonant with these lay perspectives. Utilization is thus seen as involving the application of scientific generalizations and propositions to a few critical and easily manipulable variables. When the variables in the scientist's formulation are translatable into the very terms in which the user confronts his problem the consonance is particularly great. This conception has particular appeal to scientists in that it fits the analogical association of their work with the paradigm of science associated with the best-known examples of classical physics, i.e., crucial experiments involving few variables in a closed system. When the ends posed in the practical problem formulation are accepted, the engineering model is also attractive to the scientist in that it permits him to take a purely instrumental stance in his work.

From the structural-functional standpoint, it would be anticipated that threats to group integrity will mobilize the most universally accepted core elements of a given culture. In the case of applied research, the doctrine is objectivity. The simple, predetermined ends in engineering formulations protect the value-free and disinterested stance of social scientists. In contrast to frankly service-oriented professions that define the value criteria toward which their art is directed in terms of their own systems of thought—criteria of health in the case of medicine or of justice in the case of law—the stance of value disinterestedness surrenders the formulation of criteria to clienteles. That it involves securing autonomy by a surrender of autonomy is a source of tension for social scientists that gives the engineering model greater place in the presentational culture than in the action system.

The popularity of the engineering model has followed not only from its shaping of images, but also, in turn, from the way these images have positioned social science activities organizationally. This has been particularly important in the immediate postwar era when the burgeoning of social science programs took place largely within the federal research and development structure; a structure that was particularly congenial to engineering orientations. Both then and earlier, in seeking to convert potential clienteles who were dubious about the scientific claims of social science, those who have had the roles of proselytizers, salesmen, brokers, or public relations men for social science have couched their appeals largely in terms of engineering models. To the extent that work in the social sciences was dependent upon the support of lay clienteles, what was done and how it was done was often influenced by the sales talk.

An examination of social science research programs in the military in support of per-

---

would be some more inclined to resolve the tensions arising from different scientific norms by giving primacy, say, to those favoring parsimony and specificity over those dictating value neutrality and exhaustiveness.

[1] See, for example, Storer (II.1, 1966: 1-2).

sonnel selection, management, training, and the design of man-machine systems yields numerous examples of work following engineering models. An example in our particular subject area would be psychological warfare research which often has had formulated engineering aims, such as the fashioning of political propaganda to bring about a desired change of attitudes in a target audience. The lists and "project cards" issued by offices administering research put statements of social science work into a procrustean bed, forcing its description and rationalization in such terms as "end items," "technical requirements," "test-stages," and "engineering stages."

The very limited fit of the engineering model to posited conditions of acceptance and applicability helps explain tensions that have often characterized social science relationships to the world of practice. The reasons for this are so well known that to cover them is merely to enumerate the trite: the multivariate character of practical problems; the limited control over critical, contingent conditions that administrators and social scientists can exercise; the disjunctions between the way problems confront practitioners and scientists; the complexities of the "ends" side of means-ends formulations; as well as the nonacceptance of social science as science. These and many other problems are discussed in the articles in this chapter as well as in the critiques of the model to which we have made reference earlier.

These critiques also contain examples of some of the ways in which the model has been refined and restated in order to make for a better fit with the environments in which it is being applied. In recognition of the fact that the scientist is rarely trained to make the practical judgments involved in engineering and, given prevalent role prescriptions, that he is not supposed to take part in policy formation or action, a role has been designated for a broadly gauged "middleman" or "social engineer."[1] To the chagrin of many social scientists, however, these "middlemen" have been very slow in materializing.

Simulation, various forms of systems analysis, and game theory, as discussed by Davis, have been other means of retaining the instrumental specificity of the engineering model[2] while providing approaches to more multivariate, complex, and dynamic problems and, sometimes, to phenomena that cannot be manipulated directly.

The pervasiveness of formulations in terms of engineering models persists in discussions of use, despite repeated analytic recognition of their frequent inapplicability. They guide most attempts to search empirically for the uses to which social science is put. Although these searches have produced examples of utilization, they have not yielded and, as we will show later, cannot yield comprehensive conclusions about how, when, and how much utilization takes place. As a result social science is generally perceived as having had low utility (but great potential). The resulting dubious attitudes of clienteles, and the anxieties and doubts of social scientists themselves, affect the social roles of the social sciences. In the ensuing discussion we will attempt to show that perceptions of nonutility are, in considerable measure, consequences of the low correspondence of the engineering model to the actual uses that have been made of social science.

LACK OF FIT OF THE ENGINEERING MODEL

Much social science work, and perhaps most of it, does not fit the model since:

[1] See Hauser, pp. 248–251 and Guetzkow, pp. 255–257.
[2] See e.g. Helmer (V.1, 1965).

(a) it has not always selected features of social life or study with an eye toward their manipulation or manipulability; (b) it has often had a diffuse "problem" orientation rather than a crucial-experiment one; (c) even when it may have been undertaken as a basis for providing guidance for some fairly specific problem-area, it has nonetheless been affected by the aspirations toward achieving general import that marks social scientific activities; (d) the ambition has been to have the results widely communicated within the profession and frequently outside of it rather than to a restricted clientele.

More abstractly, both the way problems have been presented to social scientists and the way in which social scientists have addressed themselves to problems have often departed from the simplest engineering model in some of the following ways:

1. Number of Variables. Problems are multivariate; simultaneous consideration has been given a multiplicity of possible means and conditions rather than a few.

2. Complexity of Means-Ends Relationships. In addition to calculating the rational means toward a given end, consideration has been given to the interrelationships of ends (*Wertrationalität* as well as *Zweckrationalität*).[1]

3. Pragmatic Specificity. The attention has been directed to the interests of many parties and broad cultural, political, and humanitarian concerns rather than to the parochial ends of a given party.

4. System Isolation. Open systems rather than closed ones have been posited.

5. Time Specificity. Problems have been approached in historical, longitudinal, and dynamic terms.

6. Manipulability. Attention has been directed to phenomena which, however well understood, remain beyond the realm of manipulation or control.

Along each of these dimensions, departures of research work from the simplest engineering model make potential use of the work less readily specifiable. It goes without saying that each extension of potential functional pertinence also is likely to carry with it losses of precision and certitude. At the same time it increases logically, if not actually, the number of potential functional relationships. With these extensions of the model, social science work becomes pertinent to many different purposes, parties, types of action, systems, environmental conditions, and points in time, as well as to inputs of knowledge from other sources. These are precisely ways in which many differentiate between "basic" and "applied" research. This is true even though there is also a tendency to define basic research in terms of closeness to the classical hard-science model.

Pushed to the nonspecific extreme along all these dimensions, research activities become hardly distinguishable from traditional forms of academic scholarship, including some not called "scientific." Despite the fundamental institutional location of scientific research in the academy and the fact that much of its symbolic legitimation derives from this institution, the functions and modes of communication of knowledge central to academic institutions have not provided the explicit rationale for the production and use of social scientific knowledge for practical problems. For example, the institutions which prepare military or foreign service officers for high-level posts (e.g., the War Colleges or the Foreign Service Institute) have not been regarded as important research clienteles by policy-oriented social scientists. Nor have these institutions generated the "requirements" or otherwise substantially influenced allocations of social science research efforts so as to meet their particular needs for knowledge concerning military or foreign policy. When social science research has been brought directly into the service of these educational systems, it has been addressed, almost exclusively, to such engineering problems as those involved in the selection of students or the measurement of training effectiveness rather than to

---

[1] See, Chapter III, p. 152.

those providing the forms and substance of curricula. This has been the case even when, as described by Croker in his article in Chapter III, a social science research program was organizationally situated within a higher military educational institution.

ENLIGHTENMENT FUNCTIONS

Yet, to a considerable degree, the influence of social science knowledge on the actions and modes of thinking of foreign and military policy makers has come about through acquiring such knowledge in the course of their general educational experience; through their general exposure to social science literature—popular and semi-popular as well as scholarly; indeed, through the role of social science in shaping the cultural ambience. The frequency with which social scientists feel impelled to talk about this as a revelation is indicative of the extent to which other formulations predominate. The report "Strengthening the Behavioral Sciences" (III.3, 1962) issued by the President's Science Advisory Committee in 1962, for instance, states:

"The impact of the behavioral sciences on our society is far greater than most people realize. At one level they are providing technical solutions for important human problems. But at a deeper level they are changing the conception of human nature—our fundamental ideas about human desires and human possibilities. When such conceptions change, society changes.

"In the past few generations, many beliefs about such diverse matters as intelligence, child rearing, delinquency, sex, public opinion, and the management of organizations have been greatly modified by the results of filtering scientific fact and theory through numerous layers of popularizing translations. The casual way in which unproved behavioral hypotheses often find widespread acceptance underscores the importance of strengthening and deepening the behavioral sciences and of securing better public understanding of what they are and what they are not (p. 234)."

The diffuse impacts of social science production illustrate what we will call the *"enlightenment function."* The labels "engineering" and "enlightenment" are functional terms in that they refer to the uses to which knowledge is put irrespective of the intentions entering into its production. But the defining dimensions also may be used to differentiate among research approaches. It is apparent that work done following the engineering model may also find its way to applications through the indirect modes of transmission that are characteristic of the enlightenment function. The importance of the discussion of these functions here, however, is that work guided by engineering conceptions is rationalized in accord with narrowly prescriptive forms of transmission and application.

Within this general framework, research whose function is conceived as enlightenment may differ in ambition as well as in focus and scope from that directed toward engineering. On the one hand the social scientist may have a more modest role. He may, for example, content himself with "sensitizing" his audience to the important variables bearing on a problem, rather than with specifying the forms of their interrelationship or with assigning precise weights to these.[1] Here mere labelling may be seen as providing clarification of an otherwise intractable reality and as making for a common language between categories of decision-makers or among other types of specialized audiences. On the other hand he may have a more ambitious role in the sense of embracing much more of what is significant to a problem and more problems that are significant to this audience. He may attempt to project long-range changes in the world political environment. Likewise

[1] For a discussion of "sensitizing concepts" see Blumer (VI, 1931). See also Shils (I, 1961) and the article by Millikan in this chapter.

work following enlightenment conceptions may orient itself toward the substance of policy and planning or it may, as suggested by Hammond, seek to develop broader systematic representations of decision-making processes and contexts.

INTELLIGENCE FUNCTIONS

In the selections in this chapter by Lasswell, Hammond, and Millikan, prescriptions for social science work are removed, in varying degrees, from the engineering end of each of the continua that discriminate engineering from enlightenment functions. But frequently the examples of functions that they suggest envisage more pragmatic specificity—that is, more specific identifiability of users and uses—than would be consistent with the general enlightenment mechanisms described here. We may call functions in this middle-range *"intelligence."* Although we use pragmatic specificity as the primary characteristic to differentiate intelligence from enlightenment functions, this tends to be associated with more feasible restriction in each of the other five discriminating dimensions: number of variables, complexity of means-ends relationships, openness of system, time specificity, and, to a lesser extent, manipulability.

Using the label "intelligence" in this fashion is different from many customary definitions which emphasize collections of facts and data. Furthermore there has been so much vulgar association, even in the academic discussion, of the term "intelligence" with espionage that a certain feature of the definition as it is used here requires particular emphasis. The departures from the engineering function that our distinction includes make intelligence knowledge fit *adaptational strategies* more readily than manipulative ones. By an adaptational strategy we mean an individual or social system acting in such a way as to accommodate to, or exploit, an environmental change from an output of some other system by behavioral change that is not directed toward altering the source of this output. Open and multivariate systems can be described and aspects of their future states predicted more easily than prescriptions can be given for their successful manipulation.

Conventional conceptions of intelligence also include more highly specific purposes that would be closer to the engineering ends of the several continua. This is the case, for instance, with both the "technical" and "ideological" intelligence discussed by Lasswell in his article in this chapter. We find "intelligence" a suitable label more for want of a precise and less encumbered term than because knowledge with this form and function is at all exclusive to agencies or offices carrying the label. Nor is intelligence as used here at all exhaustive of the roles of knowledge in such agencies.

MANIPULATIVE OR ADAPTATIONAL STRATEGIES

The effect of engineering models has been particularly marked in research pertinent to foreign affairs through the peculiarly manipulative orientation it imparts to thinking about problems. Questions of how to affect a "target system" (sometimes with literal and sometimes with nonliteral analogies to the military meaning thereof) tend to be more common than those directed to the potential adaptations a party may make to present or predicted, but uninfluenceable outputs of that system. This has been as true of those models for influencing foreign systems which yield love or GRIT as the most effective manipulative means as it has been of those which reliably prescribe force and fear. It is noteworthy that even those social scientists most immediately and directly motivated by alarm over what they see as the dangerous manipulative potential of the social sciences frequently ignore the adaptational uses to which intelligence and enlightenment oriented research are particularly well adapted. Kelman (II.2, 1965), for example, writes:

"The reason for my deep concern is that the products, procedures, and orientations of social research inherently . . . treat man as an object rather than as an active, choosing, responsible agent. There is thus a danger that the widespread use of social science approaches—of psychological tests, interviews, experiments and observations—may in itself contribute to people's sense of alienation and helplessness, . . . and that, furthermore, these approaches may lend themselves most readily to the purposes of those agencies who are concerned with manipulating and controlling the behavior of individuals—with or without the consultation or the active involvement of the social scientist himself. To the extent that this danger becomes a reality, the social scientist becomes an agent and mediator of dehumanizing forces. It is even conceivable that a caricatured and perverted version of social science principles and techniques may serve as the operational code for an efficient dehumanized society (p. 31)."

He finds the means of reconciling these anxieties with his commitment to social science in literally "more radical" manipulations of social systems on the basis of social scientific research than those usually entertained. He advocates a new brand of radical thinking:

"There are two components to the radical thinking that I am advocating. The first is that, in analyzing societal processes, it searches for causes and attempts to specify the conditions that define a given state of affairs. Thus, it views any particular social arrangement or policy as one of many possible ones, and helps us escape the trap of thinking that what is must therefore be. It throws into question the assumptions on which current arrangements and policies are based, and tests out alternative assumptions. By specifying the conditions that have made the present situation necessary, it readily guides us to thinking about those conditions that would make alternative situations possible. In short, both in the analysis of the present state of affairs and in the search for alternatives, it goes to the roots.

"But the root is man—and that is the second component of the radical thinking that I am advocating. . . . In seeking solutions to pressing social problems, it asks what institutions and what courses of action are most likely to meet the needs and enhance the dignity and self-fulfillment of individuals.

"I hope it is clear that what I mean by radical thinking is not the advocacy of extreme actions or of social upheavals. It is, rather, the willingness to view any societal arrangement, not as necessary or inevitable, but as one of many alternative possibilities, man-made and dedicated to the purposes of men, and therefore open to change if it no longer fulfills these purposes adequately (pp. 33-34)."

Although laments are frequent that astronomy and meteorology afford more profitable analogical models for many social science science problems than do physics or chemistry, such models are recognized as appropriate for research rather than application. Many of the systems studied by social science yield knowledge which is useful in the same way as meteorology. Whereas there is still relatively little we can do about the weather, we can know when to carry an umbrella, come in from out of the rain, or go out and plant seeds. There is a further analogy in that even those controls that currently and prospectively can be exerted on weather will encounter powerful obstacles to their implementation because of their massive and dimly understood effects on existing social and meteorological equilibria.

It is not our purpose here to advocate adaptational uses of social science knowledge as in any sense inherently more functional or moral than manipulative ones. It is pertinent, however, that the former seemingly have more logical consonance with many ethically-based objections to social science than do manipulative strategies. This is true both when the knowledge is produced as intelligence—that is with the specific purposes and values of a particular user or set of users as an orientation guiding the research—or as enlightenment—that is, with broader human concerns and pragmatic potential in its orientation. Both have consonance with the article of scientific culture that makes acting on explicit knowledge preferable to acting on ignorance. They also are consistent with minimum imposition of the values a particular scientist happens to hold.

The problem of ethical neutrality remains inherent in intelligence, however, in view of the differential availability of intelligence to groups that are symbiotically competitive even when they are consciously merely adapting to one another. This is because of the different pertinence and utility to the interests of different groups that a given scientific work will have.

Enlightenment also differs from engineering in its potential action implications. While the engineering model seeks to lend confidence to action, enlightenment may foster diffidence. This is because the engineering type of knowledge orders the world in simple, precise, maximum-confidence-level propositions. In contrast the enlightenment type may emphasize complexities, uncertainties, and low predictability.

STUDIES OF INFLUENCE OR USE

As indicated earlier, much of the influence of social science knowledge has eluded attempts to study "utilization." One reason is that these studies have been largely oriented by engineering conceptions of how utilization takes place. This had made for presumptive overspecification of the potential uses and users of a given product. Frequently the search for uses has not gone beyond the specific sponsoring client of a piece of research. Such an exercise becomes patently pointless, when as is often the case, individuals who sponsored a study have rotated to other duties and the sponsoring office, or perhaps its very function has been abolished by the time the research is completed.

Research results may prove of low utility to the purpose which gave rise to the effort, but of high pertinence to some other purpose and party, as illustrated by several of the projects discussed by Croker. Orienting studies of use in terms of enlightenment or intelligence conceptions of function casts a broader net over potential uses and users. Further less presumption is involved in tracing "impacts" or "influences" of knowledge, rather than "use." Taking our subject matter as an example, studies of the influence of social science knowledge on the formation and administration of foreign and military policy would not be limited to finding instances of application of scientific principles to problems of policy or planning among a defined group of users. They would be equally if not more concerned with the extent to which the concepts, assumptions, and terms of social science as well as its implicit value premises have become part of the subculture studied. If interview techniques were to be used in such studies, we would select as respondents both those administrators who by virtue of their position or function could be regarded as clients for research as well as a random sample of all administrators in the subculture.[1]

Perhaps the most important function of social science knowledge in public administration that might be examined in studies of influence is the way in which it has provided policy makers and administrators with a scientifically-based body of esoterica—a possession necessary for every grouping in society that aspires to professional status

---

[1] For a design of research on utilization which, although couched in engineering terms, in part follows the lines indicated here, see Bailey (IV.3, 1967).

(Lynn, I, 1967). To a considerable extent the ability of social science to perform this function is dependent upon its projecting the hard-nosed scientific image suggested by engineering models. Although injecting social science esoterica into administration and policy formation may not, initially, extend much beyond the use of social science lingo, eventually it may come to include not only the fancy wrappings with which social science goods are packaged, but also the content of the package. We might hypothesize that the incorporation of social science theories, concepts, and values into the administrative culture would follow lines indicated in our discussion of intelligence and enlightenment models, even while the facilitation of entree depended heavily on presentational and perceived images of an engineering sort.

The extent to which the role of social science knowledge in furthering the professionalization of government officials has been of concern to social scientists is manifested by frequently voiced complaints over the dominance of other than social scientific esoterica in administrative and policy-making work. In the field of foreign affairs these complaints are exemplified by the remarks of Gabriel Almond before a congressional committee (Subcommittee on Government Research, III.3, 1966):

> "I think the Department of State has a record of on the whole being unduly skeptical and unduly slow in stimulating and in carrying on social science research that has a direct bearing on the foreign policy interests of the United States. They are a conservative, *humanistic institution, dominated by a foreign service which is trained largely in the law, in history and in the humanistic disciplines.* They believe in making policy through some kind of intuitive and antenna-like process, which enables them to estimate what the prospects of this and that are in this or the other country (p. 114)." [Editors' italics.]

There are similar conflicts within the communities of foreign affairs and military administration that divide those who identify with a science-oriented professional culture from those attached to more traditional bases of status and expertise. The former become continually more numerous and influential as advanced, specialized professional education becomes more important in elite recruitment. Although there are varying degrees of inclination toward one or the other of the "Two Cultures" in the graduate programs from which military and foreign affairs specialists are recruited, such education provides increasingly more intensive acculturation to social science. This is particularly visible when these current governmental educational programs are contrasted with the more traditional forms of educational preparation in international law or, even more so, in undergraduate institutions largely devoted to training in an appropriate class life-style.

The study of how social science knowledge is linked to the working out of professionalization within the foreign affairs and military policy fields might illuminate the differential usefulness of knowledge in an altogether different sense from that to which studies of its functions have thus far been directed. It would identify actors possessing much fuller human and behavioral attributes than the faceless "users" commonly encountered in studies of utilization. The behavioral qualities we would examine in a given group of officials—concern with legitimacy, responsibility, and ethics, for instance—are traditionally of interest to social scientists. In such studies the political, social, and technological environments in which these officials operate can take on a new import. They may be seen as sources of many of the elements which serve to legitimate or restrict the amount of attention paid to concerns such as the ones previously mentioned. As we have stressed several times earlier in this book, these extrascientific elements of social life have undoubtedly been of more significance in shaping the relationships of government and social science than the unfolding of the inner logic of social science as a science.

ENGINEERING AND INTELLIGENCE MODELS

Social Science and Social Engineering

PHILIP M. HAUSER

There should be no disagreement with the proposal for research into the role of applied social science in the formation of policy. The relation between social science and the formation of social policy and social action is, in fact, one of the more important areas of study in the general field of social control (Parsons, III.2, 1946; Wirth, VI, 1948a; Dewey, VI, 1947). The outline for research prepared by Merton[1] constitutes a good framework for the investigation of important aspects of the relationship between social science and the world of practical affairs. But there is room for vigorous disagreement with a fundamental assumption about the role of applied social science with which he starts, ...

At the outset it should be recognized that "pure" as well as "applied" social science research has important implications for social policy and action; and that the formation of policy and the implementation of policy in action should in themselves not be regarded either as "pure" or "applied" research, but rather as forms of "social engineering." In the interest of clarity, it is important to distinguish between pure research, applied research and social engineering.

• *Philosophy of Science,* Vol. 16, July 1949, pp. 209–218. Reprinted by permission of The Williams & Wilkins Company and the author.

[1] [For this and other references to Merton, see Robert K. Merton (I, 1949). Hauser and Merton were both contributors to the *Philosophy of Science* symposium on "Applied Social Research in Policy Formation." Eds.]

PURE VERSUS APPLIED RESEARCH

Pure research and applied research have in common the fundamental characteristics of research which briefly may be stated as the task of relating data to hypotheses in a manner to permit generalization in the form of laws or probability statements in respect to the phenomena in the field of observation. In this sense, both pure and applied research are scientific endeavors. The essential difference between pure and applied research is to be found not in the point of view or methods of the investigator, not in the nature of the phenomena under investigation, but rather in the manner in which the problem is selected, in the auspices of the research and in the immediate, as distinguished from the long-run, objectives of the research. In pure research the problem under investigation is likely to be one whose selection is dependent upon imminent developments in the science itself. The investigation is generally conducted under the aegis of an organization whose primary function is research for the enrichment of knowledge, which may include not only research organizations at universities, private research institutions and foundations, but also some research organizations in government, in business or in other realms of practical affairs with a pure research assignment. Both the immediate and long-run objective of pure research is the acquisition of knowledge, understanding and control in its scientific connotation.

The problem in applied research is delineated by the client—the person or agency confronted with a situation in which decision or action is required. The investigation is usually conducted under the auspices of an organization confronted with a "practical problem." The long-run objectives of such research may well be the same as those of pure research; but the immediate objective is to obtain knowledge, comprehension and control for their bearing on the solution of the practical problem. In consequence, applied research frequently does not focus on the problem of generalizing beyond the immediate problem calling for solution.... The findings of applied research however, if conducted in accordance with the canons of science, should represent additional factual grist in the bin of funded social science knowledge, and as such is available for generalization beyond the immediate practical problem to which it is addressed.

SOCIAL SCIENCE RESEARCH VERSUS SOCIAL ENGINEERING

Both pure and applied research defined as scientific activity should differ from social engineering in that they should not involve either the formation or implementation of social policy. It would be well to recognize that the formation of social policy and social action are not scientific functions and, in consequence, should not be regarded as research functions. The formation of policy, the reaching of decisions, the conduct of action programs should not be regarded as research functions, but as administrative functions, and as such might more appropriately be referred to as "social engineering," than as "applied social science."

The difference between this conception of applied social science research and that presented by Merton ... centers about the inclusion or exclusion of value judgments as a function of applied social science research. Under Merton's conception, "All applied science research involves *advice* ... (recommendations for policy) ..." and therefore value judgments. Although I am aware this is the common concept of applied social science and one that parallels the conception of applied natural science, I should urge a conception of applied social science research in accordance with the definition above, which excludes value judgments. Applied social science research should parallel pure social science research in being restricted to existential judgments, and instrumental judgments in terms of value judgments, so far as they may be involved, of persons or agencies other than the scientist.[1] That is, applied research like pure research should restrict itself to a description of observed relationships between phenomena, to generalization of these relationships, and to predictions of alternative courses of events so far as observed relationships and possible generalization permit, within frameworks of goals and value judgments set forth by policy makers or action agencies.

These essential distinctions between pure and applied social science and between social science and social engineering may be illustrated by the differences in the types of propositions which they would produce. In pure social science, research findings are expressed in the form: "If a, b and c are observed in situation L and M, X will occur in situation L, p out of n times, and Y in situation M, p_1 out of n times, *ceteris paribus*." In applied social science research findings take the form: "*Given a and b and given* situation M, Y will occur p out of n times if c is brought into the situation, *ceteris paribus*." In social engineering the proposition takes the form: "Having decided on Y, c is to be brought into the situation to supplement a and b in situation M, and situation L is to be avoided to preclude X."

* * * * *

[1] For an apposite discussion of the relation of existential, instrumental and value judgments to social science see Benoit (VI, 1945); also Lundberg (VI, 1945).

Both pure and applied social science research are necessarily conducted within a framework of some set of values. In the former, they are the values, implicit or explicit, of the culture in which the research is conducted and of the person undertaking the investigation. In the latter, the cultural context also carries a value system although the specific values which may dominate the research are more apt to be those of the policy maker or action agency for whom the research is being conducted than those of the investigator. Under the proposed concept of pure and applied research, it should be the responsibility and obligation of the investigator explicitly to formulate the value systems involved which may affect the orientation, the character and the conclusions of the research, whether the values are his own or that of the policy maker.[1] Awareness of these values is, in fact, a first prerequisite to objectivity in the research endeavor and should lead to systematic explorations of various blueprints for research as they are affected by different value systems. Such a procedure should be required in the planning of any research, whether pure or applied. But the essential point is that the investigator as a social scientist does not assume responsibility for the formation of the values as a product of research.

REASONS FOR PROPOSED DISTINCTIONS

Ample justification is to be found for this proposed conception of applied social science. In the first place, value judgments have a quite different relation to the investigator, to the action agency, and to the public at large in applied social science than in applied natural science. Value judgments in applied natural science are not as likely to be affected by the deep-rooted emotional, sentimental and conditioned attitudes, and the predilections and prejudices of the investigator, of the action agency, or of the public at large. Second, it is much more difficult in the nature of social science subject matter to distinguish between social science knowledge and common sense knowledge (Wirth, VI, 1948a). The difficult task of making this distinction clear . . . is made even more difficult by the admixture of existential, instrumental and value judgments identified as products of social science. Practically every person feels he knows a good deal about the subject matter of the social sciences and is usually prepared to defend his value judgments.

* * * * *

A clear distinction between the roles of the social scientist and the social engineer in respect to value formation would tend also to protect social science from identification with many forms of movements and causes which profess value systems as products of research. The difficulty of distinguishing between "genuine" and "spurious" research to which Merton refers is made considerably more difficult by the confusion of existential and instrumental judgments with value judgments as products of research. The task of evaluating research methods or verifying research findings in the competition between bad research and good research is a relatively simple task compared with that of evaluating value systems presumably emanating from research.

Social science and the social scientist are generally suspect even when not identified with value judgments that align them with respect to political controversy, to vested interests or to widely accepted conventions or social codes. The social scientist is compelled to deal with subject matter that often

---

[1] It may be noted that the policy maker or action agency is also confronted with the problem of values in selecting the researcher from among potential investigators with different value systems. Within the limits of feasibility, the policy maker may seek to have available the findings of independent researches conducted by scholars with different value systems in order to control values as a variate in the research activity.

involves traditions, sacred practices and values. It is difficult enough for the social scientist to achieve objectivity in pursuing research with such phenomena; it is much more difficult to persuade action agencies or the public at large that an objective approach can be achieved; and both these tasks are made infinitely more difficult, if not impossible, if the social scientist *qua* social scientist is either identified with value judgments or attempts to achieve them as a product of research.

In addition . . . there are important positive reasons for assigning these functions to the social engineer . . . . There is ample historical and contemporary evidence suggesting the inadvisability of separating policy making from responsibility, especially in a democratic society. It is a fundamental aspect of democracy that the policy maker is held responsible for, and therefore assumes the risks of, decision making and action. The social scientist as an advisor would symbolize the divorce of policy making from risk bearing. The social engineer because of his responsibility for his decisions and actions and because he is confronted with risks may be in a better position to reach wise decisions than the social scientist, even though the latter may provide him with an important part of the knowledge on which the decision may rest. The relation between policy making and risk bearing is in itself an important area of research.

. . . . There are many problems, particularly in the field of political conflict, which are not technical problems but which are posed by conflicting value or power systems. There are aspects of such problems which social science cannot illuminate, often because no further illumination is necessary. They are problems for the statesman whose job it is to act successfully even though the act may be evil or the least evil among several expedient actions. Morgenthau (VI, 1946) describes such problems as problems for the "more than scientific man" and more than the social engineer as he defines him, "the statesman." The statesman, however, is but another form of social engineer as defined above.

But in this type of problem, . . . social science, through pure or applied research, can make important contributions. Social science research could help make the values or objectives explicit, analyze their consistency or compatibility, evaluate the extent to which they are dependent on one another, throw light on the comparative costs of varying objectives, provide knowledge about the several means to the achievement of the ends, and evaluate the consequences of policy and action in relation to the means employed and objectives aimed at (Wirth, VI, 1948a). Here is another important area of research—the study of the role of social science as the handmaiden of perhaps the most important of the social engineers—the statesman.

SOCIAL SCIENCE AND PREDICTION

The proposed distinction between applied social science research and social engineering would also affect the role of the social scientist in relation to the problem of making forecasts or predictions. Merton distinguishes between "abstract predictions" and "concrete forecasts." He recognizes the former as a product of pure research and as involving assumptions with respect to many factors which may be belied by the course of events. Although Merton recognizes that the concept *ceteris paribus* "is often an embarrassing obstacle" in applied research, he would nevertheless treat concrete forecasts, which are "contingent upon uncontrolled conditions" as a function of applied social science. In this position, there is an already evident, and potentially even greater, menace to the prestige and acceptance of social science.

If the distinction between applied social science research and social engineering is to be accepted, it would be the function of applied research also to make "abstract predictions" under varying assumptions and varying patterns of contingent conditions. That is, applied research like pure research would result in a series of predictions tied to varying explicitly stated assumptions and explicitly stated contingent conditions. It would not undertake the flat, unconditional prediction of any course of events . . . .

In its present state of development social science certainly cannot predict the actual course of many future events and in respect to many problems, will probably never be in a position to do so. The social scientist as a social scientist would be foolish to assume the burden of predicting the actual course of complex social events contingent upon conditions which he knows he cannot control either in a scientific nor in an administrative sense. To do so is to invite inevitable adverse reaction and a loss of confidence, not only in him, but in social science . . . . The task of predicting the actual course of events should be left to the social engineer. It is his job, utilizing the "abstract predictions" of the social scientist, to estimate the contingent conditions with whatever degree of certainty a given problem may necessitate and to formulate his policy and his action program accordingly. It is his privilege to reap the honor and glory of successful prediction or price of failure. The social scientist as a social scientist should recognize his limitations as a soothsayer and seek neither the fame of the successful prophet nor assume the risk of failure.

* * * * *

CONCLUDING REMARKS

The proposed distinction between social science and social engineering should not be interpreted to mean that social science should not be concerned with values or with forecasts of events. Social science most assuredly cannot escape the necessity of dealing with values as data for research, nor should social science be unmindful of the relevance of its product including abstract prediction for the formation of values in policy determination and social action. Social science itself and the utilization of the products of social science research may both gain considerably, however, if it is recognized that it is not within the province of the social scientist as a social scientist to give "advice" or to participate in policy decision and action programs . . . .

The current admixture of science and engineering in applied seocial science is easily understood as a transitional happenstance occasioned by the lag in the development and training of social engineers as a distinct profession. Social engineering tasks are today, in the main, performed by amateurs, by lay persons without special training as social engineers. This, of course, is not the universal rule, for some social engineering professions are well-established and drawn upon for the performance of specific social engineering jobs. The social worker, the teacher, the expert in public administration, the city planner and the investment counselor are examples in point. But many of the more important decisions affecting broad social policy and action programs are made usually by lay persons—politicians, businessmen, lawyers—lay persons in the sense that they have not been trained as specialists to deal with the policy and action problems for which they are responsible.[1]

A central problem for research lies then in the study of mechanisms and processes through which available social science knowledge may contribute to policy making and its implementation. This points to an important and relatively neglected area with significant research as well as practical oper-

---

[1] For elaboration of this point see Goldenweiser (VI, 1946).

ational implications. This is the area involving the role of the expert in relation to the policy maker and executive—the social engineer. Penetrating insights into this relationship are available to help frame this problem for research (Goldenweiser, VI, 1944). In part, such research is but an aspect of research into forms of effective rational, as distinct from traditional, emotional, or irrational forms of social control.

Conversion Barriers in Using the Social Sciences

HAROLD GUETZKOW

Within recent years there has been increasing interest in the social processes underlying the application of basic social science knowledge to practical affairs.[1] Little attention has been given, however, to the way the very structure of knowledge affects its conversion for application. In the social sciences the roles of scientist, engineer, technician, practitioner, and policy maker have not been well differentiated. It may be useful to sketch how the knowledge that the scientist develops may be converted by others for use and then to examine the impact of certain characteristics of basic knowledge upon the application process.

THE PRODUCTS OF SOCIAL SCIENCE

The basic products of the social scientists are tested theories, some of which have been consolidated into textbooks and summaries. In its more rigorous form this basic knowledge consists of models of concepts in their interrelations to one another. Sometimes the concepts are well formulated, even operationalized as variables; sometimes the variables so developed are formally interrelated in systems as sets of mathematical equations. The theories of the social scientist are abstract and general, as they must be to have wide usefulness.

The process of utilizing these theories is very different from the task of generating them. Applied knowledge is used toward particular ends, and the goals determine what information is relevant; theories are not valued of themselves, but only as they are applicable to the achievement of concrete, specific purposes. Although the client's own formulation of his end value often cannot be taken as a rigid given, as Gouldner (V.1, 1956: 174–179) points out, this essay does not deal with the problem of ends.

* * * * *

A SCHEMATIZATION OF THE CONVERSION PROCESS

The conversion of general knowledge into a usable form can be viewed as consisting of a threefold process: (1) the basic variables are reidentified and measured in concrete settings; (2) the relevant model involving these variables is selected and composed from among alternative theories; and (3) the magnitudes of the important constants in the selected system are determined, so that specific predictions may be made for each different situation. These three phases appear to constitute major conversion barriers to using basic social science knowledge in solving concrete social problems.

• *Administrative Science Quarterly*, Vol. 4, June 1959, pp. 68-81. Reprinted by permission of the publisher and the author. This paper was read at the meetings of the Operations Research Society of America in San Francisco in November 1956 under the title, "A Model on the Application of the Social Sciences to Management Practice."

[1] For example, Graham (IV. 1: 1954); Webbink (IV.1, 1950); Likert and Lippitt (I, 1953); Likert and Hayes (VI, 1957); Merton and Lerner (VI, 1951); Schramm (VI, 1954).

Reidentification and Measurement of Variables

The isolation and measurement of the variables in specific field situations is no little task. In given situations variables may assume a succession of magnitudes, although for periods their size may be relatively constant. Often the methodology developed by the scientist is too expensive or too elaborate for field situations. In the social sciences especially it may be necessary to use indirect techniques to get at the latent rather than the manifest expression of a given variable. The practical and ethical demands of the field sometimes require extensive modification of the original measuring devices.

Many complain that the devices of the scientist are clumsy and inappropriate for direct utilization. This is often true. Simplifying measuring devices is a prerequisite for successful application . . . . But sometimes the social scientist cannot develop his measuring devices into usable form, for he does not know the requirements of particular field situations.

Model Selection

Choice of a theory from among alternatives is a crucial step in the conversion process. In applying basic social science knowledge, one can sometimes integrate various theories, if they are concerned with phenomena which are relevant to a particular problem. But sometimes the theories are incompatible; if one procedure is applied, another simply is not possible. This situation also arises when the applier has multiple goals which demand contradictory means.

*   *   *   *   *

There are at least three roots to this difficulty, two of which may be remedied. First, because social science is still in its early stages, its theories are often inadequate for application to a particular situation. Because of this, alternatives may yield but a half-fit, which makes choice among them difficult. This inadequacy sometimes gives the impression that social phenomena are "experienced by the individual actor on the social scene in entirely different terms" from those used by the scientist. The argument claims that

". . . the social scientist *qua* theoretician has to follow a system of relevances entirely different from that of the actor on the social scene. . . . His problems originate in his theoretical interest, and many elements of the social world that are scientifically relevant are irrelevant from the point of view of the actor on the social scene, and vice-versa (Strauss, VI, 1956)."

As the coverage of social science theory broadens, all social events become relevant to the theoretician's interest. When social science theory becomes comprehensive, its description of behavior will necessarily cover those provinces of action usually reserved to men of practical affairs, even in areas where judgment and intuition now reign supreme. That the social scientist cannot predict in such complex social problems at the moment does not argue that prediction is impossible. Both researcher and applier want to predict, and for both the efficacy of their knowledge depends upon the adequacy of their prediction.

A second root of difficulty is the inadequate dissemination of basic knowledge among practitioners and lay users. The practical questions of the latter are disparate with the theoretical schemes. Often the applier merely asks for "more knowledge" instead of inquiring how a particular independent variable or two will exercise their effect upon a given, well-defined dependent variable. Both of these causes of difficulty in choosing the appropriate theory are remediable.

But the third root seems inherent in the nature of the social sciences in contrast to the biological and physical sciences. Many social situations have large numbers of highly interrelated variables with feedbacks.

Instead of being able to work with quasi-isolated, miniature models—as the natural scientist does—the user of social science must immediately work with an interrelated system. Even though scientists and applier try to simplify, both are forced to reckon with the interplay among their variables, because variables often cannot be held constant without disrupting the social process itself.

But these feedbacks do not make the social systems fundamentally different from equally intricate biological and physical systems, even when the feedbacks in social systems are generated by the self-awareness of the actors. As has been pointed out, social science generalizations must be constructed with such feedback systems incorporated as integral parts of the model being used (Simon, VI, 1954; Grunberg & Modigliani, VI, 1954).

. . . . Bales, Slater, and their associates present evidence that members often demand contradictory functions of their leaders; for example, providing idea leadership and simultaneously serving as group unifiers (Slater, VI, 1955). The Conference Research project found that leaders were valued when they were idea men with respect to the committee's procedures, but not when they determined the outcome of the agenda being considered by the group (Guetzkow, Heyns & Marquis, VI, 1951: 62). Are the theories contradictory? On the surface yes; actually no. The hypothesis resulting from the Conference Research project explains one reason why leaders in the Bales-Slater theory cannot perform both leadership functions . . . .

Parametric Determinations

Another troublesome cognitive aspect of the conversion process is the need which general, abstract knowledge imposes upon the applier for specification of the initial conditions and weightings of the isolated variables. To use a theory to produce changes one usually starts from some point which becomes the system's initial conditions. Specification of these initial conditions enables one to telescope the past and to provide data essential in making predictions about the future. In addition, one must obtain information about the relative weightings to be assigned to particular factors in a given situation. These initial constants and relative weightings are often designated as the system's parameters.

. . . . Guetzkow and Gyr (VI, 1954) were able to distinguish two conditions on the basis of the type of conflict found in decision-making groups. The two conditions were an initial situation in which there was (1) substantive conflict over agenda issues and (2) affective or emotional conflict, expressed as interpersonal strife. To obtain consensus on the final decisions in a group it is imperative to recognize the type of conflict initially dividing the group . . . .

. . . . One of the central findings of the Conference Research project was its discovery of the detrimental effect of the members' self-oriented needs (such as their demands for status, personal dominance, and so forth) to the productivity and overall success of decision-making groups (Guetzkow, Heyns, & Marquis, VI, 1951: 66). In some situations this variable may have no weight because there is little expression of such self-oriented needs . . . .

In this case of self-oriented needs the magnitude of the variable in the on-going situation is independent of the initial conflict conditions. However, with respect to such variables as facts and withdrawal, as already described, the change in weightings needed is a result of interaction with the initial conditions.

* * * * *

IMPLICATIONS OF THE SCHEME FOR USE OF THE SOCIAL SCIENCES

The Nature of Social Engineering

In order to pursue the implications of these barriers to the social processes involved in applying basic knowledge, it may be useful to differentiate various social roles involved. In 1947 Herring (V.1, 1947) posited the need for a "social science technician," using the term broadly to mean "an individual who has been professionally trained to apply to practical situations the facts, generalizations, principles, rules, laws, or formulae uncovered by social science research." Schramm (VI, 1954: 39) presented an "anatomy of utilization" by describing a four-link chain between scientist and final consumer, as follows:

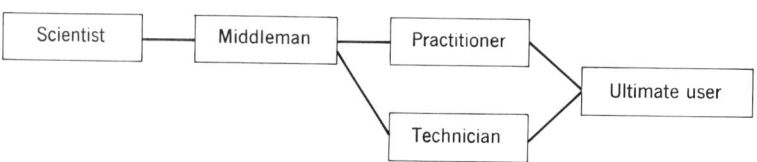

An example is found in industry: physicist—mechanical engineer—production manager and technician—product user.

If this analysis of the conversion barriers is adequate, an expansion of the "middleman" function is required. Among practitioners whose life work is concerned with individual and social behavior, such as social workers, educators, lawyers, administrators (in business and in government), and politician statesmen, there is much reliance upon intuitive knowledge, applied with skill and art derived from long experience. As information in the social sciences increases, there is more need to differentiate the expert in social science knowledge from both the social scientist and the practitioner. The social engineer is the broad-gauged "middleman" who knows how to transform basic knowledge from the various social science disciplines into usable forms. He differs, too, from the technician (the pollster in business and industry, for example) whose competence is restricted and who may be only slightly familiar with the fund of basic knowledge underlying his specialization.

What assignments should be given to these social engineers?

1. Work by social engineers on practical alternative measures of a given variable is needed, once a variable has been conceptualized and operationalized. A danger in the successful simplification of measuring devices is too easy utilization with consequent misapplication. The widespread misuse of various economic indices such as the cost-of-living measure in government, unions, and business suggests the confusion sometimes induced by partisans who distort for their particular organization's gain. But just as we have not deprived ourselves of micrometers and ammeters in the physical sciences because they are misused, so misuse should not delay efforts to accelerate simplification in the social sciences too. The reduction in costs made possible by such simplification often determines whether it is feasible to use the basic knowledge in concrete situations.

2. Social engineers must select appropriate theory from the alternatives, if they are fortunate enough to find relevant theories within a given problem area. This demands a thorough knowledge of the alternatives. Should alternative systems give about the same result, choice among them may be made on criteria other than achievement of one's immediate application goals.

Gouldner (V.1, 1957: 96-98) argues that choice of the concepts involved in an application depends on such factors as their accessibility to control and whether the "instrumental management of a variable would violate" the values of the group involved. When alternative models allow alternative interventions, such criteria become most appropriate. Economic criteria are always important in choosing among alternatives.

* * * * *

Because variables involved in practical problems are often not divided as they are among the traditional disciplines, social engineers must be broadly trained. Because the fund of knowledge is increasing, they must also be allowed adequate time for continuous updating of their knowledge across the disciplines. Exemplary demonstrations of attempts at the updating of "middlemen" are found in the seminars of the Foundation for Research on Human Behavior (Likert and Hayes, VI, 1957).

Yet to demand a competent grasp of the relevant storehouse of information does not imply that the tasks of the social engineer are identical with those of the social scientist, as Hayek (VI, 1956: 470) implies when he asserts, "We can . . . only rarely delegate the application of our knowledge but must be our own practitioners." Scientists engaged in basic research are handicapped as social engineers because they may fit practical problems to their academic traditions, instead of allowing the problems to dictate the particular fund of knowledge to tap. One of the advantages of the "operations research" approach to practical problems is its neglect of the boundaries of the traditional disciplines.

3. Perhaps the most startling implication of the foregoing analysis is that determination of initial conditions and factor weightings must be repeated by the social engineer each time the concrete situation changes. For example, in using psychometric instruments for personnel selection, one finds that each job continues to change. This requires revision of the screening devices constructed for the evaluations. Even after one has "engineered" a suitable test for a particular job specification, one must maintain monitoring devices to ensure that the solution developed for the job at one time is still applicable at a later time, when the nature of the job may have changed.

Even in the thoughtful report issued by the Russell Sage Foundation there seems to be misunderstanding of this implication. For example, in discussing the work of the Foreign Morale Analysis Division of the Office of War Information and the Military Intelligence Service, the authors say that the facts of the "inactive social science programs have now been compiled and can be drawn on for social engineering," as if to assume that such particulars will be useful ever after, despite changes in the morale of nations (Webbink, IV.1, 1950: 44). Failures in the workability of social science knowledge may be traced to inadequate assessment of initial conditions and incorrect estimates of the weightings attached to particular factors in a given problem situation.

TECHNOLOGY VERSUS SCIENCE

Gradually a large, versatile battery of practical, operational measuring devices will be accumulated. More and more useful handbooks, summarizing alternative variable systems, will be developed. Compilations will be made of the ranges over which the parameters can sweep, and some of them may even turn out to be relatively stable, approximating the ever-useful constants of the physical sciences. These developments will constitute the technology of the social sciences.

As social science theory improves, more social inventions will arise from its development. These by-products of theory—the intelligence test, the panel survey methodology, and the "process observer" for small groups—will proliferate an array of contrived social phenomenon about which more will be known than we know about the extremely complicated systems existing in nature. In the physical sciences the engineer does better in predicting the behavior of the machines he contrives than the phenomena he finds in "raw" nature. . . . Likewise, the social practitioner will understand his miniature contrived social systems better than the systems he encounters in the tradition-rooted world about him. This development will suggest to the naïve observer that social phenomena perhaps are not as difficult to predict as they were earlier thought to be. Actually, however, the engineer will now be working in areas where he has relatively more understanding than he has about social systems occurring in nature.

The difference between science and technology is not clearly drawn in the social sciences. Although the work of the scientist is the isolation of variables and the construction of theories which interrelate them, the basic researcher in the social sciences often misunderstands his task. Sometimes he squanders his limited research resources on parameter estimation, even though the size of a particular parameter (except when it is zero) usually would not disprove his theory. Nor can the parameters discovered by the basic researcher in his laboratory often be applied directly to practical, field situations . . . .

SUMMARY

The intellectual task of the social science researcher is different from the requirements imposed when the basic fund of knowledge is to be used in concrete social situations. Work in the basic sciences involves isolation of variables, development of operational measurements, and establishment of models to represent relations among the isolated variables. To apply this knowledge, however, a threefold conversion must be undertaken: (1) The basic variables must be reidentified in the field situation, and practical operational measures must be developed at practical costs. (2) Appropriate selection of alternative variable systems must be made, so that relatively accurate consequences of action may be predicted. (3) Adequate estimates must be made of the parametric values involved in specifying both the initial conditions and the variable weightings in order to apply the chosen model to a particular situation. These are three important barriers to more effective use of basic social science knowledge.

Problem situations often demand systems which cross the traditional academic disciplines. There are distinct differences in the intellectual tasks confronting the social scientist and the user of social science knowledge. Indications are that experts needed for using knowledge are different from those needed for its discovery.

The Relation of Ideological Intelligence to Public Policy

HAROLD D. LASSWELL

The intelligence function adapts itself to changing conceptions of policy and to innovations in the procedures by which facts are gathered, analyzed, and presented. New policy ideas are today resulting from the vast transformations that are taking place in the structure of society, state, and government. New methods of observing, analyzing, and reporting data have arisen as an outcome of the growth of modern social and psychological sciences. So swift is the stream that we may fail in every effort to chart the banks within which it flows; yet the importance of seeking to understand the complex relationship of policy and intelligence is great enough to justify the risks involved. Greater clarity may reduce the amount of fumbling that is invariably associated with new efforts to adapt old functions to different conditions.

A canvass of the existing literature reveals that very little systematic and unified treatment has been given to the intelligence function. In limited spheres, notably in relation to military policy, there are theoretical discussions and practical manuals.[1] It has long been an axiom that command depends on adequate intelligence of the resources and plans of the enemy. In the realm of diplomacy there are valuable hints on how information may be obtained (Thompson & Padover, VI, 1937). Concern for the internal security of the state and aspirations toward revolutionary action have both inspired contributions to the intelligence problem. The literature of democracy has reiterated the need of an intelligent public opinion; however, there has been a minimum of advance toward specifying the criteria by which relevant intelligence for the citizen and the official may be recognized.[2]

It is possible to fathom some of the factors that have contributed to the comparative neglect of the intelligence function as a whole. In preliberal, predemocratic states, ideological policy was simple. The aims of policy in this field were to detect sedition at home and conspiracy abroad and to encourage the reverent acceptance of state-friendly religions. In liberal, democratic states, however, there is nothing simple about the ideological goals, if we take these aspirations literally. Democracy means respect for human dignity. This implies a commonwealth of mutual deference. (To be deferred to is to be taken into consideration; in a democratic government or state this calls for participation in the making of important decisions.) Policy is democratic when it is consistent and compatible with human dignity. Obviously this calls for deeper knowledge of reality than the simple recording of momentary approval of contemplated lines of action.

● *Ethics,* Vol. 53, October 1942, pp. 25-34. Reprinted by permission of The University of Chicago Press and the author. Copyright 1942 by The University of Chicago Press.
[1] Concerning World War I see Ronge (VI, 1930).

[2] An effort like that of Merriam (VI, 1939) is most exceptional. The leads suggested by Wallas (VI, 1914: Chapters X-XIII) have never been adequately followed up.

Although the ideal of human dignity is positive, it entered the stage of the large-scale modern state clad in the scanty garments of negativism. Private businessmen were out to get government out of the market. The expanding business society expressed itself through the competitive market and representative government. The focus of attention of the businessman was limited to the market; the focus of attention of the government man was restricted to auxiliary functions . . . . No positive conception of the relationship between the parts and the whole of a democratic state was sought. It was not missed.

In recent times the re-expansion of government has redefined the focus of attention of the policy-makers of liberal, democratic states. More and more they are compelled to try to find a unified set of positive objectives, to "reconcile" business and government. At the same moment that the internal structure of the state is changing, the key symbols and symbol elaborations of the state are under attack. Communist revolutionaries deride the democratic aspirations of such states as hypocrisy; Nazi revolutionaries deride them as decadent and contemptible. The Nazis reject both symbols and practices; the Marxists reject only the practices.

The sheer intellectual task of clarifying the goals and instruments of democratic idealism has gone largely by default. If we look back to the seventeenth and eighteenth centuries in England, we are impressed by the strength of the intellectual currents that were running toward unity of state aim. When David Hume wrote about social processes, his contributions included not only essays on the balance of trade but on the balance of power. The doctrines of mercantilism[1] were a rather coherent body of policy ideas: states were conceived as succeeding or failing in terms of power (by which was meant political fighting effectiveness); power was believed to depend on stimulating exports in return for precious metals. Goals were so clearly defined that intelligence operations could count goods and weigh bullion and apply this practical meter stick to the measurement of policy success and failure.

The liberal, democratic state did not succeed in harmonizing professed ideal and effective policy, partly because the democratic elements in the ideal were left undeveloped . . . . The cardinal value was the dignity of man, but prosperity was not translated in terms of human dignity. Bentham's calculus of felicity was pointed in this direction, but it was not specified in terms capable of being operationally applied to an extremely complicated division of labor.

Some shortcomings of liberal, democratic states have been failures of policy and intelligence; the urgent question of the moment is how these deficiencies can be surmounted. Can the policy-makers who profess ideals of human dignity learn to specify what they mean in operating terms? No doubt the intelligence function can aid, to some extent, in the task of clarification; unquestionably the intelligence facilities of modern society can provide relevant knowledge when goals are put in definite terms.

Modern procedures do make it possible for the first time in the history of large-scale social organization to realize some of the aims of democracy. Social and psychological sciences have developed procedures that are capable of reporting the facts about the thoughts and feelings of our fellow-men. In the Great Society, with its thousands of specialized material environments, its enormous geographical spread, and its instantaneous communication, special measures must be taken to learn the significant facts of life. By means of quick interviews, we can supplement some of the guesses that are made about what men think; and by prolonged interviews and participation we can probe more deeply into the texture of experience.

---

[1] On the full range of mercantilism consult Heckscher (VI, 1932).

By disciplined methods we can locate the zones of poor democratic performance and determine the factors that contribute to their continuation.... By using our new instruments of mutual understanding, we can specify our goals and report on their state of realization. The very act of specifying the meaning of human dignity disciplines both our policy-makers and our scientists. The gathering of knowledge can be synchronized with the needs of policy and with the formal standards of science.

We can actually study the thoughts and feelings of each of the major divisions of modern social structure and perfect means of making them fraternally intelligible to one another.... Policy decisions need to be tempered in the light of racial, confessional, and other group attitudes. If democracy includes a decent regard for the thoughts and feelings of others, our procedures can and should be applied to the enormous task of making these facts available to the various components of our society (Smith, VI, 1941). By examining the contents of the channels of public communication[1] we may determine the degree to which even the opportunity exists of taking the other fellow into proper account. Up to the present time, it must be conceded, our press, film, and radio channels of mass communication have not adequately performed this task (Lasswell, VI, 1941b).

Each public policy calls for two types of intelligence: ideological and technical. By ideological intelligence is meant facts about the thoughts, feelings, and conduct of human beings. Other facts are technical. It makes no difference whether the policy goal is phrased in ideological or technical terms; both kinds of information are involved in any complete consideration of goals or alternatives. Ideologically phrased objectives are to strengthen the will to victory of the home population; to demoralize the fighting will of the enemy; and to win allies. The attainment of these objectives depends upon many technical considerations, such as geophysical factors affecting radio reception. If goals are phrased in technical terms (tanks, guns, planes), they depend upon data about the thoughts and feelings and conduct of factory workers and of many other elements of the population. It is evident that we are compelled to pass back and forth between ideological and technical facts in contemplating each and every line of policy.

Whatever scheme is used to classify policy, each policy and each category of policy must be properly integrated with every other. By policy we understand the making of important decisions. A decision adds energy and determination to preference; it is part of an act of striving. Values, therefore, are not only indorsed; they are sought by mobilizing a significant part of the values already at hand. The importance of decisions may be appraised according to the magnitude of this potential mobilization of resources. In the most vital personal decisions, character, material goods, friendship, and life are at stake. In the realm of public policy the stakes are comparable: moral integration, material assets, diplomatic position, and continuity.

For any personality, individual or collective, policy is concerned with total value position. Within the field of total policy, distinctions may be drawn that aid decisions by classifying ends and means. In the realm of high policy a fourfold classification has often been serviceable, according to which the four fronts of policy are military, diplomatic, economic, ideological. Each sphere of policy is to some extent an end and to some extent a means; successful policy proceeds by continuous integration. Thus every proposed military policy must be evaluated with reference to other objectives in the sphere of military policy and to goals in the

---

[1] Representative recent contributions to this emerging science include: Waples (VI, 1942); Lazarsfeld (VI, 1940); Gallup and Rae (VI, 1940); Murphy and Likert (VI, 1938). On content analysis see Lasswell (VI, 1935: Chapter IX; VI, 1941a).

sphere of diplomacy, economics, and ideology . . . .

For purposes of brief definition we may sum up the four fronts of policy as ends and means. The end of military policy is predominance over enemies in battle; the distinctive means are instruments of violence. The end of diplomatic policy is favorable agreement, whatever the substantive character of the agreement; the distinctive means is negotiation. The end of economic policy is production; the distinctive means are productive instruments. The end of ideological policy is favorable attitudes; the most distinctive means are symbols. We may subdivide each policy front into internal and external. If this is done, some clarification is needed about the internal diplomatic front, since usage has limited diplomacy to external relations . . . . At present, there is no consensus on how these internal processes are classified. Sometimes they are assigned to the internal ideological front. Often what are here called diplomacy and ideology are bracketed together as "political" policy—despite the patent advantages of reserving the term "politics" for the overall term. A threefold division thus results: military, economic, political. Nearly every other thinkable breakdown is sometimes made and is often useful. If a two-term classification is desired, the most satisfactory is the one hinted at above: ideological and technical. In the former the emphasis is upon thoughts and feelings and upon the symbols that circulate through the channels of radio, film, press, and conversation. In the latter the starting-point is material objects. The usual instruments of ideological policy are speeches, news conferences, news releases, magazine articles, . . . [and the like]. Propaganda is the positive guidance of such material; censorship eliminates. Personnel selection for symbolic rather than technical reasons also comes within the field of ideological action . . . .

What the intelligence function can contribute to policy may be exemplified in certain simple instances on different policy fronts. The contributions can be summed up in three points: intelligence can (1) clarify goals, (2) clarify alternatives, and (3) provide needed knowledge.

. . . . [A]n example from diplomacy: Policy instructions may be to negotiate a trade agreement, but the time period may be left vague. Intelligence may report that peaceful persuasion would produce the result in about six months; that an opportunity to receive stock in American business concerns would diminish opposition so much that success could be hoped for in three months. The supporting facts include knowledge of the attitudes of influential leaders . . . . [Another] example is ideological: Are atrocity stories to be played up more in the future than in the recent past? Intelligence may report that if more atrocity stories are circulated among the wives of skilled workers, it may give them a more vivid sense of what war is and stimulate their aggressive interest in helping their husbands keep on the job . . . .

These instances have deliberately been selected on a low level of abstraction, but they show the essential interrelations between policy and intelligence. In practice, decision-makers of every level are finding new goals and subgoals, contemplating new alternatives, asking for new information as a means of evaluating future probabilities. Policy thinking is "forward" thinking; it is manipulative and responsible. It is always guided to some extent by knowledge; and a recurring problem is to perfect the intelligence function so that it brings to the focus of attention of the decision-maker what he most needs to think about and what he most needs to think with.

We may classify the types of knowledge needed for ideological policy as follows: (1) distribution of attitudes, (2) trend of attitudes, and (3) comparisons of available alternatives with past situations and with scientific findings . . . .

Attitudes are hypothetical patterns of reality; the terms used to name attitudes must be given operational definitions from the standpoint of many different observers. In giving instructions for the identification of carbon, we have no trouble in choosing a definitive index. But this is not true of an attitude, like hatred of the President or of Hitler. We must work with many indices and construct rather arbitrary rules to govern the inclusion or exclusion of the resulting profiles.

Attitudes may be inferred from many kinds of data: (1) what people say and do; (2) what is said to people; (3) what is done to people. We may record what people say and do when they are unaware that they are being interviewed or when they are unaware that they are being observed for scientific or policy purposes. Our observer may be so situated that he may affect the result by influencing the attitude of the subject, or he may not . . . .

By examining what is said to people we may be able to foresee their responses. Policy-makers are accustomed to rely upon inferences that they make from what is brought to the focus of public attention in the mediums of mass communication. Many decisions are affected by inferences about public response that are made when the policy-maker reads a newspaper or listens to a broadcast on the way to the office. Inferences may also be based upon knowledge of what has been done to people and of how they have responded in the past. Thus, if we hear of acute housing congestion, of speed-up, of rising prices of consumption goods, of shortages of consumption goods, of rapid introduction of groups against which there is a local bias (racial, religious, partisan), we may construct many plausible inferences that are often confirmed by additional data.

The terms used to describe people are of cardinal importance, since they imply hypotheses about the factors that significantly affect response. We are concerned both with position in the social structure and with personality structure.

The organization of the intelligence function calls for the proper articulation of many specialists with policy-makers. Some problems arise because of the novelty of the procedures involved. Since the science of communication is itself in its infancy, the opportunities now open stimulate both imagination and ambition. Specialists who have become associated with the development of one specific procedure of observation are often prone to exaggerate its place in the total picture. Hence they may "oversell" one group of policy-makers on the results that can be expected from polling or psychiatric interviewing or content analysis or organizational analysis. Acceptance of a given skill group may be followed by disillusioned rejection, and the growth of a mature and well-developed intelligence operation may be retarded.

Policy-makers in business and government are well acquainted with the idea of describing the distribution of attitudes in a given group. They are also familiar with the idea of describing the distribution of politically significant symbols at the focus of attention of a group. The former has come from the counting of votes in elections and in poll interviews. The second has come from the practice of clipping the press of selected groups. Clipping bureaus are long-established institutions inside and outside government. The opinion poll has made rapid progress since the appearance of the American Institute of Public Opinion.

Although the idea of quantitative summaries of significant material is widely accepted, their interpretation is capricious. If you believe in the importance of world-organization after the war, you will probably be less critical of data that purport to show that a great many Americans look forward to such an outcome. If, on the contrary, you reject this goal, you may dismiss entirely the procedure by which the data were obtained or you may engage in vigorous methodological controversies about it. It is not generally recognized that, while the words recorded in brief polling interviews are highly valid in predicting elections, they are of indeterminate validity in forecasting how people will respond in situations that are as yet unorganized. The focus of attention of the group is in an advanced state of organization with respect to action when mid-election polls are taken; but remarks about price regulation may have no more significance than showing that the term itself is a negative word to most of the responders. Hence if something is to be done, it may be useful to reselect the validating symbols.

Another difficulty arises from the task of selecting and presenting certain kinds of information in a form deemed useful by policy-makers. Policy-makers are usually poised toward action. They want to choose between clear-cut courses of action. Hence intelligence material must be processed in a way that commends it to decision-makers.[1] Now scientists are accustomed to think in intervariable ("equilibrium") terms and to appraise their data as pertinent or not if they confirm or disconfirm a general proposition that is part of the systematic structure of their science. Hence they are not accustomed to considering the timing of their results in terms of policy objectives. If they find that experimental animals show more scratching and biting behavior when they are put on short rations than when they are cut down in sexual opportunities, they may take it for granted that these results are pertinent to policy. But what policy? Do they expect policy-makers to cut down on sex opportunities rather than rations? If so, when and where? Notice that there may indeed be policy implications; my only point is that the act of processing intelligence material must find an acceptable relationship to the policy-maker's conception of his policy alternatives.

Scientists who are accustomed to long interviews are faced with the problem of cutting their results down to a form that is valuable for policy and yet preserves something of the depth perspective of their data.

From brief polling results we may know that 60 per cent say "Yes," 20 per cent say "No," and 20 per cent are noncommittal in reply to a question. If we look at the replies in the perspective of intensive knowledge, we may rearrange them in many different ways. Ten per cent of those who say "yes" may do so because they want to bring about a negotiated peace; 20 per cent may say "Yes" because they want to block a "peace without victory." But the 10 per cent may own and affect by advertising newspapers that reach millions of people. It is a sterilizing process to limit the description of how people feel and think to an overterse bar chart; yet the busy executive may be impatient of the time it takes to read a set of qualifying riders.

Intensive procedures can be most effectively used when they are guided toward the "sore spots" or the "success spots" revealed by quick, extensive procedures like polling or brief content analysis. Also, intensive procedures can be pointed toward policy problems that can be dealt with at rather long intervals . . . .

We are able to adapt to the needs of ideological intelligence many of the presentation forms developed for limited use in our society. In some ways the best and the most characteristic intelligence report is the prospectus offered to potential investors in new undertakings. The prospectus may rest on a foundation of vast research conducted by production engineers, market analysts, and many other technicians. No matter how elaborate the factual groundwork, the final results are put in clear-cut and inviting synoptic form . . . . Good prospectus writers have successful careers because of the exceptional utility of the function they perform as go-between uniting promoter, technician, and investor.

Documentary reports cannot take the place of personal presentation if full advantage is to be taken of research and planning. Ideological material is less definitive than technical reports, and, if it is

---

[1] Mannheim (II.1, 1948: Part IV) contains a classical discussion.

to be correctly related to policy, the head of intelligence must be a member of the inner policy councils. Only by constant emphasis can policy-makers come to recognize the full degree of their reliance upon certain facts for basic clarification of their task.

The intelligence operation constantly asks for new specifications of objectives. Policy-makers often leave goals phrased in ambiguous language, hence open to misunderstanding. One function of the intelligence branch is to point out any handicapping ambiguousness and to bring about authoritative declarations. Often the goals enunciated by makers of policy are inconsistent or even contradictory; hence the policy branch must often call for new directives at every level of decision. Often, too, authoritative statements are entirely missing in reference to many zones of action; one duty of an intelligence branch is to call attention to these omissions.

When the process of goal discovery had been carried to the most inclusive objective, we come to the key ideals of the state. The specialists on integrating the flow of fact cannot bring about goal clarification unless the need of integrated policy is widely felt. Intelligence specialists who try to force rigorous proclamation of purpose may fail to carry the policy group along with them. During our present period of transition from a business-dominant to a government-dominant state, the relationships between those who formulate authoritative declarations of policy and those who perform the intelligence function will be in a constant state of redefinition. To push ahead too far and too fast will often lead to the rejection of disciplined fact-gathering. And yet failure to keep the need of clarity at the focus of attention of policy-makers is to delay needed adjustments to reality.

[*Editors' Summary of Author's Conclusions*. World War I showed that the legalistic and diplomatic aims of nontotalitarian states were insufficient for policy needs. There is at present a reluctance by influential elements to put the objectives of these states in basic terms of social structures; this arises from deep timidities and a basic pessimism about the prospects of maintaining the character and pattern of our society. The deep distrust of the possibility of any order but one distinguished by total governmentalization of organized activity means that in a sense, Marxist predestinarianism has everywhere triumphed. Not even the meaning of a social order compatible with human dignity secured by a balanced structure has been clarified by our intellectuals. For example, no rules of balance have been specified for a balanced income structure—the condition considered most favorable to a free society. A unifying conception of democratic policy may be discovered in these years of stress; then ideological intelligence will be smoothly articulated with policy. Until then, there can be a persistent, clarifying interplay between intelligence and policy-making.]

ENLIGHTENMENT MODELS

Foreign Policy Making and Administrative Politics

PAUL Y. HAMMOND

Serious literature about foreign policy, when it is not primarily historical, can be classed in three ways.[1] It is either pragmatic, attempting to solve specific problems through a mastery of specific data; or it is what I will call unitary, arguing for comprehensive solutions on the basis of some general vision of the truth; or it is pluralistic, asserting the value of many approaches and denying the certainty of any one.

Of the three, the pragmatic argument is the most satisfactory only because it makes the most modest claim: that it applies to the immediate case only. Despite its specificity, however, it involves criteria which are either dogmatic (i.e., they claim standing as truth) or pluralistic (i.e., they claim validity as a method of pursuing truth when confidence is low that it will ever be captured). The unitary approach has survived remarkably well side by side with scientific skepticism, perhaps owing to the attractions of *raison d'état,* or the appeal of expertise, or simply the grace and charm of writings like those of George Kennan, or the authoritative ring of other postwar realists like Hans Morgenthau and Henry Kissinger. The pluralistic approach is supported by a growing body of serious writing on democratic political processes, but it does not begin to cope with the demands of necessity when confronted by *raison d'état,* or by the postwar realities.

In particular cases, the issue between the unitary and the pluralistic approach may be focused on whether one should seriously rely upon the development and skillful application of a satisfactory set of tools for analyzing and making policy, or on whether the analysis of policy making should be confined predominantly to describing the political process of policy making. This article is an attempt to deal quite explicitly with the relation between the two approaches in a discussion primarily confined to United States foreign policy.

I. THE DIALECTIC OF ADMINISTRATIVE POLITICS

In its fullest conception, the problem of political control in the field of external affairs assumed the general dimensions it now presents in the late nineteenth century—after the Franco-Prussian War, by one reckoning, or after the extension of the suffrage and the rise of the yellow press, by another. At any rate, the problem is composed of elements that can be associated with both reckonings. On the one hand, the enormous possibilities for combining resources in time and space in the prosecution of wars and, equally, the potential consequences of not being able to do so put governments contingently in the hands of their military. On the other hand, the development of mass electorates and the mobilization of a mass

• *World Politics,* Vol. 17, July 1965, pp. 656-671. Reprinted by permission of The RAND Corporation and the author.

[1] Any views expressed in this paper are those of the author. They should not be interpreted as reflecting the views of The RAND Corporation or the official opinion or policy of any of its governmental or private research sponsors.

public opinion in the politically developed states of Western Europe tended to loosen the material and political constraints on the size of national effort in war.

The issue of control thus had to be defined in two ways . . . . First, the question was how to keep the military establishment nonpartisan, yet still sensitive to and flexible about matters involving domestic values . . . . Second, given the mobilization requirements made evident by the Franco-Prussian War and the centralization of authority usually considered essential in military operations, . . . how was it possible to maintain political control over war? Two additional factors are commonly associated with this second control problem—the nature of war itself, and the radical separation of war and policy in certain Western political traditions . . . . They, in turn, posed additional questions: How to control war when it seemed to be so uncontrollable? How to control the actions of those assigned to prosecute war when it seemed essential to the success of their efforts that they be free from controls or restraints? It should be noted that, together, these questions pose the dilemma of strategic efficiency and domestic political control in which authoritarian rationality is pitted against egalitarian pluralism. . . .

The state as actor in foreign relations may be thought of as a political system composed of three sectors: the public governmental, the privileged governmental, and the nongovernmental, or private, sectors. The public government consists primarily of the national legislature, together with the chief executive and his leading political associates or subordinates in the executive branch. The privileged governmental sector is roughly the bureaucracy, or the executive branch beneath the highest political levels. It is called privileged because its ultimate assertion of hierarchical loyalty is in the claim of executive privilege. The boundary between the public and privileged sectors is plain enough where it falls between the legislature and the bureaucracy, because of a convenient constitutional arrangement in the United States and, in some degree, in other modern constitutional governments. But where the boundary segregates executive branch officials from each other, it is, like the distinction between policy and administration, more an analytical convenience than a denotable fact. The private sector consists of a network of political interests that provide a political environment within which the government, public and privileged, functions. Together, the three sectors constitute, in one carefully explicated term, the national governmental process. (Truman, VI, 1951.)

The network of relationships that binds the private sector to the governmental sectors is the instrument of domestic political control. It may be considered to perform three major functions: cognitive, responsive, and aggregative. The cognitive function is to produce, transmit, and evaluate the information which serves as the basis of policy making. The responsive function is to meet the objectives of policy with appropriate actions and programs. The aggregative function is to gain support for courses of action decided upon as government policies.

In this article our attention will be limited as much as possible to the cognitive and responsive functions . . . . To be sure, the distinction between response and aggregation is no more than a point of emphasis. Response deals with what to do, and aggregation with how to gain consent and support for what to do . . . . In politics, however, the two are ultimately integrated.

In democratic political systems—and certainly in the United States—responsiveness to political pressures is a legitimate mode of behavior in many, though not in all, cases. But it is also legitimate for government to respond to its own internally derived standards—to standards of consistency and efficiency, and to the requirements for and the advantages of organized effort. Political responsiveness and operational efficiency, then, form a kind of dialectic, a coexistence in which each imposes control upon the other....

II. EMPIRICAL METHODS IN THE STUDY OF ADMINISTRATION

Some of the problems of analyzing administrative politics lie in the methods used. It may therefore be helpful to begin with a discussion of these methods, even if it is brief and somewhat arbitrary.

Pluralism has been nothing if not fashionable in American political studies. Among other things, it has helped to justify the enlarged bureaucracies and the expanded executive powers—the neo-Hamiltonianism —which were a consequence of the economic and social crises of the interwar period.... More broadly, it provided the basis for the development of what has been called empirical democratic theory. Political pluralism has served not only to tame by explanation the executive and administrative power requirements of a democratic age but also to explicate other political functions associated with the modern democratic state.[1]

In the field of defense policy and politics, Huntington (VI, 1961) published a powerful elaboration of the pluralist argument in *The Common Defense*.... In an earlier work, *The Soldier and the State,* he had attacked administrative pluralism as it applied to civilian control of the military, insisting that only if a clear line of division was maintained between military and civilian functions could control be "objective" and effective, and the military profession be kept professionally intact (Huntington, VI, 1957: 189-192, 260-263).... In *The Common Defense,* on the other hand, he surveyed from several perspectives the development of American military policy since World War II, each time explaining these developments in terms of a bargaining process within the executive branch of the federal government which he characterized as "legislative." According to Huntington, this process cut across, though it did not eliminate, distinctions like those upon which he had depended earlier in his concept of "objective" civilian control of the military.

Huntington's qualified optimism that the system works poses an issue which is fundamental to any appraisal of national security policy. It is the contention that rationality in administrative politics rests upon the same premise that rationality in the outcome of the legislative process does; that an open system of bargaining and debate will produce the most rational policy possible, even though the legislative process can be seen as wholly "political." The question, then, is whether administrative politics is, as Huntington asserts, comparable to legislative politics.

Rationality can be defined broadly according to two standards. One is internal consistency; the other, correspondence. Bureaucracies try to be consistent, but get out of touch with reality. Popular assemblies are by design sensitive to certain elements of the real political world, public perception and opinion, but pay the price of internal consistency. Sometimes they are also more sensitive than the bureaucracies they sponsor to other elements of political reality, such as the political ramifications of nuclear proliferation or the impact of aid programs on foreign business activities. This is so, however, not because they have more competent intelligence facilities. On the contrary, bureaucracies are likely to be superior in their perception of reality to the extent that perception depends upon an organized intelligence operation which gathers and processes information systematically, where-

---

[1] For example, Almond (I, 1950) has provided an enrichment of the systematic concept of public opinion, with particular reference to the potentiality of public opinion for rational behavior despite the notable inadequacies in individual opinions revealed by opinion surveys (i.e., gross inconsistency and a frighteningly meager and inaccurate information base).

as the advantage enjoyed by the popular assembly in collecting and processing information derives from the very lack of routinization and consistency.

We may therefore as a schematic convenience identify legislative bodies with correspondence and executive bodies with internal consistency....

Pluralism, or group political analysis—in the present context they can be taken as the same thing—has many strengths but suffers from three important inadequacies when it is used to analyze the problems of control and efficiency in the modern democratic state. (1) It explains the bureaucracy's cognition of political data found within the domestic political system far better than it does any sensitivity of the bureaucracy to data located outside it. (2) It is often dependent upon perspectives of extreme detachment which limit its utility to participants in the political process. And (3) it is a culture-bound, "shallow" analysis of what are in fact "deep" political phenomena.

Bargaining is only one of several plausible versions of group political dynamics which can be used for analytical purposes, but it is seemingly precise and analytically convenient. It is a model of a single event or of a small cluster of events—a transaction, as it is sometimes termed. Its limitations can be demonstrated, first, by placing it in a larger analytical context (though still one of group political processes) where other explanations of what happened can be shown to account for as much or more data; and, second, by exposing the prerequisites for effective bargaining. In the larger analytical context, aggregative models which describe the building of a majority in terms of an intricate process of mutual self-adjustment do not afford bargaining an explicit role, or possibly any role at all. Explicitness, of course, may not be important. It may be possible to do a great deal of what amounts to bargaining implicitly without any actual negotiations and without an expressed "deal." This leads us to the second limitation.

The more that bargaining is understood in political analysis to depart from the explicitness of a formal negotiation ending with an enforceable contract—the more, that is, that the political phenomena to be interpreted are taken as amounting to informal and implicit bargaining—the more the political analysis involved is dependent upon the existence of a basic political or social order. Bargaining requires a capability to signal and communicate, to discern one's interests and derive means for achieving them, to interact, to predict the behavior of the other party, and possibly to sanction that behavior. Where these capabilities are formal and explicit, patently they are a part of the social and political order. Where they are implicit, they are equally dependent on that order.... The terms of the tacit bargain, as well as the means by which they are reached, should reflect expectations about enforcement which in turn rest on interpretations of the social and political order. However, since the selection and interpretation of the available data will depend upon their conformity to an abstract (if also implicit) mode, it should be expected that similarities among cases, not their variations, will be stressed. Put this way, it should be clear that bargaining analysis can be only the beginning of a political analysis, although it may be a very good beginning indeed.

One effect of concentration on discrete or individual political transactions in bargaining analysis is the emphasis which it gives in turn to lateral political relationships....

In order to comprehend the underlying dimensions of the social phenomena involved it is necessary to probe beneath the formal prescriptions which must persist in the official versions of public and private organizations. But these formal organizations cannot simply be dismissed in political analysis. At the minimum, their existence will affect the structure of social phenomena. Beyond that, in a nontraditional society—one in which the bureaucracy is viewed as an instrument of governing which should be modified whenever necessary—the continued existence in the public bureaucracy of any particular formal arrangement must be taken as largely intentional, and as the consequence of some fairly vigorous and influential convictions about its desirability.

* * * * *

By looking for the evidence that behavior in a public or a private bureaucracy consists of implicit or informal contract-making, one can normally fulfill his expectations readily, but quite possibly to the neglect of phenomena which have organic rather than individualistic analogues. To neglect these is to miss the crucial characterictics of administrative politics, the mixture of authoritarian *and* equalitarian elements, the hierarchy of authority *and* the lateral relationships. It is this hierarchical relationship which empirical political studies have been the least prone to take seriously.

III. ADMINISTRATIVE POLITICS: THE SETTING AS DETERMINANT

Similar political methods will have dissimilar uses and consequences as they are applied in different sets of circumstances. An obvious categorization which will help to explicate the bureaucracy as a political arena in developed constitutional orders is one intended to distinguish the differences in context imposed by the legal order within which bureaucracy works. Legal orders could be listed as extraconstitutional, constitutional, statutory, and administrative. Classes of politics could then be described by variations in the mixture of these four classes of the legal order. Partisan politics, for example, would have a high proportion of extraconstitutionality, a growing but still small element of statutory constraints, some structuring to accord with the constitutional entities whose control is the objective of party activity, and very little constraint by governmental administrative act. . . . Leaving aside the question of whether executive and administrative politics should be regarded as separate classes, let us examine the setting of administrative politics.

What is striking about this setting in comparison with that of legislative and party politics is the prominent role that intention or conscious choice has played in its development. The bureaucracy operates within certain fixed limits which are traditional-conventional and legal-constitutional, but the predominant components of its setting are statutory and administrative—rules provided by act of Congress or by the executive chain of command. It is difficult to characterize the consequences of this mixture. The setting can be, and has been, changed more rapidly and readily than that of partisan politics; yet partisan politics is more flexible than administrative politics, for it operates in a less structured setting. Being more the consequence of recent deliberate actions than is legislative politics, moreover, administrative politics might be regarded as more rational. (This is, of course, an antihistorical standard of rationality. One might argue quite the opposite—that the longer the basic structures which control politics have remained unchanged, the more rational they are, because they have withstood the test of time.) Yet legislative politics coincides more nearly than does administrative politics with at least one model of antihistorical rationality—the marketplace for the free exchange of ideas. What we can say at the very most, then, is that the administrative setting can be and probably is controlled by deliberate act more than are legislative or partisan politics.

Theoretically, it should be possible to rank political acts along a continuum from an extreme one-to-one lateral relationship to an extreme superior-subordinate hierarchical relationship. We could approach the task of analyzing the lateral-hierarchical variation as a distributional-description problem, summarizing our findings with schedules or profiles of executive-branch and legislative-branch phenomena. But it might be very difficult as a practical matter to rank phenomena according to their lateral-hierarchical value. The difficulty would be that each phenomenon occurs within a more general context in which the immediate relationship might have the characteristics, say, of a strongly lateral relationship, while the behavior of each actor would in fact have been strongly influenced by hierarchical pressures not in the foreground of the phenomenon. This multiple effect, for example, has often been the problem in analyzing cabinet-level activities in the United States government. Even when one keeps in mind the primacy of the President in relation to each and every person involved in cabinet and National Security Council deliberations, it is possible to overestimate the lateral quality of cabinet-level discussions. In the American system, the Presidential cabinet is a forum that provides the chief executive with advice which presumably he cannot get as conveniently in any other way. But a President cannot count on his cabinet members' either thinking of or telling him everything he wants to be told in a cabinet meeting. In particular, cabinet members may be more willing to talk to the President in private. . . .

Conceiving of the cabinet as a set of lateral relationships actually depends upon viewing the President as an observer of its deliberations rather than as one who directs its course. When one recognizes that the President has an interest intrinsic to his office, as it were—in who attends a meeting, what the agenda is, what positions are explored or staffed out beforehand, and where the best data and the best expert judgments concerning an agenda item can be obtained—the apparent lateral character of the deliberation begins to yield to its hierarchical elements. In fact, to the extent that the cabinet is a President's cabinet—i.e., to the extent that it deals with issues and interests in *his* terms—it would perhaps be more appropriate to consider it a predominantly hierarchical phenomenon . . . .

Administrative politics takes place in an environment in which it is impossible to neglect either hierarchical or lateral relations. . . . In addition to the openness of a public bureaucracy—particularly one in the American setting, including the competition in means and over ends, the flexibility, the redundancy, the sensitivity to fragmentary public wishes, the skepticism about collective judgments and objectives—there exists something quite the opposite, a commitment to consistency, and hence to inflexibility, to a centralized determination of policy and organizational objectives. . . .

Ultimately, the administrative dialectic can be resolved into a difference about cognition. The ultimate authoritarian position is that the truth (i.e., the correct perception and analysis of relevant conditions) can be known, and that the place it is most likely to be known is at the top, the only place where the cognitive resources of the whole organization can be fully exploited. The ultimate liberal position is that perhaps there is no truth beyond what the individuals in the system perceive, or claim to perceive, and that if any truth is to be uncovered it will be done through individualistic methods in pursuit of individual interests, which implies free and equal discussion. Since the results of even these methods will be highly imperfect, it is a good thing for the organization not to commit itself wholly to any single answer or set of answers.

IV. ADMINISTRATIVE POLITICS AND NATIONAL SECURITY

The administrative politics of national security has its own particular, if not unique, setting. Policy and programs must be responsive to both domestic and foreign political considerations. These two sets of considerations impose somewhat different requirements upon the cognitive and responsive capacities of a government bureaucracy —the privileged government sector. Of the cognitive requirements, the domestic set are the least peculiar. They are met, as they are in other areas of governmental activity, by the networks of political communication and transaction which are indigenous to the domestic political system and which link both the public and privileged government sectors with the non-governmental or private sector of the system.

* * * * *

At one end of these communication links are the sensors and transmitters of the government. As receptors, they may be armed with the power of subpoena, or with the statutory right to know—the right to ask and to require an answer. They may search discriminately for information by means of investigators and researchers, or they may be passive, at least as initial receptors, recording or conveying whatever they encounter in the conduct of their business. What they sense may be data about the substantive problems with which the government is faced—facts about economic conditions, scientific developments, social conditions. Or they may sense views and opinions about issues. Much of the time they will sense a combination of the two —what we might call political information in the form of representations more or less partisan in character which at once provide data, express interests, and convey opinions . . . .

The cognitive requirements of the foreign set of considerations depend in part upon the same networks, though in different proportions. In comparison with the domestic pattern, the mass media probably play a proportionately more important role in providing information about foreign conditions pertinent to American interests. Private interest representation probably plays a smaller role, though by no means a negligible one. The government, on the other hand, takes a proportionately more active and prominent part in the collection and processing of data. The data about the foreign sector are collected and processed chiefly through what is called the intelligence community.

Presumably the government could utilize many of the same methods and at least devote as many—or even more—resources to the collection of data about domestic conditions, although such activities when directed at domestic affairs are always more likely to have discernible partisan uses than do their foreign counterparts . . . .

It is not difficult to draw contrasts in responsive requirements. In the domestic realm, the government is not expected to encounter or respond to situations in which its total physical security capabilities will be challenged, nor does it have to deal with unified aggregates of power units or actors on a sovereign-to-sovereign basis. Both of these situations are precluded by the character of the domestic order, including the monopoly of organized violent means permitted the government. In the external realm, however, the government must be prepared to cope with both situations. In both an obvious advantage is unity, the capability of speaking with one voice and acting in a consistent and coordinated manner as a sovereign state . . . .

This contrast in cognitive and responsive requirements between those originating domestically and those which derive from external conditions suggests why the most commonly used analytical methods of illuminating empirical democratic theory can be inappropriate for analyzing government, even democratic government, in the performance of its national security function. For example, as Stanley Hoffmann (VI, 1963: 11) has pointed out in a criticism of group political analyses, models of political integration simply ignore the fact that the processes involved in political integration can be fostered or suppressed by national governments as an important matter of state policy, and that therefore a major determinant of political integration is the political decision of the states involved.

V. THE ANALYTICAL CHALLENGE

It may well be enough in the pursuit of democratic theory merely to illuminate the political processes of which democratic orders are composed. That is not enough, however, for the development of policy analysis and the methods appropriate to it. A major advance in policy analysis where complicated operational capabilities are involved, such as in defense and foreign aid functions, is in the development and application of operations and systems analysis techniques . . . . These methods are, in effect, a powerful tool for specifying in particular contexts standards of internal consistency. Their uses are limited to the capacities of those who practice them to explicate and quantify policy objectives and operational functions.

One need not approve of every application or outcome of systems and operations analysis in the Defense Department in order to consider the extensive changes brought about there by the incumbent administration an important improvement in the Department's operation . . . . [T]o impose the task of quantification is to force the production and distribution of data organized, correctly or incorrectly, with reference to some purpose. Data of any reliability, organized in this manner, are not to be taken for granted.

The liberal ideal of the marketplace for the free exchange of ideas as the model of social rationality refers to a setting in which it is expected that reason will be articulated and hence will prevail. But articulation is not without costs. If these costs are not offset by expectations of substantial gains to be made from articulation, it is difficult to justify . . . .

When it is working well, operations analysis forces a consideration of issues on specified merits within a specified policy frame of reference and with questions of fact systematically linked to questions of policy. But, like any intellectual or professional discipline or any rational system, it sacrifices comprehensiveness and correspondence for precision and internal consistency. One can, therefore, without contradicting oneself, be enthusiastic about the utilization of operational analysis techniques in the Defense Department for their linking of data, analysis, and choices; be critical of certain applications of them; and be anxious to see the particular constraints of the analytical methods involved pushed back or transcended. Shifts in emphasis along these lines are already discernible in the Defense Department . . . .

Cost effectiveness analysis can be as useful and as limiting in policy analysis as the bargaining mechanism can be in the analysis of group political behavior. It would appear that both are capable of considerable further adaptation, but both need to be better understood in their political context than they now are. The interest of political science in political systems as well as in political transactions encourages the expectation that the narrowness of bargaining analysis will be reduced and possibly overcome. The challenge for policy analysis in the national security sphere, quite apart from the structural questions which it raises, is not only to refine the new, pragmatic "theologies" of operations and systems analysis as disciplines in cognitive consistency, but also to develop broader systematic representations of the context in which they are applied, and to find ways of dealing with political as well as material resources which will strengthen the cognitive correspondence capacities of internally consistent policy making.

Inquiry and Policy: The Relation of Knowledge to Action

MAX F. MILLIKAN

People do research for two reasons: first, because it is interesting, and second because it may be useful. The relations of researchers with men of action are sometimes complicated by the fact that useful knowledge is not always interesting, or interesting knowledge necessarily useful. Thus, although researchers and decision-makers enjoy flirting with each other, if they are to make a serious and congenial marriage both parties must recognize—more than they usually do —the kinds of circumstances in which usefulness and interest coincide.

In the natural sciences a *modus vivendi* has been evolved over the past few generations which, although it does not avoid occasional domestic conflict, at least permits the necessary degree of cooperation on matters of importance. The engineer knows that he needs the natural scientist and has a pretty good idea of how to use him; the natural scientist in turn has learned something about which of his discoveries have action implications, and how these implications can be elaborated usefully for the operator.

In the social sciences, on the other hand, attempts to effect such a union have too frequently resulted in frustration and disillusion. Recently, and especially since World War II, there has been a growing feeling among both operators and social scientists that the growing body of social science knowledge should be applied to the solution of some of the pressing policy problems of our time. The remaining question is that of how it is to be applied. In certain fields this has been done with some success. Economic theory has proved relevant to the problem of controlling economic fluctuations in the more advanced countries. The work of students of the psychology of learning has influenced educational policy....

The contributions of social science to the solution of the great international problems of our time have not been notable. In the United States, at least, this has not been for want of trying. Here, the government has financed a variety of social science research projects designed in one way or another to illuminate foreign policy, and the great American foundations have supported a great deal of work directed to the same end. Yet the results to date have been disappointing to both the operators and the researchers.

The disappointment of those who have commissioned the research shows itself in a number of ways. They feel in the first place that much of what has been done is either useless or irrelevant to the problems they are struggling with. The work is obviously painstaking and thorough, a great deal of material has been surveyed, elaborate classifications have been developed, and a great many facts have been assembled. But there is a frustrated and irritated feeling that, when one has waded through a fat re-

• Daniel Lerner, Ed., *The Human Meaning of the Social Sciences,* New York: World Publishing Company, 1959, pp. 158-180. Reprinted by permission of The World Publishing Company and the author. Copyright by Meridian Books, Inc., 1959.

search report, one is no nearer to the answers he is seeking than when he began. When projects are formulated there seems to be agreement as to the problems to be explored; yet, when the results emerge, the problems the social scientist has been grappling with appear to be quite different from those the operator is interested in . . . .

All this is complicated by the operator's impression that the researcher is playing with complex intellectual machinery for its own sake . . . .

Similarly, and as often, the social science researcher emerges from the experiment angry and resentful at its failure. He probably undertook an applied research assignment with grave misgivings in the first place. There is a tradition in the academic world that to undertake research on behalf of a customer, particularly for pay, is to sell one's soul to the devil. The scientist is apt to have a strong conviction that applied research cannot be "fundamental," that there is something inherently contradictory in the advance of knowledge and the service of practical ends, and that to work for a policy-maker is therefore somehow to prejudice one's professional standing . . . .

The recent history of social science is the history of a struggle on the part of social scientists to make their work more positive and less normative, to eliminate from the analysis of human behavior the influence of the value judgments of the researcher. Undoubtedly the clearer separation of social observation from judgments about social goals has been important to scientific advance. The researcher pressed to work on policy problems is plagued by the fear that this will plunge him back into the confusion between norms and observed reality from which he has been struggling so hard for decades to free himself.

These varied initial doubts are often compounded by the researcher's experience as an applied project proceeds. The researcher may face a growing conviction either that the operator has asked the wrong questions, that the questions are too vaguely or too narrowly formulated, or that as formulated they are incapable of being clearly answered . . . .

In any case, he submits his report only to find that his customer, though he appeared to be most eager to get it, makes little or no use of it. In many cases there is evidence that his reports have not even been carefully read; in many others they seem to have had little or no effect on the operational decisions subsequently taken. Not uncommonly, the researcher concludes in restrospect that his initial doubts about the wisdom of engaging in applied research were fully confirmed, and he withdraws once more into academic isolation.

In this essay I would like to analyze some of the reasons for this state of affairs. In a sense, they can all be described as failures of communication between researchers and policy-makers. But the roots of these failures do not lie merely in the semantic problems associated with the use of different terminology. Rather, they can be traced to a series of misconceptions on the part of both researchers and operators as to the relation of knowledge to action in the field of human affairs. Action specialists seriously misconstrue the kinds of help they can expect to get from social scientists, and social scientists have a variety of misapprehensions as to what the policy-making process involves . . . .

The operators, on the one hand, commit their elementary error in an inductive fallacy —the assumption that the solution of any problem will be advanced by the simple collection of fact. This is easiest to observe in governmental circles, where research is considered as identical with "intelligence" . . . . Roger Hilsman (IV.2, 1956), in his interesting interview study of the views of the role of research and intelligence held by policy-makers in the U. S. government, has thoroughly documented the pervasiveness of the notion among operators that, if only they were supplied with more raw facts of almost any kind, they could make much wiser decisions on the issues that confront them.

The operator who holds this view of the utility of new facts may find himself disenchanted with research on one of two grounds. In the first case, the social scientist may refuse to pander to this taste for new facts and concern himself instead with restructuring the concepts in terms of which previously known facts are to be interpreted. In this event the operator clearly does not get what he originally expected. Furthermore, what he does get fails to persuade him that he expected the wrong thing . . . .

In the second case, the researcher, frequently against his own better judgment, tries to be responsive to this expressed demand for new "factual information" and assembles a handbook containing a large amount of such material. The operator gets what he expected, but finds to his frustration that it gives him very little help in solving his problems. For example, a request for a report on the nature of the leadership of a foreign country may elicit a vast amount of data on the social origins, pattern of incomes, religious beliefs, and past affiliations of all key members of the foreign élite—information that leaves the operator in no better position than before to estimate the probability, for instance, that this élite will be susceptible to Communist blandishments. Indeed, some interesting experimental psychological work has been done by Alex Bavelas and Howard Perlmutter, at the Center for International Studies, which suggests that an individual's capacity for making sound judgment about a complex situation may be seriously impaired by supplying him with a lot of information which he believes should be relevant but whose influence on the situation is not clear to him . . . .

A somewhat different misconception, logically incompatible with that just described but frequently held by the same people, is that the usefulness of social science research can be tested by its ability to predict complex social behavior in some detail. Whereas the obsession with the illuminating power of fact expects too little of social science research, the test of prediction expects too much. Here the analogy with physical science research, instead of being imperfect, is carried too far. In the natural sciences it is reasonable to assign a research team of scientists and engineers the task of designing an instrument that will with fair certainty achieve certain specified physical results . . . .

. . . . Even abstracting from the philosophical question of whether a completely deterministic explanation of human behavior will ever be possible, it is clear that social science has not yet reached the stage where its formal models can often yield even a statistical prediction of a complex social event.

Our best formal models are still partial; they explicitly exclude consideration of some of the factors at work in any actual situation. The relative weight of the factors explicitly analyzed can seldom be measured, and their combined influence seldom computed. Prediction of a sort is, of course, a necessary component of policy-making. Any decision to act must be based upon a judgment that the net consequences of the preferred course of action will be more favorable than those of some alternative. But in social situations such a judgment can seldom be effectively made by "scientific" procedures. If the policy-maker simply desires advice as to what he should do, he had better rely on the intuition of a man of wide experience and demonstrated understanding rather than on the intellectual skills and techniques of the social scientist . . . .

If the contribution of the social scientist to policy is neither the collection of facts nor the making of predictions, what is it? First, we must recognize that every practical judgment is based upon a structure of concepts and assumptions that is largely implicit and poorly understood. One of the functions of science is to make these implicit concepts and assumptions explicit, to test their generality, and to set forth more precisely the circumstances in which they are valid. Thus, although social science cannot often predict, it can make very important contributions to effective prediction. Social science cannot replace intuition and experience, but it can greatly enrich them, clarify them, and make them more general. Each of the social sciences concentrates on the relations between certain limited aspects of human behavior. Social science research on a problem can illuminate the variety of forces at work, can place limits on the range of possible outcomes, can force implicit, partial judgments into explicit form in which they can be systematically examined and their applicability tested, and can explore the internal consistency of a variety of intuitive expectations. Most policy judgments involve an implicit appraisal of resources of motivations, of organizational and administrative possibilities, of political interests, and the like. Economic, psychological, political, and sociological analysis can expose these judgments to systematic scrutiny....

If this picture of how the policy-maker can use social science research is correct, the operator must approach social science research with very different expectations from those he normally has. The operator's normal impulse is to ask for the conclusions of a social science research project and to regard the argument as none of his concern. But the payoff for him will usually be precisely in the argument rather than in the conclusions. The purpose of social science research should be to deepen, broaden, and extend the policy-maker's capacity for judgment—not to provide him with answers....

In one respect particularly the intuitive process may be misleading. A great many contradictory things can, by a skillful impressionistic presentation of a case, be made to appear obvious. There is a reasonable, "commonsense" interpretation of almost every form of individual and social behavior. Whatever regularities a study reports, a number of people are likely to feel that no study was required to reach this "obvious" conclusion. This would be equally likely if the findings of the study were precisely the opposite. When Samuel Stouffer's exhaustive study of the attitudes of the American soldier appeared after the war, it was greeted by widespread lay criticism that its findings were apparent before the work was begun and that the whole enterprise was, accordingly, a waste of time and money. To meet this criticism, Paul Lazarsfeld (VI, 1949) in a review, began by citing a series of soldier attitudes so described as to leave the reader feeling that these were precisely the attitudes any of us would expect. He then went on to say:

"But why, since they are so obvious, is so much money and energy given to establish such findings? Would it not be wiser to take them for granted and proceed directly to a more sophisticated type of analysis? This might be so except for one interesting *point* about the list. *Every one of these statements* is the direct opposite of what actually was found" (p. 380). It is the task of a social science study to determine which of the contradictory but intuitively obvious conclusions about a situation is in fact true and in what circumstances it may be expected to obtain....

An effective marriage of knowledge and action is seriously inhibited in the modern world by an exaggerated emphasis on the virtues of the division of labor. Decision-making and the pursuit of systematic knowledge have come to be regarded as separable activities, and it is supposed to be inefficient for the researcher to concern himself with policy decisions or for the policy-maker to probe too deeply into research techniques. The policy-maker is supposed to recognize what it is he needs to know and to be able to levy a clear requirement on the researcher to supply the missing knowledge. The researcher, using techniques which it is his business and nobody else's to understand, is in turn supposed to answer the questions put to him. In fact, of course, the relations between knowledge and action are infinitely more complex and reciprocal than this image would suggest and cannot be adequately mastered unless each kind of specialist develops an extensive knowledge of the other's mental processes. Indeed, the most important task for both policy-makers and researchers is a better and more communicable definition of the problem to be solved.

* * * * *

The dominant American theory and practice of administration in both government and industry contributes to this excessive division of labor between specialists in action and specialists in knowledge. In government there is a long-standing tradition of sharp separation of research and intelligence from policy-making and execution. The analyst in a research or intelligence organization is virtually prohibited from speculating about policy alternatives or even from intimate intellectual contact with policy makers. Organizational procedures, based on the false premise that the operator knows what it is that he needs from research, call for the formulation on paper of research "requirements" by operating organizations, the vetting of these requirements by various intermediaries, and their ultimate delivery by courier to the research group. This group, in turn, is supposed to "fill" these requirements by its own occult means and to mail the "answers" back to the operators . . . . This procedure virtually forecloses any opportunities for a fruitful attack on the really central problem the joint reformulation of the policy problem by both researcher and operator.

* * * * *

The researcher's conception of the relation between knowledge and action is likewise plagued by a number of false perspectives. Like the operator, the researcher tends to have an exaggerated faith in the division of labor and, derived from this, an idealized image of the policy maker. If the function of the man of action is, by definition, to act, then what he must want is conclusions, not analysis. Here again is an emphasis—this time from the researcher—on the answer rather than on the process of thinking by which the answer is supported. This leads to a research product consisting either of conclusions regarded as obvious by the operator in advance of research or of recommendations which are not persuasive because they are inadequately supported. The situation reflects a tendency on the part of the researcher to underestimate the intellectual content of the policy-making process . . . . Because the policy-maker usually does not articulate in social science terminology his judgments about the variables he is trying to manipulate, the researcher often assumes that the man of action is guided to effective decision-making by some intuitive process beyond the reach of rational argument.

This misconception is frequently associated with another—inconsistent with it—that the operator knows what he wants from research and that his questions are therefore to be taken at face value . . . . [T]ime and again projects are begun with only the most cursory mutual consideration of just how they are expected to be used. The subsequent result is apt to be bitter disenchantment on both sides. Conversely, the most valuable product of many applied research projects considered successful has been a new conception in the mind of the operator of how the problems with which he is confronted are to be defined.

The researcher frequently, although he recognizes the inadequacy of the statement of the problem he has been given, is inhibited by the difficulties of communication from insisting on being provided with a better one. Instead he goes off to his library or his laboratory and makes his independent attempt to describe what he is planning to do in the language of his own discipline.

Here another difficulty arises. His first impulse will be to discard, sometimes without realizing it, those aspects of the problem which do not interest him. He can defend this on the ground that there is no point in his doing research on problems which are inherently not researchable. The higher his standards of scientific research, the narrower will be his selection of problems and the greater the eventual frustration of the customer with the result.

The clash of interest and utility is likely to be most marked in the early stages of a science, which are characterized by a great deal of attention to careful classification, to precise definition, and to the establishment of useful tautologies—that is, to the elaboration of all the logical consequences of a few simple assumptions .... The early stages are therefore likely to consist of the construction of an elaborate intellectual tool whose cutting edge for shaping practical problems is small and weak.

What the researcher may justifiably regard as a major intellectual achievement in bringing order out of chaos may well strike the operator, who is uninterested in the machinery for its own sake, as a scholastic exercise of little relevance. To establish the proposition that business leaders tend to have a high level of achievement motivation, or that caste inhibits social mobility, or that social overhead capital has a high capital-output ratio may be scientifically significant but of little help to the policy-maker who has asked for an estimate of the "vigor" of the private sector in the Turkish economy or of the probability of "mass conflict" in India or of whether China's economic development plan "will work."

* * * * *

Certain other characteristics of the stage in which the social sciences presently find themselves further limit the utility to the policy-maker of much social science research, especially in the analysis of the relations between states. In many countries there is a vast amount of social science research going forward on the structure and characteristics of foreign societies from which the policy-maker feels he should be able to benefit. He finds, however, when he examines this research, that it has a strong static bias ....

From the standpoint of scientific development this bias is thoroughly understandable. Dynamics is always more complicated than statics; rates of change are harder to measure and analyze than states of affairs ....

On the other hand, from a policy point of view the most important characteristic of our times is that societies are changing in almost all their fundamental dimensions at a rate unprecedented in history. All our most crucial international policy problems require an appraisal not of states of affairs but of patterns of evolution. Economic development, newly emergent nationalism, trends in the character of Communist society, the political implications of changing weapons technology—these are all questions which cannot even be posed in other than dynamic terms. If the social scientist is to help the policy-maker deal with these situations at all, he must find ways of introducing process explicitly into both his analytic frameworks and his empirical observations. The social sciences are moving toward the formulation of dynamic theories and their empirical testing, but at this stage realistic dynamic analysis can be undertaken only at considerable cost in rigor and precision.

There is the further difficulty of the requirement, in the analysis of most policy alternatives, that a number of factors lying within the focus of interest of a variety of social science disciplines be considered simultaneously .... The most critical policy issues of our times are those relating to the interaction of complex national states. The international behavior of states, however, is conditioned in important ways by their own internal dynamics. National states, especially the more recently created ones, are not, of course, homogeneous entities possessing a common will but are themselves collections of interacting communities and groups. Thus research on the behavior of larger social units such as nations requires research in turn on the behavior and interactions of smaller units such as provinces, business communities, castes, and even families and individuals. The relation of macro- to micro-studies poses a serious dilemma for applied research. To study intensively all the thousands or millions of micro-units that make up the macro-units is obviously a task beyond the resources of any academic community....

The different social sciences have developed different capabilities for handling different levels of social aggregation. By and large, psychology and anthropology are most confident and most at home in applying a microscope to individuals or small groups. Political science, on the other hand, has traditionally taken as its province the study of national and international institutions and organization. Economics, similarly, has concentrated a good deal of its attention on national aggregates, though it is the one social science discipline that, more than any other, has mastered the problem of integrating the analysis of the behavior of individuals in small economic units with the study of national and international aggregates. But systematic interdisciplinary research is complicated by the fact that each discipline is most at home in the study of a different kind of social unit. We do not yet have even an embryonic science of social change that offers a framework for integrating the kinds of work carried on by different social scientists. We are moving in the right direction. Political science has been increasingly concerning itself with the intensive study of the political behavior of individuals and small groups. Psychologists and anthropologists are more frequently asking, with the help of sociologists, how representative the phenomena revealed by their micro-studies are in the larger populations with which the political scientist deals. But the bridges between micro- and macro-studies need much more strengthening before they will bear the weight policy analysis places on them.

The final problem relates to the scientific respectability of an explicit analysis of values and goals as a subject for scholarly inquiry.... [It is frequently suggested that] the scientist [should] concern himself only with the world as it is, and [should] let the policy-maker or someone else worry about the directions in which we should be trying to push it. The trouble is, of course, that there is an inherent interdependence between the concepts we use to interpret events and those we use to articulate our values.

Three kinds of elements must be appraised in any policy analysis: goals, environment, and instruments. The policy-maker must sort out carefully the various ends the policy is designed to pursue as well as the costs that are acceptable in terms of other values foregone. He must understand the forces at work in the world which are beyond his control and the directions in which they are likely to carry the environment, whatever he does. Finally, he must appraise the capabilities and limitations of the various policy instruments available to him to influence the environment in what he believes to be desirable directions. The social scientist tends to regard his tools as applicable only to the second of these three elements. But rational analysis of the first and third requires at least as great intellectual subtlety and precision. More important, these three elements cannot be examined in isolation, since each can be defined only in terms of the other two. A study of what is happening in Soviet society will be useful to the policy-maker only if it is written in the light both of what he would like to have happen there and of the instruments he can use to affect what happens. Equally, he cannot even state his goals or enumerate his instruments with clarity except in terms of an implicit or explicit theory of Soviet evolution. The division of labor among different analysts according to the distinction between normative and positive propositions cannot be carried very far without depriving social science of most of its operational utility.

* * * * *

I have already suggested my reasons for believing that the policy-maker can broaden his insights and deepen his intuition by learning more of what is going on at the scientific end of the spectrum, if the policy-maker learns to share some of the perspectives and motivations of the social scientist. If he has the intellectual curiosity and persistence to learn some of the uses and limitations of social science tools, he can substantially improve the wisdom of his own practical judgments. But he will be continually disappointed if he expects rigorous scientific inquiry to yield conclusions directly and mechanically applicable to the fuzzy problems he confronts.

What of the social scientist? Does he stand to benefit from wrestling with the insoluble problems of the policy-maker, inextricably enmeshed as they are in a value context, or will such an activity threaten to compromise his scientific integrity and prevent him from making the fundamental contributions to communicable human knowledge which are his central responsibility? Much depends on how he approaches his task, and how self-consciously aware he is of what he is doing. If he confuses the distinction between a wise judgment and a communicable scientific truth he is likely to make little progress toward either. If, however, he devotes the bulk of his attention to his central scientific objective, uncompromisingly maintaining the highest scholarly criteria in these activities, his work can benefit greatly from an occasional concern with the muddy normative problems of policy. The rules of scientific method do not tell us what it is important to work on. The ultimate objective of social science is a scientific explanation of human behavior in all its complexity. An occasional effort to assist the statesman serves to emphasize not only our ignorance of social forces but also the extent to which our knowledge is intuitive and imprecise. The effort to sort it out, to give it precision, and to make it communicable, even where this effort is largely doomed to failure, can enormously stimulate the selection of promising areas for scientific inquiry. The principle of the division of labor is indeed a powerful one, but only if each of the specialists—in this case specialists in action and specialists in knowledge—devotes some effort to trying to understand both intuitively and logically the total human problem to which his specialty can make a contribution.

Bibliographic Appendix

INTRODUCTION

This bibliographic appendix lists references to some 225 books, articles, and reports dealing with organizational and methodological aspects of the relations between social science and public policy. The writings listed have been annotated and organized in an analytic framework that points up major trends, dimensions, and issues in the interactive patterns that have developed between the Federal government and the scholarly community over the last 25 years.

The selective character of the bibliography makes it important to point to some of the limitations of the compilation. First, the bibliography is limited to works dealing with the American experience. Second, it lists only materials that are available to the scholarly community at large. Excluded are the numerous internal governmental reports that deal with our subject matter. Third, the bibliography lists references to congressional materials only when an entire report or hearing has been devoted to the social sciences and government.

For most social scientists the kind of self-examination that is contained in these writings has been a subsidiary interest and has been undertaken only sporadically. The writings that deal with these subject matters are consequently scattered throughout the literature. There are, however, some types of source that are likely to yield more of these writings than others. As a guide to those who may want to stay abreast of developments, we indicate some of the more fertile sources in the periodical literature which are also those that have been searched systematically in the preparation of the bibliography.

The digests reporting on new literature often have sections devoted to applied research activities and matters of professional concern to social scientists. This is the case, for instance, for both *Sociological Abstracts* and *Psychological Abstracts*. The *American Behavioral Scientist's* listing of "New Studies in Behavioral Science and Public Policy" is particularly useful because of its emphasis on policy-oriented research.

In the periodic literature the journals of the professional associations, especially *The American Psychologist* and *The American Sociologist,* are valuable sources. Among the journals devoted to applied social science that have proved to be particularly useful are *The American Behavioral Scientist, Human Organization,* and the recently issued *Journal of Applied Behavioral Science.* Here we should also mention *Public Opinion Quarterly,* which for a long time has been a major forum for social scientists active in government survey and public opinion research. Among journals devoted to international and military problems there are a few in which discussions of policy applications of social science research are likely to be found: *World Politics, Journal of Conflict Resolu-*

tion and the *International Studies Quarterly*. Let us finally mention two other journals aimed at a general science audience that frequently branch out into the area of social science: *Science,* the journal of the American Association for the Advancement of Science, and the *Bulletin of the Atomic Scientists*.

The annotated bibliography consists of five parts: Part I. Social Roles of the Social Sciences: General and Introductory Writings; Part II. Approaches to the Study of the Role of Social Science in Public Policy: Theory and Method; Part III. The Organization of Policy-Oriented Social Science; Part IV. Decision-Making Structures and the Use of Social Science Research; Part V. The Substance of Social Science Knowledge and Policy Concerns in International and Military Affairs.

Part VI lists works that have been cited in our book but fall outside the scope of the main bibliography. Consequently they have been listed separately and have not been annotated.

PART I. SOCIAL ROLES OF THE SOCIAL SCIENCES: GENERAL AND INTRODUCTORY WRITINGS

The first part lists works examining the overall nature and content of social science and its roles in society. These include, but are not limited to, considerations of the role of social science in public policy. In most cases the content of these writings cuts across two or more subsequent parts or sections.

Also included are writings by social scientists who at different times during the past two and a half decades have attempted programmatic formulations of the social and political roles of social science. Among the works that have had a considerable impact on past and present discussions of how social science knowledge can be brought to bear on the problems of the time are anthologies, such as Lerner and Lasswell's *The Policy Sciences: Recent Developments in Scope and Method* and Linton's *The Science of Man in the World Crisis,* and books, such as Lynd's *Knowledge for What?* and Leighton's *Human Relations in a Changing World.*

Almond, Gabriel A. *The American People and Foreign Policy.* New York: Harcourt, Brace & World, 1950. 269 pp. In this pioneering study of the social basis of American foreign policy social scientists receive attention as a particular interest group. Their shortcomings in this role are attributed to their lack of political bargaining power, their inability to give usable advice, and the absence of channels through which they can influence public opinion.

Archibald, Kathleen. "The Utilization of Social Research and Policy Analysis." Unpublished Ph.D. dissertation, Washington University, 1968. 456 pp. Based in part on the existing literature, in part on interviews with government officials and policy-oriented scholars, this thesis discusses alternative role orientations of policy-oriented social scientists with particular reference to international security. The three alternative orientations to the applied role are labelled the *academic,* the *clinical,* and the *strategic.* Utilization of social science in policy formulation is regarded as a relatively unstructured exchange process between members of different social systems. The historical and institutional contexts of social research and policy analysis are set forth in two appendices entitled "Federal Interest and Investment in Social Science" and "Social Science and International Security."

The first appendix was reprinted in Research and Technical Programs Subcommittee, Committee on Government Operations, U. S. House of Representatives. *The Use of Social Research in Federal Domestic Programs, Part I.* 90th Cong., 1st Sess., 314-340 (1967).

Bennis, Warren G., et al. (Eds.). *The Planning of Change: Readings in the Applied Behavioral Sciences.* New York: Holt, Rinehart, and Winston, 1961. 781 pp. "The influence of Kurt Lewin's pioneering studies of planned social change is evident throughout this volume." The purpose of the book is to bring together "some of the best current conceptualizations of different aspects of application and change process and to tie these contributions together with extensive critical and theoretical introductions."

Engler, Robert. Review of *Knowledge for What? The Place of Social Science in American Culture,* by Robert S. Lynd, *Washington Post,* Book Section, 14-15 (April 11, 1965). "Robert Lynd wanted the social scientist to be the critic of the absurd, not its high priest. In other words, to be relevant to the young and the living, to see the present as history." Engler's major criticism is that

Lynd's appraisals and challenges may have been too harsh.

Gilpin, Robert, and Wright, Christopher (Eds.). *Scientists and National Policy-Making.* New York: Columbia University Press, 1964. 408 pp. Among these essays prepared for the Council for Atomic Age Studies at Columbia University are selections on national science policy as well as on the political involvements of scientists—called here "The Apolitical Elite" by Robert Wood. Includes "Scientists, Foreign Policy and Politics" by Warner R. Schilling, "Strategy and Natural Scientists" by Alfred Wohlstetter, and "The Scientific Strategists" by Bernard Brodie.

Glock, Charles Y., et al. *Case Studies in Bringing Behavioral Science into Use.* Stanford, Calif.: Institute for Communication Research, Stanford University, 1961. 135 pp. A series of case studies of the utilization of social science research in civilian and military agencies and departments. See particularly Glock's introductory article, "Applied Social Science Research: Some Conditions Affecting its Utilization," and George W. Croker, "Some Principles Regarding the Utilization of Social Science Research within the Military."

Gouldner, Alvin W., and Miller, S. M. (Eds.). *Applied Sociology: Opportunities and Problems.* New York: The Free Press, 1965. 466 pp. A collection of papers dealing with such aspects of applied social science as the relationship between clients and practitioners, the interaction of applied and general sociology, and that of applied sociology and public policy.

Hauser, Philip M. "Are the Social Sciences Ready?" *American Sociological Review,* 2, 379-384 (August 1946). The author stresses the urgent need for strengthening research in the social sciences to avert danger of future war. He finds that the "failure of society to utilize the knowledge we have gained is in itself a subject for social science research" and suggests that the situation would be ameliorated if the concept of "social engineering" was clarified.

Herring, Pendleton, et al. *Research for Public Policy: Brookings Dedication Lectures.* Washington: Brookings Institution, 1961. 126 pp. Contains three lectures and accompanying panel discussions given at the dedication ceremonies for the Brookings Institution's new Center for Advanced Study in November 1960. The purpose of the lectures was "a brief stock-taking of where we are in the social sciences, and in their application to public problems." The lectures were given by Pendleton Herring, Philip Moseley, and Charles J. Hitch, to name only a few.

Horowitz, Irving Louis (Ed.). *The New Sociology.* New York: Oxford University Press, 1964. 512 pp. A series of essays organized for a double purpose: first, as studies in sociology and social theory, and second, as a tribute to C Wright Mills. Some sample titles are: "C. Wright Mills: Social Conscience and Social Values," and "Social Science and Value: A Study in Interrelations."

Kecskemeti, Paul. "The 'Policy Sciences': Aspiration and Outlook," *World Politics,* 4, 520-535 (July 1952). Review of Daniel Lerner and Harold D. Lasswell (Eds.). *The Policy Sciences: Recent Developments in Scope and Method,* Stanford, Calif.: Stanford University Press, 1951. 344 pp. The author finds "that a fruitful application of scientific knowledge to problems of policy is not possible if the separation between the 'expert' and the 'practical man' remains complete. . . . When science is to be applied to 'policy,' the practical man must 'know' something and the expert must desire and value something. The gap between the unenlightened 'wish' and the goal-neutral 'information' must be filled."

Lasswell, Harold D. *The Future of Political Science.* New York: Prentice Hall, 1963. 256 pp. Lasswell assesses the adequacy of political science as a tool for problem-solving in Federal, State, and local governmental bodies. The frame of reference is his seven functions or stages of decision process.

Lazarsfeld, Paul, Sewell, William, and Wilensky, Harold (Eds.). *The Uses of Sociology.* New York: Basic Books, Inc., 1967. 901 pp. The origin of this book was the American Sociological Association Annual Meeting in 1962 which was devoted to the topic "The Uses of Sociology." Contains papers by more than 40 present-day sociologists on sociology's different social purposes and different institutional contexts. The introduction by Lazarsfeld suggests typologies for the problems toward which sociology is applied and the roles of applied sociologists.

Leighton, Alexander H. *Human Relations in a Changing World: Observations on the Use of the Social Sciences.* New York: E. P. Dutton and Co., 1949. 354 pp. Based upon a "particular experience in applying some of the principles and methods of social science, especially cultural anthropology, sociology, and psychiatry, to the war-time analysis of Japanese morale." The author's wartime service in the Office of War Information, Foreign Morale Analysis Division, provides a point of reference for his discussion of the use of social science research "in the service of peace."

Lerner, Daniel (Ed.). *The Human Meaning of the Social Sciences*. New York: Meridian Books, Inc., 1959. 317 pp. Based on a symposium organized by the French journal *Esprit*, this anthology discusses the values, methods, and uses of social science. Among the contributors are Margaret Mead, Harold Lasswell, and Edward Shils. Although they deal with the American experience, the essays were written for a European audience.

Lerner, Daniel, and Lasswell, Harold D. (Eds.). *The Policy Sciences: Recent Developments in Scope and Method*. Stanford, Calif.: Stanford University Press, 1951. 344 pp. This collection of symposium papers launches the "policy sciences" as a new branch of applied social science. Noted social scientists, among them Mead, Shils, Speier, and Merton, review the research procedures which have been developed within these sciences and their application to policy formation. Harold Lasswell gives the historical development of the "policy sciences."

Likert, Rensis. "Behavioral Research: A Guide for Effective Action," in *Some Applications of Behavioral Research*. Rensis Likert and Samuel P. Hayes, Jr. (Eds.). Paris: UNESCO, 11-43 (1957). The Director of the University of Michigan Survey Research Center discusses the applicability of behavioral research to a wide range of problems confronting public and private organizations.

Likert, Rensis, and Lippitt, Ronald. "The Utilization of Social Science," in *Research Methods in the Behavioral Sciences*. Leon Festinger and Daniel Katz (Eds.). New York: The Dryden Press, 581-646 (1953). The book pays systematic attention to major types of research settings. Likert's and Lippitt's chapter focuses on ways in which citizens can use the resources of social psychology to improve policy making and program planning.

Linton, Ralph (Ed.). *The Science of Man in the World Crisis*. New York: Columbia University Press, 1945. 532 pp. This anthology contains articles by many specialists in the field of anthropology on the basic concepts applicable to the comparative study of culture. The book is an attempt to involve the "science of man" in planning the post-war world by making its findings available to laymen and representatives of other disciplines.

Lynd, Robert S. *Knowledge for What? The Place of Social Science in American Culture*. Princeton, N.J.: Princeton University Press, 1948. 268 pp. These lectures, presented at Princeton University in 1938 and later made into a book, combine a critique of social science scope and method with a discussion of the role of the social sciences in American culture. It is a plea for improving the tools of the social sciences and for using them in dealing with the problems of the time.

Lynn, Kenneth S., et al. (Eds.). *The Professions in America*. Boston: Beacon Press, 1967. 273 pp. This *Daedalus* symposium includes a specific paper on the scientific professions (by John J. Beer and W. David Lewis) and places this group within a common treatment of several different professions, which is especially useful.

Merton, Robert K. "The Role of Applied Social Science in the Formation of Policy: A Research Memorandum," *Philosophy of Science*, 16, 161-181 (July 1949). A contribution to the *Philosophy of Science* Symposium on "Applied Social Research in Policy Formation," this memorandum is a plea for more extensive analysis of the role of applied social research in policy. Provides a catalog of the contexts (organizational situational, etc.) in which applied social research is conducted and utilized and the function of research as perceived by social scientists and policy makers. The discussion of these variables includes a critical examination of the status and potentialities of applied social science.

Mills, C. Wright. *The Sociological Imagination*. New York: Oxford University Press, 1959. 234 pp. "The sociological imagination enables us to grasp history and biography and the relations between the two within society." Mills' aim is to define the meaning of the social sciences for the cultural tasks of the time and to specify the kinds of effort that lie behind the development of the sociological imagination.

Myrdal, Gunnar. *Value in Social Theory: A Selection of Essays on Methodology*. Paul Streeten (Ed.). New York: Harper, 1958. 269 pp. This selection of essays contains the address by Myrdal given at the British Sociological Association conference in 1953. It is published under the title "The Relation between Social Theory and Social Policy." Included are excerpts from *An American Dilemma* concerning the role of values in empirical analysis.

Shils, Edward A. "The Calling of Sociology," in *Theories of Society: Foundations of Modern Sociological Theory*. Vol. 2. Talcott Parsons, et al. (Eds.). New York: Free Press of Glencoe, Inc., 1405-1448 (1961). Traces the reasons for the gradual acceptance of sociologists into the intellectual community by showing such influences as the German university and the development of psychoanalytic thought. Deals with a definition of the substance of sociology, its methods and aims, as well as the relation of the social scientist to policy making.

Young, Donald. "Limiting Factors in the Development of the Social Sciences," *Proceedings of the American Psychological Society*, 92, 325-335 (November 1948). In a printed version of a paper read at a "Symposium on Research Frontiers in Human Relations," the Director of the Russell Sage Foundation lists four conditions limiting the development of the social sciences. Among these are: a lack of organization in the distribution of financial support, and a confusion of the functions of social engineering and social research.

PART II. APPROACHES TO THE STUDY OF THE ROLE OF SOCIAL SCIENCE IN PUBLIC POLICY: THEORY AND METHOD

The writings listed in Part II represent several different strands of theoretical and methodological thought, each of which in its own manner, contributes to the development of a theoretical framework for the study of the role of social science in public policy, as exemplified by works in the following three subsections:

1. Sociology of Knowledge, Sociology of Science, and Sociology of Social Science. Salient characteristics of each of these "sociologies of . . ." were discussed in the Editors' Introduction. This section includes representative materials taken from each subfield with special emphasis on writings providing overviews or syntheses of developments in these fields (e.g. Merton, 1945; Kaplan, 1964; and Storer, 1966).

2. The Value-Contexts of Policy-Oriented Social Science. The problem of how the use of social science research for specific political and social ends can be reconciled with the requirement that scientific inquiry be conducted in a spirit of "value neutrality" is a long-standing concern among social scientists. In this section we have attempted to broaden such discussions by including works which examine the social and political ideas influencing American social scientists and the ideological climate in which a policy-oriented social science has attempted to take root.

3. Theories of Decision-Making and Bureaucracy. Theories of decision-making in public organizations contribute to the study of the role of social science in public policy in the following important ways: (a) examination of the intellectual and other processes by which decisions are made helps clarify the intelligence and information needs of decision-makers; (b) study of the contexts—organizational, situational, and philosophic—affecting decision-making procedures and choices provides insights into conditions affecting the use of scientific knowledge; (c) models of decision-making systems (governmental, Congressional, Executive, etc.) enable us to locate the points where social scientists have gained or may gain access to the system.

II.1 SOCIOLOGY OF KNOWLEDGE, SOCIOLOGY OF SCIENCE, AND SOCIOLOGY OF SOCIAL SCIENCE

Barber, Bernard. *Science and the Social Order.* New York: Free Press, 1952. 288 pp. An attempt to provide a theoretically systematic and factually comprehensive account of the sociology of science. In the final chapter entitled "The Nature and Prospects of the Social Sciences," the author argues that the natural and social sciences are essentially the same in principle, but that they are at significantly different stages of development and acceptance.

Barber, Bernard, and Hirsch, Walter (Eds.). *The*

Sociology of Science. New York: Free Press, 1962. 662 pp. A collection of writings dealing with science as a social phenomenon—its social character, its sociohistorical development, its patterns of organization, the social images of science, social influences on the processes of discovery, and the social responsibilities of science.

Barton, Allen. "The Sociology of Reading Research," *Teachers College Record,* 63, 94-101 (November 1961). The field of reading research is depicted as a social system in which different status groups and institutions interact. "It is the interaction among these many status groups which ultimately determines what research is done, how it is interpreted to administrators and teachers, . . . and how much is applied by the classroom teachers."

Ben-David, Joseph, and Zloczower, Awraham. "Universities and Academic Systems in Modern Societies," *European Journal of Sociology,* 3, No. 1, 45-84 (1962). Examines relationships of universities to the political and social structures of the countries of Western and Central Europe as they affected the organization and functions of academic institutions and conceptions of the roles of science and the university. Major attention is given to the development of the modern university in Germany, to class higher education in the United Kingdom, and to the influence of these conceptions on the large-scale academic enterprise in the United States.

Biderman, Albert D. "Social Indicators and Goals," in *Social Indicators.* Raymond A. Bauer (Ed.). Cambridge, Mass.: MIT Press, 68-153 (1966). This paper recommends "the application of the perspectives of the sociology of knowledge to the evaluation of the adequacy of social indicators for assessing and directing the social consequences of large-scale programs, such as the space effort." Includes analysis of the use of quantitative data in State of the Union Messages.

Bramson, Leon. *The Political Context of Sociology.* Princeton, N.J.: Princeton University Press, 1961. 164 pp. A treatment of the influence of social and political theories on sociology, this book centers on the concepts of the mass and mass society and shows how these concepts were received by American sociologists functioning within a liberal milieu. It can be viewed as a case-study of the influence of a social and political milieu on presuppositions of theory and research.

Coser, Lewis. *Men of Ideas: A Sociologist's View.* New York: The Free Press, 1965. 374 pp. A study of the background and emergence of the modern intellectual. Part I deals with the institutions that have nurtured the intellectual vocation since the eighteenth century. Part II explores relations between men of power and men of ideas. Part III treats American conditions today, scientific institutions, the academy, and intellectuals in Washington.

Gerver, Israel, and Bensman, Joseph. "Towards a Sociology of Expertness," *Social Forces,* 32, 226-235 (March 1954). Expertness as a social phenomenon is discussed from different aspects; the relation of experts to social institutions, criteria for judging expertness, perspectives of expertness, and the career mobility of the expert.

Harter, Carl L. "The Power Roles of Intellectuals: An Introductory Statement," *Sociology and Social Research,* 48, 176-186 (January 1964). The role played by intellectuals in the power structure of society is discussed and an assessment is made as to whether or not the expertise of intellectuals enables them to play an important role in influencing public opinion, and if so, how they accomplish this task.

Hinkle, Roscoe C., and Hinkle, Gisela J. *The Development of Modern Sociology.* New York: Random House, 1954. 74 pp. The authors trace the growth of American sociology during three discernible stages: the period of the pioneers in the nineteenth and early twentieth centuries, the emphasis on empirical research and fact finding in the 1920's and early 1930's, and the merging of theory, research, and application during and after World War II.

Kaplan, Norman. "Sociology of Science," in *Handbook of Modern Sociology.* Robert E. L. Faris (Ed.). Chicago, Ill.: Rand McNally and Co., 852-881 (1964). A review of developments in the sociology of science since early 1950. Contains extensive references to empirical research concerning the communications system in science, selection and recruitment of scientists, research organization, and the advisory roles of scientists in government.

Kecskemeti, Paul. *Sociological Aspects of the Information Process.* Santa Monica, Calif.: The RAND Corp., 1952. 32 pp. An attempt to formulate a theory of a particular aspect of the "sociology of knowledge," the sociological determinants of knowledge defined as *beliefs*. Key roles in the transmission and valuation of knowledge are identified and related to postulates and hypotheses regarding the properties of "belief networks" in various societies.

Kelly, George. "The Expert as Historical Actor," *Daedalus*, 92, 529-548 (Summer 1963). A consideration of the expert as policy counselor. Kelly discusses the expert's historical role in the construction of knowledge systems, his collaboration with the state in crisis periods, his mediation between the systems of knowledge and the systems of power, and his right to trespass in politics.

Kuhn, Thomas S. *The Structure of Scientific Revolutions*. International Encyclopedia of Unified Science, Vol. II, No. 2. Chicago, Ill.: University of Chicago Press, 1962. 172 pp. The concept of "normal science," that is, the paradigms of scientific practice consensually accepted at a particular time, is central to this essay's propositions regarding the sociology and social psychology of scientists. The author—a scientifically trained historian of science—concentrates on the inner dynamics of the scientific institution rather than its relation to other institutions as he explains the progress of science through transformations of the scientific community's conceptions of its legitimate problems and standards.

Lasswell, Harold D. "Attention Structure and Social Structure," in *The Communication of Ideas*. Lyman Bryson (Ed.). New York: Harper and Brothers, 243-276 (1948). One of 16 articles of a symposium on different aspects of communication, Lasswell's discussion concentrates upon the interconnections between social structure and frame of attention. He points to the reasons behind efforts to control knowledge and the discrepancies between the elite's picture and what the public at large sees and concludes that "the structure of attention in world politics conforms to the general pattern of power."

Mannheim, Karl. *Man and Society in an Age of Reconstruction*. New York: Harcourt, Brace & World, 1948. 469 pp. "The strand in *Man and Society* which links it with the author's previously translated work is the conception that contemporary changes include the spheres of thought as well as the social, political, and economic worlds. . . . It formulates live problems answerable by observation and analysis out of abstract 'issues' and constructs methodological controls by not merely thinking of the objects of study, but by also forming clear concepts of our ways of thinking about them." [From a review by C. Wright Mills in *American Sociological Review*, 5, 965-969 (October 1940).]

Mannheim, Karl. *Ideology and Utopia*. New York: Harcourt, Brace & World, 1951. 318 pp. "Despite the vast number of specialized accounts of social institutions, the primary function of which centres around the intellectual activities in society, no adequate theoretical treatment of the social organization of intellectual life exists. . . . In *Ideology and Utopia*, Professor Mannheim presents not merely the outlines of a new discipline . . . but also offers a much needed clarification of some of the major moral issues of to-day. . . ." [From Preface by Louis Wirth.]

Mannheim, Karl. *Essays on the Sociology of Knowledge*. New York: Oxford University Press, 1952. 327 pp. This collection, with an introduction by Paul Kecskemeti, contains six essays written by Mannheim during the early part of his academic career in Germany. General, methodological principles of Mannheim's "sociology of knowledge" are discussed.

Merton, Robert K. Review of *The Social Role of the Man of Knowledge*, by Florian Znaniecki, *American Sociological Review*, 6, 111-115 (February 1941). "Rich store of hypotheses which often derive from Znaniecki's earlier work, and so have a measure of empirical confirmation at the outset . . . thus is a prospectus which no future student dare neglect; it is a promise of things to come which is in part its own fulfillment."

Merton, Robert K. "The Sociology of Knowledge," in *Twentieth Century Sociology*. Georges Gurvitch and Wilbert E. Moore (Eds.). New York: The Philosophical Library, Inc., 399-405 (1945). Merton is not concerned here with historical and intellectual origins, but with the question of the basis of contemporary American interest in the sociology of knowledge. He calls his scheme of analysis a "Paradigm for the Sociology of Knowledge."

Merton, Robert K. *Social Theory and Social Structure*. Glencoe, Ill.: The Free Press, 1957. 645 pp. Part III "The Sociology of Knowledge and Mass Communications" contains a discussion of "Karl Mannheim and the Sociology of Knowledge" which places Mannheim in the perspective of his intellectual predecessors. Part IV contains "Studies in the Sociology of Science." Also included is the essay, "The Role of the Intellectual in Public Bureaucracy."

Mills, C. Wright. "The Powerless People: the Role of the Intellectual in Society," *Politics*, 1, 68-72 (April 1944). It is Mills' thesis that because the "worlds of mass-art and mass-thought are increasingly geared to the demands of politics . . . it is in politics that intellectual solidarity and effort must be centered." The intellectual must, for the sake of objectivity, remain sufficiently detached from society, and at the same time become involved enough to feel responsibility to it.

Schatzman, Leonard, and Strauss, Anselm. "A Sociology of Psychiatry: A Perspective and Some Organizing Foci." *Social Problems*, 14, 3-15 (Summer 1966). Several sociological models are suggested for viewing the field of psychiatry. In setting up these models, the authors draw their knowledge from the study of professions and professional practices, of social movements, and of institutional forms in the field of mental health.

Schelting, Alexander von. Review of *Ideologie und Utopie*, by Karl Mannheim, *American Sociological Review*, 1, 664-674 (August 1936). Review is a critique from the point of view of traditional epistemology.

Storer, Norman W. *The Social System of Science.* New York: Holt, Rinehart, and Winston, 1966. 180 pp. An attempt to develop a theory of the social organization of science based upon a general model of "social systems," their basic characteristics and dynamics. Certain basic parallels between the "social system" of science and other social systems within society are indicated.

Wilson, Logan. *The Academic Man.* New York: Oxford University Press, 1942. 248 pp. A work designed to provide an objective basis for understanding professional life as it exists within the social organization of the contemporary American university. The book examines the various levels of the academic hierarchy, the problems of status —status evaluation, socio-economic status, and professional status—and concludes with a discussion of the social processes and functions found in academic endeavor.

Wirth, Louis, "American Sociology, 1915-1947," in *The American Journal of Sociology, Index to Volumes I-LII, 1895-1947*. Chicago, Ill.: The University of Chicago Press, 273-281 (n.d.). Wirth finds that the pages of the *American Journal of Sociology* "reflect fairly faithfully . . . how, in the course of 32 years, the transformation of sociology from a more or less undifferentiated body of ideas into a set of highly specialized interests has been accomplished."

Znaniecki, Florian. *The Social Role of the Man of Knowledge.* New York: Columbia University Press, 1940. 212 pp. Classical work in the "sociology of knowledge" concerned with what is meant by "systems" of knowledge. Are the systems of knowledge which scientists build and their methods of building them influenced by the social patterns with which scientists are expected to conform . . . ?"

II.2 THE VALUE-CONTEXTS OF POLICY-ORIENTED SOCIAL SCIENCE

Bell, Daniel. *The End of Ideology: On the Exhaustion of Political Ideas in the Fifties.* New York: Collier Books, 1961. 474 pp. These essays deal with the social changes in America in the 1950's. The author's interest lies in "social description and explanation" rather than in the testing of hypotheses. "It is sociology as a 'perspective' as a way of being sophisticated about the world."

Benne, Kenneth D., and Swanson, G. E. (Issue Eds.). "Values and the Social Scientist," *The Journal of Social Issues*, 6 (1950). 82 pp. (Whole issue.) A symposium organized around a paper by George Geiger with commentaries by economists, psychologists, philosophers, and a theologian. Bruce Raup's "Choice and Decision in Social Intelligence" and Ronald Lippitt's "Action-Research and the Values of the Social Scientist" are particularly relevant.

Easton, David. "Harold Lasswell: Policy Scientist for a Democratic Society," *Journal of Politics*, 12, 450-477 (August 1950). "In the writings of Harold Lasswell there is adumbrated the most extreme claim that social science can make. The suggestion appears that to convert political science to a policy science, a discipline contributing to the solution of social problems, new referential principles are required; there appears in embryo the further claim that even the goals upon which social policy must be based can be established with the procedures of a fully developed science of man."

Gerth, H. H., and Mills, C. Wright (Eds.). *From Max Weber: Essays in Sociology.* New

York: Oxford University Press, 1946. 490 pp. Of particular interest here are the two essays "Politics as a Vocation" and "Science as a Vocation."

Kelman, Herbert C. "The Social Consequences of Social Research: A New Social Issue," *The Journal of Social Issues*, 21, 21-40 (July 1965). In this presidential address, Kelman discusses the role of social science in relation to the forces that work toward the dehumanization of the present society. He expresses concern "that the products, procedures, and orientations of social research inherently reflect these forces in the sense that they treat man as an object rather than as an active, choosing, responsible agent." This stems in part from the manipulative orientation of much social research; in part from the invasion of privacy, as well as the elements of deception that are inherent in some types of research procedures.

Lane, Robert E. "The Decline of Politics and Ideology in a Knowledgeable Society," *American Sociological Review*, 31, 649-662 (October 1966). The growing and changing role of knowledge in contemporary society, Lane argues, leads to the increased application of scientific criteria for policy determination at the expense of short-term political criteria and ideological thinking.

Lasswell, Harold D. "The Garrison State," *American Journal of Sociology*, 48, 455-468 (January 1941). The aim of Lasswell's article is to consider the possibility that we are moving toward a world of "garrison states," in which specialists on violence are the most powerful group in society. Presented as a developmental construct, it is not a "dogmatic forecast," but a picture of the probable. The aim is to sensitize the specialist to impending events, and to aid in the timing of scientific work.

Reprinted in Leon Bramson and George W. Goethals (Eds.). *War*. New York: Basic Books, Inc., 309–319 (1964).

Lasswell, Harold D. *National Security and Individual Freedom*. New York: McGraw-Hill, 1950. 259 pp. Lasswell discusses the problem of maintaining a balance between national security and individual freedom in a time of continuing crises of national defense. He deals directly with the contribution of scientists and scholars and urges them to infuse their knowledge into the decison-making structure.

Lasswell, Harold D. "The Political Science of Science: An Inquiry into the Possible Reconciliation of Mastery and Freedom," *The American Political Science Review*, 50, 961-979 (December 1956). Presidential address delivered at the annual meeting of the American Political Science Association in Washington, D.C., 1956. A discussion of why political scientists have failed to foresee and comprehend wartime and postwar breakthroughs in science and technology, especially the development of atomic and nuclear energy.

Lasswell, Harold D. "The Garrison-State Hypothesis Today," in *Changing Patterns of Military Politics*. Samuel Huntington (Ed.). New York: The Free Press of Glencoe, Inc., 51-70 (1962). The object of this essay is to consider the significance of the garrison-state hypothesis, formulated about 25 years ago, "in the light of scholarship and the flow of history to date." Lasswell concludes that the master challenge of modern politics is "to civilianize a garrisoning world, thereby cultivating the conditions for its eventual dissolution."

Opler, Morris E. "Social Science and Democratic Policy," *Applied Anthropology*, 4, 11-15 (Summer 1945). The author assesses some of the reactions and obstacles that social scientists face in attempting to apply their techniques and ideas "to the problems of contemporary America."

Riesman, David. *Individualism Reconsidered*. Glencoe, Ill.: The Free Press, 1954. 529 pp. A series of essays by a noted sociologist which focuses upon such subjects as individualism, the intellectual's role, and the importance of values in society.

Shils, Edward A. *The Torment of Secrecy: The Background and Consequences of American Security Policies*. Glencoe, Ill.: The Free Press, 1956. 238 pp. Shils points to the exaggeration and distortion of the loyalty and security problem which comes about as a result of the clash between events of the real world and certain traditional fantasies and passions. He seeks to analyze "some features of the role of secrecy in modern society and its interplay with privacy and publicity."

"The Freedoms and Responsibilities of Social Scientists," *Social Problems*, 1, 77-102 (January 1954). Collected under this heading are: (a) a revised version of the panel discussion, *Challenges to the Freedom of Sociologists* held at the annual meeting of the Society for the Study of Social Problems, Berkeley,

1953; and (b) articles contributed by sociologists, among them Arnold Rose.

Weber, Max. *The Methodology of the Social Sciences.* Edward A. Shils and Henry A. Finch (Eds. & Trans.). Glencoe, Ill.: The Free Press, 1949. 188 pp. Methodological essays written in the years between 1903 and 1917. Of particular interest here is "The Meaning of 'Ethical Neutrality' in Sociology and Economics" which was directed toward university social scientists who made assertions about the right ends of policy in the name of their scientific or scholarly disciplines. It was intended to clarify the extent to which statements about policy could be based on scientific knowledge.

Wooton, Barbara. "The Long Term Impact of the Social Sciences on Democratic Political Practice," *Confluence,* 3, 16-28 (March 1954). A discussion of the effect of the activities of social science upon democratic political institutions. Points to the insecurity of the foundations of our political life and the implication of the spread of scientific method. New breakthroughs in the science of administration necessitate a clarification and redefinition of the boundary between expert and amateur.

II.3 THEORIES OF DECISION-MAKING AND BUREAUCRACY

Braybrooke, David, and Lindblom, Charles E. *A Strategy of Decision: Policy Evaluation as a Social Process.* New York: The Free Press of Glencoe, Inc., 1963. 268 pp. A collaborative effort by a professor of economics (Lindblom) and a professor of philosophy (Braybrooke), this book discusses discrepancies between decision-making theory and decision-makers' actual practices.

Bryson, Lyman. "Notes on a Theory of Advice," *Political Science Quarterly,* 66, 321-339 (September 1951). An analysis of the effect of rational, objective information on the decision-making process and the problems involved in trying to put knowledge at the service of power.

    Reprinted in Nelson W. Polsby et al. (Eds.). *Politics and Social Life: An Introduction to Political Behavior.* Boston, Mass.: Houghton Mifflin Co., 93-106 (1963).

Deutsch, Karl. *The Nerves of Government.* New York: The Free Press of Glencoe, Inc., 1963, 316 pp. Utilizes communications theory to build an "information flow" model of policy making. Emphasizes the need of the decision-maker for "creative intelligence" concerning the needs of the public.

Lasswell, Harold D. *The Decision Process: Seven Categories of Functional Analysis.* College Park, Md.: Bureau of Governmental Research, College of Business and Public Administration, University of Maryland, 1956. 23 pp. In this printed version of a lecture given at the University of Maryland, the intelligence function is presented as one among seven categories of functions used for analyses of decision processes. The author points out that "the intelligence function has received little systematic treatment" and suggests promising lines of inquiry.

Lindblom, Charles E. "Policy Analysis," *The American Economic Review,* 48, 298-312 (June 1958). In seeking to formalize methods for policy analysis, the author first clarifies the characteristic procedures of the "conventional" method of policy analysis. He then proceeds to describe in detail a contrasting method, less reliance on theory and a fragmented view of important variables.

Lindblom, Charles E. "The Science of 'Muddling Through,'" *Public Administration Review,* 24, 79-88 (Spring 1959). A significant theoretical formulation of decision-making processes in which the "rational comprehensive method" of arriving at policy decisions is contrasted with the method of successive limited comparisons or the "incremental method."

Lindblom, Charles E. *The Intelligence of Democracy.* New York: The Free Press, 1965. 352 pp. Using the market mechanism as a model, Lindblom defines his concept of "mutual adjustment" as a process by which people can coordinate themselves without a common purpose and without rules that prescribe their relation to each other. The book proposes systematic comparative analysis of centrality and partisan mutual adjustment among various kinds of decision-makers as competing methods for rational coordination of governmental decisions.

Long, N. E. "Public Policy and Administration: The Goals of Rationality and Responsibility," *Public Administration Review,* 14, 22-31 (Winter 1954). Long rejects the idea of a value-free science of administration. Bureaucracy is not a neutral instrument solely devoted to the "unmotivated presentation of facts and the docile execution of orders from political superiors." The fund of knowledge in a bureaucracy should present the political superiors with alternative solutions to problems, and thus increase the possibility of rational action.

Merton, Robert K. "Role of the Intellectual in Public Bureaucracy," *Social Forces,* 23, 405-415 (May 1945). Merton examines the role of the professional intellectual in society focusing on the intellectual who exercises advisory and technical functions within a bureaucracy.

Simon, Herbert A. *Administrative Behavior.* New York: The MacMillan Company, 1947. 259 pp. Through his study of decision-making in administrative organizations, the author sheds light on such questions as the role of value and fact in administrative decision, the effect of the organization on individual behavior, the role of authority, and organizational loyalty.

Simon, Herbert A., Smithburg, Donald W., and Thompson, Victor A. *Public Administration.* New York: Alfred A. Knopf, 1950. 582 pp. An unusual textbook of public administration which draws heavily on sociological and psychological concepts and theories. The behavior of individuals in organizations forms the starting-point for an increasingly complex analysis of organizational units and the structure of large-scale organizations.

Snyder, Richard C., Bruck, H. W., and Sapin, Burton. *Foreign Policy Decision-Making.* Glencoe, Ill.: The Free Press, 1962. 274 pp. Contains an essay presenting a tentative formulation of an analytical scheme which may serve as a frame of reference for the study of international politics. Foreign policy decision-making is taken as a special case of decision-making in complex organizations. Its methods and findings are held to be capable of general application. Organizational and intellectual process analyses are differentiated.

Snyder, Richard C., and Robinson, James A. *National and International Decision-Making: Toward a General Research Strategy Related to the Problem of War and Peace.* [n.p.: n.d.]. 228 pp. Part of the Institute for International Order series on research in the social sciences having a bearing on problems of war and peace. The authors stress research on decision-making processes as an important way of assessing where social science knowledge should be infused in order to have maximum impact on problems of war and peace. The volume includes an inventory of past and current research in the area of decision-making and extensive bibliographic references.

Wildavsky, Aaron. "The Analysis of Issue-Contents in the Study of Decision-Making," *Journal of Politics,* 24, 717-732 (November 1962). This study of decision-making focuses upon the personal and social characteristics of the participants, the institutional settings in which they work, and the flow of information and advice which they receive. The thesis of the paper is that the study of decision-making would gain by making explicit and systematic an analytic category—the contexts of the issues—specifying the situations in which issues occur and their impact on the decision-makers.

Wilensky, Harold L. *Organizational Intelligence: Knowledge and Policy in Government and Industry.* New York: Basic Books, 1967. 226 pp. The book aims "to bring together the scattered literature on organizational intelligence and to develop hypotheses about (a) the determinants of the uses of intelligence and (b) the structural and doctrinal roots of intelligence failures; and to infer from these the conditions that facilitate the flow of high quality intelligence." [Preface.]

PART III. THE ORGANIZATION OF POLICY-ORIENTED SOCIAL SCIENCE

An understanding of the problems and potentialities of policy-oriented social science requires knowledge of the organizational forms developed for the funding and conduct of research. Part III lists writings which describe and analyze both the general question of how the social sciences have developed organizationally in the last 25 years and the more specialized questions of the origins and present status of governmental support of social science, the characteristics of organizations producing research for public policy, and the problems emanating from a growing dependence on federal funds for research.

The writings listed in this part have been arranged under the following four headings:

1. An Overview of Organizational Developments in Applied and Policy-Oriented Social Science. The empirical and policy orientations in the social sciences have given rise to large-scale facilities and complex procedures for the conduct of research. Among the writings included in this section is Lazarsfeld's "Observations on the Organization of Social Science Research in the United States" which contains the results of a survey of organizational arrangements within the universities for conducting empirical social science research.

2. The Involvement of the Federal Government in Social Science Research. (General). General writings on federal sponsorship of social science research are important background materials in studying policy-oriented research activities. Among writings of this type are: (a) those tracing the historical and institutional background of federal support of scientific and social scientific research; (b) several reports and discussions aimed at formulating a "national social science policy," (c) reports on past, present, and future levels of governmental support for social science research.

3. The Involvement of the Federal Government in Social Science Research on International and Military Affairs, 1940-1966. World War II marks the beginning of large-scale governmental support of research in international and military affairs. The extensive involvement of social scientists is reflected in the literature by the several case histories recorded by social scientists acting as participant-observers. Among postwar trends are the rise of a branch of social science which concerns itself with problems of strategy and national security, and the appearance on the scene of such new breeds of policy-oriented research organizations as profit-making and "captive" ones.

4. Problematic Aspects of the Relationship of the Government and the Social Science Professions. In the postwar period social scientists have shown concern that their growing dependence on federal support for research would entail loss or scientific freedom and unwarranted control over the conduct of research and research findings. The cancellation in 1965 of "Project Camelot," an Army-sponsored research program on counter-insurgency, had the effect of highlighting major political, ideological, and ethical issues.

III.1 AN OVERVIEW OF ORGANIZATIONAL DEVELOPMENTS IN APPLIED AND POLICY-ORIENTED SOCIAL SCIENCES

Bennis, Warren G. "The Effect on Academic Goods of Their Market," *The American Journal of Sociology*, 62, 28-33 (July 1956). The growth of large-scale research organizations, sponsored by foundations and other private bodies, has made research groups sensitive to their market. When the attitudes toward work among social scientists on two research projects with contrasting financial outlook were compared, it was found that those on the project with tenuous and unstable financing maintained a market orientation, while those on the financially secure project were oriented to the task.

Compton, Bertita. "Psychology's Manpower: Characteristics, Employment and Earnings," *American Psychologist*, 21, 224-230 (March 1966). The data presented in this article were obtained from a survey conducted for the National Register of Scientific and Technical Personnel in 1964. The article summarizes data concerning those 16,804 respondents who indicated a specialty within the field of psychology.

Eaton, Joseph W. "Social Processes of Professional Teamwork," *American Sociological Review*, 16, 707-713 (October 1951). The purpose of this essay is to discuss the advantages and difficulties of team research. Emphasis is upon the structure and processes of the interpersonal relationships of the participating scientists.

Glock, Charles Y. "Some Implications of Organization for Social Research," *Social Forces*, 30, 129-134 (December 1951). The then Director of the Bureau of Applied Social Research of Columbia University discusses the interplay between the nature and role of research and its organization. Provides categorization of characteristics necessary for the survival of social research organizations and explains how these attributes may foster the attainment of research objectives.

Gordon, Gerald, and Marquis, Sue. "Freedom, Visibility of Consequences, and Scientific Innovation," *The American Journal of Sociology*, 72, 195-202 (September 1966). Using experts' evaluations of the innovativeness of 245 projects addressed to social-psychology aspects of disease, the authors test certain hypotheses concerning the effect of research settings on innovativeness in scientific research. Among their findings: research conducted in academic social-science departments clearly was less innovative than similar research in institutions such as hospitals or health agencies.

Hopper, Janice A. "Sociologists in the 1964 National Register of Scientific and Technical Personnel," *The American Sociologist*, 1, 71-78 (February 1966). This first report on sociologists in the National Register contains data on the number of sociologists registered, their primary work activity, the most frequently reported subfields within sociology, and salaries. The article also contains a critical examination of the sociological specialties list in the Register.

Hopper, Janice A. "Preliminary Report on Salaries and Selected Characteristics of Sociologists in the 1966 National Science Foundation Register of Scientific and Technical Personnel," *The American Sociologist*, 2, 151-154 (August 1967). Reports preliminary data on the 1966 survey of sociologists for the National Register of Scientific and Technical Personnel. Also included are comparisons with data collected in the 1964 survey.

Lazarsfeld, Paul F. "Observations on the Organization of Social Research in the United States," *Information, Bulletin of the International Social Science Council*, 29 (December 1961), 35 pp. (Whole issue.) Based on a survey (usually referred to as the "Columbia Survey"), this article deals with the rapid expansion of empirical work in the social sciences and the types of arrangements by which American colleges and universities have tried to make room for empirical social research.

Lazarsfeld, Paul F. "The Sociology of Empirical Social Research," *American Sociological Review*, 27, 757-767 (December 1962). This presidential address at the 57th Annual Meeting of the American Sociological Association in September, 1962, deals with the interrelation between the organization of social research and methodology.

Lazarsfeld, Paul F., Klein, Lawrence R., and Tyler, Ralph W. *The Behavioral Sciences: Problems and Prospects*. Boulder, Colo.: Institute of Behavioral Science, University of Colorado, 1964. 40 pp. Papers presented at the dedication ceremonies for the new building of the Institute of Behavioral Science, June 21, 1962. Lazarsfeld's paper traces the historical development of organized research in the social sciences and gives an assessment of its present status.

Lee, Alfred McClung. "Individual and Organizational Research in Sociology," *American Sociological Review,* 16, 701-707 (October 1951). A comparison of "individual" and "organizational" research, this article includes definitions of both, the techniques used, criticisms made against group research, and the problems associated with these two forms of research.

Parsons, Talcott. "Some Problems Confronting Sociology as a Profession," *American Sociological Review,* 24, 547-559 (August 1959). This article prepared by Parsons in the capacity of Chairman of the Committee on the Profession of the American Sociological Society gives "unequivocal primacy to the sociologist's role as a *scientist."* In talking about the "applied function," Parsons argues that it be mediated through the professional schools which he sees as centers for "action research."

Record, Wilson. "Some Reflections on Bureaucratic Trends in Sociological Research," *American Sociological Review,* 25, 411-414 (June 1960). The author points to the constricting character of institutional demands and how these inhibit the quest for truth.

Rosengren, William I. "Institutional Types and Sociological Research: An Hypothesis in Role Systems and Research Models," *Human Organization,* 20, 42-48 (Spring 1961). The purpose of the essay is to suggest some of the ways in which sociologists and other social scientists have become entwined in the organizational structures in which research is conducted. Two types of institutional or organizational settings for research—"urban" and "folk"—are discussed with particular reference to medical—psychiatric organizations.

Sibley, Elbridge. *The Education of Sociologists in the United States.* New York: Russell Sage Foundation, 1963. 218 pp. A comprehensive examination of numerous aspects of the training of professional sociologists. Included are topics such as the following: the graduate schools in sociology, the educational background and aptitude of the students, the content of graduate training and the graduates' appraisal of their training.

Somit, Albert, and Tanenhaus, Joseph. *American Political Science: A Profile of a Discipline.* New York: Atherton Press, 1964. 173 pp. Basing their profile on data from a sample survey of 832 members of the American Political Science Association, the authors treat such varied matters as prestige departments and figures in political science, the issue of "behavioralism," and the bases of career satisfaction among political scientists.

"The Structure of Economists' Employment and Salaries, 1964," *American Economic Review,* 55 (December 1965). Supplemental issue. Reports data on economists in the National Register of Scientific and Technical Personnel gathered in the course of a survey conducted in 1964. This year was the first time that the economics profession was included in the register.

Waldo, Dwight (Ed.). *The Research Function of University Bureaus and Institutes for Government Related Research.* Berkeley, Calif.: Bureau of Public Administration, University of California, 1960. 222 pp. A report on a conference held at the University of California, Berkeley, in August, 1959. Papers of special interest include one by Amin Alimaid, which examines "Origins, History and Directions of the University Bureau Movement in the United States," and one by Vincent Ostrom entitled "Public Policy Studies: An Approach to Governmental Research."

Wohl, Richard R. "Some Observations on the Social Organization of Interdisciplinary Social Science Research," *Social Forces,* 33, 374-383 (May 1955). A discussion of social and intellectual conditions conducive to bringing specialists together in a cooperative research effort. Wohl traces "the mood and milieu" of concerted research through a hypothetical interdisciplinary research project.

Young, Donald. "Organization for Research in the Social Sciences in the United States," *International Social Science Bulletin,* 99-107 (1949). Outlines the changes that have taken place in the organization for research since World War II, and the aims and problems of various types of research situations.

III.2 THE INVOLVEMENT OF THE FEDERAL GOVERNMENT IN SOCIAL SCIENCE RESEARCH (GENERAL)

Alpert, Harry. "Congressmen, Social Scientists, and Attitudes toward Federal Support of Social Science Research," *American Sociological Review,* 23, 682-686 (December 1958). The former director of the National Science Foundation research program in the social sciences gives a retrospective view on development of congressional attitudes and actions toward the social sciences during the twelve years since the Senate voted to exclude these disciplines from the National Science Foundation Act.

Alpert, Harry. "The Government's Growing Recognition of Social Science," *Annals of the American Academy of Political and Social Science,* 327, 59-67 (January 1960). Points to the new developments which have strengthened the standing of the social sciences in the federal government. Factors contributing to this are: changing congressional attitudes, executive acceptance of the social sciences, and the broad definitions of scientific disciplines.

"Congress and Social Science," *American Psychologist,* 22, 877-1041 (November, 1967). (Whole issue.) "In years to come, the 90th Congress, opening in 1967, may be viewed as the place and time of the take-off point for the underdeveloped social and behavioral sciences." [Introduction.] This issue includes testimony before the Senate Subcommittee on Government Research of the Committee on Government Operations relating to a proposed National Foundation for the Social Sciences and on the "Full Opportunity and Social Accounting Act of 1967."

Ellis, William W. "The Federal Government in Behavioral Science," *The American Behavioral Scientist,* 7, 51 pp. (May 1964). (Whole issue.) This issue provides an extensive examination, based on a mail-questionnaire survey, of the federal government's involvement in behavioral science research—areas of investigation, methods, and sources of support. Includes article by the Editor (Alfred de Grazia) titled, "The Government in Behavioral Science: Some Critical Notes."

Federal Funds for Research, Development and Other Scientific Activities, Vols. 1-15. Washington, D.C.: National Science Foundation, 1952-1966. Published annually since 1952, these reports contain the annual Federal expenditures for research and development according to sponsors, performers, and fields of science. Actual expenditure as well as estimates are reported.

Lundberg, George A. "The Senate Ponders Social Science," *The Scientific Monthly,* 64, 397-411 (May 1947). Discussion of the reasons for not making social science part of the National Science Foundation. Analyzes the attitudes of legislators toward the social sciences in an attempt to find clues as to the nature of the obstacles to overcome.

MacGregor, Gordon. "Anthropology in Government: United States," in *The Yearbook of Anthropology.* New York: Wenner-Gren Foundation for Anthropological Research, 421-433 (1954). A survey of the support given anthropological studies by Federal agencies and departments.

Parsons, Talcott. "The Science Legislation and the Role of the Social Sciences," *American Sociological Review,* 11, 653-666 (December 1946). Against the background of a brief history of legislative proposals to establish a National Science Foundation, Parsons discusses federal support of basic research in the social sciences.

Pfaffman, Carl. "Behavioral Sciences," in *Basic Research and National Goals.* A Report to the Committee on Science and Astronautics, U.S. House of Representatives. Washington, D.C.: U.S. Government Printing Office, 203-236 (1965). Provides information on the support given basic research in five social science disciplines by the Federal government. Concludes that the "consensus seems to be that support for basic research in the behavioral sciences should be improved, but that any increase substantial enough to match the physical sciences is not called for. . . ."

Price, Don K. *Government and Science.* New York: New York University Press, 1954. 203 pp. The thesis is that the processes of research and discussion are more responsible for the development of public policy and administration than are the processes of conflict among political parties and social or economic pressure groups. The book consists of seven lectures delivered as the James

Stokes Lectures on Politics at New York University.

Research and Technical Programs Subcommittee, U.S. House of Representatives. *The Use of Social Research in Federal Domestic Programs,* Parts I-IV, 90th Cong., 1st Sess., 1967. A staff study by the committee which makes extensive use of writings by social scientists and others on numerous aspects of the relationship of government agencies, primarily domestic ones, and social science disciplines. The results of surveys of federal research programs and of the attitudes of some social scientists toward government support are included in Parts I and III, respectively.

Rice, Stuart. "The Federal Reports Act," *The American Sociologist,* 2, 73-75. (May 1967). One of the authors of the *Federal Reports Act of 1942* describes the conditions that gave rise to its provisions for Bureau of the Budget review of questionnaires used in government-sponsored research. The Act represented one achievement of long efforts by American social scientists to integrate and upgrade the statistical services of the Federal government.

Scientific Activities of Non-Profit Institutions, 1964. Washington, D.C.: National Science Foundation, 1967. 111 pp. A summary of information obtained in the National Science Foundation's survey of scientific activities of independent non-profit institutions during 1964. Organizations surveyed include: research institutes, federal contract research centers managed by non-profit institutions and private foundations.

U.S. National Resources Committee, Science Committee. *Research—A National Resource.* Washington, D.C.: U.S. Government Printing Office, 1938. 255 pp. An examination of the federal government's role in relation to scientific research. Contains the results of a government-wide survey of social research programs as well as a report by Samuel A. Stouffer on the production and use of social statistics by federal agencies and departments.

Wilson, John T. "Government Support of Research and its Influence on Psychology," *The American Psychologist,* 7, 714-718 (December 1952). Traces the evolution of the federal government's contract and grant program in psychology and its effect on the discipline.

III.3 THE INVOLVEMENT OF THE FEDERAL GOVERNMENT IN SOCIAL SCIENCE RESEARCH ON INTERNATIONAL AND MILITARY AFFAIRS, 1940–1966

Bennis, Warren G. "The Social Scientist as Research Entrepreneur: A Case Study," *Social Problems,* 3, 44-49 (July 1955). A version of a paper read at the 1954 Annual Meeting of the American Sociological Society. Based upon a Ph.D. thesis, it deals with a new type of intellectual organization which has grown up in response to the need for interdisciplinary and team research to deal with world problems.

Cartwright, Dorwin. "Social Psychology in the United States during the Second World War," *Human Relations,* 1, 333-352 (1948). Prepared at the request of the American Council of Learned Societies, partly for foreign scholars. Gives an overview of wartime development stressing heavy involvement of social psychologists in government. Extensive bibliography.

Crawford, Elisabeth T., and Lyons, Gene M. "Foreign Area Research: A Background Statement," *The American Behavioral Scientist,* 10, 3-7 (June 1967). A discussion of the current problems of foreign area research introduced against a background of how social science research in foreign and military affairs have developed organizationally and substantively in the last 25 years. Originally prepared for a conference on foreign area research held under the auspices of the Advisory Committee on Government Programs in the Behavioral Sciences, National Academy of Sciences in 1966.

Darley, John G. "Psychology and the Office of Naval Research: A Decade of Development," *American Psychologist,* 12, 305-323 (June 1957). An analysis of the financial support given psychology by the Psychological Sciences Division of the Office of Naval Research. During the period treated the division supported some 143 separate research projects in psychology.

Embree, John F. "Anthropology and the War," *Bulletin of the American Association of University Professors,* 32, 485-495 (Autumn 1946). The article sets forth "why" and "how" anthropologists were drawn into government service in World War II.

Friedman, Saul. "The RAND Corporation and Our Policymakers," *The Atlantic Monthly,* 212, 61-68 (September 1963). A journalist's description of the RAND Corporation which details origin, objectives, structure, and functions. Presents a critical appraisal of the impact of RAND research on government policy making in the fields of foreign affairs and strategy.

Gosnell, Harold F., and Moyca, David C. "Public Opinion Research in Government," *American Political Science Review,* 43, 564-572 (June 1949). Describes potentialities of public opinion research in government and presents examples of government agency activities in public attitude and opinion research. Provides detailed description of the research activities of the Office of War Information.

Halperin, Morton. "Is the Senate's Foreign Relations Research Worthwhile?" *American Behavioral Scientist,* 4, 21-24 (September 1960). A generally favorable evaluation of the series of studies from private research organizations in 1958 commissioned by the Senate Foreign Relations Committee. Despite their limitations these studies are regarded as indicating a way in which social science can help provide the expertise Congress needs in order to share in foreign policy making.

Katzenbach, Edward L., Jr. "Ideas: A New Defense Industry," *The Reporter,* 24, 17-21 (March 2, 1961). A professor of history at Princeton University looks at the practice of government "purchasing" of advice and ideas pertinent to both the "hard" and "soft" aspects of defense planning. Describes proliferation of organizations engaged in production of ideas and advice.

Kraft, Joseph. "RAND: Arsenal for Ideas," *Harper's Magazine,* 221, 69-76 (July 1960). A former staff member of the *New York Times* depicts the nature, function, and importance of a research organization like RAND.

Lanier, Lyle H. "The Psychological and Social Sciences in the National Military Establishment," *The American Psychologist,* 4, 127-147 (May 1949). An exposition on the organizational and administrative structure of the National Military Establishment as it concerns agencies conducting or sponsoring research in the psychological and social sciences. Organizational charts, tables, and refences are included.

Leighton, Alexander H. and Opler, Morris Edward. "Psychiatry and Applied Anthropology in Psychological Warfare Against Japan," *The American Journal of Psychoanalysis,* 6, 20-27 (1946). Outline of the research findings of the Foreign Morale Analysis Division with respect to wartime morale of Japanese soldiers and civilians. A plea is made for using the same methods and concepts in dealing with postwar problems in Japan and elsewhere.

Lyons, Gene M., and Morton, Louis. *Schools for Strategy: Education and Research in National Security Affairs.* New York: Frederick A. Praeger, 1965. 356 pp. The first full-length study of teaching and research in national security affairs—institutions, approaches, personalities, and accomplishments. The authors delineate the field of national security research and describe academic programs in national security affairs and the growth of research institutes. Extensive notes and bibliographic references.

McDiarmid, John. "The Mobilization of Social Scientists," in *Civil Service in Wartime.* Leonard D. White (Ed.). Chicago, Ill.: University of Chicago Press, 73-96 (1945). McDiarmid first comments briefly on social scientists in the federal service in 1938, then reviews the wartime demands for social scientists and the nature of their contribution, and finally describes the activities of the U.S. Civil Service Commission and operating agencies in bringing demand and supply together.

Nichols, Roy F. "War and Research in Social Science," *Proceedings of the American Philosophical Society,* 87, 361-364 (January 29, 1944). Nichols discusses the mobilization of social scientists during World War II for work in the fields of population studies, economic control, and public opinion. He stresses the need for further development of social science techniques better suited to cope with more complex problems and poses questions as to the postwar demobilization of researchers and research offices.

"Planners for the Pentagon," *Business Week,* 56-90 (July 13, 1963). The complexity and seriousness of defense in the nuclear age necessitate the utilization of knowledge possessed by civilian intellectuals. Roles and types of these so-called "defense intellectuals" are discussed. The policy research of RAND and the Institute for Defense Analyses is given special emphasis.

Smith, Bruce Lee Raymond. *The RAND Corporation*. Cambridge, Mass.: Harvard University Press, 1966. 332 pp. The first extensive study of RAND's history, organization, and operation which also includes some data on the role of the social sciences at RAND.

Stouffer, Samuel A. "Studying the Attitudes of Soldiers," *Proceedings of the American Philosophical Society,* 92, 336-340 (November 1948). This contribution to a symposium on "Research Frontiers in Human Relations" provides an analytic summary of the experiences of the Research Branch of the Information and Education Division of the War Department in bringing survey results to bear on policy.

"Strengthening the Behavioral Sciences," *Science,* 136, 233-241 (April 1962). An assessment of the status and aims of behavioral science. The Behavioral Sciences Subpanel of the President's Science Advisory Committee surveys the underlying needs of the development of the scientific study of behavior and recommends action to meet them.

Subcommittee on Government Research, Committee on Government Operations, U.S. Senate. *Federal Support of International Social Science and Behavioral Research.* 89th Cong., 2nd Sess., 1966. 273 pp. Conducted a year after "Project Camelot," this examination of government sponsored foreign area research programs focuses on the content and scope of these programs, administrative procedures for review of research proposals, and efforts to "civilianize" such research. Among the individuals who testified were government social science research administrators, representatives of professional associations in the social sciences, and academic social scientists conducting foreign area research.

Subcommittee on International Organizations and Movements, Committee on Foreign Affairs, U. S. House of Representatives. *Winning the Cold War: The U.S. Ideological Offensive. Hearings, Parts I-VIII, Reports Nos. 1-2.* 88th Cong., 1st and 2nd Sess., March 1964-December 1965. See next entry.

Subcommittee on International Organizations and Movements, Committee on Foreign Affairs, U. S. House of Representatives. *Behavioral Sciences and the National Security. Hearings, Part IX, Report No. 4.* 89th Cong., 2nd Sess., 1966. Hearings held for the purpose of taking "a close and searching look at all nonmilitary and economic programs . . . intended to support our foreign policies, and to advance the cause of peace and freedom in the world." Includes information on the research programs of the Department of State, AID and USIA, as well as testimonies by social scientists on the role of research in U.S. propaganda efforts. See particularly Report No. 4, "Behavioral Sciences and National Security," and Part IX of the hearings held December 6, 1965.

"The New Intelligence Requirements: Proceedings and Papers," *Background,* 9, 171-198 (November 1965). Remarks by John Gange, Gabriel Almond, William Marvel, and William Nagle dealing with the role of government in the support of social science research in international affairs. Also included are discussions between audience participants and panelists.

U.S. Department of State, *Foreign Affairs Research.* Washington, D.C.: U.S. Department of State, Bureau of Intelligence and Research, 1967. 83 pp. This directory records the resources available in government offices for the study of foreign affairs. Includes an "Introduction" which gives facts and figures on government support of research in international and military affairs.

Woodward, Julian L. "Making Government Opinion Research Bear upon Operations," *American Sociological Review,* 9, 670-677 (December 1944). A sociologist serving in the Office of War Information outlines the special features and conditions of the wartime research climate in Washington. "The most important of these new conditions is the requirement that most of the research done on government funds in wartime agencies be immediately useful in operations."

III.4 PROBLEMATIC ASPECTS OF THE RELATIONSHIP OF THE GOVERNMENT AND THE SOCIAL SCIENCE PROFESSION

Archibald, Kathleen. "Social Science Approaches to Peace: Problems and Issues," *Social Problems,* 11, 91-104 (Summer 1963). Analyzes "factors affecting the contribution of social science to, and the role of the social scientist in, the peace and international security area." Based on interviews and discussions with social scientists and policy makers.

Reprinted in Alvin W. Gouldner and S. M. Miller (Eds.). *Applied Sociology: Opportunities and Problems.* New York: The Free Press, 266-284 (1965).

"Background Information on Problems of Anthropological Research and Ethics," *Fellow Newsletter*, 8, 1-13 (January 1967). (Whole issue.) Contains a report prepared by Ralph Beals and the Executive Board of the American Anthropological Association on government sponsorship of anthropological research, especially as it relates to research in foreign areas. Discusses problems of disclosure of sources of funds and relationships of American anthropologists to host nation scholars. This report and a subsequent *Statement on Problems of Anthropological Research and Ethics* adopted by the Fellows of the Association in 1967 were prompted by "Project Camelot."

Boggs, Stephen T. "The Organization of Anthropology in Action," *Human Organization*, 23, 193-195 (Fall 1964). In a discussion of the organizational problems involved in bringing anthropological research to bear on policy, the then Executive Secretary of the American Anthropological Association suggests that anthropologists be given full-time rather than consultant positions in agencies concerned with programs overseas.

Boulding, Kenneth E. "The University, Society and Arms Control," *Journal of Conflict Resolution*, 7, 458-463 (September 1963). The author, of the Department of Economics and the Center for Research on Conflict Resolution at the University of Michigan, advocates that every operating agency and government division should have a research division operating in close contact with a research agency in the university.

Bray, Charles W., Lanier, Lyle H., and Darley, John G. "The Effects of Government Research Contracts on Psychology," *The American Psychologist*, 7, 710-721 (December 1952). Three contributions to a symposium held at the Midwestern Psychological Association in 1952. A variety of issues and problems linked to government support of research in psychology are discussed. Among these are: conflicts of interest between buyers and sellers, the "overselling" of psychological research and external control of academic research.

"Camelot and Psychological Tests," *American Psychologist*, 21, 401-477 (May 1966). (Whole issue.). An issue on the theme of current controversy over psychological research and services. The year 1965 is viewed as one of continuing controversy over the use of psychological testing but will also be remembered as the year of "Project Camelot." Among articles discussing the latter are "Foreign Affairs Research: Review Process Rises on Ruins of Camelot" by John Walsh; "Scholars and Foreign Policy: Varieties of Research Experience" by Thomas L. Hughes; and "Project Camelot: An Interim Postlude" by Theodore R. Vallance.

Carter, Luther J. "Social Sciences: Problems Examined by Senate Panel," *Science*, 153, 154-156 (July 8, 1966). The U.S. Senate's Subcommittee on Government Research of the Government Operations Committee has initiated hearings on the problems of government's relations with the social science community. Carter reviews developments of government-sponsored social science research and shows the diversity of opinion among social scientists by citing the views of prominent people in the field.

Crawford, Elisabeth T. "Organization and Values in Socal Science Research on International and Military Policy," *Background*, 10, 131-149 (August 1966). Suggests as conceptual models for studying policy-oriented research: the networks of communication among social scientists, their sponsors and clienteles; social science as a status system; as a community; and as a system of values. In applying each of these models, values held by social scientists form an important structuring variable, as Crawford illustrates by discussing attitudes of social scientists toward sources and forms of financial support.

"Editor's Column," *The American Sociologist*, 1, 182-184 (August 1966). In one of a series of editorial comments Talcott Parsons discusses the relationship of sociology to political-ideological conflicts. He fears that too close an involvement of sociologists with political bodies can "divide sociology into ideological motivated 'schools' which stand opposed to each other and judge each other's work, not mainly on grounds of objective validity and scientific significance, but of ideological correctness."

"Editor's Column," *The American Sociologist*, 2, 62-64 (May 1967). A discussion of "value-neutrality" (*Wertfreiheit*) as it relates to acute problems in the relations of the sociology profession to the surrounding society.

Goldstein, Walter. "Informed Dissent and Academic Research," *Background,* 8, 101-104 (August 1964). Goldstein argues that university establishments have failed to question the basic policy choices of the administration and calls for more platforms for informed discussion and dissent. He suggests that military contractors be approached to assist in the financing of controversy.

Goodenough, Ward H. "The Growing Demand for Behavioral Science in Government; Its Implications for Anthropology," *Human Organization,* 21, 172-176 (Fall 1962). The article was followed by "A Comment" by Anne Parsons; "Reply to Anne Parsons" by Goodenough; and Parson's "Rejoinder . . ." in *Human Organization,* 23, 93-98 (Summer 1964). An exchange of letters, giving widely divergent opinions concerning the role of the social scientist in the bureaucracy.

Horowitz, Irving Louis (Ed.). *The Rise and Fall of Project Camelot: Studies in the Relationship Between Social Science and Practical Politics.* Cambridge, Mass.: MIT Press, 1967. 385 pp. The book examines the "Camelot affair" under five different headings and from five different perspectives. These are: the setting of "Project Camelot," its design and purposes, the academic response to its cancellation, the political response, and the general implications of the "Camelot affair." Included are articles by Irving Louis Horowitz, Robert Boguslaw, J. W. Fulbright, Johan Galtung, and Robert A. Nisbet.

Mainzer, Lewis C. "Scientific Freedom in Government-Sponsored Research," *Journal of Politics,* 23, 212-230 (May 1961). The question is asked: ". . . is proper scientific discretion retained by those doing scientific research within federal agencies or elsewhere with federal funds?" Mainzer points out that it is necessary to distinguish between the value of science as an intellectual discovery and science as a means toward certain goals.

Orlans, Harold, "Ethical Problems in the Relations of Research Sponsors and Investigators," in *Ethics, Politics, and Social Research.* Gideon Sjoberg (Ed.). Cambridge, Mass.: Schenkman Publishing Co., Inc., 3-24 (1967). A staff member of the Brookings Institution discusses ". . . some of the more common ethical problems . . . that arise in the sequence from the application for research funds through the use, and to the completion of a research report." A section of the article examines reasons for boycotts by scholars of certain programs, such as those of the military.

Pool, Ithiel de Sola. "The Necessity for Social Scientists Doing Research for Governments," *Background,* 10, 111-123 (August 1966). The author presents the arguments that extensive use of the social sciences by government is essential if the government is to be humane and intelligent. Likewise social science is also needed to make foreign policy and other international activities more rational. [Reprinted in Irving Louis Horowitz (Ed.). *The Rise and Fall of Project Camelot: Studies in the Relationship Between Social Science and Practical Politics.* Cambridge, Mass.: The MIT Press, 267–280 (1967).]

Silvert, Kalman H. "American Academic Ethics and Social Research Abroad: The Lesson of Project Camelot," *American Universities Field Staff Reports,* 12, 21 pp. (July 1965). (Whole issue.) A political scientist discusses ethical problems in the social science profession which he feels have been sharpened by Project Camelot. The article focuses on three relationships: "The first between social science and government; the second between professional competence and integrity; and the third between Latin American Studies as such and the general performance of the American academic community." [Reprinted in Irving Louis Horowitz (Ed.). *The Rise and Fall of Project Camelot: Studies in the Relationship Between Social Science and Practical Politics.* Cambridge, Mass.: The MIT Press, 80–106 (1967).]

Subcommittee on Government Research, Committee on Government Operations, U.S. Senate. *National Foundation for Social Sciences, Parts I-III, Hearings on S.836.* 90th Cong., 1st Sess., 1967. With Chairman Fred R. Harris, one of the most vigorous supporters of social science in Congress, doing most of the questioning, an array of government officialdom, science officialdom, and academic notables offer statements, testimony, and exhibits in hearings on the bill to establish a national foundation for the social sciences "in order to promote research and scholarship in such sciences." The post-Project Camelot controversies set the stage for much of the discussion, but it ranges extensively in matters affecting the organization, financing, and uses of the social sciences.

PART IV. DECISION-MAKING STRUCTURES AND THE USE OF SOCIAL SCIENCE RESEARCH

The relationship between governmental support of social science research and the actual use made of research findings is sufficiently tenuous to warrant the treatment of the latter problem in a separate part (Part IV). The many ways in which research find its way into the minds and actions of decision-makers makes the study of utilization unusually difficult. The works listed in Part IV represent three approaches to this problem. The first section lists some of the few existing writings containing description and analysis of those general characteristics of the governmental structure that affect the use of research (bureaucratic restraints, the problem of "sensitizing" decision-makers, etc.). Inferences regarding conditions favoring or impeding the use of research can be drawn from studies of the organizational machinery for policy formation, the belief systems of policy-makers, and their education into the policy-making "culture" (IV.2). Case studies of the uses made of social science research in agencies and departments with policy-making or operational functions is another way of approaching the study of utilization (IV.3).

The three subsections contained in this part have been given the following headings:

1. The Use of Research in the Federal Government (General).

2. Characteristics of International and Military Decision-Makers and Decision-Making Structures Affecting the Use of Research.

3. The Use of Social Science Knowledge and Expertise in Departments and Agencies Concerned with International and Military Affairs.

IV.1 THE USE OF RESEARCH IN THE FEDERAL GOVERNMENT (GENERAL)

Graham, Milton D. *Federal Utilization of Social Science Research: Exploration of the Problems.* Washington, D.C.: The Brookings Institution, 1954. 146 pp. Description of trends in federally supported research in the social sciences. Included is a discussion of the problems of utilization of research in governmental agencies, and suggestions of methods to be used in studying utilization.

Kecskemeti, Paul. *Utilization of Social Science Research in Shaping Policy Decisions.* Santa Monica, Calif.: The RAND Corporation, April 24, 1961. 14 pp. The contention is that the most extensive utilization of social scientific methods of fact-finding and analysis is found in economic policy. Open problems and uncertainties arise when one turns to other social sciences. Three ways of utilizing scientific theory and research in governmental policy making are suggested.

Robinson, James A. "The Social Scientists and Congress," in *International Conflict and Behavioral Science.* Roger Fisher (Ed.). New York: Basic Books, Inc., 266-271 (1964). A brief examination of the two products of modern social science—public opinion polls and organizational theory—that the author finds would merit more attention by Congressmen. His conclusions regarding the present use made of these products in Congress are largely negative.

Webbink, Paul. *Effective Use of Social Science Research in the Federal Service.* New York: Russell Sage Foundation, 1950. 47 pp. A brief discussion of the government's role in increasing and improving the utilization of the social sciences in the accomplishment of government objectives. Against the background of uses of social science research in government during World War II, it discusses such issues as the need to make applied research cumulative, the role of the social science technician, and the problems of obtaining adequate personnel serving both as "users" and "producers" of research.

IV.2 CHARACTERISTICS OF INTERNATIONAL AND MILITARY DECISION-MAKERS AND DECISION-MAKING STRUCTURES AFFECTING THE USE OF RESEARCH

Barber, Arthur. "The Citizen, the Scholar and the Policymaker," *Background,* 8, 79-92 (August 1964). In a discussion of the role of research in public policy, Barber contends that the intellectual community has had little effect on the American policy process. The paper is followed by a critique by Vincent Davis.

Evans, Allan. "Intelligence and Policy Formation," *World Politics,* 12, 84-91 (October 1959). A discussion of Roger Hilsman, *Strategic Intelligence and National Decisions;* Washington Platt, *Strategic Intelligence Production;* and Harry H. Ransom, *Central Intelligence and National Security,* by Allan Evans of the State Department's Bureau of Intelligence and Research.

Feld, Maury D. "Military Self-Image in a Technological Environment," in *The New Military: Changing Patterns of Organization.* Morris Janowitz (Ed.). New York: Russell Sage Foundation, 159-194 (1964). Changing self-images of military professionals are studied by systematic content analysis of service journals. Among the indicators used to trace the change from primitive self-conceptions to competitive or managerial ones are the distribution of military and civilian authors in these journals, and the military rank distributions of contributors.

Hilsman, Roger. *Strategic Intelligence and National Decisions.* Glencoe, Ill.: The Free Press, 1956. 187 pp. Study of the role and workings of U.S. intelligence agencies. The contention is that "it is in the strategic intelligence agencies that research—and even the social sciences—will find their real home within the formal structure of government." Included is a "working model" outlining relationships between knowledge and action in foreign policy decision-making.

Holsti, Ole R. "The Belief System and National Images: A Case Study," *The Journal of Conflict Resolution,* 6, 244-252 (September 1962). It is argued that decision-makers act upon their images of states and that these images are dependent upon the decision-maker's belief system. The study focuses upon John Foster Dulles, his belief system, and his perceptions of the Soviet Union. The implications for the problem of resolving international conflicts are discussed.

Janowitz, Morris. *The Professional Soldier: A Social and Political Portrait.* Glencoe, Ill.: Free Press, 1960. 464 pp. "Never before have so many critical sociological facts been presented in one place regarding central questions which political and social scientists are asking about military institutions and their role in the contemporary world. More important, by applying a sociological perspective to these issues, Janowitz raises new questions that others should be asking." [From a review by Albert D. Biderman in *The Annals,* 332, 162–163 [November 1960).]

Janowitz, Morris, and Little, Roger. *Sociology and the Military Establishment.* New York: Russell Sage Foundation, 1965. 136 pp. The authors appraise the state of and outlook for sociological analysis of the military establishment and discuss problematic issues in applying sociological theory and research to the analysis of important problems to the military.

Kissinger, Henry A. "The Policymaker and the Intellectual," *The Reporter,* 20, 30-35 (March 5, 1959). In a discussion of the need for new approaches and policies in the field of foreign affairs, Kissinger also reviews the role of the intellectual in bringing about such changes. Finds that the "expert" not uncom-

Langer, William L. "Scholarship and the Intelligence Problem," *Proceedings of the American Philosophical Society,* 92, 43-45 (March 1948). A discussion of the role of scholarly research in intelligence production. Professor Langer headed the Research and Analysis Section of the Office of Strategic Service during World War II and subsequently was chief of the Research and Intelligence Section in the Department of State.

Masland, John W., and Radway, Laurence I. *Soldiers and Scholars: Military Education and National Policy.* Princeton, N.J.: Princeton University Press, 1957. 530 pp. Described in the "Preface" as "a study of military education with emphasis upon the preparation of career officers for positions involving participation in the formulation of national policy." Discusses relations between military and civilian educational institutions and the use of research in teaching at undergraduate and higher military schools.

Polk, William R. "Problems of Government Utilization of Scholarly Research in International Affairs," *Background,* 9, 237-259 (November 1965). A far-ranging discussion of major issues in the relationship of scholarship and decision-making by a former member of the State Department Policy Planning Council. An important portion of the paper is devoted to the question of a "middle ground" where scholars and "operators" can meet. [Reprinted in Irving Louis Horowitz (Ed.). *The Rise and Fall of Project Camelot: Studies in the Relationship Between Social Science and Practical Politics.* Cambridge, Mass.: MIT Press, 239–266 (1967).]

Ransom, Harry H. *Central Intelligence and National Security.* Cambridge, Mass.: Harvard University Press, 1958. 287 pp. The purpose of the book is to describe the growth and function of central intelligence in the United States since World War II. Stresses the importance of information for rational decision-making and the potential rewards of an efficient intelligence system. Ransom also points to the need for basic research.

Rostow, Walt W. "The Fallacy of the Fertile Gondolas," *Harvard Alumni Bulletin,* 633-634 and 639 (May 25, 1957). In a discussion based on allegory, Rostow, a former professor at MIT and Chairman of the State Department's Policy Planning Council, points to the importance of linking university thought with government action. "Policy must be based on an assessment which achieves a unified view of the field of action. . . . Ideally, the synthesis in the President's head . . . should bear a close relation to the synthesis achieved by our scholars."

U.S. Department of State. *The Scholar and the Policy Maker.* (External Research Paper 151.) Washington, D.C.: Department of State, 1964. 23 pp. A series of talks given at the plenary session of the Association of Asian Studies in Washington, D.C., 1964. A far-ranging discussion of the role of scholarship in policy-making with emphasis on the contribution of area studies. The participants are Robert Blum, Roger Hilsman, George E. Taylor, Charles Wolf, Jr., and Henry S. Rowen.

Yarmolinsky, Adam. "Confessions of a Non-User," *Public Opinion Quarterly,* 27, 543-548 (Winter 1963). Paper presented by the former Special Assistant to the Secretary of Defense at the Annual Conference of the American Association for Public Opinion Research in May 1963. Yarmolinsky feels that the complex nature of decisions makes them less susceptible to influence by public opinion and hence limits the usefulness of public opinion research.

IV.3 THE USES OF SOCIAL SCIENCE KNOWLEDGE AND EXPERTISE IN DEPARTMENTS AND AGENCIES CONCERNED WITH INTERNATIONAL AND MILITARY AFFAIRS

Alger, Chadwick F. "The Role of the Private Expert in the Conduct of American Foreign Affairs." Unpublished Ph.D. dissertation, Princeton University, 1958. 399 pp. A study of the utilization of private experts by the *civilian* foreign affairs agencies of the U.S. government based on interviews with some sixty government officials and private experts.

Alger, Chadwick F. "The External Bureaucracy in U.S. Foreign Affairs," *Administrative Science Quarterly,* 7, 50-78 (June 1962). Utilizing data from a study of the participation of private experts in the conduct of U.S.

foreign affairs, this paper analyzes the behavior of outside experts.

Bailey, Gerald. *Utilizing Simulation of International Behavior in Political-Military Affairs.* Part I and II. McLean, Va.: Human Sciences Research, Inc., 1967. 21 and 46 pp. Part I of this report includes a survey of simulation activities in government agencies concerned with international and military affairs. Part II presents a theoretical analysis and an approach to research on the utilization of simulation products. Utilization of these as well as other intellectual products is viewed as a social process in which researchers, policy-makers, and liaison persons are the principal actors.

Beals, Ralph L. "The Uses of Anthropology in Overseas Programs: Introduction," *Human Organization,* 23, 184-186 (Fall 1964). In an introduction to a series of papers dealing with the uses of anthropology in action programs, the author discusses the benefits of using anthropologists in overseas programs.

Bennett, Meridan. "Evaluation and the Question of Change," *The Annals of the American Academy of Political and Social Science,* 365, 119-128 (May 1966). A description of the position of the Peace Corps' Division of Evaluation and its relationship to research and planning. Changes in and current problems of evaluation are outlined. The social sciences are viewed as crucial in creating an integration of research, planning, and evaluation.

Bowers, Raymond V. "The Military Establishment," in *The Uses of Sociology.* Paul F. Lazarsfeld, William Sewell, and Harold Wilensky (Eds.). New York: Basic Books, Inc., 234-274 (1967). Describes the uses of sociology for military intelligence, strategic planning, and psychological warfare from the beginning of World War II to the present time. The author concludes that ". . . well over 200 professional sociologists have contributed to the post-war use of sociology by the military establishment, and the list approximates a *Who's Who* of current American sociologists."

Carter, Launor F. "Survey Results and Public Policy Decisions," *Public Opinion Quarterly,* 27, 549-557 (Winter 1963). Paper presented by System Development Corporation director and former Chief Scientist of the Air Force at a Conference of the American Association for Public Opinion Research, May 1963. Deals with the uses of surveys by Air Force decision-makers and planners.

Davison, W. Phillips. "Foreign Policy," in *The Uses of Sociology.* Paul F. Lazarsfeld, William Sewell, and Harold Wilensky (Eds.). New York: Basic Books, Inc., 391-417 (1967). Describes the use of sample survey techniques by the Department of State, the United States Information Agency, and the Agency for International Development. The author points out that "more difficult to find are cases in which the behavioral sciences have directly affected the planning or execution of foreign policy." A potentially larger contribution by behavioral scientists to foreign policy is discussed in the section "Is Greater Utilization Possible?"

Elder, Robert E. "The Public Studies Division of the Department of State: Public Opinion Analysts in the Formulation and Conduct of American Foreign Policy," *Western Political Quarterly,* 10, 783-792 (December 1957). Describes the organization and functioning of the Public Studies Division of the Department of State. This division is no longer in existence.

Evans, Allan, and Gatewood, R. D. "Intelligence and Research: Sentinel and Scholar in Foreign Relations," *The Department of State Bulletin,* 42, 1023-1028 (June 27, 1960). Brief discussion of the operation of the State Department's Bureau of Intelligence and Research.

Gollin, Albert. "The Role of Research and Evaluation in the Peace Corps: Retrospect and Prospect," *Proceedings—Peace Corps Contractors' Conference.* Estes Park, Colo.: Estes Park Center for Research and Education, 1965. Raises some of the issues involved in the use of research and evaluation techniques in organizations in general and in the Peace Corps in particular. Emphasis is placed upon the role that systematic study, analysis, and experimentation must play in improving methods of development assistance.

Hall, Edward T. "Orientation and Training in Government Work Overseas," *Human Organization,* 15, 4-10 (Spring 1956). The author examines the anthropological training given government personnel in preparation for overseas assignments (TCA and Point IV). He finds it inadequate in many respects.

Miniclier, Louis. "The Use of Anthropologists in the Foreign Aid Program," *Human Organization,* 23, 187-189 (Fall 1964). The Director of the Community Development branch of the U.S. Foreign Aid program discusses some of the problems involved in using anthropologists in overseas missions.

Schaedel, Richard P. "Anthropology in AID Overseas Missions: Its Practical and Theoretical Potential," *Human Organization,* 23, 190–192 (Summer 1964). Work accomplished by anthropologists in AID missions overseas is examined in the light of four major types of activities in which they are involved: program evaluation, planning, operations support, and community development.

Smith, Bruce Lee Raymond. "Strategic Expertise and National Security Policy: A Case Study," *Public Policy,* 13, 69-106 (1964). A member of the staff of the RAND Corporation reviews the origins, execution, and eventual communication to Air Force policymakers of a RAND study: *The Strategic Bases Study* (Rand Report 266). The postwar trend to include social scientists in a scientific advisory function is pointed out.

PART V. THE SUBSTANCE OF SOCIAL SCIENCE KNOWLEDGE AND POLICY CONCERNS IN INTERNATIONAL AND MILITARY AFFAIRS

The relevance of social science theories and methods to problems of international and military policy is at the core of the relationship of governmental decision-makers and the social science community. Among the questions having a bearing on this problem are some of the following: Are the social sciences sufficiently advanced, theoretically and methodologically, to make a contribution to policy making? To what extent are social scientists guided by considerations of policy relevance in their choice of research topics? What strategies should be employed in order to bring about optimum applicability of research findings to policy problems?

Part V has been divided into the following three subsections:

1. Translating Basic into Applied Social Science. The general methodological problem of the distinctive characteristics of basic and applied social science and the mechanisms through which basic social science knowledge is put to use in an applied setting is an important basis for consideration of some of the previous questions raised.

2. The Applicability of Social Science Methods and Materials to International and Military Policy Problems. In this section representatives of several disciplines examine the types of social science concepts, theories, and data that apply to policy formulation and evaluation in such areas as psychological warfare, limited war and deterrence strategies, and problems of socio-political development. The question of how the social sciences can adapt themselves to changing knowledge needs in these and other areas is a concern of several of the writers.

3. Applying Social Science Knowledge in the Area of Peace and International Cooperation. Research aimed at the resolution of conflicts between nations and the furtherance of international cooperation represents a major branch of the policy-oriented social sciences. The social science concern with problems of world peace dates back to the prewar period and has been heightened by the nuclear threat and the Cold War. In recent years the discussion of how social science research can be applied to the solution of these problems has been actively pursued by the "peace research" school.

V.1 TRANSLATING BASIC INTO APPLIED SOCIAL SCIENCE

Cartwright, Dorwin. "Basic and Applied Social Psychology," *Philosophy of Science,* 16, 198-208 (July 1949). Using an analysis of the war and postwar concentration on applied research in the field of social psychology as his point of departure, Cartwright discusses the relationship between basic and applied social science and suggests means for bridging the gap between the two.

Gouldner, Alvin W. "Explorations in Applied Social Science," *Social Problems,* 3, 169-181 (January 1956). A discussion of differences between basic and applied research in terms of concepts, methodology, and theory. The author contends that the needs of applied social science are not met by present models for the conversion of basic into applied knowledge.

> Reprinted in Alvin W. Gouldner and S. M. Miller (Eds.). *Applied Sociology: Opportunities and Problems.* New York: The Free Press, 5-22 (1965).

Gouldner, Alvin W. "Theoretical Requirements of the Applied Social Sciences," *American Sociological Review,* 22, 92-102 (February 1957). Discussion based on a model of the value-orientation of the applied social scientist. Gouldner identifies the theoretical and conceptual needs of applied social science.

> Reprinted in Warren G. Bennis, et al. (Eds.). *The Planning of Change: Readings in the Applied Behavioral Sciences.* New York: Holt, Rinehart, and Winston, 1961. 781 pp.

Helmer, Olaf. *Social Technology.* Santa Monica, Calif.: The RAND Corporation, February 1965. 40 pp. The author argues that the social problems facing both affluent and developing countries are so pressing that one cannot afford to wait until satisfactory theories of human relations are available. He proposes as an alternative, "a reorientation of some of the effort in the social science area toward social technology, employing operations-research techniques."

Herring, Pendleton. "The Social Sciences in Modern Society," Social Science Research Council, *Items,* 1, 2-6 (March 1947). A Director of the Social Science Research Council and member of its Committee on Problems and Policy examines the nature and responsibility of social science with special emphasis on an expanded role in the formation of public policy. The training of social science technicians, meaning individuals who can apply social science theory and concepts to practical problems is the key to such an expanded role.

Katz, Fred. "Analytic and Applied Sociologists: A Sociological Essay on a Dilemma in Sociology," *Sociology and Social Research,* 48, 440-448 (July 1964). In a revision of a paper presented at the 1963 meetings of the American Sociological Association in Los Angeles, Professor Katz presents a challenge to sociologists to use applied research to further analytic or basic sociology.

Lundberg, Craig C. "Middlemen in Science Utilization: Some Notes Toward Clarifying Conversion Roles," *The American Behavioral Scientist,* 9, 11-14 (February 1966). An attempt to define and understand the major roles involved in converting social science knowledge into practical use. The hope is to clarify the terms 'scientist' and 'practitioner.' Lundberg offers a scheme for examining conversion roles with examples of the use of the scheme.

Thompson, Laura. "Some Perspectives in Applied Anthropology," *Applied Anthropology,* 3, 12-16 (June 1944). The author argues that the applied role of the anthropologist should be one of being a "social physician" as well as a "social engineer."

Zetterberg, Hans L. *Social Theory and Social Practice.* New York: The Bedminster Press, 1962. 190 pp. A program of applied social theory for use in social service organizations. Topics discussed are the knowledge of social practitioners and social theorists, and the uses of social theory.

V.2 THE APPLICABILITY OF SOCIAL SCIENCE METHODS AND MATERIALS TO INTERNATIONAL AND MILITARY POLICY PROBLEMS

Almond, Gabriel A. "Anthropology, Political Behavior, and International Relations," *World Politics,* 2, 277-284 (January 1950). Almond illustrates the relevance of psychoanthropological insights and methods to problems of government policy by using Clyde Kluckhohn's *Mirror for Man* and Alexander H. Leighton's *Human Relations in a Changing World* as cases in point.

Bell, Daniel. "Ten Theories in Search of Reality: The Prediction of Soviet Behavior," in his *The End of Ideology: On the Exhaustion of Political Ideas in the Fifties.* New York: Collier, 315-353 (1962). In this essay the Columbia University sociologist examines critically some of the extraordinary amount of research and writing on the Soviet Union produced in the United States in the postwar period. He poses two questions: (a) Which theories or approaches have "stood up" in explaining events, and which have not? (b) If one were a policy-maker, which research would one underwrite in the future, and why?

Boguslaw, Robert. *The New Utopians: A Study of System Design and Social Change.* Englewood Cliffs, N.J.: Prentice-Hall, Inc., 1965. 213 pp. A sociologist, whose career has involved extensive participation in systems design, analyzes the assumptions about the nature of a society and various old utopian theories that are implicit in the work of the "new utopians"—computer-oriented system designers.

Bray, Charles W. "Toward a Technology of Human Behavior for Defense Use," *American Psychologist,* 17, 527-541 (August 1962). A summary of the recommendations of the Research Group in Psychology and the Social Sciences established at the Smithsonian Institution for the purpose of planning a long-range research program on human behavior for defense use. The author, a member of the Research Group, discusses the objective of defense research in psychology and the social sciences.

Brodie, Bernard. *Scientific Progress and Political Science.* Santa Monica, Calif.: The RAND Corporation, November 30, 1956. 20 pp. Discussion of the deficiencies of political science in coping with policy decisions affecting national security in an atomic age. The author points out several factors which have worked against an expanded role for political scientists in national security policy.

Casagrande, Joseph, and Gladwin, Thomas (Eds.). *Some Uses of Anthropology: Theoretical and Applied.* Washington, D.C.: The Anthropological Society of Washington, 1956. 120 pp. A selection of eight papers, presented at the Washington, D.C. Anthropological meetings in 1954-1955, examining the "relationship of anthropology to other fields . . . and its contributions to administrative problems and programs."

Davison, W. Phillips. "Political Communications as an Instrument of Foreign Policy," *Public Opinion Quarterly,* 27, 27-36 (Spring 1963). The author contrasts popular conceptions of political communication and propaganda with the approach to foreign propaganda suggested by social science research. He emphasizes the importance of making groups and organizations the principal target of foreign propaganda rather than an amorphous mass of individuals.

Davison, W. Phillips. *International Political Communication.* New York: Frederic A. Praeger, 1965. 400 pp. In a comprehensive analysis of international political communication prepared for the Council on Foreign Relations, the author traces the flow and effect of communications in democracies, communist states, and developing nations. References are made to the role of research in planning and conducting international communication programs.

George, Alexander L. "Communications Research and Public Policy," *World Politics,* 3, 251-268 (January 1951). A review article focusing on the contribution of the research reported in Daniel Lerner's *Sykewar: Psychological Warfare against Germany, D-Day to VE-Day* and Harold Lasswell's *Language of Politics* to the development of the "policy sciences."

Guetzkow, Harold. "A Use of Simulation in the Study of Inter-Nation Relations," *Behavioral Science,* 4, 183-191 (July 1959). In this description of simulation activities at Northwestern University, Guetzkow traces the origins of simulation to the war game and, in part, to social psychological group experiments. He discusses applications of internation simulation and finds that it may be used "as exercise material in the training of policy-makers. . . ."

Hennessy, Bernard. "Psycho-Cultural Studies of National Character: Relevance for International Relations," *Background,* 6, 27-49 (Fall 1962). An extensive review of the use of the concept of "national character" in anthropological research on primitive and modern cultures. The author concludes that the concept has limited relevance to the study of international relations because it does not account for the fact that policy is formed by elites, a class greatly deviant from the modal personality of national groups.

Kelman, Herbert C. (Ed.). *International Behavior: A Social-Psychological Analysis.* New York: Holt, Rinehart and Winston, 1965. 626 pp. Society for the Psychological Study of Social Issues sponsored this collection of 15 essays dealing with "social-psychological processes that occur where nationals and governments interact." The first half of the volume includes four papers in which national and international "images" figure as the dependent variable and three in which such images form the independent variable. The second half of the volume includes papers concerned with interactional processes in international relations—including strategies, decision-making, bargaining and negotiation, and personal contacts. The contributors are some of the most prominent behavioral students of international affairs.

Lasswell, Harold D. "Psychological Policy Research and Total Strategy," *The Public Opinion Quarterly,* 16, 491–500 (Winter 1952–53). It is the hypothesis of this paper that exposure to the results of research on communication can make a difference in the outcome of the decision-making process. Lasswell is concerned with the aggregate impact of psychological policy research on political decisions.

Lasswell, Harold D. "The Scientific Study of International Relations," *The Yearbook of World Affairs,* 12, 1–28 (1958). The main concern is the infusion of scientific thinking into the field of international studies in recent years.

Lasswell, Harold D. "The Policy Sciences of Development," *World Politics,* 17, 286–309 (January 1965). A review of Lucian W. Pye (Ed.), *Communications and Political Development,* Joseph LaPalombara (Ed.), *Bureaucracy and Political Development,* and Robert E. Ward and Dankwart A. Rustow (Eds.), *Political Modernization in Japan and Turkey.* Lasswell finds that the three books give evidence that "the policy sciences of development are beginning to emerge as an identifiable problem-oriented frame of reference, intersecting every specialized field of knowledge."

Lippmann, Walter. *Public Opinion.* New York: Penguin Books, 1946. 323 pp. The general subject is public opinion formation and control with particular reference to World War I and the immediate postwar era. Part VIII (Organized Intelligence) contains a discussion of the role of expert knowledge and advice in government opinion-formation and decision-making carried out in the framework of Wallas's "Great Society."

Lybrand, William A. (Ed.). *Symposium Proceedings: The U.S. Army's Limited-War Mission and Social Science Research, March 26, 27, 28, 1962.* Washington, D.C.: Special Operations Research Office, June 1962. 393 pp. The general objectives of this symposium were the following: (a) to present a clear picture of the Army's limited war mission, with special emphasis on its counterinsurgency mission; (b) to identify the Army's requirements for behavioral and social science research; and (c) to promote understanding of the Army's research and development efforts.

Packenham, Robert A. "Approaches to the Study of Political Development," *World Politics,* 17, 108-120 (October 1964). Drawing on the scholarly literature on political development, the author sets forth a typology of conditions viewed as prime correlates or determinants of political development. These are: a legal-formal constitution, a level of economic development, an administrative capacity, a social system that facilitates popular participation in governmental and political processes, and a political culture.

Pool, Ithiel de Sola, et al. *Social Science Research and National Security.* A Report Prepared by the Research Group in Psychology and the Social Sciences. Washington, D.C.: Smithsonian Institution, 1963. 261 pp. A research effort for the Defense Department. The central question of the nine topics in this volume is: "How can a branch of social science be produced which takes upon itself a responsible concern for national security matters, and how can talented individuals from within social science be drawn into this area?" Extensive bibliographic references.

Singer, J. David (Ed.). *Human Behavior and International Politics.* Chicago: Rand McNally, 1965. 466 pp. The purpose of the work is to help carry the discipline of international politics from the prescientific to the scientific stage in its development. Indicated is the nature of the possible contribution of the behavioral sciences to international politics as a systematic, scientific field of investigation. The volume is organized as a textbook on international politics.

Windle, Charles, and Vallance, T. R. "The Future of Military Psychology: Paramilitary Psychology," *The American Psychologist,* 19, 119-129 (February 1964). An analysis of the future of military psychology. The authors predict a trend toward emphasis on human components of social systems and an increase in the study of human interaction and communication across cultural boundaries. They see a significant increase in research on such psychological aspects of nation building as persuasive communication, diffusion of innovations, and political behavior.

V.3 APPLYING SOCIAL SCIENCE KNOWLEDGE IN THE AREA OF PEACE AND INTERNATIONAL COOPERATION

Albertson, Maurice L. "Peace Research—Past, Present, and Future," *Background,* 6, 29-40 (Winter 1963). Albertson analyzes the contributions made by universities, government agencies, and private organizations to the effort of bringing about a stable and permanent peace. He points out that the magnitude of the current effort is microscopic in comparison with what is needed to accomplish this objective, and encourages scholars to engage in peace research.

Angell, Robert C. "Governments and Peoples as Foci for Peace-Oriented Research," *Journal of Social Issues,* 11, No. 1, 36-41 (1955). The author examines the type of social science research that would point the way to peace. The analysis is made in terms of two broad categories of research: research on governments and research on peoples.

Blake, Robert R. "Psychology and the Crisis of Statesmanship," *The American Psychologist,* 14, 87-94 (February 1959). Presidential address, Southwestern Psychological Association, 1958. Examines several approaches for resolving differences between nations against the background of psychological theory and research.

Cohen, John. "Peace Research," *Bulletin of the Atomic Scientists,* 19, 35-36 (May 1963). Calls for a sharper critique and definition of the objective of peace research. Who are the people competent to engage in such research and what are the assumptions under which they work?

Hart, Hornell R. "Social Science and the Atomic Crisis," *The Journal of Social Issues,* Supplement Series No. 2, 30 pp. (1949). (Whole issue.) The author suggests an operational plan for bringing about the needed upsurge in the social sciences to meet the atomic crisis. An important part of this project is the social scientific study of the role of social science.

Inkeles, Alex, "Understanding a Foreign Society: A Sociologist's View," *World Politics,* 3, 269-280 (January 1951). Drawing the illustrative materials from his experience in interdisciplinary research on the Soviet Union, Inkeles discusses characteristics of the sociologist's orientation that enable him to contribute to the understanding not only of particular social systems, but to "social systems as such."

Kluckhohn, Clyde. "Anthropological Research and World Peace," in *Approaches to World Peace.* Lyman Bryson, Louis Finkelstein and Robert MacIver (Eds.). Fourth Symposium, Conference on Science, Philosophy and Religion. New York: Harper & Bros., 143-152 (1944). The anthropologist's experience with "whole" cultures and sharply contrasting peoples has given him insights which are crucial for the statesman and administrator and which, if applied, may make the world a safer place to live. A lively discussion by five anthropologists follows the paper.

Kreith, Kurt. "Peace Research and Government Policy," *Background,* 8, 269-277 (February 1965). An attempt to broaden the definition of peace research in order to distinguish between academic and applied research. Kreith sees value in having social scientists outside the government pursue policy research.

Maccoby, Michael. "Social Scientists on War and Peace: An Essay Review," *Social Problems,* 11, 106-116 (Summer 1963). An examination of the independent social scientists and their contribution to policy analysis in the areas of Soviet studies, deterrence, post-attack survival and the effect of the arms race on American society. Maccoby finds that "the independent social scientist, unlike those working for the government . . . is able to question basic assumptions of policy."

McNeil, Elton B. (Ed.). *The Nature of Human Conflict.* Englewood Cliffs, N.J.: Prentice-Hall, Inc., 1965. 315 pp. With the emphasis upon the responsibility of the social scientist for understanding the violent affairs of man, the author undertakes a systematic account of social science and the issues of war and international relations. The article "The Anthropology of Human Conflict" by Margaret Mead and Rhoda Metraux shows that the contribution of this discipline to understanding the problem of conflict resolution on the world scene lies essentially in the anthropologist's familiarity with the concept of culture.

Myrdal, Gunnar. "Psychological Impediments to Effective International Cooperation," *The Journal of Social Issues,* Supplement Series No. 6, 31 pp. (1952). (Whole issue.) Approaches the matter of psychological impediments to effective cooperation from the institutional angle and emphasizes the importance of bringing these problems to the attention of all social scientists. "The psychological impediments to overcome in making international cooperation more effective are all concerned with how to get governments . . . and ultimately the peoples, to experience allegiance to the common cause . . . The main means of fostering this larger allegiance are the actual experience of cooperation, ..."

Pachter, Henry M. "Amateur Diplomats and the Peace Literature," *Social Research,* 39, 95-107 (Spring 1963). A critical review of social scientists' proposals to end the arms race. The books reviewed have in common that they are authored by individuals whose primary expertise lies in areas other than international politics. Among the books reviewed are Amitai Etzioni's, *The Hard Way to Peace: A New Strategy* and Erich Fromm's, *May Man Prevail?*

Russell, Roger W. "Roles for Psychologists in the Maintenance of Peace," *The American Psychologist,* 15, 95-109 (February 1960). An analysis of psychological components of the values and practices underlying the "maintenance of peace." Includes suggestions for more extensive study of these components.

Schwartz, Leonard E. "Social Science and the Furtherance of Peace Research," *American Behavioral Scientist,* 9, 24-28 (March 1966). The demands of modern government require the articulation of new dimensions in the social sciences—peace research. The contention is that the complex problems confronting the twentieth century demand a probing examination of the adequacy of the social sciences for offering constructive alternatives to the use of force. ". . . A dialogue among universities, government officials, and private foundations might very well be in order to jointly determine the optimum rationale and scope of research institutions for the resolution of conflict."

Singer, J. David. "Peace Research, Peace Action," *Bulletin of the Atomic Scientists,* 19, 13-17 (January 1963). Reports the results of "a modest survey and appraisal of the peace movement as it now exists among American intellectuals." The survey elicited responses on such items as what substantive questions and issues were considered most important and most researchable and preferences regarding research strategies.

PART VI. OTHER WORKS CITED

Abt, Clark C. "War Gaming," *International Science and Technology,* August, 1964, 29-37.

Acheson, Dean. "The American Image Will Take Care of Itself," *New York Times Magazine,* February 28, 1965.

Adams, Brooks. *The Theory of Social Revolutions.* New York: The Macmillan Company, 1913.

Apter, David. *Ideology and Discontent.* New York: Free Press, 1964.

"Armed Forces and Society in Western Europe," *European Journal of Sociology,* 6, No. 2, (November 1965). (Whole issue.)

Asher, Robert E., et al. *Development of the Emerging Countries: An Agenda for Research.* Washington, D.C.: The Brookings Institution, 1962.

Bailey, Stephen K. "New Research Frontiers of Interest to Legislators and Administrators," in *Research Frontiers in Politics and Government.* Stephen K. Bailey (Ed.). Washington, D.C.: The Brookings Institution, 1–22 (1955).

Banfield, Edward C. *American Foreign Aid Doctrines.* Washington, D.C.: American Enterprise Institute, 1963.

Bauer, Raymond, Pool, Ithiel de Sola, and Dexter, Lewis. *American Business and Public Policy.* New York: Atherton Press, 1963.

Behavioral and Social Sciences Survey Committee. Washington: National Academy of Sciences-National Research Council, 1967. (Pamphlet.)

Bell, David. "The United States and World Progress." Address at Pomona College, June 11, 1961. Processed.

Bello, Francis. "The Young Scientists," *Fortune,* 49, 142-148, 172, 175-176, 181-182 (June 1954).

Benedict, Ruth F. *The Chrysanthemum and the Sword: Patterns of Japanese Culture.* Boston: Houghton Mifflin, 1946.

Benoit, Emile. "Value Judgments and the Social Sciences," *The Journal of Philosophy,* 42, 197-210 (April 1945).

Blumer, Herbert. "Science Without Concepts," *The American Journal of Sociology,* 36, 515-533 (January 1931).

Boguslaw, Robert. "Situation Analysis and the Problem of Action," *Social Problems,* 8, 212-219 (Winter 1960-61).

Boguslaw, Robert, Davis, Robert H., and Glick, Edward B. *Plans—1: A Vehicle for Studying National Policy Formation in a Less Armed World.* Falls Church, Va.: System Development Corporation, 1964.

Brand, Horst. "Disarmament and American Capitalism," *Dissent,* 9, 236-251 (Summer 1962).

Brody, Richard A. "Some Systematic Effects of the Spread of Nuclear Weapons Technology: A Study Through Simulation of a Multi-Nuclear Future," *Journal of Conflict Resolution,* 7, 663-753 (December 1963).

Bronfenbrenner, Urie. "The Mirror Image in Soviet-American Relations: A Social Psychologist's Report," *Journal of Social Issues,* 17, No. 3, 45-56 (1961).

Brookings Institution Study Group. "Political Development in the Emerging Countries: Challenge to United States Foreign Policy." Washington, D.C.: Brookings Institution, 1961. Mimeographed.

Brown, David S. "The Key to Self-Help: Improving the Administrative Capabilities of the Aid-Receiving Countries," *Public Administration Review,* 24, 64-77 (June 1964).

Buchanan, William, and Cantril, Hadley. *How Nations See Each Other.* Urbana, Ill.: University of Illinois Press, 1953.

Cantril, Hadley. "Opinion Trends in World War II: Some Guides to Interpretation," *Public Opinion Quarterly*, 12, 30-44 (Spring 1948).

Cantril, Hadley. *The Pattern of Human Concerns*. New Brunswick, N.J.: Rutgers University Press, 1965.

Caplow, Theodore. *Principles of Organization*. New York: Harcourt, Brace and World, 1964.

Carroll, Holbert N. "The Congress and National Security Policy," in *The Congress and America's Future*. David B. Truman (Ed.). Englewood Cliffs, N.J.: Prentice-Hall, 150-175 (1965).

Churchman, C. West, Ackoff, Russell L., and Arnoff, E. Leonard. *Introduction to Operations Research*. New York: John Wiley & Sons, 1957.

Cohen, Bernard C. *The Influence of Non-Government Groups on Foreign Policy Making*. Princeton, N.J.: Center of International Studies, 1959.

Committee on Appropriations, U.S. Senate. *Hearings, Mutual Security Appropriations, FY 1961*. 86th Cong., 2nd Sess., 1960.

Committee on Armed Services, U.S. Senate. *Hearings, National Defense Establishment*. 9 vols., 80th Cong., 1st Sess., 1947.

Committee on Foreign Affairs, U.S. House of Representatives, *Hearings on Foreign Assistance Act of 1962*. 87th Cong., 2nd Sess., 1962.

Committee on Foreign Relations, U.S. Senate. *Hearings on Foreign Assistance Act of 1962*. 87th Cong., 2nd Sess., 1962.

Committee on Government Operations, U.S. House of Representatives. *Operations of the Development Loan Fund*. Report No. 1526, 86th Cong., 2nd Sess., 1960.

Crow, Wayman J. "A Study of Strategic Doctrines Using the Inter-Nation Simulation," *Journal of Conflict Resolution*, 7, 580-589 (September 1963).

Dahl, Robert A. *Congress and Foreign Policy*. New York: Norton, 1964.

Davis, Robert H. "Arms Control Simulation: The Search for an Acceptable Method," *Journal of Conflict Resolution*, 7, 590-602 (September 1963).

Davison, W. Phillips. *The Berlin Blockade: A Study in Cold War Politics*. Princeton, N.J.: Princeton University Press, 1958.

De Grazia, Alfred (Ed.). *Congress: The First Branch of Government*. Washington, D.C.: American Enterprise Institute, 1966.

Dewey, John. "Liberating the Social Scientist: A Plea to Unshackle the Study of Man," *Commentary*, 4, 378-385 (October 1947).

Dexter, Lewis A. "Congressmen and the Making of Military Policy," in *New Perspectives on the House of Representatives*. Robert A. Peabody and Nelson W. Polsby (Eds.). Chicago: Rand McNally, 305-324 (1963).

Dyer, Murray. *The Weapon on the Wall: Rethinking Psychological Warfare*. Baltimore, Johns Hopkins Press, 1959.

Ericson, Martha C. "Social Status and Child-Rearing Practices." Paper delivered at the Fifty-fourth Annual Meeting of the American Psychological Association, University of Pennsylvania, 3-7 (September 1946).

Etzioni, Amitai. *A Comparative Analysis of Complex Organizations*. New York: The Free Press of Glencoe, 1961.

Etzioni, Amitai. *The Hard Way to Peace*. New York: Collier Books, 1962.

Etzioni, Amitai. *Modern Organizations*. Englewood Cliffs, N.J.: Prentice-Hall, Inc., 1964.

Free, Lloyd A. *Six Allies and a Neutral*. Glencoe, Ill.: The Free Press, 1959.

Free, Lloyd A. *Attitudes of the Cuban People Toward the Castro Regime*. Princeton, N.J.: Institute for International Social Research, 1960.

Free, Lloyd A. *Attitudes, Hopes and Fears of the Dominican People*. Princeton, N.J.: Institute of International Social Research, 1965.

Free, Lloyd A. *Some International Implications of the Political Psychology of Brazilians*. Princeton, N.J.: Institute for International Social Research, 1961.

Fyfe, Henry Hamilton. *The Illusion of National Character*. London: Watts and Co., 1946.

Gallup, George, and Rae, Saul F. *The Pulse of Democracy*. New York: Simon and Schuster, 1940.

Garthoff, Raymond. *Soviet Strategy in the Nuclear Age*. New York: Frederick A. Praeger, Inc., 1958.

Glazer, Nathan. "The Ideological Uses of Sociology," in *The Uses of Sociology*. Paul F. Lazarsfeld, William H. Sewell and Harold L. Wilensky (Eds.). New York: Basic Books, Inc., 63-77 (1967).

Goffman, Erving. *The Presentation of Self in Everyday Life*. Garden City, New York: Doubleday and Co., Inc., 1964.

Goldenweiser, E. A. "Research and Policy," *Journal of the American Statistical Association*, 39, 1-9 (March 1944).

Goldenweiser, E. A. *Translating Facts into Policy*. New York: National Bureau of Economic Research, 1946.

Goode, William. "Community within a Community: The Professions," *American Sociological Review*, 22, 194-200 (April 1957).

Gorer, Geoffrey. *The American People: A Study in National Character*. New York: W. W. Norton, 1948.

Grunberg, Emile, and Modigliani, Franco. "The Predictability of Social Events," *The Journal of Political Economy*, 62, 465-478 (December 1954).

Guetzkow, Harold, and Gyr, John. "An Analysis of Conflict in Decision-Making Groups," *Human Relations*, 7, No. 3, 367-382 (1954).

Guetzkow, Harold, Heyns, Roger W., and Marquis, Donald G. "A Social Psychological Study of the Decision-Making Conference" in *Groups, Leadership and Men*. Harold Guetzkow (Ed.). Pittsburgh: Carnegie Press, 55-67 (1951).

Hacker, A. "The Spector of Predictable Man," *The Antioch Review*, 14, 195-207 (June 1954).

Halpern, Manfred. "Toward Further Modernization of the Study of New Nations," *World Politics*, 17, 157-181 (October 1964).

Hammond, Paul Y. "NSC-68: Prologue to Rearmament," in *Strategy, Politics and Defense Budgets*. Warner R. Schilling, Paul Y. Hammond, and Glenn H. Snyder (Eds.). New York: Columbia University Press, 267-378 (1962).

Hartz, Louis. *The Liberal Tradition in America: An Interpretation of American Political Thought Since the Revolution*. New York: Harcourt, Brace, & World, Inc., 1955.

Haviland, H. Field Jr. "Foreign Aid and Foreign Politics," *AID Digest*, 21-33 (August 1962).

Hayek, Friedrich A. "The Dilemma of Specialization," in *The State of the Social Sciences*. Leonard D. White (Ed.). Chicago: The University of Chicago Press, 462-473 (1956).

Heckscher, Eli F. *Der Merkantilismus*. Jena: Verlag von Gustav Fischer, 1932.

Hoffman, Stanley. "Discord in Community: The North Atlantic Areas as a Partial International System," in *The Atlantic Community: Progress and Prospects*. Francis Wilcox and H. Field Haviland (Eds.). New York: Frederick A. Praeger, Inc., 3-31 (1963).

Hofstadter, Richard. *Anti-Intellectualism in American Life*. New York: Vintage Books, 1966.

Holton, Gerald. "Scientific Research and Scholarship: Notes Toward the Design of Proper Scales," *Daedalus*, 91, 362-399 (Spring 1962).

Huitt, Ralph. "The Outsider in the Senate: An Alternative Role," *American Political Science Review*, 55, 566-575 (September 1961).

Hull, Clark. *Principles of Behavior*. New York: Appleton, 1943.

Huntington, Samuel P. *The Soldier and the State: The Theory and Politics of Civil-Military Relations*. Cambridge, Mass.: Belknap Press of Harvard University Press, 1957.

Huntington, Samuel P. *The Common Defense: Strategic Programs in National Politics*. New York: Columbia University Press, 1961.

Huntington, Samuel P. "Political Development and Political Decay," *World Politics*, 17, 386-430 (April 1965).

"The Image of America Abroad," *Public Opinion Quarterly*, 24, 517-523 (Fall 1960). (A Symposium under the chairmanship of Leo P. Crespi.)

Inkeles, Alex. "Sigma Xi Lectures delivered at University of Connecticut." January 11, 1950.

Inkeles, Alex, and Levinson, Daniel J. "The Study of Modal Personality and Socio-cultural Systems," in *Handbook of Social Psychology*. Cambridge, Mass.: Addison-Wesley Publishing Company, 977-1020 (1954).

Janowitz, Morris. *The Military in the Political Development of New Nations*. Chicago: The University of Chicago Press, 1964.

Jordan, Nehemiah. "International Relations and the Psychologist," *Bulletin of the Atomic Scientists*, 19, 29-33 (November 1963).

Joseph, Franz M. (Ed.). *As Others See Us: The United States Through Foreign Eyes*. Princeton, N.J.: Princeton University Press, 1959.

Kaldegg, Ann. "Responses of German and English Secondary School Boys to a Projection Test," *British Journal of Psychology*, 39, 30-53 (September 1948).

Kardiner, Abram, et al. *The Psychological Frontiers of Society*. New York: Columbia University Press, 1945.

Kardiner, Abram, and Linton, Ralph. *The Individual and His Society: The Psychodynamics of Primitive Social Organization*. New York: Columbia University Press, 1939.

Key, V. O. Jr. *Public Opinion and American Democracy.* New York: Alfred A. Knopf, 1964.

Klineberg, Otto. "A Science of National Character," *Journal of Social Psychology,* 19, 147-162 (February 1944).

Kofmehl, Kenneth. *Professional Staffs of Congress.* East Lafayette, Ind.: Purdue University Press, 1962.

Lasswell, Harold D. *World Politics and Personal Insecurity.* New York: McGraw-Hill Book Co., 1935.

Lasswell, Harold D. "The Achievement Standards of a Democratic Press," in *Freedom of the Press Today.* Harold L. Ickes (Ed.). New York: The Vanguard Press, 171-178 (1941a).

Lasswell, Harold D. "World Attention Survey," *Public Opinion Quarterly,* 5, 456-462 (Fall 1941b).

Lasswell, Harold, and Kaplan, Abraham. *Power and Society.* New Haven: Yale University Press, 1950.

Lazarsfeld, Paul F. *Radio and the Printed Page.* New York: Duell, Sloane, and Pearce, 1940.

Lazarsfeld, Paul F. "The American Soldier—An Expository Review," *Public Opinion Quarterly,* 13, 377-404 (Summer 1949).

Lee, Alfred McClung. "Social Pressures and the Values of Psychologists," *The American Psychologist,* 9, 518-522 (September 1954).

Legislative Reference Service, Library of Congress. *U.S. Foreign Aid: Its Purposes, Scope, Administration, and Related Information.* House Document No. 116, 86th Cong., 1st Sess., 1959.

Lerner, Daniel. "Toward a Communication Theory of Modernization," in *Communications and Political Development.* Lucian Pye (Ed.). Princeton, N.J.: Princeton University Press, 327-350 (1963).

Likert, Rensis, and Hayes, Samuel P. Jr. (Eds.). *Some Applications of Behavioral Research.* Paris: UNESCO, 1957.

Linton, Ralph. "Speech delivered at University of Connecticut." December 5, 1949.

Lundberg, George. "Can Science Save Us?," *Harper's Magazine,* 191, 525-531 (December 1945).

Matthews, Donald R. *U.S. Senators and Their World.* New York: Vintage Books, 1960.

McClelland, David C. *The Achieving Society.* Princeton, N.J.: D. Van Nostrand and Co., 1961.

McClelland, David C. "National Character and Economic Growth in Turkey and Iran," in *Communications and Political Development.* Lucian Pye (Ed.). Princeton, N.J.: Princeton University Press, 152-181 (1963).

McDonald, Thomas J. "JCS Politico-Military Desk Games," in *Second War Gaming Symposium Proceedings.* Murray Greyson (Ed.). Washington, D.C.: Washington Operations Research Council, 63-74 (1964).

McGranahan, Donald V., and Wayne, Ivor. "German and American Traits Reflected in Popular Drama," *Human Relations,* 1, 429-455 (August 1948).

Mead, Margaret. *And Keep Your Powder Dry: An Anthropologist Looks at America.* New York: W. Morrow and Co., 1942.

Meeker, Robert J., Shure, Gerald H., and Moore, William H. Jr. "Real-Time Computer Studies of Bargaining Behavior: The Effects of Threat Upon Bargaining," in *AFIPS Conference Proceedings.* Baltimore: Spartan, 115-123 (1964).

"Memorandum from Richard Neustadt to Roger Hilsman." U.S. Bureau of Intelligence and Research, Department of State, October 12, 1962. Mimeographed.

Merriam, Charles E. *The New Democracy and the New Despotism.* New York: McGraw-Hill Book Co., 1939.

Merton, Robert K., and Lerner, Daniel. "Social Scientists and Research Policy," in *The Policy Sciences.* Daniel Lerner and Harold D. Lasswell (Eds.). Stanford, Calif.: Stanford University Press, 282-307 (1951).

Milburn, Thomas W. "The Concept of Deterrence: Some Logical and Psychological Considerations," *Journal of Social Issues,* 17, No. 3, 3-11 (1961).

Millen, Bruce. *The Political Role of Labor in Developing Countries.* Washington, D.C.: Brookings Institution, 1963.

Miller, George A., Galanter, Eugene, and Pribram, Karl H. *Plans and the Structure of Behavior.* New York: Holt, Rinehart, and Winston, 1960.

Morgenthau, Hans J. *Scientific Man Vs. Power Politics.* Chicago: University of Chicago Press, 1946.

Morris, Charles. *The Open Self.* New York: Prentice-Hall, 1948.

Murphy, Gardner and Likert, Rensis. *Public Opinion and the Individual.* New York: Harper and Brothers, 1938.

"The Need for More Specific Criteria in Programming Economic Assistance." State Department Memorandum, August 14, 1962. Mimeographed.

Neutralization in Southeast Asia: Problems and Prospects. A Study Prepared at the Request of the Committee on Foreign Relations, U.S. Senate, Washington, D.C.: Government Printing Office, 1966.

Orlansky, Jesse, and Blumstein, Alfred. *Behavioral, Political and Operational Research Programs on Counterinsurgency Supported by the Department of Defense.* Washington, D.C.: Institute for Defense Analyses, 1965.

Osgood, Charles E. *An Alternative to War or Surrender.* Urbana, Ill.: University of Illinois Press, 1962.

Parrington, V. L. *Main Currents in American Thought: An Interpretation of American Literature from the Beginning to 1920.* New York: Harcourt, Brace, & Company, 1930.

Parsons, Talcott. *The Social System.* Glencoe, Ill.: The Free Press, 1951.

Pilisuk, Marc, and Rapoport, Anatol. "Stepwise Disarmament and Sudden Destruction in a Two-Person Game: A Research Tool," *Journal of Conflict Resolution,* 8, 36-49 (March 1964).

Pool, Ithiel de Sola. *Satellite Generals: A Study of Military Elites in the Soviet Sphere.* Stanford, Calif.: Stanford University Press, 1955.

Pool, Ithiel de Sola and Prasad, Kali. "Indian Student Images of Foreign Peoples," *Public Opinion Quarterly,* 22, 293-304 (Fall 1958).

"Presidential Advice to Younger Sociologists," *American Sociological Review,* 18, 597-604 (December 1953).

Price, Derek de Solla. *Little Science, Big Science.* New York: Columbia University Press, 1963.

Pye, Lucian W. *Guerilla Communism in Malaya: Its Social and Political Meaning.* Princeton, N.J.: Princeton University Press, 1956.

Pye, Lucian W. *Politics, Personality and Nation Building: Burma's Search for Identity.* New Haven, Conn.: Yale University Press, 1962.

Pye, Lucian W. (Ed.). *Communications and Political Development.* Princeton, N.J.: Princeton University Press, 1963.

Pye, Lucian W. "The Developing Areas: Problems for Research," in *Studying Politics Abroad: Field Research in Developing Areas.* Robert E. Ward (Ed.). Boston and Toronto: Little Brown and Co., 5-25 (1964).

Pye, Lucian W. and Verba, Sidney. *Political Culture and Political Development.* Princeton, N.J.: Princeton University Press, 1965.

"Report on Viet Nam Survey," *The American Sociologist,* 2, 271 (November 1967).

Research in Arms Control and Disarmament, 1960-1963. New York: Ford Foundation, 1963.

Riesman, David. *Faces in the Crowd.* New Haven: Yale University Press, 1952.

Riesman, David. *Constraint and Variety in American Education.* New York: Doubleday and Co., 1958.

Riesman, David. "From Morality to Morale," in *Personality and Political Crisis.* Alfred H. Stanton and Stewart E. Perry (Eds.). Glencoe, Ill.: The Free Press, 81-120 (1951).

Ronge, Maximilian. *Kriegs- und Industrie-Espionage.* Vienna: Amalthea-Verlag, 1930.

Roosevelt, James (Ed.). *The Liberal Papers.* New York: Quadrangle Books, 1962.

Rose, Arnold. "The Social Responsibility of the Social Scientist," *Social Problems,* 1, 85-90 (January 1954).

Rusk, Dean. "The Bases of the United States Foreign Policy," *Proceedings of the Academy of Political Science,* 27, 100-110 (January 1962).

Rustow, Dankwart A. "The Vanishing Dream of Stability," *AID Digest,* 3-6 (August 1962).

Sargeant, Howland. "American Information and Cultural Representation Overseas," in *The Representation of the United States Abroad.* Vincent M. Barnett, Jr. (Ed.). New York: Fredrick A. Praeger, Inc., 75-128 (1965).

Schelling, Thomas C. *The Strategy of Conflict.* Cambridge, Mass.: Harvard University Press, 1960.

Schramm, Wilbur. *Utilization of the Behavioral Sciences: Report of a Planning Review for the Behavioral Sciences Division.* New York: Ford Foundation, 1954.

Shepard, Harold A. "The Value System of a University Research Group," *American Sociological Review,* 19, 456-462 (August 1954).

Shils, Edward A. "Social Inquiry and the Autonomy of the Individual," in *The Human Meaning of the Social Sciences.* Daniel Lerner (Ed.). New York: Meridian Books, Inc., 114-157 (1959).

Shure, Gerald H., Rogers, Miles S., and Meeker, Robert J. "Group Decision Making Under Conditions of Realistic Complexity," *Human Factors,* 5, No. 1, 49-58 (1963).

Simon, Herbert A. "Bandwagon and Underdog Effects and the Possibility of Election Predictions," *The Public Opinion Quarterly,* 18, 245-253 (Fall 1954).

Simon, Herbert A. *Models of Man.* New York: John Wiley and Sons, Inc., 1957.

Singer, J. David. *Deterrence, Arms Control, and Disarmament.* Columbus, Ohio: Ohio State University Press, 1962.

Slater, Phillip. "Role Differentiation in Small Groups," *American Sociological Review,* 20, 300-310 (June 1955).

Smith, Bruce Lannes. "Propaganda Analysis and the Science of Democracy," *Public Opinion Quarterly,* 5, 250-259 (June 1941).

Smith, Bruce L. R. "The RAND Corporation: Case Study of Nonprofit Advisory Corporation." Unpublished Ph.D. dissertation, Harvard University, 1964.

Social Science Research Council. *The Pre-Election Polls of 1948: Report to the Committee on Analysis of Pre-Election Polls and Forecasts.* New York: Social Science Research Council, 1949.

Somit, Albert and Tanenhaus, Joseph. "Trends in American Political Science: Some Analytical Notes," *American Political Science Review,* 57, 933-947 (December 1963).

Speier, Hans. *German Rearmament and Atomic War: The Views of German Military and Political Leaders.* Evanston, Ill.: Row, Peterson, and Co., 1957.

Stagner, Ross. "Personality Dynamics and Social Conflict," *Journal of Social Issues,* 17, No. 3, 28-44 (1961).

Strauss, Leo. "Social Science and Humanism," in *The State of the Social Sciences.* Leonard D. White (Ed.). Chicago: The University of Chicago Press, 415-425 (1956).

Thompson, James Westfall and Padover, Saul K. *Secret Diplomacy: A Record of Espionage and Double-Dealing, 1500-1815.* London: Jarrold, Ltd., 1937.

Truman, David B. *Governmental Process: Political Interests and Public Opinion.* New York: Knopf, 1951.

U.S. Agency for International Development, Program Coordination Staff. *Principles of Foreign Economic Assistance.* Washington, D.C.: Government Printing Office, 1963a.

U.S. Agency for International Development, Program Coordination Staff. *Program Guidance Manual.* Washington, D.C.: Government Printing Office, 1962 and 1963b.

U.S. Agency for International Development, Program Coordination Staff. "Types of AID Strategy: Outline." 1963C. Mimeographed.

United States Foreign Policy. Compilation of Studies Prepared Under the Direction of the Committee on Foreign Relations, U.S. Senate. Washington, D.C.: Government Printing Office, 1966.

United States Information Agency, Research and Reference Service. *Some Indications of World-Wide Public Opinion Toward the U.S. and the U.S.S.R.* Washington, D.C.: U.S.I.A., 1963.

Uyeki, Eugene S. "Behavior and Self-Identity of Federal Scientist-Administrators," in *Research Program Effectiveness.* M. C. Yovits, et al. (Eds.). New York: Gordon and Breach, 495-527 (1966).

Vidich, Arthur J., and Bensman, Joseph. *Small Town in Mass Society: Class, Power, and Religion in a Rural Community.* Garden City, N.Y.: Doubleday & Company, Inc., 1960.

Vidich, Arthur J., Bensman, Joseph, and Stein, Maurice (Eds.). *Reflections on Community Studies.* New York: John Wiley and Sons, Inc. 1964.

Vollmer, Howard. *A Preliminary Investigation and Analysis of the Role of Scientists in Research Organizations.* Menlo Park, Calif.: Stanford Research Institute, 1962.

Wallas, Graham. *The Great Society.* New York: The Macmillan Co., 1914.

Walsh, John. "AID: Almost Everyone Favors Research on Development Problems but Going Has Not Been Smooth," *Science,* 792-795 (May 17, 1963).

Waples, Douglas (Ed.). *Print, Radio and Film in a Democracy.* Chicago, Ill.: The University of Chicago Press, 1942.

Whitehead, A. N. *Science and the Modern World.* New York: Macmillan, 1950.

Wiener, Norbert. *The Human Use of Human Beings: Cybernetics and Society.* New York: Doubleday, 1954.

Wirth, Louis. "Responsibility of Social Sciences," *Annals of the American Academy of Political and Social Science,* 249, 143-151 (January 1948a).

Wirth, Louis. "Consensus and Mass Communication," *American Sociological Review,* 13, 1-15 (February 1948b).

Wolfenstein, Martha. *Disaster: A Psychological Essay*. Glencoe, Ill.: The Free Press, 1957.

Wriggins, W. Howard. "Politics: Purpose and Program," *AID Digest*, 17-20 (August 1962).

Young, Donald. "Sociology and the Practicing Professions," *American Sociological Review*, 20, 641-648 (December 1955).

Znaniecki, Florian. *The Method of Sociology*. New York: Farrar and Rinehart, 1934.

Author Index

Page numbers in italics are in Bibliographic Appendix.

Abt, Clark, 229, *318*
Acheson, Dean, 216, 218, 221, *318*
Ackoff, Russell L., 225, *319*
Adams, Brooks, 67, *318*
Albertson, Maurice L., *316*
Alger, Chadwick, *309*
Almond, Gabriel A., 156, 214n, 243, 271n, *287, 304, 313*
Alpert, Harry, 136n, 234–235, *301*
Angell, Robert C., *316*
Apter, David, 148, *318*
Archibald, Kathleen, 10n, *287, 304*
"Armed Forces and Society," 132, *318*
Arnoff, Leonard E., 225, *318*
Asher, Robert E., 113n, *318*

"Background Information...," *305*
Bailey, Gerald, 78, 242n, *310*
Bailey, Stephen, 136n, *318*
Banfield, Edward C., 116, 121, *318*
Barber, Arthur, 53, *308*
Barber, Bernard, 18, *291*
Barnett, Vincent M., Jr., *322*
Barton, Allen, 69, 72, 73, *292*
Bauer, Raymond, 138, 218n, *292, 318*
Beals, Ralph, *305, 310*
Beer, John J., *289*
Behavioral and Social Sciences Survey, 24, *318*
Bell, Daniel, 79, *294, 313*
Bell, David E., 124, *318*
Bello, Francis, 93, *318*
Ben-David, Joseph, 152n, *292*
Benedict, Ruth F., 156, 157, 211, *318*
Benne, Kenneth D., *294*
Bennett, Meridan, *310*
Bennis, Warren G., 52, *287, 299, 302, 312*
Benoit, Emile, 170, 172, 248n, *318*
Bensman, Joseph, 16, 24, *292, 312*
Biderman, Albert D., 11n, 55, *292*
Blake, Robert R., *316*
Blumer, Herbert, 239n, *318*
Blumstein, Alfred, 71n, *322*
Boggs, Stephen T., *305*

Boguslaw, Robert, 230, 231, *306, 314, 318*
Boulding, Kenneth, 75, 170, 172, *305*
Bowers, Raymond V., 10n, *310*
Bowles, Chester, 118
Bramson, Leon, 4, *292, 295*
Brand, Horst, 172n, *318*
Bray, Charles W., 156n, 235n, *305, 314*
Braybrooke, David, 135, *296*
Brodie, Bernard, *288, 314*
Brody, Richard A., 229, *318*
Bronfenbrenner, Urie, 230, *318*
Brookings Institution Study Group, 114n, 118n, *318*
Brown, David S., 121, *318*
Bruck, H. W., *297*
Bryson, Lyman, *296, 316*
Buchanan, William, 219n, *318*

"Camelot and Psychological Tests," 2n, 15, *305*
Cantril, Hadley, 214, 219n, 221n, *318, 319*
Caplow, Theodore, 72, 73, *319*
Carroll, Holbert N., 136n, 139, *318*
Carter, Launor F., *310*
Carter, Luther J., *305*
Cartwright, Dorwin, *302, 312*
Casagrande, Joseph, *314*
Churchman, C. West, 225, *318*
Cohen, Bernard C., 218n, *318*
Cohen, John, *316*
Committee on Appropriations, 122, *319*
Committee on Armed Services, 13, *319*
Committee on Foreign Affairs, 123, *287, 319*
Committee on Foreign Relations, 118n, *319*
Committee on Government Operations, 117n–118n, *319*
Compton, Bertita, 70n, *299*
"Congress and Social Science," 2n, *301*
Coser, Lewis, *292*
Crawford, Elisabeth T., 10n, 154–155, *302, 305*
Croker, George W., *288*
Crow, Wayman J., 229, *319*

Dahl, Robert, 126, 136n, *319*
Darley, John G., *302, 305*

325

Davis, Robert H., 230, *318, 319*
Davis, Vincent, *308*
Davison, W. Phillips, 10n, 133, 214n, 217, *310, 314, 319*
de Grazia, Alfred, 141n, *301, 319*
de Rivera, Joseph, 168
Deutsch, Karl, 54, 224, 226, *296*
Deutsch, Morton, 172
Dewey, John, 247, *319*
Dexter, Lewis A., 136n, 138, 139, 218n, *318, 319*
Durkheim, Emile, 32, 151
Dyer, Murray, 196n, *319*

Easton, David, *294*
Eaton, Joseph W., *299*
"Editor's Column," 2n, *305*
Elder, Robert E., *310*
Ellis, William, 23, 70, 71, *301*
Embre, John, *302*
Engler, Robert, *287*
Ericson, Martha C., 210, *319*
Etzioni, Amitai, 69n–70n, 72, 122n, 170, *317, 319*
Eulau, Heinz, 141n
Evans, Allan, *308, 310*

Federal Funds..., 10, 23, 71, 153, *301*
Feld, Maury, 130, *308*
Feldman, Sheldon, 168
Festinger, Leon, *289*
Finklestein, Louis, *316*
Fisher, Roger, *307*
Free, Lloyd, 215, 216, 217, 218n, *319*
Friedman, Saul, *303*
Fromm, Erick, 170, *317*
Fulbright, J. W., *306*
Fyfe, Henry Hamilton, 208, *319*

Galanter, Eugene, 225, *321*
Galbraith, John K., 147
Gallup, George, 261n, *319*
Galtung, Johan, *306*
Garge, John, *304*
Garthoff, Raymond, 133, *319*
Geiger, George, *294*
George, Alexander, *314*
Gerth, H. H., *294*
Gerver, Israel, *292*
Gilpin, Robert, 74, *288*
Gladwin, Thomas, *314*
Glazer, Nathan, v–vi, *319*
Glick, Edward B., 230, *318*
Glock, Charles Y., 235n, *288, 299*
Goethals, George, *295*
Goffman, Erving, 16, *319*
Goldenweiser, E. A., 251n, 252, *320*
Goldstein, Walter, *306*
Gollin, Arthur, *310*
Goode, William, 69, 73–74, *320*
Goodenough, Ward H., *306*

Gordon, Gerald, 52, *299*
Gorer, Geoffrey, 156, 212, 213, *320*
Gosnel, Harold I., *303*
Gouldner, Alvin W., 235n, 253, 256, *288, 305, 312, 313*
Graham, Milton D., 253n, *307*
Greyson, Murray, *321*
Grunberg, Emile, 255, *320*
Guetzkow, Harold, 169, 229, 237n, 255, *314, 319*
Gyr, John, 255, *320*

Hacker, A., 92n, *320*
Hagen, Everett, 113n
Hall, Edward T., *310*
Halperin, Morton, 56, 136n, *303*
Halpern, Manfred, 113, *320*
Hammond, Paul Y., 136n, *320*
Hart, Hornell R., *316*
Harter, Carl L., *292*
Hartz, Louis, 126, *320*
Hauser, Philip M., 235n, 237n, *288*
Haviland, H. Field, Jr., 114n, *320*
Hayek, Friedrick A., 257, *320*
Hayes, Samuel P., Jr., 253n, 257, *289, 321*
Heckscher, Eli, 260n, *320*
Helmer, Olaf, 235n, 237n, *312*
Hennessy, Bernard, *314*
Hero, Alfred, 214n
Herring, Pendleton, 7, 235n, 256, *288, 313*
Heyns, Roger W., 255, *320*
Hilsman, Roger, 13n, 53, 278, *308*
Hinkle, Gisela J., 4, 17, *292*
Hinkle, Roscoe C., 4, 17, *292*
Hirsch, Walter, *291*
Hitch, Charles J., *288*
Hoffman, Stanley, 275, *320*
Hofstadter, Richard, 148, *320*
Holsti, Ole R., *308*
Holton, Gerald, 89, *320*
Hopper, Janice, 19n, 70n, *299*
Horowitz, Irving Louis, 15, 173, *288, 306, 309*
Hughes, Thomas L., *305*
Huitt, Ralph, 137, *320*
Hull, Clark, 224, *320*
Huntington, Samuel, 113, 271, *295, 320*

Ickes, Harold L., *321*
"Image of America Abroad, The," 219n, *320*
Inkeles, Alex, 211, 221, *316, 320*

Janowitz, Morris, 129, 132, *308, 320*
Jordon, Nehemiah, 223, *320*
Joseph, Franz M., 219n, *320*

Kaldegg, Ann, 210, *320*
Kaplan, Abraham, 137n, *321*
Kaplan, Norman, 19n, 22, 52n, *291, 292*
Kardiner, Abram, 208, 209, 210, *320*
Katz, Daniel, *289*

Katz, Fred, *313*
Katzenbach, Edward L., *303*
Kecskemeti, Paul, 235n, *288, 292, 307*
Kelly, George, *293*
Kelman, Herbert, 241, *295, 314*
Key, V. O., Jr., 214n, *321*
Kissinger, Henry A., *308*
Klein, Lawrence R., *299*
Klineberg, Otto, 207, 211, *321*
Kluckhohn, Clyde, 157, 235n, *316*
Kofmehl, Kenneth, 142, *321*
Kraft, Joseph, *303*
Kreith, Kurt, *316*
Kuhn, Thomas S., 22, 226, *293*

Lane, Robert, *295*
Langer, William L., *309*
Lanier, Lyle H., *303, 305*
Lasswell, Harold, 3n, 113–114, 126, 137n, 261, *287, 288, 289, 293, 295, 296, 314, 315, 321*
Lazarsfeld, Paul F., 51, 52, 86, 261n, 280, *288, 299, 310, 319, 321*
Lee, Alfred McClung, 92n, *300, 321*
Legislative Reference Service, 116, *321*
Leighton, Alexander A., *287, 288, 303*
Lens, Sidney, 173
Lerner, Daniel, 3n, 123, 218n, 253n, *287, 288, 289, 314, 321, 322*
Levinson, Daniel J., 221, *320*
Lewis, W. David, *289*
Likert, Rensis, 136n, 235n, 253n, 257, 261n, *289, 321*
Lindblom, Charles E., 135, *296*
Linton, Ralph, 208, 210, *287, 289, 320, 321*
Lippitt, Ronald, 235n, 253n, *289, 294*
Lippman, Walter, 6, *315*
Little, Roger, *308*
Long, N. E., *296*
Lundberg, Craig C., 235n, *313*
Lundberg, George, 248n, *301, 321*
Lybrand, William A., 156n, *315*
Lynd, Robert, 8, 92n, *287, 289*
Lynn, Kenneth S., 22, 243, *289*
Lyons, Gene M., 10n, *302, 303*

McClelland, David C., 114n, 126n–127n, *321*
Maccoby, Michael, *316*
McDiarmid, John, *303*
McDonald, Thomas J., 229, *321*
McGranahan, Donald V., 211, 212, *321*
MacGregor, Gordon, *301*
McHale, Thomas, 118
MacIver, Robert, *316*
McNeil, Elton B., *316*
Mainzer, Lewis C., *306*
Mannheim, Karl, 17, 151, 152, 264n, *293, 294*
Marquis, Donald G., 255, *320*
Marquis, Sue, 52, *299*
Marnel, William, *304*
Masland, John W., *309*

Matthews, Donald R., 140n, *321*
Mead, Margaret, 156, 157, 211, *289, 316, 321*
Meeker, Robert J., 229, 230, *321, 322*
Melman, Seymour, 170, 172
Merriam, Charles, E., 259n, *321*
Merton, Robert K., 8n, 15, 17n, 18–22, 247, 248, 249, 250, 253n, *289, 291, 293, 297, 321*
Metraux, Rhoda, *316*
Milburn, Thomas W., 230, *321*
Millen, Bruce, 114n, *321*
Miller, George A., 225, *321*
Miller, S. M., *288, 305, 312*
Mills, C. Wright, *289, 293, 294*
Miniclier, Louis, *310*
Mitford, Jessica, 16
Modigliani, Franco, 255, *319*
Moore, William H., 230, *321*
Morgenthau, Hans J., 250, *321*
Morris, Charles, 96, *321*
Morton, Louis, *303*
Mosely, Philip, *288*
Moyca, David C., *303*
Murphy, Gardner, 261n, *321*
Myrdal, Gunnar, 1, 3, 7, 235n, *289, 316*

Nagle, William, *304*
"Need for More Specific Criteria . . . , The," 122n, *322*
Neustadt, Richard, 118, 120, *321*
Neutralization in Southeast Asia, 142, *322*
"New Intelligence Requirements," 23, *304*
Nichols, Roy F., *303*
Nisbet, Robert A., *306*

Ohly, John, 124n
Orlans, Harold, 12, 155, *306*
Orlansky, Jesse, 71n, *322*
Osgood, Charles E., 168, 170, 171, 223, 225, 226, 229, *322*

Pachter, Henry M., 172n, *317*
Packenham, Robert A., 112, *315*
Padover, Saul K., 259, *323*
Parrington, V. L., 92n, *322*
Parsons, Talcott, 132, 247, *290, 300, 301, 305, 322*
Peabody, Robert A., *319*
Perry, Stewart E., *322*
Pfaffman, Carl, 235n, *301*
Pilisuk, Marc, 230, *322*
"Planners for the Pentagon," *303*
Polk, William R., 53, *309*
Polsby, Nelson W., *296, 319*
Pool, Ithiel de Sola, 132, 138, 156, 218n, 219n, *306, 315, 318, 322*
Prasad, Kali, 219n, *322*
"Presidential Advice to Younger Sociologists," 98, *322*
Pribram, Karl H., 225, *321*
Price, Derek de Solla, 89, *322*
Price, Don K., 11, *301*
Pye, Lucian W., 114n, 126, 132, 221, *321, 322*

Radway, Laurence, *309*
Rae, Saul F., 261n, *319*
Ransom, Harry, *308, 309*
Rapaport, Anatol, 173, 230, *322*
Raup, Bruce, *294*
Record, Wilson, *300*
"Report on Viet Nam Survey," 158n, *322*
Research and Technical Programs Subcommittee, 10n–11n, 157, *302*
Research in Arms Control and Disarmament, 71n, *322*
Rice, Stuart, 12, *302*
Riesman, David, 4, 92n, 96n, *295, 322*
Robinson, James, 149n, *297, 307*
Rogers, Miles S., 229, *322*
Ronge, Maximilian, 259n, *322*
Roosevelt, James, 165, 171, *322*
Rose, Arnold, 92n, *322*
Rosengren, William I., 52, *300*
Rostow, Walt W., 53, *309*
Rusk, Dean, 116, *322*
Russell, Roger W., *317*
Rustow, Dankwart A., 114n, *322*

Sapin, Burton, *297*
Sargeant, Howland, 214n, *322*
Schaedel, Richard P., *311*
Schatzman, Leonard, 18, *294*
Schelling, Thomas, 231, *322*
Schelting, Alexander von, 30, *294*
Schilling, Warner R., *288, 320*
Schramm, Wilbur, 253n, 256, *322*
Schwartz, Leonard F., *317*
Scientific Activities . . . , 11n, *302*
Sewell, William, *288, 310, 319*
Shepard, Harold A., 97, *322*
Shils, E. A., 15, 235n, 239n, *289, 290, 295, 322*
Shure, Gerald H., 229, 230, *321, 322*
Sibley, Elbridge, 52, *300*
Sibley, Mulford, 173
Silvert, Kalman, 15
Simon, Herbert A., 55, 73, 169, 231, 255, *297, 323*
Singer, J. David, 225, 226, *315, 317, 323*
Sjoberg, Gideon, *306*
Slater, Philip E., 255, *323*
Smith, B. L. R., 71, *304, 311, 323*
Smith, Bruce Lannes, 261, *323*
Smithburg, Donald W., 73, *297*
Snyder, Richard C., *297, 320*
Social Science Research Council, 15, *323*
Somit, Albert, 52, 126, *300, 323*
Speier, Hans, 133, *323*
Spencer, Herbert, 32
Stagner, Ross, 230, *323*
Stanton, Alfred E., *322*
Stein, Maurice, *323*
Storer, Norman, 18, 20–22, 236n, *293, 294*
Stouffer, Samuel, 5, *304*
Strauss, Anselm, 18, *294*
Strauss, Leo, 354, *323*
"Strengthening the Behavioral Sciences," 239, *304*

"Structure of . . . , The," 12n, 70n, *300*
Subcommittee on Government Research, 155, *304, 306*
Subcommittee on International Organizations and Movements, 157n, *304*
Swanson, G. E., *294*

Tanenhaus, Joseph, 52, 126, *300, 323*
Thompson, James Westfall, 259, *323*
Thompson, Laura, *313*
Thompson, Victor, A., 73, *297*
Truman, David B., 270, *323*
Tyler, Ralph, *299*

U. S. Agency for International Development, 111, 119, 120, 122, 123, *323*
U. S. Arms Control and Disarmament Agency, 172
U. S. Department of State, 71, *304, 309*
United States Foreign Policy, 142, 148, *323*
U. S. Information Agency, 219, *323*
U. S. National Resources Committee, 5, 6, 7, 8, 10, *302*
Uyeki, Eugene S., 56n, *323*

Vallance, T. R., 235n, *305, 315*
Verba, Sidney, 221, *322*
Vidich, Arthur, 16, 24, *323*
Vollmer, Howard M., 86n, *323*

Waldo, Dwight, 4, 7, *300*
Wallas, Graham, 259n, *323*
Walsh, John, 124n, *305, 323*
Waples, Douglas, 261n, *323*
Ward, Robert E., *322*
Wayne, Ivor, 211, *321*
Webbink, Paul, 253n, 257, *308*
Weber, Max, 151, 152, *296*
White, Leonard D., *303, 320, 323*
Whitehead, A. N., 224, *323*
Wiener, Norbert, 224, *323*
Wilcox, Francis, *320*
Wildavsky, Aaron, *297*
Wilensky, Harold L., 54, *288, 297, 310, 319*
Wilson, John T., *302*
Wilson, Logan, *294*
Windle, Charles, 235n, *315*
Wirth, Louis, 5, 247, 249, 250, *294, 323*
Wohl, Richard R., *300*
Wohlstetter, Albert, 76, *288*
Wolfenstein, Martha, 132, *324*
Wood, Robert, *288*
Woodward, Julian L., *304*
Wooton, Barbara, *296*
Wriggins, Howard W., 114n, *324*
Wright, Christopher, 74, *288*

Yarmolinsky, Adam, 53, *309*
Young, Donald, 198, *290, 300, 324*
Yovits, M. C., *323*

Zetterberg, Hans L., *313*
Zloczower, Awraham, 152, *292*
Znaniecki, Florian, 30, 34, *294, 324*

Subject Index

Administration, 65–66, 67
  preparation for, 67–68
  of research, 46, 56, 156
  scientists in, 67
  university, 67
Agency for International Development (AID), 111–112, 115, 117–120, 122–123, 125
  Program Coordination Staff, 111, 120, 122
  research in, 124
Air Force, U. S., 164, 177, 185
  Air University, 187
  Chief of Staff of, 186, 187, 192
  code of ethics for, 186–188
  Human Resources Research Institute (HRRI), 185–194
  Russian Research Center (Harvard University), 131, 192–193
American Political Science Association, 76, 150
American Psychological Association, 15, 187
  Committee on Psychology in International Affairs, 166, 167
Americans for Democratic Action, 164
American Sociological Association, 15, 158
American Sociological Society, 7, 98, 198
American Statistical Association, 15
American University, 175
  and Project Camelot, 179
Applied research, 2, 3, 90
  defined, 38–39, 247–248, 253
  dynamic, 38–39
  therapeutic, 40
  value-judgments in, *see* Policy-oriented social science, value-questions in
Area studies, 77–78, 202
Arms Control and Disarmament Agency (ACDA), 154
Army, U. S., 130, 174, 175, 176, 177, 178, 180, 181, 185
  and academic psychologists, World War I, 5, 37–38
  and Project Camelot, *see* Camelot, Project

Basic research, 49
  and applied research compared, 204, 238, 248
  defined, 168, 247, 253

  see also "Robin-hooding"
Bay of Pigs invasion, 216
Behavioral and Social Science Survey (National Academy of Sciences), 24
Behavioral scientists, 9, 96, 97
  in Congress, 145, 147, 149
  see also Social scientists
Boulding, Kenneth, 170
Brookings Institution, 146
Bureau of Applied Social Research (Columbia University), 87, 88
Bush, Vannevar, 64

Camelot, Project, 15–16, 75, 154, 157, 158, 175–176, 180
  criticism of, 174, 178–179
  participants' conceptions of, 177–178
Census, social research in, 5–6, 87
Center for Advanced Study in the Behavioral Sciences, 164, 165
Center for International Studies (MIT), 200, 279
Center for Research on Conflict Resolution, 170
Central Intelligence Agency (CIA), 13, 14, 154–155
Civilian strategists, 75, 76–77, 170
Cold War, 10, 156–157, 159
  role of images in, 171–172
Communications research, 9, 74, 78, 79–80, 198, 199, 221–222
  organization of, 195–196
  political, 199–200
  theory, 200–202
Conference Research Project, 255
Congress, U. S., 167, 192
  diffusion of power in, 138
  and foreign policy decision-making, 138–139
  and the social sciences, 23, 135–136, 148–150
  as a social system, 137
  see also Congressional committees; House of Representatives, U. S.; Senate, U. S.
Congressional committees, foreign policy and defense, 139
  background and review hearings, 140, 144, 148
  legislative hearings, 139, 144

membership, 140–141
social scientists testifying, 140, 143–147
sponsorship of research, 142–143
staffs, 141–142
Contract and grant system, 11, 181
and social science, 11–12
Cost-effectiveness analysis, 76, 276
Council on Foreign Relations, 147
Councils for Correspondence, 170
Counterinsurgency, 78, 133; *see also* Camelot, Project
Craigie, L. E., 190, 191
Crespi, Leo P., 214

Darwin, Charles R., 4
Decision-making, 61–62, 65–66, 270–274, 280–281
foreign policy, 231–232, 274–276
and scientific advances, 64
and scientific research, 61, 62–64
Decision-making theories, 53, 135
role of knowledge in, 54
Department of Defense, 12, 139, 153, 157, 175, 177, 178, 276
Defense Documentation Center, 57, 175
Research and Development Board, 186
Department of State, 53, 62, 118, 125, 139, 157, 174, 176, 177, 178, 182, 195
Bureau of Intelligence Research (INR), 14, 79, 118, 119, 122
Office of External Research (INR), 57, 79
Policy Planning Staff, 119
support of research, 14, 57, 78–79
Deterrence, *see* Influence processes, international
Disarmament, 165
economic consequences of, 172–173
Dulles, John Foster, 214, 215
Dungan, Ralph, 174

Economics, 3, 7, 35, 39, 76
Eisenhower, Dwight D., 214, 215

Federal government, and agricultural research, 6
civil service, 2, 66–67
collection of socio-economic data, 5–6
educational institutions, 238, 239
expenditure for social science research, 23, 71, *see also* Social sciences, economic requirements of
"in-house" research organizations, 7
support of university research, 10–11
system for support of research, 6, 9, 11, 155; *see also* Contract and grant system
see also individual agencies and departments
Financing of research, *see* Foundations; Federal government, expenditure for social science research; Social sciences, economic requirements of
Foreign aid, 124–125, 148; *see also* Political development; Agency for International Development
Foreign area research, *see* Policy research, international and military
Foundation for Research on Human Behavior, 257
Foundations, 8
support of social science research, 5
Fulbright, William, 137, 174

Galtung, Johan, 176
Giddings, Franklin H., 4
Goldhammer, Herbert, 191
GRIT (Graduated and Reciprocated Initiatives in Tension Reduction), 165, 171, 223, 229, 240
Groves, Leslie R., 64

Hopper, Rex, 175
House of Representatives, U. S., 137, 139, 157
Committee on Foreign Affairs, 176; *see also* Congressional committees, foreign policy and defense
Human Relations Area Files, 200
Humphrey, Hubert, 137

Influence processes, international, 156
models of, 171–172, 225–228
and psychological research, 168–169, 223–224, 229–230
simulation of, 228–229
Information science, 55
Institute for Defense Analyses, 76
Institute for International Social Research (Princeton, New Jersey), 221
Institute for Social Research (University of North Carolina), 87, 88
Intelligence research, 9, 13–14, 79, 202–203
covert sponsorship of, 14
International Studies Association, 76

Johnson, Lyndon B., 176, 182, 215, 217
Joint Chiefs of Staff, Joint War Games Agency, 78, 228

Kennedy, John F., 116, 215, 216, 219
Keynes, Maynard, 4, 97, 149
Knowledge systems, 30–32, 62
and social systems, 31
validity of, 30–31
Korean War, 129, 131, 157, 188; *see also* Policy Research, international and military, Korean War
Kuter, Lawrence, 191

Le May, Curtis E., 187, 188

McCarthy, Eugene, 141
McNamara, Robert, 174, 178
Malthus, Thomas Robert, 3
Marx, Karl, 4
Military elites, 128–129
career development of, 129–130, 133
Military-scientific programs, 10, 56, 67
security and loyalty requirements for, 12, 179
social scientists in, 9–10

SUBJECT INDEX   331

Military services, and international relations, 133
  personnel research in, 78, 130
  and political indoctrination, 129
  psychological warfare functions of, 131
  social science programs in, 153, 185–186, 236–237
  and strategic intelligence, 131
  see also individual services
Millikan, Max, 146
Models, 224
  mechanistic, 224
  organismic, 224
Morgenthau, Hans J., 126
Morse, Wayne, 137

NASA (National Aeronautics and Space Agency), 182
National Academy of Sciences–National Research Council, 24, 201
National character studies, 207
  predictive value of, 210–211
  and U.S. Navy, 157
  validity in, 211–213
  World War II, 156, 207
National Foundation for the Social Sciences, 155
National Institute of Health (NIH), 89, 90, 182
National Opinion Research Center (NORC), 87, 88, 89
National Science Foundation, 70, 89, 90, 154, 182, 234
  Register of Scientific and Technical Personnel, 70
National Security Council, 66, 274
Nations, 209
  and cultures, 207–208, 209–210
  patterns of evolution in, 208
Natural sciences, 36–37
  and social sciences compared, 37
Navy, U. S., 130, 185
  and national character studies, 157
  Naval Ordinance Test Station, China Lake, 170
Nonuse of research, 55
Nutini, Hugo G., 176

Office of Education, 90, 182
Office of Strategic Services, Research and Analysis Branch, 13
  research in, 101–103
Office of War Information, Overseas Branch, 100–108, 257
Osgood, Charles E., 147, 171

Peace research, 73, 75, 76–77, 167, 170
  psychologists in, 163–165, 166
  and social change, 170–171, 173
Policy, 259, 262, 269
  analysis, 283–284
  intelligence in, 6, 261, 262–263; *see also* Uses of social science knowledge, intelligence
  process of formulating, 260–261
Policy-making elites, 42–43
  attitudes toward social science, 43–44, 45, 54, 126

judgments of research, 47
  and scientific esoterica, 2
  studies of, 53–54
  see also Military elites; Foreign aid; Congressional committees, membership
Policy-oriented social science, 69–70
  contributing disciplines, 3
  and domestic welfare programs, 158–159
  functions of, 233; *see also* Uses of social science knowledge: engineering, enlightenment, intelligence
  history, pre-World War I, 3–4, 35–38
  and interdisciplinary research, 42
  international and military affairs; *see* Policy research, international and military
  and the New Deal, 7–8
  organizations producing, 10, 52, 71–72
  "overselling" of, 45
  and political democracy, 47
  and scientific developments, 44, 257–258, 282–283
  value questions in, 8, 37, 42, 47, 248, 249–250, 251
Policy research, international and military, 74, 277
  as case for sociology of social science, vii
  by Congress, U. S., *see* Congressional committees, foreign policy and defense, sponsorship of research
  ethical issues in, 154–155, 157, 181–182
  foreign nationals in, 103
  Korean War, 189–192
  networks of communication in, 75–81
  promotion of, 104–106
  recruitment into, 74
  status groups in, 72–73
  subfields in, 74
  use of, *see* Uses of social science knowledge
  World War II, 8–10
  see also Area Studies; Behavioral scientists; Camelot, Project; Communications research; Intelligence research; Military services; Peace research; Political development studies
Policy roles, of social scientists, 151, 166–167
  advisory, 39–40
  advocatory, 146–147, 153–154, 165–166
  lobbying, 167–168
  study of, 1–2; *see also* Sociology of social science
Political development, 111–112
  economic approach to, 123–124
  and foreign policy goals, 115–116, 118, 126–127
  meanings of, 116–118
  strategies for, 119–123
Political development studies, 80, 112–114
  action implications of, 114–115
Political scientists, 4, 37
  before Congressional committees, 145
President's Committee on Social Trends, 6
Prisoners-of-War Studies; *see* Policy research, international and military, Korean War
Professional groups, 21–22
  community in, 73
  military, *see* Military elites

scientific, 22; *see also* Social scientists
self-scrutiny by, 15–16
Propaganda, 214
data-sources of, 107
effectiveness of, 104
and research, 107
World War II, 100–101
Psychological warfare research, *see* Communications research
Psychology of international relations, *see* Peace research
Public opinion, 168, 217
and attitudes, 216–217
and foreign policy decisions, 215–216, 220–221
international, 218–220
Public opinion polls, 149, 214–215
foreign, 133–134, 156
use in Congress, 136

RAND Corporation, 71, 76, 133, 177, 190, 191, 200
Research ethics, 24, 106–107; *see also* Policy research, international and military, ethical issues in
Research techniques, 40
gaming, 156, 230–231, 237
operations research, 40
sample surveys, 87
simulation, 156, 169, 237; *see also* Influence processes, international, simulation of
sociometric, 70
systems analysis, 76, 156, 237
Ricardo, David, 4
"Robin-hooding," 90
Rockefeller, Nelson, 214
Roosevelt, Franklin D., 214
Rusk, Dean, 176
Russell Sage Foundation, 198, 257
Russian Research Center (Harvard University), 192, 200

Science, systems, 19–21, 233
action, 20–23
extra-system influences, 21
internal dynamics of, 21–22
philosophical and cultural, 19–20
Senate, U. S., 137, 139
Committee on Foreign Relations, 56, 174; *see also* Congressional committees, foreign policy and defense
Smith, Adam, 4
Social change, 185; *see also* Peace research, and social change
Social engineering, 248, 256
and government intervention, 3, 7
personnel for, 194, 198, 251–252, 257
see also Uses of social science knowledge
Social roles, 32–34
knowledge-producing, 32, 34

Social Science Research Council, 201
Committee on Comparative Politics, 80
Committee on National Security Policy, 134
Social sciences, 35–36, 45–46, 234–235, 237–238
autonomous nature of, 180
economic requirements of, 23, 25, 41, 89–90
national policy for, 24
relevance to practical affairs, 156, 247, 254–255
state of knowledge in, 40–41, 48, 64
Social scientists, 278
career lines of, 95–99
defined, 136
as policy-makers and operators, 7, 8, 39, 196–197
politico-ideological beliefs, 8, 74–75, 93, 153
population of, 5, 70
as professional group, 234
views of policy process, 281–282
see also Policy roles of social scientists
Society for Social Responsibility in Science, 170
Society for the Psychological Study of Social Issues (SPSSI), 166, 172
Sociology, 2, 3, 4, 7, 35, 36–37
fact-gathering in, 5
military, 78, 131–133
of war and peace, *see* Peace research
Sociology of knowledge, 16–18, 29–34, 207
defined, 17, 29–30
empirical orientation of, 17–18, 30–32
subareas of, 18
Sociology of science, 18–23, 52
models for study in, 20, 22–23
normative orientation of, 22
and social science, 15
Sociology of social science, v–vi, 14–15, 18, 23–25
and "big social science," 23, 24
conceptual models in, 53
legitimacy of inquiries in, 14, 17
as professional self-scrutiny, 15–16
specialized inquiries in, 24, 25
Special Operations Research Organization, 174, 175, 179; *see also* Camelot, Project
Spencer, Herbert, 4
Stouffer, Samuel A., 189
Survey Research Center (University of Michigan), 87, 88
Symington, Stuart, 146

Tavistock Institute, 40
Truman, Harry, 64, 214

United States Information Agency, 79, 195, 214, 215, 219
University, 36, 49
and federal research funds, 8, 10–11
University social research centers, 51, 85–86, 92
organizational structure of, 87–88, 93–94
staffs of, 88–89
and teaching departments, 86, 88, 91

University social science, 4–5
 government support of, 8, 10–11
 prosperity of, 5, 12
 "pure science" influence, 4
Uses of social science knowledge, 46
 adaptational, 241–242
 empirical study of, 54–55, 185, 237, 242–243
 engineering, 235–236, 238
 enlightenment, 239–240, 279–280
 and formulations of research problems, 193
 intellectual processes of, 253–254, 258
 intelligence, 38, 146, 240, 263–265, 278–279
 for justification of decisions, 106
 manipulative, 240–241
 and "middlemen," 197–198, 203, 237
 nonscientific, 55–56, 188–189
 and operative contexts, 51, 55, 193–194
 and operators' attitudes, 56, 106, 189; *see also* Policy-making elites, attitudes toward social science
 predictive, 250–251, 279
 systemic view of, 56–57
 see also Congress, U. S., and the social sciences; Policy, intelligence in; Policy-making elites, attitudes toward social science; Policy roles, of social scientists; Political development studies, action implications of; Public opinion, and foreign policy decisions; Public opinion polls, use in Congress; Social Engineering

Value-free social science, 152; *see also* Policy-oriented social science, value questions in
Vietnam War, 132, 158, 221

Walker, Francis A., 5
Ward, Lester F., 4
Warfare, 129
 limited, 129
 nuclear, 163
 political control of, 129, 130, 269–270
Washington Center of Foreign Policy Research, 146
Wilson, Woodrow, 37, 39
World Association of Public Opinion Research, 221
Wright, Carroll D., 5